Africa Now

Africa Now is published by Zed Books ⟨...⟩ nationally respected Nordic Africa In⟨...⟩ cutting-edge research from leading a⟨...⟩ the big issues confronting Africa tod⟨...⟩ wide-ranging in its scope, *Africa Now* engages with the critical political, economic, sociological and development debates affecting the continent, shedding new light on pressing concerns.

Nordic Africa Institute

The Nordic Africa Institute (Nordiska Afrikainstitutet) is a centre for research, documentation and information on modern Africa. Based in Uppsala, Sweden, the Institute is dedicated to providing timely, critical and alternative research and analysis of Africa and to co-operating with African researchers. As a hub and a meeting place for a growing field of research and analysis, the Institute strives to put knowledge of African issues within reach for scholars, policy-makers, politicians, the media, students and the general public. The Institute is financed jointly by the Nordic countries (Denmark, Finland, Iceland, Norway and Sweden).

www.nai.uu.se

Forthcoming titles

Maria Eriksson Baaz and Maria Stern, *Sexual Violence as a Weapon of War: Perceptions, Prescriptions, Problems in the Congo and Beyond*

Amanda Hammar (ed.), *Displacement Economies in Africa*

Fantu Cheru and Renu Modi (eds), *Agricultural Development and Food Security in Africa*

Titles already published

Fantu Cheru and Cyril Obi (eds), *The Rise of China and India in Africa: Challenges, Opportunities and Critical Interventions*

Ilda Lindell (ed.), *Africa's Informal Workers: Collective Agency, Alliances and Transnational Organizing in Urban Africa*

Iman Hashim and Dorte Thorsen, *Child Migration in Africa*

Cyril Obi and Siri Aas Rustad (eds), *Oil and Insurgency in the Niger Delta: Managing the Complex Politics of Petro-violence*

Prosper B. Matondi, Kjell Havnevik and Atakilte Beyene (eds), *Bio-fuels, Land Grabbing and Food Security in Africa*

Mats Utas (ed.), *African Conflicts and Informal Power: Big Men and Networks*

Prosper B. Matondi, *Zimbabwe's Fast Track Land Reform*

About the author

Prosper B. Matondi is executive director of the Ruzivo Trust, a not-for-profit organisation based in Harare, Zimbabwe. He holds a PhD in rural development from the Swedish University of Agricultural Sciences based in Uppsala, Sweden. He has more than 18 years of experience researching on land, natural resources management, environmental policy and planning in Zimbabwe, within the southern African region and internationally. He has published widely and has contributed to many national, regional and international networks on land and agrarian reform issues. His latest publication by Zed Books is *Biofuels, Land Grabbing and Food Security in Africa*, edited with with Kjell Havnevik and Atakilte Beyene (2011). He sits on various advisory forums on land, agriculture and livelihood issues in Zimbabwe and beyond.

Ruzivo Trust

Ruzivo Trust is a not-for-profit organisation registered as a trust in Zimbabwe. The trust carries out action-based research on land, livelihoods, food security, climate change, biofuels and a variety of other subjects relating to development. The trust has specialist skills derived from practice in policy research and the action-oriented nature of the approaches that it uses. Furthermore, the multidisciplinary composition of the teams that run its programmes allows for in-depth understanding of socio-economic and policy processes in different contexts. The Ruzivo Trust works with communities on livelihood practices and widely shares its knowledge. The vision of the Ruzivo Trust is to promote 'secure and prosperous families and communities' and its mission is to 'influence development processes based on action-generated knowledge for securing and sustaining life'.

Zimbabwe's Fast Track Land Reform

Prosper B. Matondi

RUZIVO TRUST

Nordiska Afrikainstitutet
The Nordic Africa Institute

Zed Books
LONDON | NEW YORK

Zimbabwe's Fast Track Land Reform was first published in association with the Nordic Africa Institute, PO Box 1703, SE-751 47 Uppsala, Sweden in 2012 by Zed Books Ltd, 7 Cynthia Street, London N1 9JF, UK and Room 400, 175 Fifth Avenue, New York, NY 10010, USA

www.zedbooks.co.uk
www.nai.uu.se

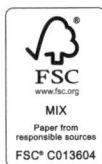

Set in OurType Arnhem, Monotype Gill Sans Heavy
by Ewan Smith, London
Index: ed.emery@thefreeuniversity.net
Cover design: www.roguefour.co.uk
Printed and bound by CPI Group (UK) Ltd, Croydon, CRO 4YY

FSC
www.fsc.org
MIX
Paper from
responsible sources
FSC® C013604

Distributed in the USA exclusively by Palgrave Macmillan, a division of St Martin's Press, LLC, 175 Fifth Avenue, New York, NY 10010, USA

A catalogue record for this book is available from the British Library
Library of Congress Cataloging in Publication Data available

ISBN 978 1 78032 149 3 hb
ISBN 978 1 78032 148 6 pb

Contents

Figures, tables and boxes

Figures

Tables

Boxes

Abbreviations

AER	agro-ecological region
Agribank	Agricultural Bank of Zimbabwe
Agritex	Agricultural, Technical and Extension Services
AIDS	acquired immunodeficiency syndrome
ARDA	Agricultural Rural Development Authority
ASPEF	Agricultural Sector Productivity Enhancement Facility
BIPPA	Bilateral Investment Promotion and Protection Agreement
CFP	Champion Farmer Programme
CFSS	Commercial Farm Settlement Scheme
CFU	Commercial Farmers' Union
CONPI	Certificate of No Present Interest
DA	district administrator
DDF	District Development Fund
DLC	District Land Committee
FGD	focus group discussion
FTF	Fast Track Farm
FTLRP	Fast Track Land Reform Programme
GMB	Grain Marketing Board
GoZ	Government of Zimbabwe
GPA	Global Political Agreement
Ha	hectare
HIV	human immunodeficiency virus
ICA	Intensive Conservation Area
JAG	Justice for Agriculture
LSCF	large-scale commercial farm
MDC	Movement for Democratic Change
MLRR	Ministry of Lands and Rural Resettlement
MRDC	Mazowe Rural District Council
NGO	non-governmental organisation
ORA	Old Resettlement Area
PLC	Provincial Land Committee
PSF	Productive Sector Facility
RBZ	Reserve Bank of Zimbabwe
RDC	Rural District Council
SADC	Southern African Development Community

SIRDC	Scientific and Industrial Research and Development Centre
SSCF	small-scale commercial farm
ZANU-PF	Zimbabwe African National Union – Patriotic Front
ZNA	Zimbabwe National Army
ZNLWVA	Zimbabwe National Liberation War Veterans Association

Glossary

A1 – defined by government as the decongestion model for the majority of landless people. Originally, it had a villagised and a self-contained variant; the latter was discontinued in 2005. Beneficiaries have access to the following average allocations – agro-ecological region (AER) I: 1–12 hectares (ha); AER IIa: 15 ha; AER IIb: 20 ha; AER III: 30 ha; AER IV: 50 ha; AER V: 70 ha. Each household is allocated 3 ha for arable land, with the rest being for grazing. Settlers have basic social services with administrative and social management systems. In this model, 20 per cent of all resettlement land is reserved for War Veterans (GoZ, 2001).

A2 – this model is administered under the Agricultural Land Settlement Act (Chapter 20:01). The model is said by government to increase the participation of black indigenous farmers in commercial farming through the provision of easier access to land and infrastructure on a full cost-recovery basis. The model aims to empower black entrepreneurs through access to land and inputs and to close the gap between the white and black commercial farmers. The land is issued on a 99-year lease with the option to purchase. Land is allocated as follows – peri-urban: 2–50 ha; small-scale commercial farm: from 20 ha in AER I to 240 ha in AER V; medium-scale farm: from 100 ha in AER I to 1,000 ha in AER V; large-scale farm: from 250 ha in AER I to 2,000 ha in AER V.

Agro-ecological region – Zimbabwe is divided into five AERs based on soil type, rainfall patterns, climatic conditions and agricultural production potential. Before the Fast Track Land Reform Programme (FTLRP), the AERs were broadly and loosely characterised by distinct farming systems: communal lands (AERs III, IV and V); small-scale commercial farms (AERs IIb, III and IV); and large-scale commercial farms (AERs I, IIa and IIb). There were, however, some large-scale commercial farms located in AERs III, IV and V, predominantly livestock and game ranching farms.

Committee of Seven – the governance structure set up by the land beneficiaries of the FTLRF. Usually, the first people allocated land on a farm would set up the committee; in some areas the War Veterans were responsible for ensuring that committees were in place to perform various governance and administrative tasks.

Communal areas – land under customary tenure where land rights are acquired and held in terms of customary law. Only access to and use of grazing land is communal in the strict meaning of the word; the rest of the land is owned under usufruct arrangements by families. The land is effectively state land, because it is held in trust by the president, with management rights given to the Rural District Council and traditional leaders. There are several thousand communal areas in Zimbabwe, averaging 0.6 acres per family; sizes differ marginally by agro-ecological region.

District – an administrative subdivision of a province. The district is run by a local authority called the Rural District Council (RDC), with a chief executive officer (secretariat) and a council, which is a political governance body (led by a council chairperson). Committees can be formed according to the RDC Act 1988; this led to the creation of District Land Identification Committees (later to be reconstituted as District Land Committees), chaired by a district administrator.

Fast Track Farms – farms established as a result of the land reform programme taking place from 2000 to the present day. This land reform programme is generally known as the FTLRP. The farms known as Fast Track Farms were basically divided into the A1 model (for the benefit of the poor) and the A2 model (for the benefit of the resource-rich commercial farmers), as defined above.

Jambanja – in the Shona language, this means 'mayhem', or causing violence to achieve a certain social objective. In the case of the land occupations prior to the FTLRP, it was appropriated as a term for effecting successful land occupations through violence or intimidating actions such as constant singing, press-ups and the beating of drums close to the farmhouses.

Land occupation – various terms have been used to describe the forcible takeover of land (outside the law) in Zimbabwe. Land occupation is one such term. Other terms used by different stakeholders include land squatting, land invasions, trespassing, land demonstrations and land grabbing, the different terms reflecting their views and ideological standing.

Large-scale commercial farms – agricultural land held by or under the authority of a title deed, either by a private individual or by an institution. In the latter case, the farm can be private land held by an individual under a title deed, or it can be held by the state either directly or through a state entity under a title deed (in which case it is freehold state land). Before the FTLRP, there were approximately 8,000 commercial farms (of which 6,250 were acquired) with 4,500 owners, i.e. some farms were held under multiple ownership arrangements. The farms averaged 2,200 ha.

Old Resettlement Areas – resettlement areas established between 1980 and 1997. Some 76,000 people benefited from resettlement on about 3.6 million ha of land. The average size of the land allocated was less than 50 ha but depended on location. They have been termed 'old' to distinguish them from the FTLRP resettlement.

Plot – the land allocated to an individual beneficiary. Each farm was divided to create many plots; for example, one farm of 2,000 ha could end up as anything between 4 and 100 plots of smaller but varying sizes (see A1 and A2 above). These plots acted as a reference point for land allocation and became the new beneficiaries' farms. The terms 'plot' and 'farm' are used interchangeably in the land reform discourse in Zimbabwe.

Province – a territory governed as an administrative or political unit. A province has an average of seven districts. Zimbabwe has ten provinces; Mashonaland Central, Matabeleland South, Matabeleland North, Mashonaland West, Mashonaland East, Manicaland, Midlands, Masvingo, Harare and Bulawayo.

Scheme – at the time of the land acquisition, each gazetted farm created what was officially referred to as a 'scheme'. The scheme comprised a number of plots allocated to individuals who shared infrastructure in the form of irrigation equipment, roads, etc. In addition, unallocated land was designated state land and was reserved for public infrastructure such as schools and service centres. The boundary of the scheme was determined by the original farm boundary before the land was compulsorily acquired. The planning for the farms therefore took into consideration the resources within the boundary (rivers, forests, roads, etc.), while the former farmhouse was a focus point for the scheme.

Small-scale commercial farms – these were known as Native Purchase Areas during the colonial period before independence in 1980. They tended to be a buffer between large-scale commercial farms and communal areas and were allocated to better-resourced Africans who purchased the land on freehold titles. It is estimated that there are about 8,000 such farms on about 4.1 million ha; the average size is 512 ha.

Village – the lowest governance unit in Zimbabwe, each with an average of 100 households. There are two structures at village level: the Village Development Committee (a select committee chaired by the village head) and the Village Assembly (attended by people over 18 years of age and presided over by the village head on behalf of the chief of the area).

Ward – a subdivision of a municipality or district. There are two structures within wards: the Ward Development Committee (WADCO), chaired by an elected councillor; and the Ward Assembly, chaired by a village head appointed by the chief. A ward usually comprises about 30 villages. In Mazowe District, for example, there are 29 such subdivisions.

Acknowledgements

This book is part of a collective effort by Zimbabwean scholars who have dedicated themselves to carrying out research into the land reform programme in Zimbabwe as it has evolved. Since 2004, I have led a team of researchers through action-oriented research on land and agrarian reform, specifically focused on the local level. In this team, I want to personally thank Dr Chrispen Sukume, Mr Norman Moyo, Mr Godfrey Magaramombe, Dr Mabel Munyuki-Hungwe, Dr Rudo Sanyanga, Mrs Patricia Masanganise, Dr Precious Zikhali, Dr Nelson Marongwe, Dr Emmanuel Manzungu, Mr Tapiwa Edwin Mapenzauswa, Professor Carroll Themba Khombe and Mrs Melta Moyo for the research we have engaged in over the years. My earnest hope is that over the next couple of years we shall continue to build and strengthen this intellectual capital to contribute to knowledge and policy engagement on agrarian issues. Special thanks for the help and input provided by the following people: Chapter 5 – Patricia Masanganise; Chapter 6 – Dr Manase Chiweshe; Chapter 7 – Dr Rudo Sanyanga; Chapter 8 – Dr Patience Mutopo.

This book benefited from contributions from young colleagues over the years, some of whom have developed their educational careers as a result of this work: Memory Mufandaedza, Cuthbert Kambanje, Dr Patience Mutopo, Dr Manase Chiweshe, Thobekile Zikhali, Gospel Matondi, Sheila Chikulo, Mukundi Mutasa and Allan Majuru. Many thanks to Mukundi for also assisting in checking the final manuscript. I hope that this young crop of scientists will continue to engage in research into these issues in Zimbabwe. In over ten years of fieldwork in Mangwe, Mazowe and Shamva Districts, we worked with teams of technical officials grappling with the challenges of land and agrarian reform. I remain indebted to the Rural District Councils that welcomed our research activities and continue to support our work.

I have benefited immensely from the inputs of many colleagues who have shaped my ideas over the years. Some of the notable individuals who influenced my work in positive ways include Professor Kjell Havnevik, Dr Atakilte Beyene, Professor Mandivamba Rukuni, Professor Robin Palmer, Professor Lionel Cliffe and Professor Amanda Hammar, and too many others to mention. I would like to thank the current and past staff members of the Ruzivo Trust, namely Mrs Esther Paradza, Sheila Chikulo, Tandiwe Musiyiwa, Sheila Jack, Alfred Mafika and various office support staff for their efforts in providing an environment for research and analysis. The assistance provided by

Godfrey Mutowo at the end of the writing of the manuscript is appreciated, while Dr Peta Jones assisted with the initial editing of the original manuscript, which led to further analysis and interpretation of the data. I appreciate the meticulous copy-editing of Judith Forshaw on the final manuscript and I would like to thank the team behind the scenes at Zed Books.

Behind the scenes, my family has had to endure my many absences from home in the last couple of years. Joane, Takudzwa, Tafadzwa and Tamanda remain a special treasure for their continued support and love.

Financial support for this project was provided by several donors who funded the research activities of Ruzivo Trust that led to the publication of this book. The opinions in this book are those of the author and do not reflect the views of the funders, the publishers of this book, nor of the Ruzivo Trust as a whole.

Preface

The Fast Track Land Reform Programme (FTLRP) in Zimbabwe has been the focus of heated, intellectually stimulating debate in Zimbabwe and beyond in the last ten years. In 2006, I was involved in a major book project, *Zimbabwe's Agricultural Revolution Revisited*. The book examined a wide range of issues underpinning the FTLRP, with a view to understanding not just Zimbabwe's land question but also its meaning in the present and future. The team motivation then was that the FTLRP pointed to much deeper transformative change that required better understanding. Such change began before independence in 1980 (what was described as the First Agricultural Revolution), and was followed by a period from the 1980s to 1990 (what the book described as the Second Agricultural Revolution). In that book, a range of questions were posed as to whether the FTLRP represented the basis for the 'Third Agricultural Revolution' in terms of its construction and objectives. The reason why it was described in this manner was that elements from both the previous revolutions could be linked into the FTLRP, pointing to a new agrarian revolution.

By 2006, Zimbabwean society had been transformed by the FTLRP and the politics surrounding it, with a telling effect on our understanding of land reforms globally. A key question that was raised throughout the decade of the FTLRP, and still lingers today, is: does the FTLRP represent the demise of the colonial land question in Zimbabwe? This question grew out of the specific history of Zimbabwe, which has been dominated by the nagging question of land. The situation before 1980 was shaped by land as a colonial question – a question that was overtly about the displacement of blacks from the most productive land. After 1980, blacks regained political control, but, on the whole, they did not substantively transfer land, nor did they change societal relationships. Significant land acquisition and transformation of the agrarian society has occurred only in the last decade, since 2000. Does it then follow that the FTLRP has finally resolved the land issue?

This question cannot simply be answered using generalised information. In fact, there should be a sufficient gathering of evidence of the changes that have occurred, and of what has happened at the local level and on the farms. With this understanding, in 2003 I led a team of scientists in a Land and Livelihoods project that sought to unpack the empirical evidence based on research on farms in Mazowe and Shamva Districts in Mashonaland Central Province. In 2006, Ruzivo Trust's research team decided to examine the same issues in Mangwe District in Matabeleland South (see the map on page xvii for the case study areas). The research focused on understanding what change means for people and agriculture at the local level. As a research team, we were mainly concerned that closely connected questions relating to transformation at the local level were still being neglected. This was because many of the debates about Zimbabwe's land reform were happening at the national and international level, yet the impact of that reform was being felt more intensely at the local level. Local stories and issues did filter into the national and international debates, but in a selective and contradictory way that made it difficult to get a clear picture of what was happening on the ground.

The FTLRP clearly divided society, with people being for or against the methods employed in the takeover of land. The initial land occupations created the basis for land acquisition and were the catalyst for the evolution of the programme, making land reform a fully fledged, complex political issue. The research in three districts (Mangwe, Mazowe and Shamva) identified a range of issues, such as land tenure, land rights and agricultural production outcomes, and the forces that shaped them. The work also examined the changes in who had control and ownership of assets and what this meant for economic livelihoods. The particular challenges faced by women were examined as a core cross-cutting issue, and at the same time the research focused on social transformation in terms of relationships, access to services and people's take on their new life in the new context of the Fast Track Farms. The overarching objective of the land reforms was to improve the welfare of ordinary people. However, socio-economic development based on farming triggered a range of internal and external forces that placed agriculture in a quandary.

This book synthesises some of the processes that have taken place at the local level, examining the long-term consequences of a major restructuring of society. The new resettlement schemes stand at the heart of several contradictory processes, which touch on people's livelihoods and their well-being. There are still questions to be answered about how to encourage local people to have confidence in the land reform programme now and in the future. This also relates to the internal and external processes and pressures that help or obstruct production, the development of new farmers, and the building of a national identity, as well as the role of politics in that. All of this resonates in the forms of development adopted by the state, and in how to express the will and rights of the people with regard to land. This book is therefore an opportune contribution to the Zimbabwean literature aiming to help shape the land reform programme as a means of prosperity for the nation.

Prosper B. Matondi
Harare, 27 April 2012

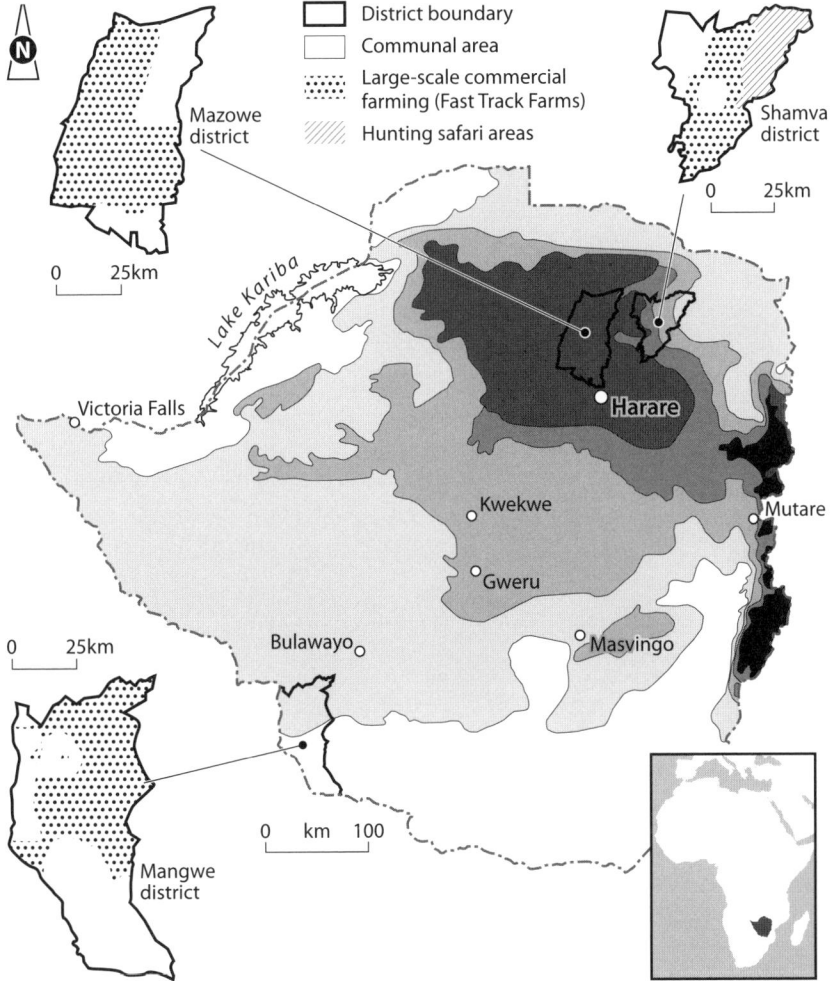

Zimbabwe's agro-ecological zones with study sites

Legend:
- District boundary
- Communal area
- Large-scale commercial farming (Fast Track Farms)
- Hunting safari areas

Mazowe district

Shamva district

0   25km

Lake Kariba

Victoria Falls

Harare

Kwekwe

Mutare

Gweru

Bulawayo

Masvingo

0   25km

0   km   100

Mangwe district

Zimbabwe's agro-ecological regions

AER 1: Eastern highlands covering less than 2 per cent of the country, annual rainfall 1,000mm or more, experiences low temperatures, suitable for commercial forestry, intensive diversified agriculture (tea, coffee, deciduous fruit and horticulture), intensive livestock and dairy production.

AER 2a North-eastern high-veld covering 16 per cent of the country, annual rainfall between 750–1,000mm, and suitable for intensive cropping and livestock production.

AER 2b

AER 3: Middle-veld covering 18 per cent of the country, annual rainfall between 500–750mm, suitable for cattle ranching and semi-intensive crop farming.

AER 4: Low-veld in the north and south of the country covering 37 per cent of the country, annual rainfall between 450–650mm, experiences periodic seasonal droughts, and suitable for cattle ranching, while crops require irrigation.

AER 5: Low-veld covering 27 per cent of the country, receives erratic rainfall of 650mm or less, suitable for extensive cattle or game ranching.

1 | Understanding Fast Track Land Reforms in Zimbabwe

Introduction

The Fast Track Land Reform Programme (FTLRP) has been inscribed on Zimbabwe's political and socio-economic map since 2000. In the early years of the reforms, the programme captured international attention and imagination, while in Zimbabwe itself it radically altered people's lives and livelihoods, and at the same time reawakened people's memories of the past. Therefore, the land reform programme was not simply about land, but also about people, especially the farmers and the communities in which they lived, originated from and settled in. It was also about the institutions they interacted with on multiple levels, and with whom they intersected at different times as the programme was speedily implemented. The programme radically transformed society, with former landowners being pushed aside, farmworkers having their livelihoods 'withdrawn', and new beneficiaries walking into new commercial land, without structured or sustained support. Yet the majority of people saw the FTLRP as the final embodiment of empowerment following Zimbabwe's independence in 1980. The FTLRP, therefore, comprises a complex mix of ingredients that have attracted the attention of both the domestic and the international community, in terms of what land reform means and how it should be delivered, but more importantly of what model works best to deliver land to the people, without tinkering with broader livelihoods. But perhaps the most difficult question is whether the reforms represent the final resolution of the colonial question or not (Okoth-Ogendo, 2007).

The title of this book is shaped by the history of land reform in Zimbabwe, which has been a constant societal feature for over a century. Such a history shows that radical land transformations have been a dominant feature of the country since the late eighteenth century, played out against a racial background characterised by whites dispossessing blacks. Yet, 2000 saw the beginning of a radical repossession, when blacks took over land from white farmers, amending policies and laws to effect the repossession. Given the time that has passed since 2000, when this massive land repossession occurred, critical questions now have to be asked: what is the significance of the reforms? Will the reforms retain their hold into the future? Is the FTLRP so flawed and unjust that it should be reversed? Or, despite it being unjust, does it provide the basis for finally resolving the colonial question with regard to the land? What are the promises that provide a sense of optimism? During implementation of the programme, President Mugabe seemed inclined to confirm that, for his leadership, the land issue was a 'done deal'. President Mugabe indicated that land reform was the key issue preventing him from relinquishing office. He said, in a radio interview on Independence Day, 18 April 2003: 'We are getting to a stage where we shall say fine, we settled this matter [land redistribution] and people can retire.'[1] Following speculative reports sparked by this statement, he further fuelled that speculation by, on 29 May 2003, calling for an open debate on his succession within the ruling ZANU-PF. Two years later, on 9 August 2005, President Mugabe declared:

> Without doubt, our heroes are happy that a crucial part of this new phase of our struggle has been completed. The land has been freed and today all our heroes lie on the soil that is declaration. Their spirits are unbound, free to roam the land they left shackled, thanks again to the Third Chimurenga. (Quoted in Derman, 2006: 2)

This book takes a cue from the fact that there is little knowledge about Fast Track Farms (FTFs) in Zimbabwe. Yet the impact of land reforms on people, in a country such as Zimbabwe where agricultural production almost collapsed, has become a contested subject. There are difficult questions with no easy answers, but questions still have to be asked: how can we build more and better bridges between knowledge and practice? How can the desired changes be encouraged and enhanced, changes that reflect the strength of individuals managing the land as an economic asset? A major issue covered in this book is an unpacking of the meaning of the FTLRP as seen from a local perspective, to try to answer some of the critical questions relating to the long-term influence of this radical programme. The best approach to judging whether the FTLRP will endure is to understand the situation as it now exists on the ground, through analysing the shifts that have happened with respect to the agrarian base. A key argument regarding the significance of the transformation brought about by the programme should be based on the situation that has unfolded, and continues to unfold, on the FTFs. While broader political statements matter, ultimately practices and people's responses on the ground are what define the character of the reforms and their future. In this book, the aim is to show what has happened on the ground and what this means for the land question as a contested colonial issue.

Understanding the context from a local perspective

The implementation of the FTLRP has dominated Zimbabwe's socio-economic and political landscape over the last decade. Some four years after 2000, I led a research team (see the Acknowledgements) that started to gather information about how the national discourse on land was translating into practice on the large-scale commercial farms (LSCFs), which were the focus of transformation. As independent, concerned scientists, in 2003/04 the research team decided to find out how the programme had evolved and how it was affecting the people entering and leaving large-scale commercial farming areas. At the same time, the government, through its institutions, was planning revolutionary changes to the large-scale commercial farming sector, mainly through the process of land downsizing, thus effectively creating a new model of small- to medium-sized farms on land that for over 100 years had been characterised by LSCFs.

Since 2000, the radical land reform programme had become a theatre of contests, policy attention and government interests, especially in the farming areas themselves. The research team sought to establish the nature of the land reform process in places far away from Harare (the centre of policy-making) and on an international border (with South Africa and Botswana): Mangwe District in Matabeleland South (see the map on page xvii for the location of the case study sites). The research team also selected places closer to Harare (Mazowe and Shamva) in order to establish whether there were any discernible differences in terms of how the programme had evolved. Research in the case study locations showed that land reform is diverse and complex, and therefore further site-specific studies were needed to capture social, political and institutional issues. The FTLRP included several processes that required better understanding, such as: the shifting relationships among farmers, as well as between farmers and the state; the transformation of the chain of production and the links between the producers themselves and mixed production outcomes; the evolution of new farming systems; the social and cultural processes that enabled individuals or groups to benefit from land reform, or prevented them from doing so, thus exacerbating rural differentiation; the local politics of land access, control and management; the governance practices that emerged from controlling not only people but also the resources necessary for farming; the stated and unstated rules that were used to resolve and manage conflicts; the rights, duties and responsibilities that a community put in place to manage land in convoluted policy spaces; and the formal and informal administrative practices that were emerging in the new resettlement areas.

Ruzivo Trust's exploratory study (2004–09) traced Zimbabwe's land question historically and analytically, to understand further how history had shaped the evolution of the FTFs; the study started from the history of land and agrarian issues as a basis for explaining the period of the FTLRP. Ruzivo's research concerns were to examine the ways in which the FTLRP was expanding at a local level, by tracking the objectives, goals and context of the programme against its implementation and outcomes. At the same time, the team analysed the broad statements made regarding the FTLRP in the media (nationally and internationally) as well as in academic circles, its broader political context, and the positioning that developed over time (either for or against the programme). These issues informed the manner in which the FTF data were interpreted.

Fast track land reform radicalism and speeding up of the reforms

The research was concerned with the fact that land reform policies were made centrally, with little direct local input or perspective. Political statements and action were pitched very high in order to hide certain local tendencies (some of the action relating to the land takeovers was permeated by violence), which made it difficult to discern what was happening on the ground. At the same time, land-related policy-making seemed to have been reacting indirectly to how people responded to the government taking over 'white'-owned farms. In fact, the government's aim was first and foremost to generate significant widespread support for its land takeover actions in Zimbabwe. In order to control policy, the government re-centralised decision-making relating to land matters, ostensibly because it perceived itself as fighting against external forces bent on reversing the gains of the programme. For this reason, local officials were simply told to implement policy as it stood. However, the cases documented demonstrate that local officials came up with ingenious ways of getting on with their work despite overwhelming challenges.

Starting in 2000, farmers began a journey that was to transform their lives for ever. This journey took the new land beneficiaries through a minefield of institutions, both formal and informal, new spaces and new people with unfamiliar systems and cultures, which determined whether one succeeded or failed. The beneficiaries' stories link policy-making to practice through an analysis of the way in which the resettlement programme dealt with local decision-making. The research alternates between accounts of action on the ground and analytical reflections. This approach differs from traditional research in that it does not test data against a chosen set of hypotheses according to a model, but instead it engages directly with people and practitioners on their terms, accepting their perspectives in their environment.

To have a fuller understanding of the FTLRP, it was essential to examine the traditional concepts of political economy; these have largely focused on top-down, macro-level approaches and on institutions and their rules. This institutional analysis is based on the belief that good political and economic institutions are central to the promotion of sound economic development and the welfare of society. More recently, institutional economics and other political economy methodologies have emphasised the need for a bottom-up, micro-level, 'game theory' approach that looks at individual interactions and individual incentives to follow (or not follow) institutional rules – in order to understand why and how institutions persist and change (Leftwich, 2008).

A major element of the research was an analysis of the interaction of people and institutions and how this shaped the progress of the reforms.

The context described above was influenced by the very nature of the FTLRP. A multiplicity of institutions emerged as the FTLRP was being implemented, chiefly with the formation of District Land Committees, and as situations changed rapidly during the first two to three years; old habits were discarded, ineffective mechanisms were set aside, and the different sets of rules were changed constantly. This often happened in a contradictory manner, creating chaos in the process; however, the programme proved to be unstoppable. I was, therefore, concerned with understanding how people co-existed in the FTF territories, which were geographically fixed communities. By looking at the situation in specific locations, the research was able to decipher the significant shifts on the FTFs and how they were shaped by people's movement and stability. Institutional engineering also had an effect on the FTF communities, and made it easier to understand local processes better.

Decision-making in the turbulent times of the fast track

The land reform programme created complexities in the everyday lives of ordinary people seeking land and better economic opportunities. A collective of people, most of whom did not necessarily know each other, rallied to achieve the common goal of reclaiming land, based on the opportunities opened up by the War Veterans and government. For instance, Kriger (1992: 6) powerfully argued that 'what people say and do matters', and the responses from officials working in different institutions, as well as those from farmers, provided the key to understanding people within the FTF spaces. Human agency, or what Röling (1997) called the 'soft side of land', was adopted as a reflective, process-based way in which local officials and other actors could deal with and manipulate certain constraining and enabling elements during the FTLRP. At the local level, while some actors organised communities to meet political ends, others acted as a counterbalance and were able to check one another during the implementation of the programme. This implies that there was an ongoing debate and negotiation over meanings, values and intentions. A mixture of social, technical and political actors at the local level created situations in which individuals could engage with, distance themselves from, or adopt an ambiguous stance towards certain rules and agreed frameworks; this was the hallmark of the FTLRP.

Over the years of the FTLRP, there has been an intensification of debate within resettled and non-resettled communities about who has benefited and why. Some patterns have been noted of beneficiaries leaving the land when they should be consolidating their position, but the causes of this are unclear, or have sometimes been ascribed to political reasons.[2] It also seems that there has been state paralysis following the formation in 2009 of an Inclusive Government with no clear policy positions on different categories of land or on the legal standing of either the beneficiaries or certain elements of the programme. The main worry is the future direction of the programme, given the absence of policy and disagreement over the formulation of the national constitution, which will have a bearing on matters relating to land and property rights. It is even more confusing when some large commercial farms, which had been subdivided into smaller landholdings by the FTLRP, are now re-emerging and promoting biofuels and agro-investments that apparently include foreigners (Matondi et al., 2011). These unfolding and deepening contradictions necessitate a clear understanding of national processes in relation to emerging practices on the FTFs. The narratives in this book reveal the various experiences of the people in Mangwe, Mazowe and Shamva over the past eight to ten years of land reform. They constitute a collection of conflicting ideas about the meanings and experiences of land and agrarian change. Research into the FTFs over a long time period provided a lever for understanding the knowledge of 'locals' who faced daily decisions and made sense of lives that were shaped by how they settled on the land and by the context in which they existed as the land reform programme unfolded.

Officials in government ministries came from a background that emphasised orderliness and adherence to laws and procedures. Yet the new settlers and interest groups emphasised the opposite, because to them 'order' meant 'doing nothing'. Existing laws and 'standards' were meant to preserve the status quo and therefore did not facilitate their entry into commercial farms; they were seen as part of the colonial mentality that accepted that large farms make better economic sense than small farms (Weiner et al., 1986; Van Zyl et al., 1996; World Bank, 1991), and 'procedures' were regarded as 'technical bureaucracy' to delay the resettlement programme. Both officials and farmers had to endure what seemed to be insecurity, because they were not certain how the former landowners would react.[3] The technical officials had to endure incidents of being physically threatened by former landowners, and at the same time being hounded by the new beneficiaries impatient over the delays in getting on to their farms. To survive this, officials sometimes had to make on-the-spot decisions based on scanty information; at times their decisions resolved conflict situations, but at other times they exacerbated the problems. Given that the pace of the FTLRP was accelerated, they lacked the time and resources to be thorough, and were always on the lookout for cues and extrapolated conclusions based on the information available, which at times was not necessarily accurate. For instance, while policy did not allow for an individual to have more than one farm, some officials ignored this, while others allowed the taking over of farms under international bilateral agreements: the officials seemed to have legitimised illegality, at least according to their own policy pronouncements.

Zimbabwe's Fast Track Land Reform Programme as viewed in international discourse

The FTLRP has gained widespread international attention since 2000, with the world divided between those who supported the 'forceful' commercial land takeover actions of the Government of Zimbabwe (GoZ) and those opposed to the actions for a variety of reasons. However, while the international politics of Zimbabwe's land reform gained a high profile, there was very little attention paid to understanding the complexities of the programme, especially at the point of implementation, specifically at a local level and on the farms themselves.

The international image of the FTLRP – chaos, violence, underuse of land, food insecurity, pariah state – seems in a contradictory way to have been its key driver. This image is historical (Moyo, 1995a; Selby, 2006; Sadomba, 2008; Cliffe et al., 2011) and has a specific context of race, which unfortunately the leadership of the white farmers failed to read (or denied the reality of) in political terms. As early as 1991, the Commercial Farmers' Union (CFU) claimed a position of superiority in production that they related to their 'culture' of doing things, as opposed to black farmers. Time and time again, the white farmers sought to prove their high productivity while caricaturing black agriculture as economically unviable and environmentally destructive:

> It is unfortunate that with few notable exceptions, the majority of resettlement schemes to date have led to a serious loss of productivity, denudation of resources, insufficient income and even food aid being required for settlers. (CFU, 1991: 1)

Evidence from a longitudinal household survey on Old Resettlement Areas found that many households who settled on commercial land developed their farms and invested strongly in building assets and social relationships (Barr, 2001). For instance, in good rainfall seasons the settlers were able to grow enough food to feed themselves, and most also grew some cash crops (Dekker and Kinsey, 2011). The CFU was also of the opinion that:

> the situation is not sustainable. The pressure on the communal lands from too many people and too many animals and the mismanagement of resources has led to widespread and sometimes irreversible degradation. The communal nature of land ownership and traditional agricultural methods, together with the traditional role of livestock, has aggravated the situation. (CFU, 1991: 2)

Through these seemingly technical statements on land use, they reinforced the politics of apportioning blame to the largely majority blacks. The effect of this was to re-create the dualism of 'them' (black farmers) mismanaging the land, with 'we' (white farmers) being better in modern agricultural practices. The defence of the property distribution that then existed between blacks and whites was, therefore, based on the white landowners' belief that they had better organisational and productive capabilities, were more innovative technically and made a greater economic contribution, as well as employing thousands of farmworkers. In this context, a culture of production was mapped on to race (and consequently on to the politics that came to haunt the white farmers from 2000); the white farmers created a positive identity for themselves while invalidating blacks, and showcased this internationally as their line of defence when the land occupations and FTLRP commenced.

The media image of the FTLRP was one of extensive displacement of white commercial farmers and farmworkers, mostly through violence. This attracted prominent international narratives, with scholars (Scoones et al., 2010) providing new contested paradigms of the myths and successes of the programme. The factual realities of land underutilisation and low levels of production, especially on the FTFs, have been explained in a kaleidoscope of ways, many of the explanations justifying the outcomes. However, studies have largely focused on the displaced either as white landowners or farmworkers (Hammar, 2008; Hammar, 2010; Hammar et al., 2010; Magaramombe, 2010) rather than on the replacement of people, agricultural production systems and processes, which has received hardly any attention. The creation of a new breed of farmers, known in the Zimbabwean lexicon as 'new' farmers,[4] has also received negative publicity, in terms of their capabilities (or lack of capability) to move agriculture and the economy forward. The construction and performance of the FTLRP are under scrutiny, especially with respect to how new farmers are seen in the context of development and international discourses, and how this affects their material conditions, survival and struggles in a new dispensation.

The changed and expanded agrarian base

By 2009, the GoZ had acquired some 10.8 million hectares (ha) of land for the resettlement programme out of a total of 12.3 million ha of commercial land (MLRR, 2009). The farms were classified as either A1 or A2 models, with the classifications based on what seems to have been a rational arrangement relating to equity and growth (Prosterman and Riedinger, 1987; World Bank, 1995; Moyo, 1995a); black agricultural commercialisation could be added to these criteria as well. Earlier scholarship had shown the advantages and efficiencies of small family farms in modern agriculture (Weiner et al., 1986; Roth, 1990; World Bank, 1991; Tiffen, 1996). In general, the government sought to reduce the large-scale commercial farms from an average of 2,200 ha to 500 ha or less, thereby increasing the number of commercial farmers from 3,950 (Taylor, 2002) to over 300,000 (split into small and large farms); these numbers included both the A1 and A2 classifications.

In the construction of the farming models, the A1 farms were supposed to be small farms[5] of between 12 and 30 ha in agro-ecological regions (AER) I to

TABLE 1.1 Agricultural land inventory as of 2011

Farming sectors	Area (ha)	Number of plots/ beneficiaries
A1	5,759,153.89	145,775
A2	2,978,334.08	16,386
Communal areas	16,000,000.00	1,200,000
Old Resettlement Areas (Phase 1 and 2)	3,667,708.00	75,569
Large-scale commercial farms (unacquired)[1]	648,041.27	1,154
Small-scale commercial farms[2]	1,400,000.00	8,000
Conservancies	792,009.00	–
Institutional farms[3]	145,693.42	113
Unsettled gazetted land[4]	757,577.51	517
Total	32,148,517.17	1,447,523

Notes: 1. Land that was not legally gazetted for acquisition and remains in the hands of its 'original' owners holding their title deeds. 2. These farms are owned under a Deed of Grant, and were known as the Native Purchase Areas before independence. Blacks were allowed to trade in land in these areas, which were a buffer between the large-scale commercial farms and the communal areas. They became the small-scale commercial farming areas after independence in 1980. 3. Land owned by parastatals, churches, schools, colleges, universities and mines. 4. Excluding conservancies. A commonly held view is that 300 white farmers remain on the land, but this is difficult to verify.

Source: Calculated from various GoZ sources (2009) and FAO/WFP (2010).

III, with farmers living in villagised areas; there would be an increase in size in AERs III to V (based on climate and other physical conditions suitable for different types of agriculture).[6] The main purpose of the A1 scheme was to decrease land pressure in the communal areas as well as to provide assets to the poor (GoZ, 2001). By 2011, there were 145,775 beneficiaries on 5.8 million ha (see Table 1.1).

While the tenure arrangements in the A1 areas are construed in social terms to follow the customary system of land allocation, adjudication and administration, the areas largely remain under state administration. The offer letter given to the A1 settlers explicitly states that the offer can be withdrawn at any time and that the government has no obligation to compensate for any improvements that the settler might have made. This provision has made the A1 settlement very insecure for the new farmers from an investment angle. However, the mass character of the model in terms of the potential number of people who support the government reclamation of land provides them with some semblance of political security.

Beginning in 2000, the government equally prioritised the elite and resource-driven A2 model, ostensibly to de-racialise the large-scale commercial farming areas (GoZ, 2001). The starting point for the A2 model was the decision in Phase II of the Land and Resettlement Programme in 1998 that recommended the selection of agricultural graduates as well as those blacks involved in agriculture to be the primary beneficiaries of any public resettlement scheme. This objective was broadened through specific public support of the development of a middle and upper class of blacks in agriculture as a basis for economic empowerment, and therefore broad economic growth.

The A2 farms are composed of individual plots of land that are classified as small-, medium- and large-scale commercial schemes.[7] By 2009, some 16,386 beneficiaries had received access to 2.9 million ha of land. The defining feature of the A2 farms was clarified with the enactment of the 99-year and 25-year lease arrangements. A major departure of the 99-year lease is that it also provides for the purchase of existing improvements on the farms by the farmers; these improvements can be used as collateral for borrowing from financial institutions. In terms of security, a long lease of 99 years is regarded as secure as a freehold tenure (MLRR, 2009). The essence of leasehold tenure is that land belonging to one person, either the state or an individual, is leased to another person via a contractual agreement. In Zimbabwe, leases are registered according to section 65 of the Deeds Registries Act. This model was instituted to increase the number of black commercial farmers.

Across the three districts of research, the dominance of small- and medium-scale farms is key. In Mazowe, more farms were allocated to A2, which reflected a tendency on the part of bureaucrats towards reserving more land for potentially well-resourced beneficiaries. In Shamva and Mangwe, A1 dominated, demonstrating a planning frame that aimed to appease the 'the poor' in non-strategic pieces of land. The expectation was that the A2 beneficiaries would take leadership in commercial production to meet the state objectives of high output production to meet food security, employment creation and foreign currency generation (Masanganise and Kambanje, 2008). On the other hand, A1 was about meeting the social objectives of addressing poverty, allowing the development of farmers who would go on to A2, and in essence decongesting communal areas.

Shifts in agricultural production As the government forcefully implemented the FTLRP, there were high expectations that new beneficiaries would perform at the same level as the former white commercial farmers (Hammar et al., 2003). However, the result was that the programme was heavily criticised for having impoverished farmworkers due to the land invasions, and of having been exclusionary and dominated by multiple land grabbing. One argument was that production and even full utilisation would not have been possible given the level of conflict and invasions that tended to affect farmers on the ground – and also discouraged a range of stakeholders, including financial institutions and other private sector supporting organisations. There is some truth in this, because, by and large, international development agencies indicated in private meetings that they would not assist resettled farmers as they were on 'contested lands'.

In any case, a radical shift in production patterns and outcomes was to be expected as new beneficiaries settled on the land, as attested by the government in the founding FTLRP document (GoZ, 2001). It is certain that new beneficiaries did not follow the former large-scale farmers in terms of the kind of agricultural enterprises they adopted. In Mazowe, Shamva and Mangwe there were certain continuities, for example in terms of livestock and crops (tobacco, maize, wheat, cotton and horticulture), but not wholesale imitation. This book shows that there was an increase in the land area under production, but a significant reduction in output. Further, there were discontinuities in some forms of agriculture (e.g. horticulture in Mazowe dropped to 2 per cent of its potential).

As agrarian communities in Mazowe evolved over time, they showed modest improvements in agricultural output, yet the people who had settled there indicated that their lives had been transformed for the better. While certain social fissures exist, adequate post-settlement stability, with its resultant benefits for people, will not be possible in a short time frame (Kinsey, 2004; Matondi, 2011a). In a context in which resources for settlement were limited, there were difficulties in the early years. The resources provided by government were affected by the broader macro-economic challenges. However, history has shown that welfare levels tend to be universally lower in the first years of settlement (Kinsey, 2004). In any case, post-settlement adjustments demonstrated several areas of stress, as new beneficiaries struggled to get access to basic services (schools, health facilities, etc.). However, as experience accumulates and collaborative efforts begin, benefits start to accrue. This is evidenced by modest collective action in the mobilisation of resources and asset building for farming outside government subsidies in districts such as Mazowe.

New agrarian relations An important aspect discussed in this book relates to the new agrarian relations forming on the FTFs. The previous communities of a few white owners living with black farmworkers have given way to multifarious communities dominated by people of different classes, backgrounds, professions, technical abilities and ethnicities. According to an Agricultural, Technical and Extension Services (Agritex) officer in Mazowe, the new farmers with different competences (engineers, market specialists, civil servants, ordinary people, some farmworkers, etc.) provide an opportunity for social and economic innovation and a new beginning. However, for the full utilisation of the commercial land, there is a need to harness these and future resources through focused capacity-building and skills development. For this to happen, the local people argue that the skills of former landowners should be acknowledged. At this stage, there is a lack of knowledge and analysis of the former, white, large-scale farmers' skills, how these were acquired over time, and how relevant they could be for a new agrarian model. This means that there is a need to examine the learning platforms that offer, for example, education and mentoring, farming skills development, agricultural extension and information in terms of how these were developed in the past and can be re-established.

Clear differences have emerged between A1 and A2 farmers, shaped by various factors. It is, however, at the production level that these differences have a telling effect across the three districts. Both sets of farmers recognise the broader forces that have shaped them, centred on the key objectives of the FTLRP and the circumstances in which they ended up as beneficiaries of plots of land. The A2 farmers are clearly aware of the desire for accumulation. In the new resettled areas, the ties to the benefactor – seen as the government and the former ruling party – mean that subordination no longer refers to village-level links on the chain of production. This also reflects the cosmopolitan nature of the people and communities that are emerging. New settlers are forging new forms of relationships, while also smuggling in a dominant patriarchal hierarchy against a policy context where officials pretend to balance gender interests. This is particularly the case in A1, rather than in A2. The A1 settlers are subjected to a series of social controls that A2 settlers tend to resist because they regard these social controls as a threat to commercial production.

On the FTFs the new settlers are exploring new forms of relationships. In the process, they are also breaking cultural barriers, although there is severe resistance by men who seek to impose norms adopted from traditional systems. The A2 beneficiaries also deviate from what was characterised as ordinary business people and civil servants. The dominant trend among this group of farmers is that they try to mimic the former white landowners. This is influenced by the design of the model and the message that both politicians and technical bureaucrats sent out to say that the A2 was a 'commercial model'. This message implied that the A1 was 'non-commercial' (although, in fact, this was not the case) and had the effect of softening the rigorous requirements for production auditing. However, the A2 farmers were placed on a higher pedestal, which led to their comparison with the previous commercial farmers. At times this comparison was unjust, but the overall expectation was that these beneficiaries would take a business approach to farming and, in particular, be the fulcrum of employment creation and foreign currency earning. In the three districts, the research established that the A2 is a new agrarian class that has steadily shed its ties with social and cultural networks, but which acts largely in accordance with new ideological norms constructed around the FTLRP.

'Chaos theory' in relation to the Fast Track Land Reform Programme

The FTLRP in its entirety, but especially the land allocation process, is characterised as having been 'chaotic' and lacking orderliness, being permeated by violence and self-serving interests through self-allocation of land by the well-to-do (Alexander, 2003; Alexander, 2006; Alexander and McGregor, 2005; Marongwe, 2003; Hammar et al., 2003; Derman, 2006; Zamchiya, 2011). Evidence derived from the press and selected case studies obscures the actual patterns and the stated outcomes. This is because overarching statements of failure are proclaimed about the FTLRP, but these have been based on short-term studies and derived largely from a partisan and agenda-setting press (both for and against the FTLRP). In fact, on the ground there was generally a certain level of orderliness amid the mayhem. Without condoning the violent aspects of action taken within the programme, there is a need to locate the disorderliness in terms of the context that influenced it, because this will need to be corrected. The following are keys to unlocking the factors at play:

- *Timing of the land reforms:* Zimbabwe's economy was already in a downward spiral from around 1997 due to high and unsustainable debts and the poor budgetary decisions of the government.
- *Speed of the reforms:* The reforms were deemed 'fast track' without there being a sound economic or political reason why they had to be 'fast' as opposed to being carried out at a normal rate.[8] This affected the broad planning framework to some extent.
- *Breadth and capacity to implement:* Capacity varied from district to district and province to province, so that the assumption that the government would be able to implement the programme wholesale and simultaneously may have been an overestimation of its own capacity.
- *Mechanisms for self-correction:* There was simply no time to learn from and correct mistakes that were identified even by the government's own audits, such as the Buka land audit (2002), the Utete land committee (2003), and the Ministry of Lands and Rural Resettlement (MLRR) and the Scientific and Industrial Research and Development Centre (SIRDC) land audit of 2006.

Measured against these benchmarks, the government may seem to have failed to put in place appropriate mechanisms for controlling the 'chaos'. Yet, at district level, one could identify some semblance of institutional order, even as the government struggled with various aspects of implementation. Of course, in the context of the mayhem, individuals took advantage to self-allocate or benefit their 'friends' with high political connections. At the same time, could 145,775 beneficiaries in the A1 model and 16,386 in the A2 model have all benefited through some form of corruption or nepotism? Such a very large number of friendships would be unprecedented in the history of state development programmes. This means that there is a need for thorough empirical evidence to establish local actualities and nuances. Perhaps the programme was the victim of its own high-pitched political intentions.

Evolving central government and micro-relations following the Fast Track Land Reform Programme

The FTLRP was premised on speed to conclude the programme, and was defined by the government as '... kick-starting the Phase II Resettlement with an accelerated pace, code named "Fast Track". This "Fast Track" is an accelerated phase where activities, which can be done quickly, shall be done in an accelerated manner' (GoZ, 2001: 6). On the ground, an official in Mangwe (interviews, October 2007) summarised it as a process of 'a fast track mode, where the emphasis was, do and ask later'. The research sought to establish how people and the state changed the way in which resources are accessed and used based on the premise of 'do and ask later' policy directives. In adopting such an approach to the reforms, government set itself a major undertaking unprecedented in history. Therefore, key governance and institutional weaknesses were apparent, because, at some level, the government's own institutions on the ground were not adequately prepared to undertake the programme speedily. Therefore, matters of technical or administrative deficiency could not intelligently or sensibly be eliminated from the policy processes, which established and sustained them.

On the FTFs, socio-political relations between the state and the people were being transformed by land in complex ways. As a result of this observation, a key concern of the research was to identify the causal processes and how they flow, to appreciate the economic change brought about by land reforms and the related politics. The study narrowly focused on observing people's day-to-day lives and livelihoods, and their coping strategies in rapidly changing situations brought about by the FTLRP. However, it is very difficult to attribute social and economic shifts to particular interventions without appreciating the wider context of change within which the land reform programme was implemented. It is likely that interventions aimed at increasing economic opportunities through the land reforms have played a larger role in catalysing social change. Therefore, it was important to incorporate interdisciplinary analysis in the understanding of political processes and systems – examining how economic, social and cultural systems interact with the political system and how their interactions affect people's lives on the ground.

In the end, this was about analysing people and institutions as shaped by the FTLRP, and the character of the places and spaces where people live and survive. Yet, there are unique differences of a geographical nature and in regional politics and culture that have resulted in specific differences in the outcomes of the FTLRP in the different parts of the country. Certainly, compared with other provinces, the Mashonaland Provinces differed in the way in which the reforms were carried out and in their outcomes. This book demonstrates some of these differences as well as common outcomes of the reforms.

Accumulation tendencies from above In Zimbabwe, the state could be described as having been 'betwixt and between' (Bryceson, 1999; 2000), in the sense that an uncertainty developed over what resettlement model should be promoted as a priority. In the FTLRP, both public and private elites emerged as key actors shaping the development of the FTLRP, as the commercial model (A2) seemed to take prominence, yet peasants and the poor managed to use political leverage to get concessions through the poverty reduction model (A1). Elites, especially those in associations such as the Affirmative Action Group, members of the now defunct Indigenous Business Development Centre, and the low-profile Indigenous Business Women's Organisation, seemed to have been subservient to rural forces led by the War Veterans, only to reawaken ten years down the road to start clamouring for broader economic empowerment. New forces with political connections, such as *Upfumi Kuvadiki*, have also emerged strongly in the indigenisation dialogue.

The urban-based social (and political) organisations seem to mirror the precedent set by the land reform programme; they are now trying to use the land experience to target other economic sectors (mining, businesses, etc.) for takeover, but in a modified version of 'buying shares' or appeasing the majority in specific localities through 'community share schemes'. The elites are caught between a rock and a hard place, because they seek personal accumulation of wealth, while worrying about the views of the poor, whose scope for accessing such wealth may be just a mirage. Nonetheless, the elites seem to be trying to sanitise such takeovers through reforming the laws first, rather than the other way round of taking and then reforming the laws later.

However, behind the scenes the elites have also been germane to the land movement, as they have used a variety of powers and tactics to put pressure on the government to encourage the de-racialisation of commercial agriculture. In this case, the politics of scaling – framing action and decision-making at a particular level – turned out to be an important elite strategy, which in the end tended to characterise the programme as having been led by the elite and having benefited that same elite, as pointed out in a 2011 parting shot by the past president of the CFU.[9] Yet, without denying such benefits (the extent of which still requires verification), little regard or attention has been given to what the land reforms mean personally to peasants and the poor, who benefited in greater numbers (and also more perhaps in qualitative terms) than the so-called elites and politicians.

The FTLRP transformed state–society relations – both the way in which broader interests were represented and the ways and means by which the state supported 'the people' in their action to take over key economic resources from a small elite, in this case mostly the white minority group. Nevertheless, as the short history shows, the mass benefits of the FTLRP also facilitated a few elite black groups in becoming the backbone of the local actors championing access to land for emancipation and economic empowerment. In the process, the FTLRP became an example of a programme that divided society and created conflicts between those whose land was taken, and those who justifiably were claiming the same land as having been historically expropriated. Yet, the process had the sum effect of subordinating local institutions to the whims of political elites, who were connected to a wide range of influential groups in the private sector, leadership, social circles, ethnic elites and so on (Munyuki-Hungwe, 2011). However, a key argument in this book is that, although there were elements of self-serving and skewed benefits that occurred as part of the haphazard programme, in general the majority profited. Illustrating this required much in-depth research on the ground to get to the bottom of what was going on and an assessment of the initial outcomes of the FTLRP.

Chapter overview

The following chapters elaborate on the key findings from the surveys and on an analysis of the issues and context of the last eight years based on the close reading of the evolution of the FTLRP. The research approach underpinning this book is based on an interactive analysis of macro- and micro-level forces, as well as of the ongoing context (national and international) that has shaped the nature, pace and emerging directions of the FTLRP. Based on a variety of information sources centred on original field data and secondary literature, the book exposes the emerging agrarian pattern on FTFs and uses this as a basis for defining whether this new agrarian landscape is the beginning of the end of the historical and colonial issue that has moulded the land question in Zimbabwe. It would seem that the demand side (majority blacks) of the land question has been addressed through processes that many would regard as 'the way not to do a land reform', yet the reality is that many people have now been on the land for some ten years. What does that bode for the future of the land question in Zimbabwe and elsewhere?

The land occupations discussed in the next chapter ignited the serious process of compulsory land acquisition (which differed from previous attempts), and saw an equally rapid process of putting people on the land (Chapter 3). The result is that land administrators, the judiciary and a range of stakeholders were all muscled into the programme without an iota of a chance of stopping or reversing the process. The result was that many aspects expected of a land reform programme, such as tenure security (Chapter 4), were put aside to ensure that first and foremost 'people were on the land', with the remaining problems to be addressed later. Clearly, production began to decline (Chapter 5), with a variety of reasons given to account for this. Nonetheless, the new settlers started to invest in their properties, but not optimally (Chapter 6); services have not been optimal, and improved only after the formation of the Inclusive Government. Also, women with high expectations of gaining access to land often did not have these expectations met (Chapter 7). Over time, however, new communities have been emerging (Chapter 8), with beneficiaries holding on despite an ambivalent government unsure what form of security should be provided to them.

2 | Land occupations as the trigger for compulsory land acquisition

Introduction

In much of the current academic discourse, there is an overt desire to research and discuss who got what land without revisiting the process of land acquisition (Moyo et al., 2009; Scoones et al., 2010). While this issue is critical, it is equally important to understand the genesis of the Fast Track Land Reform Programme (FTLRP) based on the transfer of land through compulsory land acquisition. This was indeed the foundation of the programme. Yet in Zimbabwe, and in much of the Zimbabwe literature on land after 2000, there is very little research into or academic study of compulsory land acquisition. A few scholars (Moyo, 1995a; 1998; 2000a; Tshuma, 1997; Moyo and Yeros, 2007a; 2007b), prior to and at the turn of the twenty-first century, did indeed analyse land acquisition processes in broad national terms. Much of the research has been at the national level, based on lists of farms gazetted in the national press by the government, without establishing the facts and issues of what happens on the ground when such farms are gazetted. Ruzivo Trust's Fast Track Farm Survey in 2004 sought to establish precisely the procedures of land acquisition at the local level, through identifying the key actors, the policies used by the authorities, and the reactions of the various players to such acquisition.

In the context of the FTLRP, land acquisition was defined by government as the process of compulsorily acquiring land for resettlement purposes based on legal instruments and a set of administrative guidelines. In practical terms, the land acquisition aspects – including the gazetting of farms (the official legal process of announcing targeted farms in the government press), the delisting of farms (a process of removing farms from the gazetted list), and policies relating to any remaining large-scale commercial farms owned by blacks and whites, farms under Bilateral Investment Promotion and Protection Agreements (BIPPAs) and strategic farms – were matters that influenced the land reform programme at the district level.

In order to understand the basis of land acquisition, it was necessary to first establish the key drivers for the FTLRP itself. Some academics have concentrated on the political motives (Alexander, 2003; 2006; Alexander and McGregor, 2001; Derman, 2006; Hammar et al., 2003) that broadly pitch the issues at the national level. This chapter examines the local social pressures for land reform and how these influenced land acquisition in the broadest sense. This required examination of the definition and meaning of land occupations in both a historical and a contemporary sense. A few studies on land demand have now emerged through field-based evidence on the process at a local level (Selby, 2006; Sadomba, 2008; Marongwe, 2008). This chapter explores how the land occupations shaped the patterns of land acquisition specifically in Mazowe District. However, it is important to locate this within the history of land issues in Zimbabwe as a whole, which influenced the formation of large-scale commercial farms (LSCFs). At the same time, the substantive interests of different players, of different genders, classes and areas of origin shaped how that land acquisition proceeded in districts such as Mazowe.

To step back into the history of independence, it can be seen that particular pressures had been building up around the need to speed up land transfers for the public resettlement programme. Specific episodes included the slowing of land reform during the Economic Structural Adjustment Programme of 1991 to 1995 (Matondi and Moyo, 2002); the failure of the bilateral negotiation for funding with the British government in 1997 (Moyo and Matondi, 2003); the demand for land by War Veterans in 1997 (Sadomba, 2008); the failure of the Inception Phase Framework Plan between 1999 and 2000 (Moyo and Yeros, 2007a); the land occupations led by the Svosve people in 1998 (Marongwe, 2008); and finally the failure of the constitutional review process in 2000, after the negative vote in the referendum. All these pressures, directed at the government, happened as a new opposition political party, founded by diverse civil society organisations, was emerging to champion poverty reduction as its ideological framework in the political and electoral competition.

The above factors influenced government to speed up land acquisition as part of a complex set of promises it wanted to deliver to the people. Land featured prominently, to the extent that government as represented by the Zimbabwe African National Union – Patriotic Front (ZANU-PF) had the widely publicised motto 'land to the people' or 'land is the economy, the economy is land', which became the basis upon which compulsory land acquisition was justified. However, beyond the politics of it, a range of reasons provided the government with a justification for massive compulsory land acquisition (GoZ, 2001): for example, the need to address poverty in communal areas, landlessness, homelessness, and the need to de-racialise commercial agriculture. This context is critical to understanding the process of land acquisition in Mazowe District, an area that first experienced compulsory land acquisition in 2000.

Squatting before 2000 as a trigger for land acquisition

One of the key factors that determined how the FTLRP evolved was the general social pressure for land reform, and specifically the pressure brought to bear on government by various classes of land claimants. Land squatting[1] before 2000 has been widely commented on by various scholars (Herbst, 1989; 1990; Moyo, 2000b; Hammar, 2007). In general, the authors have agreed that such squatting reflected problems of poverty (lack of employment opportunities), shortage of housing (especially in urban areas), a weak social security system (retired and retrenched farmworkers did not have a communal home to return to), and a shortage of land, for example in communal areas that were invaded by those without access to land (particularly grazing land not physically occupied by people). The land occupations were seen as a social nuisance by the landowners, who hoped that they were a passing phase and they could go back to living their normal lives. In 2000, some politicians, such as Dumiso Dabengwa (former Minister of Home Affairs) and the Acting President Joseph Msika, gave statements to the effect that the authorities would take action against the squatters. Yet, on the ground, a real war of attrition was taking place as the squatters built up their political power base, and squatting became a seesaw game between squatters and officials. The state was also intolerant of any disorder resulting from squatting, despite its limited attempts to address the problem through land resettlement. More often than not, the state was heavy handed as it showed that private property was sacrosanct from 'illegal' occupation, and that claiming for land based on previous historical occupation (referred to as 'restitution') was discouraged (Tshuma, 1997; Moyo, 2000b; Sadomba, 2008).

From 1998 to 2000, land issues featured prominently in the consultation and discussion over the drafting of a new constitution to succeed the Lancaster House constitution, especially aspects relating to the models of land acquisition (willing seller and willing buyer, or compulsory land acquisition). In fact, there was pressure on the government by ordinary people and War Veterans, who resorted to vigorous protests and land occupations. For instance, in June 1998 villagers in Svosve communal areas occupied Igava farm, vowing to stay on the land until the government made a written undertaking to resettle them. The villagers cited poor soils and congestion as factors that had compelled them to occupy white farms contiguous to the villages. Similar and widespread occupations of white commercial farms followed in Nyamandhlovu in Matabeleland, Nyamajura in Manicaland, Nemamwa in Masvingo and other places. However, these occupations had a short life span; by November 1998, most of the occupiers had been removed forcefully by the government or had moved voluntarily with promises that the land acquisition issues would be addressed in the new constitution.

It became increasingly clear that there was a significant number of people who would support any agency that would ensure that they obtained access to land. The ZANU-PF government in 2000 took advantage of this obvious demand by building its party politics around the issue, and thus tacitly supporting land invasions. War Veterans and peasants mostly from communal areas were well aware that by 2000 the government was at its weakest, in the face of deep economic problems and against the backdrop of the emergence of a strong opposition party, the Movement for Democratic Change (MDC). At that point, the usual state suppression of land squatting suddenly changed, as squatters received political support from the president. This support provided impetus to the land occupations and they began to go viral throughout the country. In addition, the War Veterans also dominated in the leadership of the government, thus making it possible for the rank and file outside government to succeed with the land takeovers. However, the land occupations were to take a radical political turn after 2000. Some would describe subsequent events as 'guided chaos', for divisions between the key state players were blurred. For instance, on 17 March the judiciary asked the police to take action against the squatters within 24 hours, but the War Veterans ignored the court directives. ZANU-PF was enticed by the idea of the land occupations as a 'God-given opportunity' to retain political power, but, at the same time, there was paralysis in government in terms of making and implementing policy, with some ministers condemning the squatting while the president supported the squatters' actions (Alexander, 2003; 2006; Derman, 2006).

Land occupations after 2000

In February 2000, War Veterans in Masvingo launched land occupations that received full media attention. The War Veterans, then under Chenjerai Hunzvi, already had substantial autonomy prior to 2000, as demonstrated by their success in extracting gratuity payments from the government. They had a clear position on land reform, advocating large-scale appropriation of land without compensation. The emergence of the opposition, leading to the struggles over the review of the constitution (up to February 2000) and in parliamentary elections (in June 2000), presented an opportunity for the government to appropriate the War Veteran farm invasion programme. The government had initially opposed farm occupations to the extent of using the state apparatus to evict occupiers (Moyo, 2000b; 2001; Sadomba, 2008). During the constitutional review process in 1999, the government inserted a clause, outside the Constitution Commission's procedures, making Britain liable for compensation for land, and thereby freeing the government to legally appropriate the required land. The rejection of the government-sponsored constitution probably convinced the ZANU-PF government to join the War Veterans' farm occupation programme (Sadomba, 2008). Government involvement then broadened the scope of occupations countrywide between February and June 2000, in order to win the elections and achieve fast resettlement. From 2000 onwards, the government adopted political strategies to acquire land by ignoring existing laws that countered occupation and by enacting laws to protect the occupiers, legitimising land acquisition without compensation.

The peasants, War Veterans and their supporters took to the land as a result of signals that the government would tolerate their actions. Over 1,000 farms (on less than 1 million ha of the 12 million ha designated as commercial farms) were occupied throughout the country (Moyo, 2001). The process of people placing themselves on the farms had political significance and created new definitions and terminologies. Some intellectual supporters called them land occupations (to demonstrate the political significance of land reform) or land self-provisioning (showing that people can take what they believe is theirs) (Moyo, 2000a; 2000b). Politicians wryly called them land demonstrations or demonstrating the need for land.[2] On the other hand, the bitter and resisting landowners called them squatting, land invasions or land grabbing. The law enforcement agencies called them common trespass, as referred to in their own statutes. Interested donors called them land or property grabbing depending on their mood. Despite this variety of definitions, the simple issue was that people placed themselves on the land in the new farms and took various actions to consolidate their claims.

Given the importance of land in Zimbabwe's history and economy, there is no question that land had to be delivered politically (Moyo, 1995a). Ten years later, Moyo and Yeros (2005b) were not surprised that it was politics that delivered on the land question. This was because Zimbabwe's nationalist politicians had a peasant origin and received support for liberation from communal areas as well as garnering electoral support from the peasants (including the urban poor, who originated from the communal areas and would therefore support land grabbing). Thus, earlier, Moyo (1995a: 17–18) wrote:

> It makes no sense, however, to pretend that the land question is not a political issue, and that it should only be addressed following purely economic logic, particularly of a short-term nature. The land issue is a political issue, which has to be addressed with full cognisance of the political problems it evokes, but in a manner which optimises the economic benefits to the country. Therefore the ruling party need not apologise for the utility of resolving the land question in its bid to be re-elected, especially if redistribution targets economic growth among the rural and urban poor.

In 2000, land invasions provided an impetus to resolve the land question, as the political mood changed as War Veterans and peasants sought methods of delivering land – with or without the government – through what has been termed *jambanja*. Chaumba et al. (2003b: 540) defined *jambanja* as follows:

> Literally meaning violence or angry argument, *jambanja* has been used in subtly different contexts to refer to different people and places, including the ex-combatant farm invaders themselves, the farm invasions, and more broadly politically instigated violence. A popular war veteran catchphrase was *jambanja*

ndizvo (violence is the answer). In some cases the term has also been appropriated by opposition supporters to mean fighting back against a bully, or by the workers' movement to refer to mass protest and direct action. But in essence it has come to refer to a time and space of at best confusion and nonsense, and at worst disorder and chaos.

Although *jambanja*[3] (or mayhem) can to some extent be viewed as a response to political coaching, it cannot be disputed that the beneficiaries played a more significant role; they were restive because of the pressures in communal areas, unemployment and limited economic opportunities. They were also riding on the back of promises made in the liberation struggle and at independence that land reform would be addressed (see Chapter 1). Therefore, when they placed themselves on the land, which they had done before in the 1980s and 1990s, they did not see anything wrong or illegal in their actions because they viewed themselves as the victors of the liberation struggle leading up to independence in 1980. Victors naturally take what they think belongs to them, and the promise of 'freedom farming' (*kurima madiro*) that had been the political message in the liberation struggle had to be fulfilled (Murombedzi, 1994; Nyambara, 2001).

Peasant and elite approaches to the land occupations The peasants and the elites employed different strategies in the land occupations. The peasants simply occupied land that was physically accessible to them. Usually the transportation available was a major determinant of the number of farms invaded within a time period. In addition, the human resources to be deployed on an invaded farm were also crucial, given that at any point the organisers might not have adequate numbers of people who could be left on a farm to 'defend' the occupation (key informant interview, 12 May 2004). According to an interviewee (16 May 2004), in Chiweshe they simply moved to farms 'next door', meaning that they occupied farms adjacent to their communal area. However, those with resources moved to 'inner farms', which were farms located far from their areas of domicile in Chiweshe communal area. In this case, this meant investing 'cash' for transport and for living in places far from home for long periods of time (which required food and other necessities), while they awaited visits from the 'roving occupying leaders' co-ordinated by the War Veterans. In most cases, this was not an easy option without financial backing. Most of these types of distant land occupiers tended to be men, and they were supported by networks of elites who were not willing to physically occupy land, or were reluctant to be seen as land occupiers because of their social status.

There emerged a variety of approaches (direct and indirect) to the occupation of farms. Those who expected to become beneficiary landowners, and who viewed their occupation as leading to the piece of land they occupied being officially handed to them, took a direct approach. However, some people who were interested in land did not have the courage to occupy that land themselves, and adopted an indirect approach by using proxies (hired War Veterans and youths). Some farms were occupied for speculative purposes, with the expectation that the 'big guys' would come and make a claim, and then the occupiers would be able to get a monetary windfall later. Thus the occupation of strategic farms was a calculated move to get the most from the expectant 'big guy' beneficiary, who would be willing to pay more if the farm had better infrastructure and a 'nice' farmhouse (focus group discussions [FGDs], 28 June 2004). Sadomba (2008) further noted that the role played by intellectuals and professionals, members of the petty bourgeoisie and workers was also a significant factor as it sanitised the land occupations and helped the government move ahead with the forced transfers.

In fact, many institutions watched the unfolding land drama with awe; the situation was unprecedented in a country that strongly believed in and practised the law to the letter and the spirit (Tshuma, 1997; Madhuku, 2004). Contradictions and uncertainty were also rife, as in some cases the Zimbabwe Republic Police (ZRP), the District Administrator's Office and the District Land Committee (DLC) facilitated negotiations between land occupiers and white farmers through certified agreements. Once agreed, they were immediately disregarded, which to some extent demonstrated the ineffectiveness of the institutions. In this 'confusion', white farmers did not know where they stood – the words of the state leaders, the media and their own experiences on the ground confirmed the rule of disorder and uncertainty at all levels. In fact, as some civil servants watched the land occupations, others were said to have used proxy youths to facilitate the strategic occupation of farms that became their preferred choices at the time of allocation. In general, the land occupiers were sophisticated in many ways, as they had the ability to raise the means to sustain the occupations, and many did not depend on government but on their own resources (Masuko, 2004).

The arsenal used in the occupations also included the use of physical violence, putting political pressure on the law enforcement agencies (especi-ally the ZRP) not to take action against occupiers, negotiations, incessant demonstrations at farm gates (singing, engaging in press-ups, and all-night vigils close to the homes of the white owners), using youths as the shock troopers, killing and maiming livestock, etc. According to one interviewee (Concession, 22 June 2004), when they arrived at a typical farm they behaved in a variety of ways influenced by prior information they had obtained about the farm (usually from farmworkers) and their knowledge of the farm owner (who he is, his relationship with workers, the government, etc.). Some placed themselves on underutilised land and started to 'utilise' it without interfering with the landowners; some immediately declared themselves the new owners and asked the owners to leave; others grabbed produce already on the land

and declared it theirs; some went for the farmhouses and equipment and declared ownership.

In Mazowe, a symbolic gesture of intention through the 'pegging' of land by occupiers and the subsequent 'squatting' – the realisation of that intention – occurred simultaneously. In most cases, the level of aggression of the land occupiers could not be predicted, nor could their demands to the farmer be foreseen. Occupiers who came to 'peg' land often left quite quickly after doing so. This was because, at that time, they needed to move across the farms to set a precedent to most of the white owners. In a way, it also veiled the fact that there were very few occupiers in certain areas; as Pilossof (2012) confirmed using Commercial Farmers' Union (CFU) data, only 28 per cent (1,525 farms) of the total number of 5,446 farms were occupied. In order to demonstrate their seriousness, some occupiers built huts in addition to pegging. This was interpreted as a more serious threat and a symbol of 'permanency'.

However, the government and some intellectuals came up with a new development that they christened 'co-existence'; the land occupiers would do 'what they had to do' on the land, while the owner was 'asked' to kindly support them with their equipment to use for farming (FGDs, June 2007). 'Co-existence' became the catchphrase of negotiations between farmers, police officials, government officials and land occupiers during 2002. The land occupiers liked co-existence because it controlled hostility from white landowners and their farmworkers. The land occupiers used it as an opportunity to get a foot in the farm door, to see how farms operated, and in many cases to 'share' their first crop with the white farmer. The white farmers liked co-existence because it stopped the incessant night-time farm-gate vigils (singing and drum beating), the barricading of their families, and the provocation of pets such as dogs. In addition, it gave them time to arrange their escape lines, in case of any impending danger.

The compromises allowed the white farmers to provide equipment to their new neighbours, while also showing their new neighbours the basics of farming. White farmers would prepare and plant a crop on the understanding that they would continue operating the farm and their new partners would assume a profit share. Farmers were then usually evicted before or during the harvest. However, where the negotiated compromises were successful, this resulted in crop-sharing arrangements that by 2004 (and still today) were being condemned at the national level as 'giving back land to the whites'. For instance, one politician argued that: 'We are also demanding that the government must repossess all farms owned by blacks who are leasing them out to former white commercial farmers, because it is against the law' (Chimakure, 2010). However, the co-existence period enabled victims (former landowners and farmworkers) and victors (land beneficiaries) to share information and temporarily integrate socially in the farm compounds. On the other hand, the white farmers found this to be a temporary strategy but one that bought them time to make alternative arrangements for their future livelihood, to remove assets from their farms, or to negotiate with government officials for a delay to the farm acquisition.

War Veterans in land occupations Sadomba (2008) has discussed at length the role of the War Veterans in the land occupations, and argues that, although they were the key force, most lost out on the opportunities that resulted from gaining access to land compared with politicians and other elites. In many ways, the War Veterans were a major factor in the land acquisition process, for they showed the government that they were prepared to take land by force. Initially, the land occupations were a protest against the ZANU-PF government by the landless for not utilising their two-thirds majority to speed up the land acquisition and redistribution process (Masuko, 2004).

From the outset, the War Veterans were at the forefront of what was happening. The signatures of the War Veterans were on the notices that were put up at farm gates and along farm roads as a sign of triumph; some of these read 'War Veterans ahead – detour', 'War Veterans in action – keep off', 'Third Chimurenga' or 'Land is the Economy and the Economy is Land'. They also displayed political party or national flags and other paraphernalia that demonstrated the action of the land occupiers. Sadomba (2008) argues that the War Veterans from Harare were also relatively better off, in terms of economic status. Some of them were employed in the private sector, many working in parastatals, and others were self-employed, mainly engaged in petty trading at the Mbare Musika market. The War Veterans were not inclined to negotiate at the national level, but rather churned out signals to their foot soldiers on the ground to consolidate, as Sadomba and Andrew (2006: 9) observed:

> The War Vets movement first engaged the state in a 'no-holds-barred' meeting on 25 April 1992, making these demands to President Mugabe. With Chenjerai Hunzvi at the helm of the ZNLWVA, their strategy became more militant and included direct confrontations. They organised street demonstrations, locked Ministers and top ZANU-PF politicians in their offices, disturbed an international conference and a Heroes' Day speech by Mugabe, interrupted court sessions and besieged the state house ... In 1997 they demanded their pensions and that the remaining 5 million hectares promised by the government be immediately redistributed. Mugabe ... yielded and ... War Vets were promised 20 per cent of all land that was to be acquired by the state for resettlement and residential purposes.

While some promoted physical confrontation in the invasions, most did not, and instead sought the more effective use of the legal instrument of land expropriation. Some engaged in corrupt land grabbing of large and multiple farms. The majority did not, preferring to be formally allocated land. In an effort to be effective in the occupations, the urban-based potential beneficiaries, with weak social capital in rural areas, organised themselves into associations for targeting commercial land and defending their stay on the land they wanted to occupy. These associations – such as Nyabira and Maryvale – had the effect of providing an organised force to:

- negotiate with the former landowners for a stake on the land on a shared basis;
- negotiate for peaceful co-existence, which meant allowing each other to practise farming without interference;
- negotiate with the land committee in Mazowe for choice farms for their members;
- influence the selection, and therefore the decisions about who got which piece of land, when officials moved in to do the planning;
- extract farming resources (seeds, fuel and inputs) from government upon settlement.

At an operational level, the associations – some of which were linked to the Zimbabwe National Liberation War Veterans Association (ZNLWVA) – had a role in attending to problems encountered on occupied farms, membership issues, mobilisation of sympathisers, identification of new farms to be occupied, and planned meetings with various stakeholders, plus resource and membership mobilisation. The associations, to ensure that their approaches were effective and objectives were being met, also constantly reviewed strategies and tactics. This should be viewed in the wider context of the political strategies of the occupiers. Interviews with War Veterans in 2004 showed that the land occupations and state expropriation process were not uniform and were riven by numerous internal conflicts and contradictions. In the western part of Mazowe, where some of the national leadership of the War Veterans settled, they sought the total restitution of all land and displacement of all white ('settler') farmers. Others sought to negotiate with the white farmers and accommodate them on downsized farms; hence some white commercial farmers remained on their properties, defended at times by the national leadership, especially the late Vice President, Joseph Msika.

Farmworkers' participation in the land occupations It has been noted in several publications and in the media that farmworkers either were victims of the land occupations (as they lost jobs and incomes), or were coerced into the land occupations. Sadomba (2008) notes that farmworkers were useful for the War Veterans as they had a good knowledge of both the farms and the white farmers. Interviews with land occupiers showed that some of the white-owned farms were spared occupation based on recommendations by farmworkers regarding their individual behaviour. It follows that they were not always victims, but were at times willing participants in assisting the land occupiers. As Sadomba (ibid.: 153) noted:

> In Mazowe, farmworkers living on the urban fringe, alongside unemployed youths, accepted mobilisation by War Veterans, thus constituting an element in the initial manpower moving onto farms to engage in further mobilisation and engage in planning further occupations. War Veterans in fact relied on mobil-ising these amenable 'local' farmworkers to occupy farms in the surrounding areas. But in other cases War Veterans saw farmworkers as a threat (seeking to protect their jobs by defending the land or property of their employer) and were thus anxious to immobilise them, where they could, to prevent counter-attacks, something that happened often, indicating that the farmworkers had their own competing views about the land occupation movement, perhaps tending to be negative where they lacked local connections ...

The farmworkers also used their intimate knowledge of the farms to allow War Veterans and ordinary land occupiers to roam on them unfettered. Famili-arity was, therefore, an important factor in sustaining the land occupations, which received backing from collaborating farmworkers. In some cases, farm-workers organised themselves to repel land occupiers, at times with disastrous consequences as the War Veterans and others mobilised forces to counter them. In these situations, violence was often the outcome. However, as Sachikonye (2003: 69) shows, the relationships created uncertainties because:

> In a sense, farmworkers acted as a kind of buffer between the farmer and the settlers. At the same time, the workers were hostages of the situation: they may have wanted land also, but they could not agitate for it openly and be seen to be joining the settlers. Some farmworkers did join the settlers, not in their own workplace but on neighbouring farms ...

Land occupation was a major factor that shaped subsequent land reform processes in the early period of the reforms, from 2000 to 2002 (see Chapter 3). The government had announced a policy that the land occupiers would not be moved until after alternative land had been acquired, which meant that they became de facto beneficiaries. The effect of this policy was that it provided latecomers with the courage to rush into and occupy farms, which created conflict situations with the earlier occupiers. At the same time, the rich, who were sceptical at first, also began to make forays on to the farms with gangs they hired to occupy land for them on a paid basis. In general, land occupiers from 2000 onwards gained courage from reading the signals of political leaders who directly supported them, or simply were indifferent to cases of forcible land takeovers. Where previously land occupiers had risked beatings and property destruction through forced removals by officials of the courts and the police, now they were left alone and at times even encouraged by politicians to stay on the farms.

The significance of the 2000 land occupations in Mazowe District In Mazowe District there were no land occupations before 2000. Does this mean that there was no specific demand for land expressed through land occupations targeting the rich agricultural lands in Mazowe? Selby (2006) noted that there were squatters at Rockwood camp near Concession, Somerset Farm and Ramahori Farm. The local farmers tried to evict the squatters through supportive court rulings, but to no avail. In general, Selby further noted, the squatters did not receive any national attention nor public support from local politicians. However, they continued to stay on the properties by forming various relationships with the landowners. Two local farmers even went to the extent of employing some of the squatters, to try to limit their negative impact, which in these cases was environmental rather than economic.

From 2000 to 2002, Mazowe was a hive of activity as urbanites, especially from Harare, made forays into the district in search of land. This demand for land by urbanites from a nearby district provided the context and forces that influenced the patterns of land acquisition. However, the proximity of commercial farms to the Chiweshe communal area, where most of the peasants lived, was what mostly prompted the land occupations and pressure for rapid land acquisition. In Mazowe District, the first landowner victims of acquisition were the farmers adjacent to Chiweshe communal area. The various classes – urban and peasant – pushing for access to land had the effect of pressurising land committees and the government's implementation agencies to speed up land acquisition in the district.

Mazowe District experienced intense land occupations from 2000 by different groups of people. A variety of land claimants (urban people, rural people and the state through parastatals such as the Agricultural Rural Development Authority [ARDA]) laid siege to farms in Mazowe. People from the Chiweshe communal area (some with outstanding traditional land claims – the Hwata, Zumba and Mbari people), people from mining centres, of various classes and status in society were involved in land occupations on different scales and using a variety of approaches. The reason why Mazowe generated interest for the expectant beneficiary was because the district is close to Harare and other urban centres such as Bindura, as well as to small business centres, such as Concession, and Glendale. The agricultural infrastructure of Mazowe was also an influencing factor in the occupations: the existence of paved farm roads, telecommunications, water resources (especially in the central parts of the district), dams and irrigation resources was attractive. In terms of agricultural potential, the district offered the best conditions in terms of soil types in the four Intensive Conservation Areas (ICAs)[4] of Marodzi-Tatagura ICA, Barwick ICA,

Glendale ICA, and Mvurwi ICA. Barwick ICA offered options for livestock and wildlife management, which was an added attraction to those with resources to invest in such activities. The ability to commute regularly to the occupied land, and the reduced transport costs, made the district an attractive choice.

Politically Mazowe was a good option because it was also meant to prove to sceptics that the land transfer process was a reality. For War Veterans, the significance of the district was that the land being taken was seen as a core base of white capital, as the district had not experienced government resettlement before. The flight of white farmers from the farms was an added bonus, as this provided land occupiers with some semblance of security during the actual invasions as there were no reprisal attacks. It is said that some white farmers defiantly maintained their farming operations by commuting from Harare.[5] However, such commuting provided the land occupiers with time to plan and execute invasions, and to cement their occupations, while the owners were domiciled in the city.

One issue that has arisen is the role of government in controlling or managing the land occupations. Scoones et al. (2010), following on from Moyo (2001), argued that the state lost control of the land invasions at some stage. In Mazowe this did not happen, but rather the state consolidated its control in that it created order in a district that had the potential for greater chaos than any other district. On the ground, the DLC helped the government to assert control of the process; through the use of broad guidelines and pragmatic local policy-making, the DLC was able to allow what worked in terms of meeting the objectives of land reform, while disallowing anything that did not fit their 'programme'. For instance, the DLC was very strict in disallowing land occupations after 2002, which accounts for their reduction and near cessation five to eight years after the FTLRP commenced.

Understanding land acquisition

From 2000, the FTLRP was closely associated with the process of land acquisition. Land acquisition has been a historical, ongoing process in Zimbabwe since the colonial land takeovers in the late 1880s (Ndlovu-Gatsheni, 2009). During much of the colonial period, land was forcibly acquired without any form of compensation; this involved the introduction of paper-based administrative processes, the drawing of maps, and the designation of land for particular racial groups and classes of farmers, as set out in the Land Apportionment Act of 1931. The sum effect of this process was the introduction of a segregated land market, where whites could acquire land on white designated land and blacks on land designated for blacks. This racial and political land apportionment created the large-scale commercial farms in areas such as Mazowe that became the centre of conflicts, especially from 2000 onwards, when the government sought to acquire commercial land for public resettlement purposes.

The character of land acquisition changed significantly in 1990, when the government introduced compulsory land acquisition within its laws. A key policy and administrative change was the introduction of land designation, where farms were to be identified for future acquisition, although in practice the government could delay the acquisition. This change was part of the government's attempt to speed up the process of land acquisition and resettlement. The Land Acquisition Act in 1992 followed the introduction in 1990 of Constitutional Amendment 11 (Tshuma, 1997). Under the Land Acquisition Act, land was classified as either designated (meaning that the government had sole acquisition rights) or non-designated. The non-designated land could be traded on the open market. The legislation provided a Certificate of No Present Interest (CONPI) for non-designated land, meaning that the government was not interested in acquiring the farm. Farmers from 2000 used CONPI in the courts and public campaigns to demonstrate that the government had issued them with certificates confirming that their farms were spared from compulsory acquisition.

In Zimbabwe there are private land market sales that allow for the transfer or exchange of land through 'willing seller/willing buyer' market-based principles. However, the government argued that the market-led acquisition process was slow, cumbersome and expensive, largely because of the resistance of commercial farmers (Moyo, 2000a; Utete, 2003a). In fact, the market-led principles of land acquisition favoured former farm owners, who in essence created an exclusive land market where only those with resources in the same market (mostly whites) would exchange land, in the process creating multiple farm ownership (Moyo, 1998; Rugube and Chambati, 2001; Rugube et al., 2003). In Mazowe, it was not uncommon to find individuals who owned three or four farms (some consolidated), as only 426 farmers occupied a large part of the commercial land.[6] The exclusive land market was what the compulsory land acquisition law sought to reform. Nonetheless, compulsory land acquisition has not found favour with the broader international community, even though it is accepted in situations where historical land inequities are supposed to be addressed (Utete, 2003a). The compulsory land acquisition legal instruments had the effect of freeing government from the 'willing seller/willing buyer' clause.

From 1997, the process of land acquisitions gained prominence because of the scale of the acquisition intended by government. In 1997, when the government designated 1,471 farms for compulsory acquisition by December that year, a total of 1,393 objections were received of which 510 were upheld (Moyo, 1998). The exclusions included farms owned by indigenous black people or churches, plantation farms, farms with Zimbabwe Investment Centre permits, and single-owner farms being used productively. For the remaining 883 farms, the government had to go through lengthy judicial processes. There was an immediate reaction to the designations and a land donors' conference was called; this was held between 9 and 11 June 1998 and attended by representatives from 48 countries. The government then prepared policy documents on Phase II of the Land and Resettlement Programme, as a successor to the Phase I programme that it had declared as having ended in 1997. At this conference, President Mugabe noted that black Zimbabweans were getting agitated over the slow pace of land reform and warned that: 'If we delay in resolving the land needs of our people, they will resettle themselves. It has happened before and it may happen again.'[7]

At the conference, basic principles and the framework for international assistance for the land reform programme were agreed upon. A major agreement was on the need to formulate the Inception Phase Framework Plan as a precursor to Phase II of a government donor-supported land acquisition and resettlement programme. It was proposed that several alternative approaches to land redistribution should be tried, by both government and civil society, on 118 farms that had been offered for public resettlement purposes. The Inception Phase Framework Plan provided the government with a weapon they could use to stop or discourage illegal land takeovers, such as the ones that happened at the end of 1998. However, as time went on, the government felt that the donors were not serious about their funding commitments for land reform. For example, only a Learning and Innovation Fund of US $5 million from the World Bank came to fruition, although there were pledges from several donors; the funding fell far short of what the government had expected (Matondi and Moyo, 2002). This, in essence, gave rise to the FTLRP, but it was not the sole cause: there were also complex political and economic contextual factors emerging at the turn of the twenty-first century that made the programme inevitable.

The politics of compulsory land acquisition Compulsory land acquisition, formalised in law prior to the parliamentary elections in 2000, became the key arsenal for transferring land. The law, which was challenged by commercial farmers through the CFU, was confirmed as legitimate by a Supreme Court ruling in 2001. The government rallied significant institutions to support the programme, and in the process ended up politicising the technical bureaucracy and taking a party position on the land acquisition issue (Matondi, 2008b). The ruling party then pushed for compulsory land acquisition and set aside all forms of negotiations, while providing a semblance of wanting to negotiate with white farmers (but not committing to it) through, for example, the Zimbabwe Joint Resettlement Initiative, which was never implemented. Given the high-stakes political challenge following the defeat of the 'yes' vote preferred by ZANU-PF in the constitutional referendum elections in 2000, the party increasingly hardened its position on land acquisition matters.

In the amended Land Acquisition Act of 2000, the government allowed for compensation only for improvements, as well as allocating responsibility for the payment of land compensation to the United Kingdom government. With a majority in parliament just before the national elections in 2000, ZANU-PF had effectively and legally cemented provisions for compulsory land acquisition, providing legitimacy to their actions (Madhuku, 2004). During that time, while the ruling governing party was tactful in using the land issue to gain votes, it still tried to devise legal and constitutional guidelines to sanitise the ongoing land occupations, using presidential laws to come up with legal instruments such as the Rural Land Occupiers (Prevention from Eviction) Act in 2001. Thus its political survival strategy was based on the fact that the majority of the poor (and mass voters) strongly identified with the land issue, given their extremely impoverished material conditions. Therefore, from 2000 onwards, the poor sided with the government's view of land expropriation, as evidenced by the party's recovery following the referendum setback and its consolidation in 2005. ZANU-PF, as the governing party, then became a significant factor in the design and execution of compulsory land acquisition, using all channels at its disposal. To ZANU-PF, the land occupations came as a significant masterstroke in its strategies for retaining political power. Moyo (1995a; 2001) argues that any political party could have taken land as a political agenda in order to retain power.

Statutory instruments legitimising compulsory land acquisition were used and underpinned by violence to force farmers – voluntarily and involuntarily – from their land. Yet violence had also been used in the past by government in collusion with farmers against those demanding land and illegally occupying it. In the 1980s and 1990s, the brutal violence against land squatters through national, provincial and district squatter control committees, using the courts and their brutal messengers as well as the police to evict squatters, was aimed at obstructing the demand for land. At times, because of a lack of capacity, government would also allow white commercial farmers to carry out brutal evictions and punishments of these so-called squatters and poachers (Moyo, 2001; Alexander, 2003; Sadomba, 2008).

At a political level, compulsory land acquisition progressed because there was now resolute political leadership, led by the President, that ensured that it remained on track. For instance, the highest authority of the land at one point in 2002 threatened to take over all remaining white farms, responding to indications that the electorate was strongly becoming aligned with the opposition. In response, land occupiers increased their occupation activities, while the government continued the gazetting of farms, ignoring the deadline for the end of the fast track programme (August 2002, according to indications from the government). In the ten years since then, the FTLRP has become a cliché of land reform; perhaps it would be more accurate to refer to a continuous process of fast track land reform rather than a self-contained programme. After 2002, the land occupations (and therefore the acquisition of farms) escalated, with no end in sight. More productive farmers (whether black or white) became victims if they were alleged sympathisers of the opposition or if they failed to make deals with politicians.

Policy and legal instruments for land acquisition The story of land acquisition at the national level can be told in terms of how various local institutions and people reacted to the government's resolve finally to address land ownership inequities (Matondi, 2008b). National policies were influenced by different forces within and outside government, as well as by the reaction of the large-scale farming communities in terms of how they negotiated, or failed to negotiate, with the government. From 2000 to 2002, the government was clearly on the offensive as it gazetted large-scale farms in the national press, ostensibly to demonstrate the seriousness of its intention. It is, therefore, pertinent to understand clearly the national processes surrounding the politics of land acquisition and the implications of the ways in which policy mutated in the early years of the FTLRP. Such a framework may then guide understanding of how land acquisition was carried out in Mazowe District.

In general the GoZ strongly believes in legality; although politicians appeared to be ignoring the rule of law, they actually made concerted efforts to get back to a legal framework to support their political actions relating to land acquisition. However, Zimbabwe's legal scope on land issues can be traced back to the colonial period, when white politicians used the law to dispossess blacks of their land (for example, Land Apportionment Act 1930 and Native Land Husbandry Act 1951) (Matondi, 2001; Madhuku, 2004; Bolding, 2004). Bolding (2004) quotes a series of legal instruments (Native Affairs Act 1927, Maize Control Act 1931, Cattle Levy Act 1931, Natural Resources Act 1942, Good Husbandry Act 1944, etc.) as some of the key legislation put in place by the colonial government over a short period of time. These legal weapons were used not just for land expropriation but also to control nascent competition posed by African peasants. Some of these legal weapons were used against white landowners by the post-independent government in 2000 and afterwards to effect land expropriation.

The FTLRP was associated with the Land Acquisition Act of 1992 (now Chapter 20: 10). The Act was a historical piece of legislation given that it legally allowed for compulsory acquisition of productive agricultural land for resettlement purposes. The amended Land Acquisition Act (Act 15 of 2000) streamlined the previous dual route of compulsory acquisition by eliminating designation, which tended to delay the land acquisition process. It retained the direct acquisition route but with more clearly defined procedures for compensation. At a political level, the government justified the amendments because administration of the legal process was complex and time-consuming; also, the legal process led to mostly successful litigations against compulsory acquisition by former owners between 1993 and 1999.

As far as the legislative process was concerned, the government could be judged to be lacking in foresight, as it enacted laws only after realising deficiencies in existing laws, and hence it repeatedly amended the same provisions of the expropriation legislation to correct its oversights (Madhuku, 2004). The legality of the expropriation laws and their compatibility with international laws protecting private property were questioned. The expropriation laws were enacted at a time when the executive became highly political in its conduct and pushed aside other key state bodies, particularly parliament. For instance, by using presidential temporary powers, which lasted six months, to effect land policy actions, the executive appropriated the powers of the legislature to deal with law-making matters (ibid.). The executive had the habit of making and implementing 'temporary' laws, thus blurring the separation of powers with parliament. This was at a time when the state became largely reactive and hardened its political position on land issues.

The government saw the main advantage of compulsory acquisition as having been to force unwilling landowners to release excess land for resettlement in appropriate areas. The state could also move at the right pace for the allocation of such land without undue farmer pressure to pay compensation, as the government did not have sufficient money to pay all the affected landowners simultaneously. The main disadvantage was that the instrument could be contested by the landowners who could delay the process on the basis of constitutional guarantees. Secondly, it was largely frowned upon by the international community as it was regarded as a primitive system of grabbing land, thus affecting property rights and potential investment in agriculture. Within Zimbabwe, the compulsory land acquisition instrument was at times found to be at variance with the constitution and the rights of the landowners (ibid.). Moreover, it was largely contested on the basis of the criteria for compulsory land acquisition, compensation in terms of the valuation procedures and the responsibility for compensation, among other issues.[8]

The FTLRP became the central platform for playing out the law and politics, with the former landowners exercising their rights to use the courts to fend off land takeover. However, the law did not work for politicians in a context where the government viewed the highest court of the land as being led by an anti-land reform white judge (Tshuma, 1997). The former supreme court judge, Anthony Gubbay, had been accused of making a political statement and of questioning the authority of parliament on land matters in 1991, which was seen as a serious breach of the constitution and governance, and of being politically motivated rather than making judgments purely on the basis of law (Madhuku, 2004). However, although the judiciary had been accused in the 1990s of encroaching on the executive and legislature, it was not until the height of the land reform programme that it was reformed by the executive arm of the state. Mostly black judges, apparently seen as more sympathetic to

TABLE 2.1 Land: the constitution and legal framework of Zimbabwe, 1979–2009

Year	Constitutional changes	Relevant legislation	Key provisions
1979–84	Constitution of Zimbabwe (Section 16: 1)	Land Acquisition Act (Act 15 of 1979)	Limits rights of compulsory acquisition; introduces 'willing seller/willing buyer' criteria for compensation; allows acquisition for resettlement with 'prompt and adequate' compensation
1985–90	Same as above	Acquisition Act (Act 21 of 1985)	Repeals 1979 Act; includes no reference to 'willing seller/willing buyer' criteria; offers all commercial agricultural land sold on the open market to government first; if the government is not ready or interested in the property (Right of First Refusal), it is issued with a CONPI
1990	Constitution of Zimbabwe Amendment Act (Act 30 of 1990, 11th Amendment to the Constitution)	Land Acquisition Act (Act 3 of 1992 and now Chapter 20: 10)	Repeals 1985 Act; introduces designation for up to ten years as a prelude to compulsory acquisition; confirms compulsory acquisition through designation
1992–93	Constitution of Zimbabwe Amendment Act (Acts 4 and 9 of 1993, 12th and 13th Amendments to the Constitution)	Same as above	Abolishes Right of First Refusal; confirms compulsory acquisition through designation
2000	Constitution of Zimbabwe Amendment Act (Act 5 of 2000, 16th Amendment to the Constitution) Constitutional Amendment 16A	Land Acquisition Amendment Act (Act 15 of 2000) Land Acquisition Amendment Act (Act 14 of 2001) Land Acquisition Amendment Act (Act 6 of 2002)	Absolves the government from paying compensation for land; obliges payment for improvements (section 16A); incorporates new position of no obligation to pay compensation for land; eliminates designation route; allows payment through instalments, bonds and other long-term securities; makes the maximum one-year preliminary notice of acquisition valid indefinitely; condones the government's failure to comply with time limits imposed by the Land Acquisition Act; reduces the indefinite validity of preliminary notice of acquisition to two years (increased to ten years through section 14 of Act 7 of 2004); requires the 'owners' of a farm to be acquired to cease operations within 45 days of the notification being served. The owners are also

Year	Act	Description
	Land Acquisition Amendment Act (Act 10 of 2002)	expected to vacate the living quarters within 90 days, even when they are challenging the acquisition; introduces the presumption that land to be acquired for resettlement is suitable for agricultural purposes; allows acquisition to proceed despite a failure to serve the notice on bond holders that is required by law
2001	Same as above	Prescribes the maximum farm sizes per agro-ecological region; allows for an occupier who had occupied land by March 2001 to stay on the land; Act repealed without substitution by the Gazetted Land (Consequential Provisions) Act (Act 8 of 2006, Chapter 20: 28)
	Rural Land (Farm Sizes) Regulations Rural Land Occupiers (Prevention from Eviction) Act (Act 13 of 2001, Chapter 20: 26)	
2004–06	Same as above	Provides for compulsory acquisition of farm equipment and material on agricultural land which is not being used for agricultural purposes; amends the Land Acquisition Act by extending the validity of the preliminary notice of acquisition from two years to ten years
	Acquisition of Farm Equipment or Material Act (Act 7 of 2004, Chapter 18: 23)	
	Gazetted Land (Consequential Provisions) Act (Act 8 of 2006, Chapter 20: 28)	Requires former owners of land that has been compulsorily acquired and owners whose land is identified and gazetted for resettlement and other purposes to cease operations within 45 days and vacate the living quarters within 90 days of the gazetting unless authorised to remain on the land
2005–09	Constitution of Zimbabwe Amendment Act (Act 5 of 2005, 17th Amendment to the Constitution)	Takes away the right of former landowners to contest agricultural land acquisition in the Administrative Court or in any other court in Zimbabwe, although they can still challenge the fairness of the compensation offered

Source: Matondi, 2011a.

land reform, were appointed, with some of them becoming beneficiaries of the FTLRP.[9] Nonetheless, judicial decisions on land issues have been mixed, with the land rights of some former landowners protected despite the executive's political pressure to remove white farmers. Madhuku (2004) concludes that the colonial land laws created the current land question, and states that at some stage the law became irrelevant in the context of land reform because: 'A state which passes unjust laws and complies with them is acting in compliance with the rule of the law' (ibid.: 143). Therefore any discussion of political questions or reference to justice and fairness will need to be viewed in the context of the historical facts behind the law.

At the local level, once the political decision had been made on the FTLRP, the takeover of land and its allocation continued. This was despite the legal battles that were taking place in the courts. The land occupations from 2000 onwards had the tacit approval of government, which had provided local (reformed) structures with added ammunition to move forward with land takeovers. To create order, the government facilitated the creation of DLCs and Provincial Land Committees (PLCs). However, the government allowed some leeway for the formation of sub-committees at farm level, called Committees of Seven; these were not part of the DLCs but were independent bodies charged with handling farm-level conflicts and misunderstanding, while also ensuring that the land takeovers remained intact. Given that these were not legal bodies, they did not follow the dictates of law in land acquisition, allocation or management, as will be noted in several chapters of this book.

Government administrative mechanism for land acquisition In terms of procedures, government departments in Mazowe relied on policy directives from the national level, which made the acquisition process complex and cumbersome. An official interviewed noted that it took days for policy directives to reach them, when at times they would have made a decision to acquire a particular farm immediately. In fact, the simultaneous interest from central government players meant that some farms were acquired outside the policy provision of delisting, as central government indicated that officials on the ground should always understand that all white-owned farms could be acquired. The land acquisition process thus involved several procedures, which at times ran concurrently, as well as numerous institutions and stakeholders:

- *Land Identification Committees.* These were chaired by the district administrator and were responsible for land identification. However, the District Co-ordinating Committee chair of the ruling party played a much more active role. The committee was composed of representatives from ministries, traditional leaders, councillors and other key stakeholders. Their job was to identify farms for resettlement purposes through compiling and vetting lists for submission to the provincial offices. The lists were then analysed by the PLCs and then submitted to the National Task Force or command centre. The list of farms was then submitted to the former Ministry of Lands and Agriculture for acquisition.

• *Land acquisition criteria*. The government stated that it would acquire land according to the following administrative, but not necessarily legal, criteria: a) land belonging to those who own more than one farm – multiple ownership; b) land owned by absentee landlords; c) land near communal area boundaries; d) derelict or underutilised land; and e) foreign-owned land. In addition, plantations and agro-industrial processors in the poultry, beef, dairy and seed sectors were recommended for delisting.

• *Farms under government-to-government agreements and estates or plantations*. Approved conservancies and properties protected by bilateral investment agreements were recommended for delisting or exclusion from the programme. However, in 2004 the government changed the law to facilitate the acquisition of such farms based on public resettlement requirements, with full compensation being provided.

• *Gazetting of farms*. The Ministry of Lands and Rural Resettlement led the process of gazetting the farms. The list of farms for compulsory acquisition was compiled and then gazetted in the official *Government Gazette* and other print media.

The compulsory land acquisition policy did not result in the actual acquisition of the farms, as this still had to go through the legal procedures. What it meant was that the government would prepare a standard affidavit for all farms, and when in future it was established that such farms were to be acquired, it would then use this standard affidavit in the legal process. In addition, the delisting of farms was also to be used as a basis for removing farms erroneously identified for acquisition. While this would have improved land management during the acquisition period, it remained a challenge. It was noted that some former landowners continued to negotiate with powerful politicians to obtain a delay to the acquisition. For instance, key informants said that the owners of farms in Wards 20 and 32 negotiated with powerful players, thereby creating problems for local officials trying to effect transfers as the need for them arose.

It should be noted that during the FTLRP all previous systems of land and resource administration were disabled in order to facilitate what were envisaged as action-oriented ad hoc arrangements. This included the creation of committees and task forces composed of political appointees to oversee the programme. At all levels, a number of administrators were sucked into these committees to ensure that what was agreed was implemented with speed. The result was that land administration became chaotic, with old systems collapsing and numerous power struggles at the national and local level. Many potential settlers were unable to discover who was in charge of what and who could process what when they sought information on various aspects of the land reform programme.

At the national level, a command centre supported by local structures was established to streamline the activities of the various ministries. In practice, there was horse-trading, competition and conflict between ministries (agriculture, information and publicity, legal affairs, and local government) as they sought to appropriate the political grandstanding associated with the programme. At the same time, they also collaborated effectively on certain aspects of the programme, such as the mobilisation of agricultural support to new farmers. The various committees and sub-national statutory bodies, such as the Office of the Governor, district administrators, chiefs, headmen and interest groups such as the War Veterans, all competed to have a say in the programme. However, the executive summary of the Presidential Land Review Committee's report (Utete, 2003a) noted the complexity of implementing land reform quickly:

> It should be noted that the process of acquiring and distributing land to the people under the two resettlement models, the A1 and A2, was undertaken in a complex legal framework, which rendered the process both difficult and cumbersome. As the Committee went about its work it could not fail to be struck by the number and variety of legal issues that still required resolution in respect of the acquisition procedures; the allocation of land to beneficiaries, especially under the A2 model; the assessment of the value of improvements; and ownership and access to moveable assets on the farms. Inevitably, the governmental machinery for administering these matters was taxed to the limit.

In some new resettlement schemes, settlers established their own chain of authority to represent their interests by engaging officials in higher offices. At times, traditional leaders such as Chief Negomo in Mazowe established a degree of authority over the resettlement, especially in the areas in which they were allocated land. In other areas, settlers depended on the Committee of Seven, rekindling memories of the committees of the liberation struggle before 1980. When the state moved in and attempted to re-create authority, there was bound to be real conflict.

Farms compulsorily acquired in Mazowe District

Government agencies on the ground in Mazowe District faced numerous problems in the listing of farms for acquisition. In 2003, for instance, they failed to establish the actual number of farms in the district because of the numerous subdivisions and 'remainder of farms'[10] based on a long history of private market land transfers. Some farms were listed as part of Mazowe

District when they were in fact in Bindura and Goromonzi Districts. There was a lot of administrative confusion with respect to the names of farms and trading names, or just popular names. Government, after noticing the numerous administrative problems with respect to the listing of farms, eased the situation by listing all LSCFs for compulsory acquisition. This removed one burden faced by the DLC in the land identification process, as the committee's time was being taken up with numerous contests in the courts with the former landowners.

Mazowe District holds a large percentage of the prime land allocated under the A1 and A2 schemes in Mashonaland Central Province. The province had close to 1 million ha of commercial land, of which 51 per cent of the farms (or 41 per cent of the total land area) were in Mazowe District (see Table 2.2). According to the list held by Agricultural, Technical and Extension Services (Agritex), in Mazowe District all the 426 farms (a total of 340,307.42 ha) were listed for acquisition. As of 2004, the subdivision of the 426 farms had yielded 4,905 plots, of which at least 285 plots remained unoccupied at that time. Agritex officials indicated that with a proper land management information system there was potential for over 6,000 subdivisions under both the A1 and A2 models. However, there were some farms that were not acquired, as discussed later in this chapter.

TABLE 2.2 Total number of farms in Mashonaland Central Province

District	Number of farms	%	Area (ha)	%
Mazowe	426	50.84	340,307.42	41.24
Bindura	148	17.66	149,650.81	18.13
Shamva	72	8.59	66,049.36	8.00
Guruve	67	8.00	118,127.81	14.31
Muzarabani	104	12.41	119,989.89	14.54
Mount Darwin	21	2.51	31,113.33	3.77
Total	838	100.00	825,238.62	100.00

Source: Agritex, 2004.

The distribution of acquired farms by ward showed that there was intense acquisition in areas closest to Harare. However, at the time of the research, there was a block of farms (Lowdale, Selby, Esbank) on the boundary with Harare whose status was not clear in terms of land acquisition. In that block a total of 27 farms, measuring 15,9835.39 ha, originally fell in Ward 20 of Mazowe District. However, Harare Metropolitan Province was claiming that it would require some of the farms in Ward 20 for the expansion of Harare. The Mazowe Rural District Council (MRDC) and traditional leaders claimed the farms, including land parcelled for residential areas in a new suburb called Mount Pleasant Heights, managed by Harare City Council. However, prior to 2000, most of these farms had been used for peri-urban farming. There was a standing policy of implementing a peri-urban model of FTLRP, which allows for acquisition of such farms but for a different settlement model (see Chapter 3). Some of the farms were owned by national and international institutions involved in agricultural research, and these were supposed to be excluded from acquisition. However, at the workshops in 2005 carried out in Mazowe to provide feedback on the findings of the Ruzivo Trust research project, traditional leaders and councillors claimed that Harare was taking over some farms without proper negotiation.[11]

Farms delisted during the acquisition period in Mazowe Compulsory acquisition proceeded on the basis of land policy that allowed for land delisting. The delisting was used to remove farms erroneously identified for acquisition. However, it was also part of the government's administrative process for managing the gazetting of farms for acquisition. When officials identified administrative problems, procedural problems or incorrect identification, they would 'delist' such farms and officially announce such delisting in a *Government Gazette*. However, some former landowners who had negotiated with powerful politicians for a delay to the acquisition (reputedly the owners of an estate near Harare, and another close to Glendale town) managed to have their properties delisted. In Mazowe, the Agritex files (2004) showed that farms totalling 72,039.21 ha were delisted.

Farms owned by institutions (for example, universities or ARDA) and those owned by indigenous people or companies were delisted. The delisted farms were left intact in terms of their total land area, despite the existence of specifications for maximum farm sizes for each agro-ecological region (AER). It was thus unclear to which land category maximum farm sizes applied. In fact, an examination of the sizes of farms left intact in Mazowe shows that the government's policy on maximum farm sizes for all agro-ecological zones in Zimbabwe has not been strictly adhered to. According to Utete (2003a), some individuals questioned the viability of the prescribed farms' sizes for enterprises such as livestock, yet they used these arguments to maintain large-sized farms even if the farms were under crops (Sukume et al., 2004). However, there were some delisted farms in Mazowe District that were reduced in size to accommodate new settlers already on portions of the farms occupied by peasants and War Veterans. In general, the underutilised parts of these farms were settled by occupiers who viewed such land as being in excess of the requirements of the main estates. Also, key institutions such as the Mazowe

Citrus Estates were said to have negotiated with the authorities to allow for some of their land to be used for resettlement purposes.

Some farms were listed and gazetted and then delisted. In what seemed to be a confusing process, at some later stage the same farms were re-listed and re-gazetted. According to officials, this procedure reflected the due process of the law that specifies that some time after gazetting, the provision expires and farms have to be re-gazetted. Officials simply followed the law and the prescribed process. It also reflected the ongoing politics, and policy-making that involved negotiations and trade-offs on land reform. The government had to refine policy concerning the acquisition of plantations and estates, some under foreign ownership. The provision of and international relations based on country-to-country agreements placed the government in a quandary, and they had to delicately negotiate the takeover of such farms, or find a way to move them off the list and to remove illegal land occupiers.

Some farms, such as Netherfield and Hayshott, that were relatively small were swapped and the owners were said to have been given alternative farms. There is no evidence of this being done on the ground, as the Hayshott farm seemed to have retained its tenure up to the time of this research in 2007. Farms involved in a mixture of enterprises and with high production were listed and later delisted. One farm involved in game farming and another in forestry conservation were delisted, reflecting governmental and local interest in conservation issues. In fact, in 2003, the DLC did an audit to capture irregularities in the occupation of these plantations, agro-estates and farms under bilateral agreements. This led to the delisting of farms such as Dorking, Forrester Estate, Eskbank, Glenara, Goede Hoop and The Pines. Yet, by 2004, the same farms had been occupied and settled again, leading to their acquisition.

Farms spared from acquisition because of the foreign investment protection policy Some farms were spared for economic and strategic reasons; international relations largely influenced the acquisition process. Farms involved in exports, farms under country-to-country agreements, and enterprises of strategic importance such as forestry, wildlife, citrus, roses and chicken breeding were delisted. However, farms categorised as 'protection of foreign investment farms (country-to-country agreements)' deserve special mention because they were highly contested at the national level. The Ministry of Lands and Rural Resettlement argued that they discovered that some of the farms said to be under country-to-country agreements were not, when checked against the BIPPA, held by the Ministry of Foreign Affairs (MLRR, 2009). This saw a wave of new acquisitions of such farms, but given the non-existence of a database, some farms were erroneously listed for acquisition and allocated.

In Mazowe, the Forrester Estate, under a country-to-country agreement, was listed for acquisition and then delisted. The block of farms, owned by investors from Germany, was the target of land occupations by people from Chiweshe. There were nine farms in the estate; although there were bilateral arrangements, this infringed the policy against multiple farm ownership by firms and individuals, and also the farms were relatively oversized according to the policy and law of maximum farm sizes in the agro-ecological regions IIa and IIb. The total area of the farms under the Forrester Estate (9,883.34 ha) was seen as very high. Government and local politicians indicated that they were not entirely opposed to the operations of the Forrester Estate, but that in terms of land area alone it did constitute a substantial amount of land under multiple ownership. In any case, the underutilised parts of these farms were settled by occupiers from Chiweshe communal areas. It emerged from the interviews in adjacent communal areas that people viewed the Forrester land as naturally suitable for the A1 model because of its proximity to the communal area. This tended to increase political pressure for the acquisition of these farms, irrespective of their status under a country-to-country agreement.

Farms spared from compulsory acquisition for strategic reasons in Mazowe
There was also a process of farm reservation which meant that farms were spared from compulsory land acquisition. The government reserved some farms on the basis of their strategic contribution to research and development. This was at a time when it seemed that all commercial farms were targeted for acquisition. There were also sentiments expressed in public that some land owned by institutions was underutilised, and should, therefore, be subject to compulsory acquisition. However, the land committee in Mazowe had a clear policy of excluding such farms from compulsory acquisition. There were a total of 16 farms owned by institutions in Mazowe District, including two owned by ARDA, measuring 530.64 ha, used for state agricultural development projects.

The district is in fact renowned for having some of the oldest research institutes involved in farm research and experimentation. The oldest research station, run by the Ministry of Agriculture, Mechanisation and Irrigation Development, is Henderson Research Station. The research station also housed the Mazowe District extension services personnel as well as the research arm of the ministry. It has three farms with a total area of 3,230.21 ha and is involved in a variety of crop, livestock and fisheries research programmes that were spared from acquisition. The MRDC was allocated the plantation at Mandindi Farm in Ward 26 and, at the time of the survey in 2004, was negotiating with the new settlers about taking over Glengrey and Hermiston for citrus management. Also, the MRDC obtained a Citrifresh grant for managing some of the citrus farms, which they argued should lead to the delisting of the farms for general public resettlement purposes.

The research found that some of the farms were huge, ongoing estates with strategic contributions to the overall economy, such as Mazowe Citrus Estates (owned by Interfresh). They had a total area of 10,304 ha, most of which was used for citrus production, and the core of the estate was spared from acquisition. The Mazowe Estates are renowned for the production of oranges, naartjies and lemons and have a processing plant that used to employ over 2,500 workers in different divisions at its peak. The political leadership at the national and local levels have publicly condemned any attempts to illegally occupy farms owned by Mazowe Citrus Estates. This was also influenced by the fact that the management of the estates offered parts of their land for resettlement.

The government also encouraged farm swaps, so as not to prejudice owners on farms that met the requirements for being spared; farms deemed suitable for resettlement even when they met the criteria could still be swapped. Commercial farms close to communal areas were largely targeted for swaps, ostensibly because they provided better scope for moving people in communal areas on to commercial farms. It was then expected that the DLC would process farm swaps for the affected former landowners. Some officials indicated that some white former landowners refused such swaps, others were said to have left before such a policy could be effected, while others opted to take the cash compensation (but these landowners became entangled in the politics of compensation and the government's lack of money). The total number of effectively swapped farms was unknown at the time of the research.

Indigenous-owned farms saved from compulsory land acquisition Indigenous commercial landowners were threatened with land takeovers in the same way as their white counterparts. These owners bought the farms with their own funds before the onset of the land reform programme. In Mazowe District, some white farmers regarded as good neighbours were classified as indigenous and had their farms spared, although in most cases the area was decreased or the number of farms reduced to one. In the 1990s, black commercial farmers had established the Indigenous Commercial Farmers' Union to fight for a stake in Zimbabwe's agriculture and to defend their land rights in the face of state scepticism about their ability to fully utilise land that they had bought with their own resources. However, there was continued political pressure to acquire land owned by indigenous black Zimbabweans. A member of the Politburo, the ZANU-PF supreme policy-making body, told a weekly newspaper that:

> There are some indigenous people with several farms each ... these are being targeted ... We need plenty of land to resettle the masses and it should be acquired from those who have too much of it be they black or white. (*Sunday Mail*, 3 December 1997)

President Mugabe, in a New Year's Eve speech at the end of 1996, echoed this warning to black commercial farmers:

> As we acquire land, our black commercial farmers should not think that we will favour them if they leave their farms underutilised. No. Absentee farmers should ensure they are here and that their farms are being fully utilised ... The government would not allow prestige farms and all absentee farmers running their farms by remote control would face the same fate as their white counter-parts ... (*Herald*, 3 February 1997)

This changed following the FTLRP, as the government sought broad support for its programme, including from indigenous commercial farmers. The government was willing to make concessions by excluding indigenous commercial farmers from compulsory acquisition, depending on the suitability of the farms as assessed for resettlement as well as levels of utilisation. The government also used farm swaps, with indigenous owners being provided with alternative farms.[12]

In Mazowe District there were 49 indigenously owned farms with a total area of 34,354.15 ha. This represented only 10 per cent of the total land area or 11.5 per cent of the total number of farms in the district. The average area of the indigenous farms was 500 ha, which was over the recommended farm size for agro-ecological regions IIa and IIb, according to the government's Statutory Instrument on Farm Sizes. On the other hand, some of the farms were very small, with an area of 20 to 25 ha. These farms were engaged in important farming enterprises, ranging from crops (maize, soya, tobacco, etc.), beef cattle, pork and poultry to horticulture. According to Agritex officials, these farms were also served, just like all the other farms, with notices for acquisition, but were spared for the reasons elaborated above. In addition, the farms were said to be 'fully utilised', the reasoning being that the owners went into farming of their own volition and with their own resources and were, therefore, passionate about farming as a way of life.

Broader reactions of white farmers to land occupations and compulsory land acquisition

The white farmers were the victims of the land takeovers and they reacted in various ways. While the CFU took the legal route, farmers on the ground responded in a variety of ways when their land was gazetted for land acquisition. The law enacted by government also had provisions for how farmers were to be evicted. Government officials in Mazowe encouraged a humane approach, such as:

• encouraging co-existence when land was allocated to new beneficiaries before the completion of the land acquisition process;

- allowing a period of time after the farmer was notified of the government's intentions to acquire the farm;
- allowing the farmers in some cases to move their equipment (until the government made a legal position disallowing this);
- allowing the farmers to harvest their produce (but at times the new beneficiaries claimed the produce, based on a variety of arguments); and
- carrying out the forced removal of white farmers only if they resisted the notifications.

In general, white farmers were largely disappointed with compulsory acquisition as they had to leave land they had held for decades. They viewed the land acquisition as political. Taylor (2002) has documented some of the negative reactions of the white farmers that had the effect of infuriating not just the War Veterans but also politicians; for example:

> '... this place looks like a reserve; huts, donkeys, goats, the whole thing ...' The notion of the 'reserve' was resurrected to allude to the 'backward' and unproductive nature of the consequences of land reform, which was in antithesis to the modernity and high productivity of the white commercial farm. (Ibid.: 28)

At times, the white farmers recognised their ability to manipulate conflict situations to their advantage, such as the pacification of violent occupiers through the use of humour in the Shona language. As Taylor (ibid.: 31) noted: 'Humour was a way of diffusing aggression in the crowd, and attempting to "get them on your side".' In Mazowe, the white farmers faced with invaders who came on foot, in minibuses and on tractors reacted with a defeatist stance at times. While the loud noise annoyed them and they found some of the intruders' behaviour intimidating, they noted that the occupiers were not generally violent. At Bayle Farm, the negotiations were characterised by words from the leader of the land occupiers to the effect that: 'We are not taking the land from you. We are retaking the land and you took the land from our forefathers.'[13] The white farmer responded by saying: 'I am here. I cannot stop you doing whatever you want to do' (ibid.). He mounted his bicycle and led the group of 40 across the farm to a nearby vacant and windowless square stone cottage, which he offered them as accommodation. In response, one man said angrily: 'We are not animals, cattle or sheep. We cannot stay here. Offer us something else.' But the leader of the occupiers became reasonable and sombre, as he said: 'We are not taking the whole farm ... We are going to share. As long as he understands that we can live as neighbours. But if he insists the farm belongs to him we will throw him off.'

Some landowners and farmworkers opposed the land occupations through physical scuffles. In Mazowe no deaths were recorded of any white farm owner or farmworker; much of the violence was intimidation. White farmers in Mazowe, when faced with the reality of losing their land, reacted in some of the following ways: no action, flight to urban areas, co-existence with new landowners to the extent of sharing skills and equipment (some of which was seen as political blackmail), fighting through legal challenges, obliging their union (the CFU and Justice for Agriculture) to launch legal challenges, protesting through the media and internet, and using political connections to delay acquisition of their farms. While in broad terms all white-owned land was a potential target, according to an official, it was the white farmers who had shown open support for the opposition, especially from 2000 to 2002, who were largely targeted. When other white farmers heard this, they tried to hide by 'staying out of politics' in order to increase their chances of staying on the land. But 'staying out of politics' did not guarantee security, because the majority still had their land compulsorily acquired at some point.

By 2004, there were 11 remaining individual white farmers in Mazowe. There were some farms listed as companies and the actual owners were not specified, making it difficult to establish the ownership status. No white farmers were interviewed in Mazowe and the research team had to rely on the database provided by Agritex, which included findings from their interactions with farmers during farm demarcation. In general, the research team was told that, among the remaining 11 white farmers, the majority had political connections. In fact, some of them had companies in which political players appeared to have shares. According to the Agritex officials, those who left immediately at the onset of *jambanja* tended to be the younger white farmers with children. Those who had the prospect of establishing a new life elsewhere, particularly in an urban area, were said to have been more prepared to start afresh than the older farmers were. Yet some old farmers also gave up their properties because of the violence, conflicts, old age and economic problems. The isolation of the farms had the effect of pushing them into urban-based old people's homes.

In general, the remaining white farmers had their farm sizes reduced. At a certain point, the DLC recommended some white-owned farms for delisting. These farms, owned by the white farmers who remained, were regarded as highly productive and produced strategic farming products such as seed, citrus and horticulture or were involved in crop breeding. In addition, the white farmers at farms such as Hayshott, Montgomery and R/E of Verona were seen as having had a history of social co-existence with blacks before and after the land reform programme. Many participated in various political events and provided social support to poor communities. At the same time, there were some politicians who defended the white farmers. For instance, in 2007, then Vice President Joseph Msika maintained that it was never a ZANU-PF 'policy' that 'all white farmers should be chased out', and added: 'I am not a racist and I refuse to be racist.'[14] He went on to confirm that there was chaos in implementing the land reform programme and that this had contributed to Zimbabwe's agricultural decline and needed correction. In Mazowe, Vice President Msika, according to officials in government, tried to ensure orderliness, because he hailed from the district. In fact, junior officers bent on self-gain in accessing prime lands outside the procedures were evicted at his insistence (interview with an Agritex official pushed out because of the Vice President's intervention, 13 May 2007).

However, there were allegations in the press that scores of former white commercial farmers were seeking orders to evict newly resettled farmers. The government reiterated that all new farmers should stay on their allocated pieces of land pending the issuance of offer letters. In 2006 the High Court nullified offer letters issued before the promulgation of the Constitution Amendment (No. 17) Act 2005, creating a new wave of uncertainty among scores of new farmers whose land was being contested.

From 2000 onwards, there were stories in the press alleging that officials were corruptly allowing some white farmers to subsist on acquired farms. In Mazowe, the varied elites and the predominantly urbanite people seeking land in the district created conditions where underhand deals were made (Munyuki-Hungwe, 2011). On 25 April 2004, the *Sunday Mail* indicated that some farms in Mazowe District were being returned to their former owners. The Ministry of Lands was identified as the culprit in this perceived return of land to the former owners, reflecting the convoluted politics of a reform programme that involved competing interests.

Conclusions

Land acquisition in Mazowe District was based on national guidelines, but also reflected the politics of land in Zimbabwe and specifically in Mazowe. The acquisition programme was based on the government's resolve to take over land from former commercial farmers, using all means at its disposal. While from 2000 to 2002 the government let the land occupations drive the process, it later moved in to control those occupations through a technical process of land acquisition, using set guidelines. These guidelines were followed by rapid legislative changes, especially as embodied in the Land Acquisition Acts (1992 and 2000) and Constitutional Amendments (2000 and 2005). There were, however, no clear-cut operational definitions as to how these criteria for compulsory land acquisition were to be applied by the government-appointed District and Provincial Land Acquisition Committees. In addition, there was no clear order of priority for applying the procedures to identify farms for acquisition; in the end, the government arrived at the position that all commercial gazetted land should be regarded as acquired and had to be dealt with through the courts. In addition to existing principles, various additional explanatory or supportive criteria for identifying land for acquisition were proposed at various times by government officials, and this tended to confuse the officials on the ground.

There are also cases where policy was not uniformly applied in districts. For example, some farmers had all their properties gazetted for compulsory acquisition, while others were left with more than one farm. Furthermore, in some cases the policy of 'one farm per owner' was not applied in conjunction with the maximum farm size regulations. The interaction of technocrats and politicians in managing land acquisition was a source of tension. The political leadership gave directives to government technocrats and committees, yet it had no mandate to do so (Utete, 2003a). Disagreements and conflicts were also a problem within some of the district and sub-district institutions, because the land committees comprised many interest groups, all competing to 'make policy' or to be seen as being at the forefront of policy implementation. In certain cases, such situations led to action being taken that fell outside the formal policy, such as the attempted acquisition of farms under BIPPAs or the occupation of game parks.

Land conflicts emerged during the acquisition process. Some of the problems came about because of personality clashes and differences in the interpretation of policy. At the same time, the lack of cohesion and consensus at policy implementation level tended to frustrate decision-making. Some white farmers thought they would be left on their farms, yet the same institutions who gave them this idea would recommend their farms to be acquired, thus leaving farmers in limbo. Acquisition could depend on the political interests of politicians expecting to hold on to power through land takeovers. Yet, at the same time, some officials saw the acquisition as paramount in the economic development of peasants who had languished in the communal areas.

As an anecdote it is important to observe that the challenges of weak capacity and poor co-ordination led to numerous errors in processing the acquisition of properties. The Ministry of Lands and Rural Resettlement was created at a time when land acquisition was at its peak. The transfer from the Ministry of Agriculture created a void in which some individuals bent the rules for self-gain. However, over time the new ministry reorganised and put systems in place for managing land acquisition through prioritising capacity building for the Land Information Management System. However, this was not replicated in districts such as Mazowe, which had lists different from the national list of farms acquired. The acquisition processes were further complicated by the frequent litigations that farmers brought before the courts as they sought justice. The government also took some provincial-level officials to court for delisting farms without authority. In addition, it was alleged that some former commercial farmers misled government by claiming that some of their properties were owned under BIPPAs when they were not (MLRR, 2009). This tended to delay land acquisition and further compromised the decision-making processes of local officials.

3 | Interrogating land allocation

Introduction

The allocation of land under the Fast Track Land Reform Programme (FTLRP) continues to be the most highly contested issue in Zimbabwe. In fact, the intimation in the international press has been that the allocation of land was permeated by cronyism, and specifically that members of the former ruling party were the major beneficiaries. The allocation process was the second key stage after the acquisition of land. In this chapter, the allocation process is analysed in terms of the procedures, the institutional mechanisms for allocating land, and the outcome of such allocations. The allocation was based on specific political objectives in effecting compulsory acquisition of land (Madhuku, 2004; Moyo and Yeros, 2007a) from an identifiable group of mostly white landowners, to be redistributed to the majority blacks. The acquisition process proceeded at the same time as the official allocation of land to beneficiaries who had made applications. In a way, the land allocation process seems to have been influenced more by the evolving political dynamics of the FTLRP in general. The government and its implementing bodies (formal and informal) became central to the management of land allocation and influenced that allocation in different ways.

A defining feature of Zimbabwe's land allocation was that a particular political space was provided for specific institutional and policy arrangements to effect the allocations. The method used in allocating land to new beneficiaries was the outcome of state intervention, directed from the top. Despite peasant mobilisation through self-allocation, the state had proved in 1998 that it could control land occupations (or the self-allocation of land) if it wanted to, by removing the peasants and War Veterans who had occupied land in areas such as Svosve in Mashonaland East, Nyamandhlovu in Matabeleland North, Odzi near Nyazura in Manicaland, and in other parts of the country.[1] Without doubt, political forces influenced the behaviour of the state in sanctioning what it wanted to allow in the allocation of land. Yet, the state and the beneficiaries seemed to need each other for different purposes: the state wanted support for its political project, while new beneficiaries wanted the state to finally give them the land that they had yearned for for many decades.

Background to the politics of land allocation

The local and international opponents of the FTLRP have a justifiable case in contesting the conflict and violent processes that ensued in the redistribution process (Hammar et al., 2003; Raftopoulos, 2003; Raftopoulos and Mlambo, 2009; Derman, 2006). This issue is crucial for historical analyses of the social and political alliances behind the land reform process, but, at the same time, there is also a need for empirical facts about how the allocations have evolved on the ground and the specific contexts according to which people were selected. There is no doubt that during the FTLRP there were numerous social and class-based struggles among the various factions. For example, the indigenous elites were seeking to control the state through the FTLRP, and were later to target other sectors of the economy. However, the FTLRP was seen as providing free land via a public programme, and this generated interest across social classes in Zimbabwe. At the same time, the land allocations generated political pressures that were apparent on an international stage, where Zimbabwe's type of land reform was regarded as illegal from the perspective of property rights and as being racist in reverse.

Land allocation under the FTLRP was not expected to benefit everyone, because the land acquired was limited. The government planned each farm through the creation of plots based on size and viability concerns, and these plots were divided into A1 and A2. This meant that a specific number of people could benefit, and, naturally, some people would not benefit. In a context in which land as a resource was limited and there were many people competing for access, it meant that allocation became a political act of balancing multiple interests. Some politicians sought to influence land allocation as a basis for building their support base. Some leaders saw an opportunity to reduce large populations in the communal areas through facilitating the move of some people to the Fast Track Farms (FTFs). Questions remain about who benefited and why.

Numerous political statements on the outcomes of the allocation reflect deep-seated conflicts over control of a key asset (Matondi, 2001), while also reflecting more broadly on the struggle for state control and the tendency emerging among blacks towards accumulation. Therefore, as far as the outcome of land allocation is concerned, the main thrust of policy interest lies largely in the macro-economic and commercial aspects of business and international finance. Nevertheless, preoccupation with the short-term, superficial and partisan politics of agrarian reform have overshadowed a growing interest in the salient developmental implications of the broad social change that has happened due to the FTLRP in terms of land allocation.

In reality, land allocation has been the most difficult aspect of the process because of the assumptions of cronyism. Very little empirical evidence is available on the actual patterns of land allocation among various types of beneficiaries in terms of their socio-economic status and political affiliation or across the various agro-ecological regions (AERs) (and land qualities) and provinces. Besides the work of Ruzivo Trust (2003 to the present) in Shamva, Mazowe and Mangwe, there are a few research-based studies (Marongwe, 2008, in Goromonzi; Scoones et al., 2010, in Masvingo; Zamchiya, 2011, in Chipinge; Moyo et al., 2009, in Mangwe, Chipinge, Zvimba, Mazowe, Chiredzi and Kwekwe) as well as reports by non-governmental organisations (NGOs), farmers' unions and international agencies showing the actual patterns of allocations. But some of the reports on land allocation outcomes are heavily influenced by particular policy advocacy and political lobbying interests, especially the Justice for Agriculture (JAG) report of 2002. Lobby reports of this nature sought to demonstrate the level of cronyism in A2 allocations, but were never verified in terms of their authenticity on the ground. In any case, some of the outcomes have been overtaken by events, as the government has continued to take corrective measures on land allocation anomalies. In addition, some of the Government of Zimbabwe (GoZ) audits have been useful in addressing the allocation challenges, although they are of limited scientific merit and have not been analysed fully.

However, there is no thorough, ongoing independent national survey of the land allocation process and pattern to refer to. Within the short space of time since 2000, the capacity to conduct such a survey or to gain access to fully reliable data has been limited. There is extremely varied and diametrically opposed evidence being debated in the academic and public arena, and, in particular, one special issue of the *Journal of Peasant Studies* (Marongwe, 2011; Zamchiya, 2011; Moyo, 2011b; Scoones et al., 2011). In the case of the empirical evidence used for this book, the data were carefully cross-checked against official data at both national and district level and supplemented with field-based stories from Mazowe District. There is still a need for a continuous probing into land allocation patterns.

Genesis of the models for land allocation

The process of land allocation was influenced largely by the history of land reform, both before and after independence in 1980 (Hellum and Derman, 2004; Marongwe, 2008; Chingarande, 2008; Derman and Hellum, 2007; Moyo and Yeros, 2005a; Murisa, 2009; Amanor-Wilks, 2009). In the first phase of the land reform programme, ending in 1997, the government followed strict criteria for land allocation based on the desire to settle those who were made landless by the liberation struggle. In this respect, the government modelled resettlement into A (villagised), B (co-operatives), C (out-grower schemes) and D (drier areas for livestock), and settled people based on these models. There was no distinction between commercial and non-commercial enterprises in the allocations; this distinction emerged only with the FTLRP. Post-independence land reforms demonstrated that the government, through its planning technocrats, had already developed a system of selecting those in need of resettlement based on the social criteria of landlessness, displacement and unemployment (Kinsey, 1983; Moyo, 1995a). Just as in the previous land reform (1980–97), an expectation was that, over time, the selected beneficiaries would become competent to use the land productively. For this reason, selection during the second phase of land resettlement (GoZ, 1998) was supposed to focus on those with agriculture-related skills and qualifications.

During the FTLRP, the two models (A1 and A2) according to which applicants were allocated land focused on poverty alleviation and the economic development of a class of black commercial farmers. However, for the commercial A2 model, there was no expectation that the new farmers would be anything like the former landowners, in terms of both lifestyle and productivity levels (interviews, 3 June 2007). There were several major factors that influenced the plan to develop commercial black farmers; these factors included not only the creation of an egalitarian society and the de-racialisation of the sector, but also the desire to create a powerful middle class of black farmers who could defend the programme politically in the future, while also making money out of agriculture. Therefore, the dual economy inherited from the colonial era was the target of agrarian restructuring, which meant moving mostly black people on to land that was under white ownership. Did this mean that land allocation would further change the agrarian system? Some writers (Derman, 2006) note that it was about changing the 'skin colour' of the commercial agricultural sector without tinkering with the system per se; that is to say, it was more about changing the participants than about changing the dualist system. For instance, Fontein (2009: 3) noted that:

> [If] A2 farming was supposed to be about indigenising wealth and 'African-
> ising' commercial agricultural production, A1 farming was about preserving
> that 'value system' or 'way of life' in which chiefs were understood to act
> as custodians of peoples' heritage; a distinction which resonated in tones
> suspiciously similar to the teleological colonial distinction between white
> 'commercial' and African 'communal' farming areas.

The selective promotion of black entrepreneurial interests in the 1990s through empowerment was aimed at creating and bolstering supportive economic clout through compliant interest groups.

However, the critics of the FTLRP (Hammar et al., 2003; Alexander, 2003; Hellum and Derman, 2004; Marongwe, 2008; 2011; Zamchiya, 2011) have pointed to the selection of inexperienced but politically connected people for farmland as the dominant thesis explaining what was wrong with the FTLRP. Striking underutilisation of land, agricultural stagnation and therefore food insecurity and the disruption of product supply to industry, the closure of key services along the agricultural chain and an increase in unemployment are cited as some of the implications of poor land allocation by government. The earlier allocations during the first phase of land reform (1980–97) seem to have had the opposite effect, through broadening the economic base for the poor, and, more significantly, contributing to poverty reduction and a reduction in malnutrition (Kinsey, 1999).

Land allocation as a numbers game Prior to the FTLRP in 1998, the government had to design new models in response to the scale of the programme. A key characteristic of the project was that it placed people of different backgrounds and abilities of land usage into A1 and A2 categories. The A1 model was envisioned as comprising small, integrated communities using locally evolved norms and rules to manage resources and people. The A2 model, with its generation of black commercial farmers, was seen as having the potential to increase the number of commercial farmers from around 4,500 to 54,000 at its optimum level. Economically, the idea was that, as they were allocated land, they would also unlock resources from the private sector to support agriculture. Based on this, there was a belief that, had this happened, agriculture would not have stagnated fundamentally. However, this assumption proved to be incorrect due to the fact that commercial (A2) agriculture ended up siphoning state subsidies, making money and investing it elsewhere.

In the early period from 2000, the government proudly presented statistics on the numbers settled to demonstrate its successes with land reform. However, in the national agrarian policy discourse, the number of beneficiaries has waned as a topic of discussion over time, especially since the Utete (2003a) report revelations that the government had misled the public by overstating the number of beneficiaries. The government claimed that 300,000 plots were allocated in the early period in A1; the more realistic figure from Utete (ibid.) was 127,000 plots. For the A2 model, the government was claiming 54,000 new farmers, but the real figure was closer to 14,000.

Since the Utete (ibid.) report, there have been minor increments in the number of beneficiaries for both A1 (145,775 beneficiaries) and A2 (16,386 beneficiaries) (figures from MLRR, 2009). But why did the government let the state-inclined media fasten on to the inflated figures, knowing full well that they were incorrect? The manipulation of beneficiary statistics seems to have been a political strategy to persuade the sceptics that the land reform programme was indeed proving to be a success. Although the Utete report deflated the numbers, what was remarkable was that, beyond any reasonable doubt, the Zimbabwe land reform programme had placed many people on new land in the shortest possible time, an unprecedented achievement in the international history of land reform.

TABLE 3.1 Distribution of beneficiaries and land acquired

Resettlement phase	Number of families/ farmers as beneficiaries	Acquired land (ha)	Remaining land in large-scale commercial farms (ha)
Approximate total commercial land area at independence in 1980	6,600		15,500,000
Phase I (1980-97)	71,000	3,498,444	12,001,556
Inception Phase (1998–2000)	4,697	168,264	11,833,292
Phase II: A1 resettlement (2000–08)	145,775	5,759,154	6,074,139
Phase II: A2 resettlement (2000–08)	16,386	2,978,334	3,095,805*
Approximate remaining large-scale commercial farmland (includes indigenous-owned land, white-owned land, institutions, and excluded companies and estates)	–	–	1,095,805
Total	237,858	12,404,196	

Notes: There are approximately 300 large white commercial farmers remaining. * The remaining land is also owned by parastatals and private trusts such as the Development Trust of Zimbabwe (360,000 ha), indigenous-owned farms, and what the Ministry of Lands and Rural Resettlement (MLRR) describes as unallocated land (2 million ha)

Source: Adapted from GoZ, 2009.

Procedures for allocating land to new beneficiaries

The occupation of land occurred before planning in Mazowe District, which meant that planners had to use the numbers of informal settlers to determine the appropriate model (A1 or A2). This was because, when Agritex was asked to move in and organise land allocation, they could not remove the settlers because they had received an instruction to base their plans around the people already there. In fact, it was emphasised that occupiers could only be moved to planned farms (interview with Agritex officials, 4 May 2004). Agritex officials in Mazowe argued that some farms were unsuitable for the model that was to be applied to them and for the type of beneficiaries to whom they were allocated. Galloway Farm, for example, had an advanced centre pivot irrigation system but was allocated under the A1 model, which meant that at some stage the system would have to be dismantled as the plots were only around 6 ha per individual.

There were local variations, however, as some settlers obtained larger landholdings, but they did not vary greatly from the established sizes. There are various reasons for this, such as boundary cheating, poor demarcation, topography, and allowances made for physical features such as rivers, roads and tree windbreaks. At schemes such as Ballineety, the A2 plot holders agreed among themselves not to follow the land demarcation laid out by Agritex, but rather to follow the physical features on the farm because it made more sense to them. The cartography held by the ministry does not reflect such land ownership negotiation at the scheme level, which may distort the production targets provided by the Ministry of Agriculture, as some beneficiaries ended up with less land, while others had more.

The planning system was also influenced by the cultural background associated with particular geographical spaces. Although the government had decided to downplay restitutions, these took place in practice. For instance, individuals sought land in their places of origin, thus in a way bolstering restitution from below. In addition, totems were incorporated into specific land claims. As Munyuki-Hungwe (2011) notes, over the last few years the issue of totems has become a powerful signifier of identity for people in the resettlement areas. However, some people could be claiming totems that are fake, because, according to an interviewee (5 July 2007), 'totems are not written on paper but are just a verbal expression of an identity, and anyone can claim to belong to this and that totem simply to protect what they got and to be accepted in the environment in which they live'. In the end, some players, such as chiefs, ended up arguing for cultural continuity as a way of benefiting more people from a particular clan. In Mazowe, the eland totem (*mhofu*) was used as a basis for receiving land.

The MLRR and the Scientific and Industrial Research and Development Centre (SIRDC) (2006) found an example of how cultural links could be influential: at Mugutu Farm, the initial plan was for 33 A2 small-scale plots, but the District Land Committee (DLC) decided to leave plots 1, 3 and 7 because they included important traditional shrines. Plots 1 and 7 were further subdivided into A1 plots and allocated to the Mbari clan, and plot 3 to the Mazarura clan, making a total of 24 A1 plots altogether. Yet, the same people were also making claims at Stockade Farm (402.47 ha) in Madzugetu. The farm was originally offered to a plot holder named Mr Jani (a pseudonym), after he argued that he was the leader of the Mbari clan (MLRR/SIRDC, 2006). He claimed that the farm covered very important shrines, which needed to be under the custody of the clan leaders. He was allocated the plot on the understanding that he was going to share the farm with other clan members. Instead he evicted all the members who attempted to settle on the farm. The DLC resolved to re-plan the farm into six plots, with a portion of the land allocated as state land. Mr Jani was allocated plot 6.

Disagreement regarding the allocations has led to deep conflicts between the beneficiaries. At Mugutu there have been several cases of rampant vandalism on the farm; several water pumps and other equipment were removed and the fence surrounding the former clothing factory on the farm was stolen. These examples show how weak the claims of clans and totems were, but they were utilised by individuals to consolidate traditional claims. One reason people opted for using culture was that they could have failed to make a claim politically, hence they used a cultural argument, which tended to carry weight with Zimbabwe's body politic. It can be noted, therefore, that the Mazowe DLC made pragmatic planning decisions that influenced land allocation, and in order to make their decisions they had to recognise the cultural basis of land reclamation in the district.

Reverting to planning to control chaos in allocations The government sought to create order amid chaos in the land allocation process and provided policy guidelines for land allocation such as the 'one person one farm' policy. A1 allocation decisions were to be made at the district level, and A2 allocation was to be managed centrally by the MLRR. In practice, the DLC recommended successful applicants to the Provincial Land Committee (PLC), which was led by the provincial governor and the resident minister, and their names would be forwarded to the MLRR for the issuing of offer letters. A technical criterion was used to select those recommended for A2 land allocations.

In its simplest form, land allocation is associated with the selection and giving of land to people following the acquisition of farms. However, Zimbabwean land allocation involved several processes of survey and demarcation of the plots, invitations to apply for land (for the A2 model), identification of beneficiaries, selection of the beneficiaries, and on-farm selection of the plots that had been surveyed. This process was in turn affected by a number of factors that included prior land occupation (before surveying and demarcation), occupation by illegal settlers, the interests of different groups (civil servants, those with better financial resources, and those who could manoeuvre political and administrative processes), and the flight from the farms by the previous landowners. Even confirmed allocations were not a fait accompli, because changes could still be effected after the land had been allocated.

While the land acquisition was backed by legislation, actual land allocation had no legal backing, apart from an administrative offer letter that confirmed a right to the land after the allocation. In practice, some individuals had offer letters while others did not. The MLRR/SIRDC (2006: 15) audit confirmed that in Mazowe some 167 (or 38.93 per cent) of those audited did not have offer letters. They faced challenges in getting the letters given litigation by former landowners, and amid competition to access land at the district offices. In terms of the procedures, some land occupiers sought to obtain offer letters after their occupation of plots.

For the A2 model, the actual selection was based on an application to the MLRR. However, at the sub-national level, governors and resident ministers, via the PLCs, played a role through recommending A2 farmers (Scoones et al., 2010; Moyo et al., 2009). This meant that an individual in Harare could apply to the MLRR and be given an offer letter, whereas in other cases applicants could use the bottom-up route from the district or province to get their letter. The result was that there were double allocations of the same plots, and allegations that some of the offer letters were fake.[2] Conflict was thus engendered by the allocation of the same plot to many individuals. In the meantime, the government was rushing to complete the demarcation of the plots in order to allow selected beneficiaries to occupy the land.

In Mazowe, the DLC was the key institution for streamlining orderliness in the allocations. Despite the heavy presence of state apparatus, it demonstrated a level of astuteness in dealing with political heavyweights regarding the process of land allocation. Mazowe is known for having the 'who's who' of political and security circles as owners of the new farms. Mazowe was regarded as the bread basket of Zimbabwe, and was central to the white ownership of land. Thus, political figures demonstrated the seriousness of the land takeover in this district, and generally the district is regarded as having more political and military players owning land than is the case elsewhere. But, to its credit, the DLC (which was staffed by junior and senior district-level civil servants) ensured that the 'political heavies' complied with the policy and laws of land allocation just like everyone else. The broadening of the responsibilities of the DLC, and the incorporation of other interest groups, had the effect of putting a check on corrupt practices, though not entirely stopping them, as cases elsewhere show.[3]

However, pressure from the expectant land applicants, including through picketing at the district office, kept the DLC on its toes, and ensured that the committee made an effort to allocate land fairly. In Mazowe, a number of political demonstrations took place at Concession and the DLC was quick to resolve these through facilitating the issuing of permits to some of the demonstrators. This meant that the demonstrations never filtered out to the national press, as was the case in other areas. While a number of district administrators (DAs) in other parts of the country were transferred ostensibly because they engaged in unofficial practices in the allocation, this did not happen in Mazowe District.[4] This was because the DLC was politically adept at managing volatile situations by working with technical officials. Agritex stated in discussion that its role in relation to the DLC and land allocation was to:

- advise the DLC on technical issues such as appropriate farm models (A1 or A2) and the number of settlers on any farm to be settled;
- carry out ground audits and verification of queries brought before the DLC, make recommendations and bring feedback to the committee;
- actively participate in the allocation of land to applicants after assessing their previous farming history/background; and
- provide to the DLC the names of settlers who were underutilising land and of those whose plots needed to be repossessed.

However, at some stage in 2002, the allocations got out of hand, as there were accusations that people from Mazowe were not being prioritised for A2 land. A committee called the ZANU-PF Land Allocation Joint Committee was formed. This committee had links to the MLRR and had the capacity to speed up the issuance of the offer letters, unlike the PLC or the DLC. However, according to the interviewed official, this channel was alleged to involve money changing hands, also unlike the PLC/DLC route of application. In addition, this committee was accused of incorrectly allocating farms, disrupting the agreed subdivision and allocating incorrect hectarage, and also resulting in the double allocation of farms. The offer letters that came through this committee were set aside, creating further conflicts. By 2003/04, the DLC and PLC took charge and corrected the anomalies.

Operationally, in Mazowe, the DLC met the first Tuesday of every month to discuss land resettlement issues, particularly matters relating to land allocation. The DLC considered the lists as an internal process and then announced successful applicants, who were then informed by the extension officers from Agritex or the Livestock Department in their respective areas. The DLC agreed that, at the farm level, the modus operandi was to have a simple raffle, putting numbered bottle tops into a hat for beneficiaries to pick which plot to occupy; this ensured fairness. However, there are still questions about how the participating beneficiaries were selected by the DLC in order to end up in the raffle draw. The officials tasked with selecting beneficiaries were supposed to be sensitive to local sentiments about land demand. Therefore, some communal areas organised themselves around their traditional leaders and spirit mediums so that they would be prioritised, based on land reclamation or restitution. Although the government does not have a restitution policy, this issue seems to have been considered by local authorities responsible for land reform.

The attraction of Mazowe District to potential land applicants

Land allocations in Mazowe District were affected by the proximity of the district to Harare. Mazowe was the district of choice for most applicants for the following reasons:

- *Land reform comes to Mazowe for the first time.* The FTLRP was the first resettlement programme in the district since independence in 1980. On this basis alone, potential land-seekers saw it as providing an advantage in successfully gaining access to land.
- *Proximity to Harare.* Many residents of Harare saw the FTLRP in Mazowe as an opportunity for them to own land close to a place where they lived; in other words, they could have the option of being either a full-time farmer or a part-time farmer, which gave them the epithet 'weekend farmers'.
- *Availability of high-quality land.* The huge size of the district (the farming area covered 343,377.72 ha), with farmland that was also often of good quality, and the relatively low numbers of white landowners, meant that there was a high possibility of success in obtaining land.
- *Pressure from the landless in the Chiweshe communal lands.* This group of people could easily make forays on to farms and withdraw at any moment, especially during the height of *jambanja*. By moving on to the commercial farms, they also saw an opportunity to remove the label 'resource poachers': they regularly ran into conflict as they illegally accessed grazing land, straining their relationships with commercial farmers.
- *Infrastructure.* The district was in excellent condition in terms of roads, communications and access to health facilities and schools (especially private ones). This meant an expectation of less social hardship, and the possibility of a quick gain from utilising the farms' productive infrastructure to boost agricultural performance.
- *Numerous land occupiers.* As land occupiers had effectively driven away most of the white landowners, potential landowners did not have to struggle much with white landowners, as the road was literally cleared for them to take over the farms.
- *Presence of the security forces.* These provided security guarantees, as their presence limited violent tendencies. They also obtained land themselves, so they did not want trouble to occur as they wanted to settle on the land and start making money.

TABLE 3.2 Summary of applicants for A2 plots in Mashonaland Central Province

District	Total number of applicants	Recommended applicants				Total number successful
		Large scale	Medium scale	Small scale	Peri-urban	
Mazowe	11,081	35	623	4,994	6	5,658
Bindura	3,632	22	198	1,158	5	1,383
Shamva	1,832	3	62	673	0	738
Guruve	975	1	13	263	0	277
Muzarabani	742	4	31	305	0	340
Mount Darwin	565	1	20	268	0	289
Totals	18,827	66	947	7,661	11	8,685

Source: Agritex, 2004.

A whole range of people in the urban areas of the Mashonaland provinces also wanted access to land in the district. The beneficiaries ranged from ordinary people from the communal areas of Madziwa and Chiweshe to business people, civil servants and politicians. There were also urbanites from Chitungwiza, Mbare and Kuwadzana, Glendale and Bindura who chose to seek land in areas they came from, where they were known, or where they had established social roots. The choice seemed to be based on trying to enhance the chances of success. In most cases, people applied for A2 plots nearest to their urban centre of residence, and then applied again from their original communal homes. This situation confronted the district authorities responsible for land allocation with a complex framework that needed to satisfy a disparate group of land-hungry people. The fact that land demonstrators occupied most of the farms further complicated the ability of mandated bodies to proceed with proper land allocations, because of the policy that no one should be removed from where they were until they were allocated land elsewhere.[5] As a result, many negotiations had to take place between the various stakeholders during the process of planning and the actual demarcation of plots.

The DA's office in Mazowe was a hive of activity as prospective settlers enquired about the status of their applications. The research could not establish the actual number of people who applied for land in the district in the A1 schemes because the filing system was a shambles at the time of the research in 2004.[6] For example, there were various typed and handwritten lists, some of which were misfiled, while some names appeared in many lists (lists of War Veterans, traditional leaders, councillors, women, etc.), as applicants applied many times trying to enhance their chance of getting land. Information about successful applicants was obtained after an exercise of reconstructing the files and computerising the lists.

Table 3.2 shows that by the end of 2002, there were a total of 18,827 applicants for the A2 model in Mashonaland Central Province. Applicants for land submitted their completed forms at the offices of the MLRR, through chiefs, headmen and village heads. Some directly applied at the DA's office, as the DA was allocated a quota for special interest groups such as farmworkers; data indicate that less than 5 per cent nationally made it to the final successful lists (Utete, 2003a).

During the Fast Track Land Reform period, there was a broadening of the land allocation to include diverse beneficiaries. This reflected Zimbabwe's wider interest in accessing land. The following classes of beneficiaries were noted in the districts studied:

- *Ordinary citizens.* These included those coming from urban and rural areas. The term 'ordinary' was derived from the numerous lists held by various interest groups, especially those who wanted to benefit by coming from the communal areas. It seems that these largely benefited from the A1 scheme, with fewer finding their way into the A2 schemes. The term 'ordinary' was used to separate out those individuals who did not belong to one of the special interest groups noted below.

- *Civil servants.* By the very nature of their role in managing the land reform programme, civil servants could have taken advantage of their position to allocate land to themselves. This group also includes the security forces, which at times provided logistical support in some of the schemes. They were largely beneficiaries in the A2 schemes. However, resource constraints forced some to opt out of A2 in favour of A1.
- *Farmworkers.* National studies show that less than 5 per cent of farmworkers were beneficiaries (Magaramombe, 2003a; 2003b; Chambati and Magaramombe, 2008).
- *War Veterans, war collaborators and ex-political prisoners and detainees.* These were largely already on the ground when the allocations were being made, because the majority had led occupations of the land. However, previous government policy specified a provision that 20 per cent of the allocation on any scheme would be earmarked for this group (GoZ, 2001).
- *Elites and the rural rich.* The majority were from the private sector, and were encouraged to apply on the premise of the de-racialisation of the commercial agricultural sector. Some, however, manipulated the political and administrative channels to get land, and some were accused of making corrupt payments to land occupiers and land officers to get access to land.
- *Politicians and those connected to people in power.* The greatest contest is over this group, because farmer pressure groups such as JAG and an independent Member of Parliament listed them as the beneficiaries of whole farms in 2002. In Mazowe, this group comprises fewer than 400 individuals, and also includes a mixture of War Veterans, security officials, top civil servants, heads of parastatals, private companies, etc.

Cross-cutting these categories, the beneficiaries included people of different ages, genders, ethnicities, wealth, and from different working spaces (mines, urban areas, the informal sector, the private sector, NGOs, academia, politics, etc.). The categories have attracted attention because of the diverse range of people who were beneficiaries, from the poor to the rich. In many cases, people's allocation depended on their ability to negotiate with the DLC in order to be prioritised on the lists considered for available farms. Such negotiations also meant that others failed to get the land they desired, but in the end they still received something, given that the government promised that no one interested in farming should be denied access to land.

A1 land allocation to ordinary citizens in Mazowe District The A1 model was

Box 3.1 Steps in land allocation and occupation in the A1 scheme

Step 1 – Application: people registered with local institutions (village heads, chiefs, councillors, political party, etc.) or directly with the DLC.

Step 2 – Selection: carried out by the DLC with a 20 per cent quota for War Veterans. Chiefs in some areas claimed to have a 5 per cent quota on every farm.

Step 3 – Announcement of beneficiaries: beneficiaries publicised by chiefs and councillors. Individuals pursued the allocating authority.

Step 4 – Allocation: prospective beneficiaries (participants in the *jambanja* and others) assembled at a demarcated farm where they randomly picked numbers from a hat for the plot they would take. Beneficiaries then received offer letters from the DLC signed by the DA.

Step 5 – Occupation process: beneficiaries assisted by the DLC in identifying their plots. Settlers then move on to the farm. Some moved into and utilised the existing farm infrastructure or any temporary shelters that had been erected by caretakers. Farmers then relocated with their personal equipment and livestock.

designed to empower the poor in general, with an average of 12 ha being allocated to the beneficiaries as well as a shared grazing area and access to state land (where shopping centres were to be established). At the outset, the farmers were to share the infrastructure they inherited as public resources. The A1 model was generally smaller than the A2, even in the western parts of the district, which mainly is suitable for cattle ranching and therefore land sizes could have been larger. Residents of overcrowded communal areas were intended to be the prime beneficiaries of the A1 resettlement programme, but discrepancies in the allocation of A1 plots resulted in an uneven distribution of beneficiaries across the categories, with perceptions in Mazowe that those from the Chiweshe communal areas were being marginalised. The steps taken in the A1 land allocation process are shown in Box 3.1.

Lists of beneficiaries were compiled in consultation with traditional chiefs and ward councillors from the communal areas, who then forwarded the lists to the local DLCs. However, the land allocation process was so complicated that political influence, corruption and simple misallocation affected the outcome (Human Rights Watch, 2004). As a result, communal areas close to farms acquired for resettlement were only sometimes prioritised in the allocation of plots. Some residents of communal areas, e.g. Chiweshe in Mazowe District, felt that they were bypassed by the land allocation process or were not given

TABLE 3.3 Percentages and categories of land beneficiaries in the A1 scheme

Category	Type	Total	%
Ordinary	Communal and other	924	21.25
Civil servants	Agricultural Rural Development Authority	1	0.02
	Agritex	2	0.05
	District Development Fund	1	0.02
	Other	18	0.41
Security	Army	47	1.08
	Office of the President official	10	0.23
	Air force	16	0.37
	Zimbabwe Republic Police	42	0.97
Veterans	War Veteran	316	7.27
	Collaborator	10	0.23
	Ex-detainee	2	0.05
Traditional leaders	Chief	2	0.05
Others	Business person	7	0.16
	Farmworker	3	0.07
Not specified	Not specified	2,948	67.79
Total		4,349	100.00

Source: Agritex (2004).

enough land to effect real decongestion. They took action to self-allocate land close to their resource-depleted and highly populated Chiweshe communal area. For instance, the Forrester Estate became a key target with land occupiers who indicated that they had been overlooked in the allocation, with perceptions rife that people from 'Harare' had largely benefited within the district. Moreover, the fact that people from Chiweshe chose to occupy parts of the estate they regarded as underutilised tended to vindicate the position of officials who wanted to use some estate land for resettlement.

The researchers worked with Agritex to reconstruct the allocation lists, as there was no standard centralised system at district level. This is the list used for analysis and will be referred to in this chapter as Agritex (2004). According to Agritex (ibid.), in Mazowe there were 137 farms available for the A2 model in 2004, while 11 farms were to be allocated under the peri-urban model. It was noted that farms available for the A1 model measured 105,699.19 ha (or 31 per cent of the total agricultural lands in Mazowe). These farms were officially allocated to 4,963 people.[7] On the other hand, the Utete committee (2003a), established that in Mazowe a total of 217,588.05 ha were allocated to 5,478 people. The differences in the land available for resettlement as well as in the overall number of beneficiaries between Agritex and Utete are due to the discrepancies discovered during the reconstruction of the lists. The A1 categories from the Agritex list show that 21 per cent of the plots specified in the lists were allocated to the 'ordinary' category. Curiously, 68 per cent could not be accounted for by category, which leaves speculation as to the identities of those beneficiaries (see Table 3.3).

There are allegations that due to their positioning, civil servants could have influenced land allocation for their benefit. The Agritex data show that when civil servants and security personnel are combined as government employees, some 3 per cent were beneficiaries (Table 3.3). In fact, although corruption could have happened, it was not possible to be overt given the nature of the huge interests which enabled transparency in the allocation procedures. The social pressure exerted by the committees to deliver land fairly to all categories of people worked to expose unfair processes. In the field, there were numerous stories of civil servants whose names were dropped from the initial allocations, while others were moved from the A2 to the A1 model.

Youths were a major force in the land occupation. One official indicated that youths were disruptive, and most had been hired by the elites to occupy the land for them for a fee (interview, 16 June 2004). In Mazowe District, the policy was to allocate two youths to every A1 farm, which translates to a potential 274 young people being given land. Whether or not this policy was strictly adhered to was difficult to judge from the lists presented. Youths were also allocated a complete farm known as Farm 40 of Glendale, which benefited 57 people. From the survey results, nobody below the age of 21 was allocated land in the sampled farms and only 9.2 per cent of respondents below the age of 30 were allocated land. The largest proportion of land beneficiaries (30.7 per cent) were in the 41–50 age group. In general, applicants over 41 years of age obtained land in both models. In terms of model distribution, 5.6 per cent of respondents above 61 years received land in the A1 village scheme.

The allocation of land to 'youth' raises fundamental questions about government policy on the empowerment of future leaders and producers. The fact that youth participation was critical in the demand for and effective occupation of land meant that they deserved land in their own right. However, the allocation of land to young people goes against the traditional framework of land ownership in Zimbabwe. In communal areas, it is known that land can be allocated only to household heads, in this case only married men. However, in view of the potential role of young people in rural development, as well as the fact that employment is now critically dependent on agriculture, the youth were also prioritised in land allocations.

A number of studies have shown that a very small number of ex-farmworkers have been resettled under the FTLRP (Sachikonye, 2003; Magaramombe, 2003b). Figures available from the Ministry of Local Government and Urban Development suggest that at the official close of the A1 model in March 2002, official

Box 3.2 Steps in land allocation and occupation in the A2 scheme

Step 1 – Application: people completed application forms made available by the MLRR and attached cash flow budgets and details of their source of funds. At this stage, the government (through the media) encouraged people to apply at their district office or directly through the MLRR.

Step 2 – Selection: people regarded as VIPs in government and ZANU-PF heavyweights are vetted. The selection was based on prior eligibility criteria developed during Phase I of the Land and Resettlement Programme.

Step 3 – Announcement of beneficiaries: announcement made in the local print media in 2001. However, individuals pursued the allocating authority.

Step 4 – Allocation: beneficiary given an offer letter signed by the Minister of Lands and Rural Resettlement. In Mazowe, some of those who failed to get A2 plots moved to the A1 scheme. Poor communication between the DLC and the PLC led to multiple allocations.

Step 5 – Occupation process: offer letter used to claim ownership and then evict white farm owners. In most cases, 'force' was used to evict former farm owners, who sometimes instituted legal action against land occupation. Agritex, as the agency involved in the pegging of farms, assisted beneficiaries in plot identification. Most A2 farmers moved into existing farmhouses, while some built temporary infrastructure.

---

records put the figure of farmworkers who had been resettled as 2,087. The figure had increased to 3,223 by 2003, which meant that at the time of the Utete (2003a) audit, some 2.3 per cent of ex-farmworkers had been resettled. In general, in Mashonaland Central, the average allocation to ex-farmworkers was 2.9 per cent of the total allocations, with seven ex-farmworkers allocated under the A2 model. It was the only province that allocated A2 plots to ex-farmworkers in the whole country (ibid.).

In the Ruzivo survey (2004), ex-farmworkers in the study sample of beneficiaries (n=251) constituted 12.75 per cent; this was very high by national standards. However, the ex-farmworkers were allocated smaller plots compared with other plot holders. For example, on the two farms where former farmworkers were resettled they were given a smaller hectarage (between 0.8 and 2 ha) while other farmers were given 12 ha each. An emerging pattern has been observed whereby former farmworkers who have been officially resettled maintain employment contacts as a strategy to diversify their income sources.

In terms of land size, for the A1 schemes each holding was supposed to be allocated at least 27.5 ha, derived as follows: residential area (0.5 ha), arable area (12 ha) and common grazing (15 ha). The 2004 survey (n=251) found that 84.3 per cent of beneficiaries in A1 obtained between 3 and 10 ha and 11.6 per cent got between 11 and 30 ha. Almost all the peri-urban plot holders got between 1 and 2 ha. There are, however, some larger holdings, as some farmers have more than the 12 ha of arable land. The topographical variations in land use patterns – for example for livestock production – were factors considered in the demarcation of large-sized holdings.

A2 land allocation in Mazowe District The land allocation in the A2 model has been the subject of numerous debates in the media and academia (Hammar et al., 2003; Alexander 2006; Moyo et al., 2009; Scoones et al., 2010; Sadomba, 2008; Marongwe, 2008; Zamchiya, 2011). A major theme running through criticism of the FTLRP was that land was allocated to political cronies, to elites, and to those who did not deserve land because they were 'employed' or had secure income sources. A key objective of the FTLRP was to de-racialise the commercial agriculture sector, hence those with resources were given an opportunity to go into commercial farming through the A2 model. The key steps that A2 applicants followed are elaborated in Box 3.2. The selection process under the A2 model was based on eligibility criteria determined by a scoring system based on the following indicators:

- current income (bank statement to support application);
- ownership of property (title deed as evidence);
- cash flow projections in the proposal;
- experience in farming;
- qualification and training evidenced through recognised certificates; and
- a viable project proposal.

This robust system developed by the former Ministry of Lands and Agriculture was rarely adhered to in the selection of beneficiaries; it seems that the policies and criteria developed for settler selection often were not followed.

Agritex (2004) shows that for the A2 scheme there were 1,054 people selected and allocated a combined total of 195,012.52 ha. Yet, a year earlier, the Utete (2003a) audit had established that in Mazowe some 145,692.50 ha were allocated to 873 beneficiaries, of which 355 were ordinary, 71 were War Veterans and two were farmworkers. The MLRR/SIRDC (2006) land audit had far wider categories of land beneficiaries. In Mazowe they established that there were 368 farms on 388,008 ha before the land reform programme, and that 182 farms were allocated to A2 and 1,254 plots were created, benefiting 904 people. The discrepancies and variations are possibly indications of parallel land allocation processes taking place. This theory is further strengthened by the fact that some of the A2 settlers had offer letters that came direct from the ministry's headquarters in Harare whereas the procedure was that these should go through the province and the district.

Table 3.4 shows a range of beneficiaries, with civil servants in government dominating the list from JAG (2002); this was also the perception of the A1 people engaged in focus group discussions. In general, Ruzivo Trust's 2004 survey established that 44 per cent (n=77) were ordinary farmers.[8] The Agritex list (n=1,054) showed that 54 per cent of the beneficiaries could not be accounted for in terms of their place of work.

TABLE 3.4 A2 beneficiaries in Mazowe according to a variety of reports and surveys (% of total beneficiaries)

Beneficiary category	JAG, 2002	Agritex, 2004	Ruzivo, 2004	MLRR/SIRDC, 2006
Ordinary	0	24.00	44.16	35.97
Businessman	3.45	–	15.57	5.61
Government	58.63	1.52	24.67	11.00
Security	–	2.00	–	7.67
Parastatal	3.45	–	2.6	0.69
Party activist	13.79	–	0	1.60
Private	10.34	–	0	–
War Veteran	10.34	18.00	0	20.96
Pensioner	0	–	7.8	0.46
Development worker	0	–	1.3	–
Not employed	0	–	3.9	–
Other (not specified)	–	54.26	–	16.04
Total	100.00	100.00	100.00	100.00

Source: Calculated from various lists, including the 2004 Ruzivo survey.

In JAG (2002), over 58 per cent were listed as government officials, which confirms that civil servants came top in land allocation. In Mazowe there was a range of officials – from clerks, extension workers and administrators to the top civil servants in different line ministries – who were allocated land. This also meant that land sizes for civil servants also varied, depending on one's level of employment in government, with the top civil servants commanding large A2 farms. When discussing this issue, there has been a tendency to narrow the analysis towards members of the security forces, yet many people in the civil service sought land through proper channels and at times through underhand activities. In Mazowe, the land committee was open about the allocation of

TABLE 3.5 Selected schemes with high numbers of War Veterans and other security employees in Mazowe

Farm	Total number of settlers	War Veterans	Zimbabwe National Army	Zimbabwe Republic Police	Civil servants	Central Intelligence Organisation	Ordinary
Virginia Dirmie	25	16	3		4		2
Villa Franca	25	16	3		4		2
Ruia A	33	11		1			21
Petra	35	6	2	2		1	24
Moorefields	74	9					65
Lowdale	29	3		4	4		18
Ingleborough	25	4		10			11
Hermingstone	24	12					12
Frugmore	41	12					29
Fourstreams	10	10					
Forrester	52	9					43
Elsinora	49	20	2				27
Davnar	33	7	1				25
Craigengower	84	3	3				78
Chirobi	31	6					25
California	33	7					26
Burley Bottom	50	12	1				37
Bianco	26	6					20
Bellavista	–	4	1	1		1	7
Bariff	25	6	1	1			17
Ardulla	20	4					16

Source: Original data from government records, 2004.

TABLE 3.6 Distribution of farm sizes (ha) in Mazowe for A2 beneficiaries according to a variety of reports and surveys

Area (ha)	Ruzivo, 2004		JAG, 2002		MLRR/SIRDC, 2006	
	No.	%	No.	%	No.	%
1 to 50	202	83.47	0	0	421	48.00
50.1 to 100	18	7.44	0	0	170	19.38
100.1 to 500	20	8.26	9	36.00	273	31.14
500.1 to 1,000	1	0.40	9	36.00	10	1.14
Over 1,000	0	0	7	28.00	3	0.34
Total	241	100.00	25	100.00	877	100.00
Missing data	9	3.59	29	53.70	4	0.45
Grand total	250		54		881	

Source: JAG list provided to the parliament of Zimbabwe by an independent MP, Margret Dongo; MLRR/SIRDC land audit, 2006; Ruzivo survey, 2004.

land to the Zimbabwe National Army (ZNA) as an institution, while individuals applied on their own and qualified based on the set criteria stated earlier. The land committee reserved some farms in the district for state institutions.

Land allocation to War Veterans has been highly contested, with Sadomba (2008) arguing that many lost out during the land allocation process. This was despite the fact that they were at the forefront of the demand for land through land occupations. It was difficult to establish the number of War Veterans in the district, because there were too many lists of applicants, and, in addition, many of them could have been from outside the area given that there was no standing policy that the land reform programme would only cater for those within the district. At the same time, claims about who is and who is not a War Veteran have always been complex in the context of land occupations, with accusations in the media that some who took part in the land occupations were not War Veterans as they were too young to have participated in the war of liberation. So, whichever way one looks at the numbers, the allocation of land to War Veterans gained a large amount of attention relative to their size as a group. However, land allocation did not result in a skewed distribution of land in their favour in any significant way.

The allocated land in Mazowe District varied in size, which reflected the model applied and the land use patterns in the district. In the western parts of the district, land deemed suitable for livestock was generally larger than in the central and eastern parts. The A2 farms were allocated as small (plot size average 30 ha), medium (average 100 ha) and large (average 300 ha). The largest number of beneficiaries (509) ended up in small-scale plots, followed by those in medium-scale and lastly large-scale plots. In the Ruzivo survey (2004), the A2 model showed that 84 per cent of those interviewed (n=251) received between 1 and 50 ha. For the large-scale allocations, some 8 per cent of the total beneficiaries were allocated 100 to 500 ha. On the other hand, the MLRR/ SIRDC land audit (2006) (see Table 3.6) established that 31 per cent of the beneficiaries obtained between 100 and 500 ha. The JAG list, although small in terms of the number of farms listed by hectarage in Mazowe, shows that on average they were more than 100 ha, with a few being over 1,000 ha; these were more likely to be full farms, i.e. farms allocated whole to an individual rather than being divided up for many people. However, on average, it can therefore be established that the government stuck to its criteria of maximum land sizes provided for in its policy.

Peri-urban land allocation Urban people from small towns such as Mvurwi, Concession and Glendale, as well as people from Harare, were also lumped together as 'ordinary' together with people from the Chiweshe communal lands. This distorted the patterns of who benefited from land reform as well as confused the objectives of decongesting communal areas, which had been one of the prime objectives of the land reform programme. Peri-urban land allocations were largely used as a basis for rewarding former ruling party supporters, mostly the poor. While the poor indeed deserved such land, this politicisation has led to allegations of land being denied to former opposition party members. Peri-urban farming is important in the district, as can be judged by the high number of applicants for this category of farming. There are three urban centres (Concession, Glendale and Mvurwi) in Mazowe, surrounded by former large-scale commercial farms, which ignited a large demand for land. However, Mazowe District is also unique in that some of its farms in Wards 20, 21 and 23 share boundaries with Harare.

Thus, some farms in the district were developed as residential land for suburbs of Harare. Some plots, particularly in Ward 20, have been subdivided many times and are now residential stands but with space for peri-urban farming; Christon Bank is one of the popular residential areas with some low-density housing. The Harare/Mazowe peri-urban farms provide produce for the Harare market, but the proximity of Mazowe District to Harare meant that some farms were to be re-planned and ceded to the city for the purposes of urban expansion. This re-planning has now been confirmed, and in 2010 several peri-urban wards on the outskirts of Harare were incorporated into the Harare metropolitan area. Unfortunately, some of the settlers on these farms may lose land or be transferred to other farms or another province. This is another indication of the fact that land allocation and reallocation is an ongoing affair.

There is still much controversy surrounding allocations of the peri-urban plots. There were no lists of beneficiaries available in Mazowe Rural District Council, the DA's office or the Ministry of Lands. According to Agritex planning, the maximum farm sizes for peri-urban plots, after taking into consideration variations in topography, should not exceed 50 ha (which is the largest possible area, found in the drier areas suitable for livestock in the Matebeleland and Masvingo regions); in Mazowe they decided to allocate only 2 ha for peri-urban plots, because the district is in a wetter area. However, Agritex officials complained that their main planning dilemma comes from interference from political offices, which sometimes recommend plots of more than 15 ha in peri-urban areas. In Mazowe, only four farms of over 15 ha were planned, with Umzi Farm in Glendale officially allocated to 320 households on 336 ha.

The peri-urban farms in general play a critical role for urban families as a supplement to their incomes and a means of addressing food deficits in urban areas. However, before 2000 peri-urban areas practised complex land uses such as horticulture (flowers and vegetables), ostrich farming and game, which were promoted in the district on smaller units of land. The main beneficiaries were the few white farmers, and some proprietors made huge investments in greenhouses to produce various types of crops for local and international markets. In addition, livestock production, particularly dairy, poultry and pork, as well as wildlife sanctuaries for tourism, have been key enterprises in Mazowe District. In the context of the FTLRP, the government planned the peri-urban scheme with a view of promoting food security, while also aiming to attract the urban voters who had turned to the Movement for Democratic Change (MDC).

Were the beneficiaries just political cronies?

Land reform was a political process, deriving legitimacy from complex historical, economic and social contexts. There is no doubt that those who wanted land used the political route to access it, and there was nothing extraordinary about the political approaches taken by the eventual beneficiaries of the FTLRP. Yet various writers, donors and academia have tried to deconstruct the FTLRP, and in particular land allocation, in terms of politics and governance of the nation-state. A general view in the media is that it was ZANU-PF supporters who got access to land. Marongwe (2008: 3) argues that the question of who benefited from the FTLRP is highly controversial, and is at the heart of opposing interpretations of the programme. Moyo and Yeros (2005b) argue that it was largely peasants who benefited, while others (Hammar et al., 2003; Alexander, 2003; 2006; Zamchiya, 2011) assert that it was mainly those politically inclined towards ZANU-PF who accessed the land; they apply this even to local populations, who were said to have been ZANU-PF supporters (Alexander, 2003; Chavunduka and Bromley, 2010). However, some writers (Scoones et al., 2010) argue that there is a need for empirical evidence rather than relying on assumptions derived from divided media (public media versus private media) and academics.

Most research into the outcomes of land allocation lacks an adequate empirical analysis of the forces at the national and local level that shaped who got what land, where and of what size. There is a tendency to give prominence to the broad analytical categories targeted at state officials and interest groups, especially War Veterans and political parties (Alexander, 2003; Raftopoulos, 2003; Masiiwa, 2004; Marongwe, 2003; Zamchiya, 2011). However, this approach ignores the complexity, 'embedding' and interrelatedness of the structures and processes underlying land allocation. In particular, land occupiers created alliances with political parties as well as with elements in the middle and upper classes in order to become an effective force that captured the situation on the ground. Thus stereotypical conceptions of the poor as being the pawns of politicians may not be entirely true, because the poor developed tactics and strategies to influence the state, the land allocation committees and the government's technical bureaucrats and to ensure that there was no wavering in implementation of the programme. The government's technical bureaucracy became subservient to the programme because it questioned their professional ethics and morality, and swept away what they had been trained to do. In most cases, they set aside morality and joined in the programme through what seemed to be the self-allocation of land.

Generalisations about the selection of beneficiaries in the FTLRP are problematic, because one has to revisit the geographical, economic and social spaces that influenced land access and land use in the various provinces. Conclusions about beneficiaries of land reform require a good evidence base, which is still difficult to obtain, as very few researchers have asked about the political affiliation of beneficiaries. Often, the perceived bias towards ZANU-PF is derived from partisan media, and reconstructed by researchers who usually live outside the country or have taken a position against the FTLRP, and against anything to do with ZANU-PF as a political party. However, attendance at political meetings and activities (whether voluntary or by compulsion) is not the best proxy indicator of cronyism. As pointed out elsewhere in this chapter, people were often compelled by circumstance and could have participated in those activities to avert the dangers of violence and retribution. Does that make them ZANU-PF supporters? This is a difficult question to answer, in the context in which people in rural areas found themselves.

However, blatant political statements about exclusion made by some leaders have been taken to confirm that the reforms were completely opposed to members of the opposition. Marongwe (2003), Hammar et al. (2003) and Alexander (2006) quoted sources indicating that there were complaints that card-carrying members of the ruling party got land. For instance, Marongwe (2008: 152) established that political statements were included in official correspondence when known supporters of the main opposition party, the MDC, were denied access to land. For example, minutes from the Resettlement Committee in Mazowe categorically stated: 'Councillors [names cited] ... reported that there were some people from Chiwororo who were resettled but they were MDC party members. The Governor [for Mashonaland Central] asked councillors to solve this problem. They were asked to screen the list putting Chiwororo party [ZANU-PF] members.' This fact, according to Marongwe (ibid.: 153), did not escape the attention of the Supreme Court:

> But there can be no doubt that it is unfair discrimination to target farmers who are believed to be supporters of an opposition party, and to award the spoils of expropriation primarily to ruling party adherents. If ZANU-PF party branches or cells or officials are involved in the selection of settlers and the allocation of plots, the exercise degenerates from being a historical righting of wrongs into pure discrimination. It is equally wrong to discriminate against workers of foreign origin who are lawful permanent residents of Zimbabwe. (Supreme Court Judgment SC 132/2000)

Through making this loaded statement, the highest court of the land had seen the politicisation of the process as undoing a 'legitimate' land reform programme. However, the majority of beneficiaries behaved as, or simply were, members of ZANU-PF, because the situation of land allocation was seen as a party affair on the ground; examples of this behaviour included chanting party slogans, adopting party regalia and speaking the ZANU-PF language. Several factors account for these views: a) the ruling party was in charge of the allocation through their party structures being represented on the DLC (no other political party participated); b) when redistribution was covered on television and reported in print media, events where land was given to success-ful beneficiaries were shown as being ruling party occasions, with members donning party regalia, punctuated by political rallies with anti-opposition slogans; and c) although traditional leaders (who were assumed to be non-partisan) compiled the allocation lists, they submitted the lists to the DLC, which was dominated by the ruling party.

Based on these facts alone, it can be concluded that people perceived to be in the opposition might not have benefited directly, although card-carrying members also deserved land. The key questions revolved around equity – the principle was that all Zimbabweans who wanted a piece of land could get one, whatever their political affiliation. In fact, there was a need to establish neutral (read technical and bureaucratic) institutions that were non-partisan to ensure equity in the allocations. Had this been done, perhaps one of the major problems with the FTLRP would have been resolved. But this was not the case, and even ten years later the issue of bias in land allocation still features prominently.

Nonetheless, the contests over who benefited require a much deeper analysis of the Zimbabwean societal context. In fact, within the former ruling party itself, there are perceptions that the land reform benefited people from a certain class and from certain regions. Therefore, connections to the power structures, civil servants or sophisticated urban people were seen as key instruments for successfully gaining land. There are strong simmers of discontent from farmworkers, youths, the disabled and women, all of whom were largely excluded. When carefully examined, this discontent also relates to the perceptions and realities that some people got 'oversized' farms, benefited from state-acquired equipment and, moreover, were supported through a farm mechanisation programme led by the Reserve Bank of Zimbabwe. The phenomenon of multiple 'dipping' into state subsidies was a sore point. At the same time, the beneficiaries of such dipping argue that they deserved the farm support they got, and remain very sensitive to the possibility of land audits and re-planning, which may occur when state subsidies paid out during the FTLRP period have to be accounted for.

In general, the managers (government officials) largely became beneficiaries of the programme as they placed themselves at the top in the landless lists and allocation of farms. What started as land management ended up in some cases as being a process of self-allocation of land by civil servants, whose political affiliation is difficult to tell, given that the Public Services Act prohibits civil servants from dabbling in politics. Yet at the height of the land takeover, some civil servants were involved in political sloganeering in Mazowe during farmer field-day shows, thus rendering them partisan. However, such partisanship emerged because ZANU-PF had largely politicised most government structures (and the rural space, particularly farming areas), which left no options for officials except to follow the party line to protect their jobs, families and lives. Such politicisation also provided them with the opportunity to get land, using fatalistic arguments such as 'We are already stuck in the mud, so we might as well get the land' (interview with an official, 16 June 2004).

There is also a view that ruling party elements designed and sustained the land occupations; this then became a basis for justifying allocation to party members, because they had made the land transfer possible. As one War Veteran in Mazowe noted: 'How could they [opposition members] have benefited when they didn't fight in the *Third Chimurenga*. They were cowards and opposed the programme thinking that it was a political gimmick, and now they want to do a *mucheka dzafa* [harvesting where they did not sow]' (interview, 7 June 2007).

In order to dispel allegations of cronyism, the government argued that the FTLRP provided a public opportunity for people to benefit because there was an open invitation to anyone who wanted land. However, some people were sceptical due to the political foundations of the programme at the beginning, and only got interested when the programme was running at full throttle. For instance, at a feedback workshop (16 June 2005), Chief Negomo pointed out that initially it was difficult to get people in Chiweshe on the lists, but later it was decided to list anyone interested because the government then needed a greater number of people to be on the land.

When the land occupations and their relationship to the ruling political party are correlated, one notes political motivations based on the supply side of the land issue. The idea of government was one of quick acquisition and quick allocations so that it could confirm that the process was complete. However, as noted in the FGDs, this could not easily be fulfilled, because there were too few people on the lists for allocation, which worried the government politically. A mass of people was required to signal that the programme was national, non-partisan and therefore legitimate. However, for some communal area people, engagement in *jambanja* drew tremendously on their time and personal resources and they were uncomfortable to participate in a programme that had political undertones.

A diverse range of people applied for land after the *jambanja*, and some were successful. It is extremely difficult to identify whether any were members of ZANU-PF, because at the DLC the applicants were not asked their political affiliation. While accusations of political patronage are rife, the reality is that those who had the political courage took the risk to acquire land, and no force was used to make people opt to take the land. The data show a range of beneficiaries, from 'ordinary' people and civil servants to those fulfilling specific quotas (War Veterans, women, youths, farmworkers), and with the numbers involved it cannot be the case that they all belonged to one political party.

Voting patterns on the Fast Track Farms as a proxy indicator of cronyism Since the beginning of the FTLRP Zimbabwe has undergone three presidential, three House of Assembly (parliament) and two Upper House (senatorial) elections, all with mixed results for political parties. To understand the politics of the FTLRP in relation to beneficiaries requires a deeper analysis of voter behaviour on the FTFs since 2000 and of how they have selected their political leaders. An analysis of the national elections from 2000 demonstrates changing patterns in voting outcomes in constituencies covering commercial agricultural land. Whereas in the 2000 and 2005 elections ZANU-PF, as the ruling party, dominated the popular vote, this situation changed in 2008.

In the 2008 national elections, resettlement area votes seem to have swung to the opposition MDC-T (MDC-Tsvangirai), given that the party made significant gains in the ZANU-PF stronghold of Mazowe District at the parliamentary elections. The MDC-T won one constituency and narrowly lost another, while ZANU-PF held on to three constituencies (Table 3.7). At the 2005 elections, the constituency now held by MDC-T had been dominated by ZANU-PF; from independence in 1980 until the 2008 elections, Mashonaland Central had been

TABLE 3.7 Parliamentary and senate election results in Mazowe District, 2000–08

Political party	House of Assembly votes 2000		House of Assembly votes 2005		House of Assembly votes 2008[2]				Senate votes	
	West	East	West	East	Central	North	South	West	2005	2008
MDC-T[1]	7,085	7,473	5,474	7,567	5,573	2,508	4,052	2,410	No candidate	14,193
ZANU-PF	14,024	18,824	14,397	18,041	4,136	5,466	4,109	5,148	Unopposed	19,294
MDC-M	–	–	–	–	1094	717	1401	–	No candidate	3,754
UPP	–	533	–	–	119	–	178	–	–	–
ZPPDP	–	–	–	–	79	–	–	–	–	–
Independent	–	–	–	386	–	363	–	446	–	–

Notes: 1. Before 2005, there was a single MDC political party which later split into two political formations for the elections in 2008. 2. Constituencies were re-demarcated before the 2008 elections, which saw the addition of two new constituencies, and the phasing out of Mazowe East.

Source: ZESN, 2005; ZCBC, 2008.

TABLE 3.8 Parliamentary and senate election results in Shamva District, 2000–08

Political party	House of Assembly votes				Senate votes (Bindura-Shamva)	
	2000	2005	2008 (North)	2008 (South)	2005	2008
MDC[1]	5,621	4,848				
MDC-M			No candidate	No candidate	No candidate	No candidate
MDC-T			1,333	2,669	No candidate	19,400
ZANU-PF	19,460	29,287	10,386	8,956	Unopposed	35,400
Independent	–	–	1,173	0	–	–
UPP	–	–	0	–	–	–

Note: 1. The MDC split in 2005 before the senatorial elections. The Tsvangirai formation became known as the MDC-T and the Mutambara formation became known as the MDC-M.

Source: ZESN, 2005; ZCBC, 2008; ZEC, 2000, 2005 and 2008.

regarded as a stronghold of ZANU-PF. In the council elections the main political parties had an equal number of members elected, which reflected the national pattern. As for the senatorial seat, in 2005 the ZANU-PF candidate had been elected unopposed, whereas in 2008 the ZANU-PF candidate was elected into office with a relatively small lead over the MDC-T candidate.

In Shamva District, ZANU-PF has always been the dominant party, fielding candidates and winning at both the parliamentary and senatorial elections held between 2000 and 2008. While ZANU-PF retained the voters when Shamva North and South were combined in 2008, despite giving land there was no growth in the voting numbers. As for the MDC, the voting numbers declined between 2000 and 2008, with much of their support eroded due to an independent candidate taking over some of the votes (Table 3.8). The elections from 2000 show that ZANU-PF actually increased votes during the FTLRP in both parliament and senate.

In Mangwe District, the MDC has been the dominant force in terms of the House of Assembly seats. In 2005, ZANU-PF narrowly beat the MDC senatorial candidate but the MDC claimed victory in the 2008 elections (Table 3.9). In the district (previously combined as Bulilimamangwe District), the former opposition dominated the council and national elections, while ZANU-PF held on to one constituency in Bulilima (mostly communal area). In Mangwe, in the Marula Ward for instance, the people opted for the opposition to represent them even though they benefited from the ZANU-PF-led FTLRP.

In general, it seems that there is a clear trajectory; party political affili-

TABLE 3.9 Parliamentary and senate election results in Mangwe District, 2000–08

Political party	House of Assembly votes				Senate votes (Bulilimamangwe)	
	2000 (Bulilimamangwe)		Mangwe			
	North	South	2005	2008**	2005	2008*
MDC[1]	11,767	11,761	10,145			
MDC-M				3,928	9,289	10,354
MDC-T				2,294	No candidate	6,752
ZANU-PF	8,679	5,617	5,723	2,627	9,310	9,303
ZAPU	–	556	–	–	–	–
LPZ	–	253	–	–	–	–
UP		233	–	–	–	–

Note: 1. The MDC split in 2005 before the senatorial elections. The Tsvangirai formation became known as the MDC-T and the Mutambara formation became known as the MDC-M.

Source: ZESN, 2005; ZCBC, 2008; ZEC, 2000, 2005 and 2008.

ations swing over time, depending on who has the persuasive strength and over what issues. In this case, the exhaustion of eight years of economic downfall seems to have persuaded voters to try to change leadership and national governance. If the broad base of beneficiaries is considered against the background of changed voting patterns in 2008 in newly resettled areas, the argument of 'pure' political patronage seems not to be applicable in the case study areas. Probably a political analyst would argue that patronage thrives during contexts such as better economic conditions, but, equally, a waning economic environment provides leeway for using resources such as land for patronage and to gain power and control. It would seem that a combination of both may have applied to Mazowe, in large part because the voters were quietly protesting, despite having been allocated land. At the end of the day, a new mix of political players and voters of different affiliations provides a sound basis for democracy, and democracy is key to unlocking the potential that the land represents.

Elite practices and infiltration into political structures to get choice and oversized land

Munyuki-Hungwe (2011) has categorised elites in Mazowe District and has noted that political elites drew largely on their material wealth, connections in business, education and political resources, as well as on the positions they held in society. The elites are able to influence power, decisions and opinions because of their financial resources. She classified elites into: bureaucratic elites, ethnic elites, political elites, economic elites, cultural elites and social elites. In the practice of power, domination and control of the land allocation process, the roles of these elites overlapped, and the various groups were connected by specific interlocking relationships. In fact, the elites used their power not just for land allocation, but also to ensure that they were at the front of the queue to benefit from whatever government resources were earmarked for farmer support (Daloz, 2003). However, such elites did not use their power outside government, for example in the private sector, to unlock support for the land reform process.

The question is: what approaches did 'elite' civil servants use in order to be allocated land? The elites chose unorthodox methods of accessing quality land and infrastructure, which tended to engulf the FTLRP with pure 'grabbing' par excellence. In fact, cases emerged where individuals formed consortiums to virtually loot farms. Some came up with new forms of protectionism – promising former owners protection if they surrendered their land to them. Some of the consortiums have since been taken to court by the state,[9] as their political fortunes waned within their own political party. This is a group of people who were on a perpetual search for new farms as their own booty.

This elite group claimed support from the highest level (which was difficult to prove), had the machinery and connections to convince the administrators to give them land, and also, at times, determined who got what land as they bulldozed their way through the land allocation committees. In some cases, they had the audacity to take the former landowners to court as they contested the land takeovers. The approach of the elites was facilitated by the power they wielded at the time, which the public saw via reports in the media of the direct harassment of white farmers with the government seemingly un-able (or just unwilling) to control them. Elites who took landowners to court enhanced their 'macho' public image, which gave them 'legitimacy', at least in the view of low-ranking government officials and the public, and they used this as a basis for taking over more properties. In fact, behind the scenes, the ex-farmers were compelled by fear to privately negotiate directly with the elites rather than with the land authorities. This was because these elites often used force by mobilising their own eviction teams (shock troops to get the farmers out). They also aggressively penetrated the district and provincial structures of ZANU-PF as a means of using politics to protect their wealth accumulation.

In the Chegutu area (an area outside Ruzivo Trust survey sites), for example, a notorious group emerged that engaged in political mischief, with the aim of harvesting other people's crops. Accusations arose that top politicians were involved.[10] This form of piracy on the new farms made them places where survival of the fittest held sway, and where women and political weaklings could not survive. Their targets were not only the white-owned farms, but also A1 farms that they thought were 'nicer' than those they already had. New farmers in Mazowe who initially had land adjacent to main roads became reluctant to take ownership of the land because of the fear of 'nefarious highway visitors' on the prowl for the best farms (in Mazowe it was not surprising to see underutilised land on main roads, and utilised plots deeper inside the district, in areas not easily accessible). These visitors were powerful men who wanted land close to the paved highways; they went out at the weekend in their Mercedes Benz cars and were back on Monday in their all-terrain Toyota Vigo 4x4s (*mota dzine mhopo pamusana*), claiming the land and its produce and facilitating the eviction of smaller farmers (FGD, 5 May 2007). The common pattern was that they were also interested in and attracted by the infrastructure on the farms, as well as the produce, which they could harvest immediately to 'enjoy what they did not sow'.

It must be said that, although strong criticisms can be made of the role of elites, this does not undermine the fact that it was largely the ordinary citizens who benefited from the land allocations. However, the first key issue concerns the moral question of elites and politicians taking strategic farms – in other words, taking land already allocated to others – and the continued search for land by 'the pirates of the land', individuals who changed farms from year to year. In addition, such people did not conform to the regulations on farm sizes and were involved in manipulating the system for their personal benefit. These are the moral issues underpinning the criticism of the programme, not the question of whether such people should have benefited.

Land pirating happened during the first six years of the FTLRP, and today there are few, if any, cases; many individuals have settled on their chosen farms, while the MLRR has also asserted control of land ownership.

Technical planning and the expansionist tendencies of elites At times, the state used its own discretion to allow the technical bureaucrats to do their work, for example by strictly following the technical criteria in the allocation process. The use of technical planning was seen as a way in which the state could 'hide' from the sometimes 'marauding' beneficiaries. The government's line of defence would be 'technical planning'; this allowed Agritex unfettered access to the farms and enabled them to control beneficiaries by moving them into different parts of the district without too many political problems. In this way, those with the potential to be a nuisance to the state were moved, and in the process they became compliant, because they became aware that, despite allowing chaos to happen, the government was in control. Technical planning led to the A1 farmers being made to live in an artificial form of compound system, which was an adaptation of the settlement patterns imposed on former farmworkers. The settlers felt that, although they were happy to get land, the government was at the same time infringing on their human rights, specifically on the right to choose how to live. Plot holders were required to adhere to government technical planning, and could not make individual decisions concerning investments, for example in ponds or piggeries.

This type of planning causes serious problems, but it played a crucial role in the design of farm systems that would allow for service provision in the future. At the same time, it helped disguise the government's intentions for political surveillance and control of the masses on the farms. The compound system makes it easier to call political meetings, especially among the densely settled A1 farmers, but it did not apply to A2 farmers. The A1 farmers, therefore, saw the regulations as discriminatory and based on the assumed status (or wealth) of the A2 beneficiaries. For the A1 farmers in general, the planning system was too state-centred and highly dependent on the wishes of the government. The beneficiaries constantly referred to the situation prior to the FTLRP, when the government was hardly visible on the commercial farms. After allocation, many expected this situation of light-touch government to remain, but instead the government became more visible for a variety of reasons (see Chapter 4).

The relocation of settlers, ostensibly according to government developmental planning, has been riddled with controversy. Perceptions exist that some A1 farmers were removed because the government wanted to allocate land based on cronyism. Elite expansionist desires tended to get official recognition, because some individuals with enormous political power found that they could easily trample local bureaucrats, who in turn sought legitimacy for the action they took on land matters from those same elites. But some elites have been overbearing; at times they have influenced the re-planning of some farms from A1 to A2, as in the case where an A2 farmer emerged from the private sector and not only used his enormous political capital to push A1 farmers off the land, but went as far as seeking political office in order to stay put and defend the land he had obtained.

A revolving patronage system seems to have been created, with clear top-down prescriptive structures that local stakeholders could not influence. Decisions coming from the top resulted in elites acquiring land and interfering in the planning process. For instance, at Belford North Extension in Mazowe District, an A2 beneficiary illegally annexed two subdivisions, including one allocated to a weaker A2 farmer (MLRR/SIRDC, 2006). The beneficiary of subdivisions 1 and 4 of Barwick H Farm, a retired brigadier, annexed a portion of the neighbouring Esperi Farm to expand his farming project without the consent of the owner. While these A2 fights occur, the people who have suffered most are those who are resource poor (land occupiers and A1 farmers).

The greatest anxiety is caused by the process of expulsion of A1 farmers from certain FTFs because of the government's re-planning process. The process and resulting emotional arguments, sometimes reinforced by physical action, are something that many settlers dread. It makes settlers very nervous about the long-term prospects of remaining on fast track land. Cases of powerful potential A2 farmers coming late to the resettlement programme, who then connive with the land committees or powerful politicians to get land, are seen by A1 farmers as representing the greatest threat. The relocation of settlers ostensibly on the basis of government developmental planning has been riddled with controversy.

Actual re-planning and threats of re-planning A1 farms to make way for A2 schemes, on what land occupiers regard as spurious grounds, reinforce the image of resettlement areas as places of tenure insecurity. In Mazowe the technical bureaucrats attempted to systematically relocate the settlers. However, there are cases where settlers refused to vacate some of the farms earmarked for specific models. At Mugutu Farm, some settlers officially allocated land were removed from six subdivisions to clear the way for the Mbari clan, who claimed that the land was theirs traditionally. However, according to officials, the affected settlers have not been allocated land elsewhere and by the end of 2004 were still resisting vacating the plots. At Ingleborough Farm, the Mbari clan also claimed ownership. The farm had been set aside by the land committee for the ZNA, as an institution. Evicting the settlers has been difficult to implement because people have put up permanent structures. At Lowdale Farm, the Hwata people occupied the land informally. The farm was then planned and demarcated under the A1 model. However, non-clan members allocated plots at this farm could not settle, as the Hwata people refused to accept any outsiders.

Multiple land holders

After 2000, the selection of land allocations for A2 beneficiaries was used as a less subtle means of placating key groups and individuals (Selby, 2006: 327–8). However, there was still a desire to increase the number of blacks in commercial farming. For instance, the formulation of policy instruments such as that specifying maximum farm sizes was part of a wish to create space for such farmers. The farm size regulations were meant to reduce the sizes of commercial farms from as much as 2,000 ha to between 20 and 2,000 ha for A2, and between 12 and 70 ha for A1, with smaller hectarages in the better-endowed AERs, and larger sizes in regions with poor ecological conditions. These changes meant that there would be an increase in the number of farmers from 4,500 to over 160,000 in both the A1 and A2 models.

The problem, though, was that some large whole farms were left for individuals said to be politically powerful or connected to people with influence. Utete (2003a) confirmed cases of multiple farm ownership due to what the committee termed the multiplicity of 'allocating authorities', which gave rise to double allocations, multiple allocations, and favouritism in land allocations. The President of Zimbabwe, while addressing the ruling party's top decision-making body, the Politburo, in late July 2003, condemned multiple

farm owners and chided them for possessing more than one farm. According to Utete (ibid.), he 'ordered top ZANU-PF officials with multiple farms to
relinquish them within two weeks'. This was welcomed by War Veterans.[11] Vice
President Msika also stressed the point and said that the government was
going ahead with the repossession of farms from politicians with more than
one farm and from other farmers who had not taken up the land they were
allocated.[12] The directive was also extended to non-politicians; for example,
the National Task Force on Land Reform warned 52 ZANU-PF officials and
senior civil servants who owned more than one farm to surrender the land
to the state.[13] In 2003, the President's Office, through the Central Intelligence
Organisation, was said to be probing a number of captains of industry for
ignoring a directive by the President to give up their farms if they had more
than one. Among them were the President of the Confederation of Zimbabwe
Industries and the Chief Executive of the Jewel Bank, now the Commercial
Bank of Zimbabwe.[14]

Government reports maintained that such multiple landowners were no
more than 100 in number. Several lists of multiple owners were discussed in
the Buka land audit (2002) and the MLRR/SIRDC (2006). The MLRR (2009) had
this to say about multiple land ownership:

> Multiple farm ownership is a scenario where an individual or a husband
> and wife(s) (household) own more than one farm. This should include those
> who bought farms, which have not been acquired. A total of 71 multiple farm
> owners were identified during the audit. There were also 18 families found with
> more than one farm per family. These statistics reflect findings of the A2 Land
> Audit only and do not capture other land categories.

An observation made by a key informant (16 June 2004) was that multiple
land ownership emerges from the acts of greedy elites bent on accumulation
of free public goods. First, many try to hide accumulation tendencies through
their children, spouses and relatives who are officially on the list of allocations but are not using the land, which in essence is used by the multiple
owners. The second problem is that land owned in this way is rarely used to
its optimal level as the multiple owner struggles to get access to inputs, given
the general shortages of these on the market. In general, the key challenge
is that multiple farm ownership is a hidden practice, which is difficult to
establish for four key reasons:

- First, there is general fear that the multiple landowners are politically powerful and therefore untouchable.
- Second, there is a general problem in handling land ownership because of
  poor registration systems. There are also several variations, such as 'deliberate multiple ownership' or 'blind multiple ownership', which is caused by

registration problems. It may be that plots are regarded as under multiple ownership even in cases where individuals do not even know that they are in possession of another plot. The use of a manual system of registration at the beginning of the land allocation process partly contributed to this problem.

- Third, there was the following problem that Utete (2003a) encountered: 'instances of polygamous marriages and spouses who are both ex-combatants. In these instances, female spouses would like to retain the ownership of land in their own right.' In addition, some helped their children to gain access to land, creating de facto family multiple farms. Yet because there was no clear policy, they argued that the children deserved the land as long as they were above the age of majority (18 years). However, the moral argument is weak when there were so many people marginalised from the land allocations.

- Fourth, the listing of beneficiaries was also a grey area contributing to blind and deliberate multiple ownership. People tended to apply at many levels and through many organisations. Some applied in several provinces or districts to enhance their chances of getting land. The issue of multiple allocations partly stems from this process, as there was no national information system for checking double or multiple allocations. Thus the same people appeared in different lists, and when they were allocated multiple plots, they did not cede them to the authorities. Some benificiaries do not know that they have multiple farms, which partly explains the massive number of abandoned farms. According to an Agritex official (4 May 2004), they were faced with problems relating to the speed at which action was taken. There was no proper filing of information and little reference to previous land records (that were changing almost on a daily basis). There was no computerisation of the information coming from the bottom (A1 applicants) nor from the top (A2 applicants). When the officials were given computerised printouts from head office, they faced difficulties in filing them because the offices were poorly furnished. In addition, the offices were shared and had no security. Some files were lost completely, and some of the handwritten ones could have been altered.

The ultimatums coming from the central authority seemed to yield results. For instance, the *Sunday Mail* reported that some senior ZANU-PF officials in Matabeleland North had complied with the president's directive and surrendered additional farms they owned. The governor and resident minister of the province gave up two farms to the government. Two other senior government officials from the same province were also reported to have given up their farms for resettlement.[15] The *Herald* reported that 102,000 ha had been recovered from multiple farm owners and given to a committee set up by the president to co-ordinate the implementation of recommendations made by the Utete Committee.[16] The *Financial Gazette* also reported that a governor had been 'booted out' of Rockland Farm in Mashonaland East and was told 'to stick to his one farm in Manicaland Province'. The governor responded by arguing that he had ceded ownership of Rockland Farm, but denied that the farm belonged to him personally, claiming that it belonged to his wife. Influential politicians in the ruling party were said to have abused their positions by holding multiple farms under land reforms meant to resettle landless peasants.[17] It was reported that the Minister of Lands and Agriculture said that the government would continue repossessing land from multiple farm owners, despite resistance from some senior cabinet and ruling party officials.[18]

The government was against multiple land ownership on the basis that it entrenched the earlier system of land being concentrated in a few hands. Yet there was a group of well-connected individuals who not only had oversized farms, but owned more than one farm. This seems to suggest that some elites largely positioned themselves to get control of large-scale commercial farming, posing a threat to the equity that was strongly espoused as the basis for the reforms. At the same time, the government extolled the virtues of commercial farming through advancing arguments about farm viability. To give government the benefit of the doubt, viability concerns could apply to some areas, for example drier areas within well-endowed AERs IIa and IIb, and this could have been used by some as a justification for accessing larger holdings and whole farms. As can be seen in Chapter 5 of this book, the government then pursued macro-economic and agricultural policies that reinforced the bias of resource allocation towards larger farmers. The government generally subsidised agricultural credit, most of which targeted larger farmers in the post-fast track period.

Ambiguous institutional land allocation arrangements

The land allocation and administrative system was centred on government official structures and ZANU-PF structures. However, Dekker and Kinsey (2011) argue that critics have read too much into the role of politicians, because Phase I of the Land and Resettlement Programme was more autocratic as far as settlers were concerned than the FTLRP. They argue that '... the first generation of land reform farmers spent 20 years under a completely top-down, authoritarian administrative system whereas the current generation was resettled in almost an administrative vacuum and, as a result, seems to be developing some grassroots managerial innovations' (ibid.: 996). This innovation is what new beneficiaries exploited to get access to land, as the state literally weakened the government machinery to make it possible for people to be allocated land quickly, though in a chaotic manner.

Underlying all the new resettlement models, there are four kinds of land administration authority in operation, which are broadly categorised as: a) central government authority; b) political authority; c) traditional authority; and d) interest group authority. There is competition among the four over who has the power to identify land beneficiaries, demarcate and allocate land, and administer and resolve land disputes. This vagueness over the roles of the four and their tendency to jostle for supremacy, rather than complementing each other, created problems in land allocation. Utete (2003a: 31) noted that: '... many of the institutional problems were compounded by the activities of "certain persons" who, though lacking any official status or authority, nonetheless proceeded to allocate land, mainly in districts adjacent to the main towns and cities'.

The land committees presented contradictory sources of influence (positive and negative) on national policy and implementation procedures (Moyo et al., 2009). In Mazowe, almost all members of the DLC were said to own farms, which was not atypical of the country as a whole. There were also cases where urban people without adequate social capital in rural areas used porous policy guidelines to manoeuvre the committees into allocating them land. In some cases, however, the stakeholders in the land committees forced a downsizing of allocated landholdings, and therefore challenged the plans drawn up by Agritex. Moyo et al. (2009: 11) note that:

> The fact that land committees and local War Veterans' associations tended to interact with other institutions, such as traditional leaders, local peasant groups and others, tended to create a bulwark of pressure against influential central government officials and urban elites on matters of enforcing policy principles or on checking corrupt tendencies. Land committee members and War Veterans, who had led land occupation movements, became key sources of exposing corruption in land allocations and in mobilising wider social support for broadened land reform, demanding land policy adaptations and the corrections of unequal or unfair land allocations. Traditional leaders generated both equity-inducing influence by seeking more land for their 'communities' and inequity-inducing effects by seeking larger commercial plots for themselves.

In Mazowe, for instance, Chiefs Negomo and Chiweshe played a key role in mobilising their populace to access land. This was despite the view that they were being undermined in accessing land by urban people, especially from Harare. Moyo and Yeros (2007a) correctly noted that chiefs also sought to gain access to larger pieces of prime land and the homesteads of the former landowners, being themselves politicians in the state bureaucracy and private sectors. They supported the larger A2 landholdings, which they justified on grounds of respecting the *mambo* (chief).[19] Moyo and Yeros (ibid.: 111) then suggested that: 'This pattern suggests that chiefs became a special type of

89

lower tier "policy elite" which promoted both equity and inequity within a broad context of support for the land reform.'

A key point of the acquisition and allocation scenario was the suspension of bureaucracy, a process that began in the context of land acquisition. The suspension of bureaucracy, which saw the formation of land committees at the local level, meant that an institutional framework for facilitating land acquisition was transformed into an institution for land allocation, especially for the A1 model. The land committees worked in tandem with central government when responsible for land allocation for the A2 model. Moyo and Yeros (ibid.: 112–13) argued that these agencies served a useful purpose in the land reform programme through regulating people who wanted to access land:

> The suspension of bureaucracy in the rural areas was the climax of the revolutionary situation ... The emergence of a heterodox development plan under sanctions has obliged the state to extend its direct control over monetary, fiscal, pricing, trade, investment, and land policy, and to resurrect planning agencies and parastatals. This centralisation of power has both enabled the state to maintain its confrontational stance against sanctions and widened the gulf between state and society.

While Moyo and Yeros (ibid.) argue that the bureaucracy was suspended, in Mazowe the bureaucracy operated albeit at a reduced capacity. For instance, Agritex and the district office of the MLRR, in a direct sense, backed by the DA's office, continued to function based on clearly set out legal definitions of their existence and roles. If the bureaucracy had been suspended, it would have meant the suspension of legal structures completely, and the government was aware that this would be unconstitutional. However, the state simply incorporated extra-legal bodies into the functions of the state through the creation of land committees and task forces. In this case, the bureaucracy could still do its work with varying degrees of autonomy from the extra-legal and non-technical interest groups. In some cases, the decision-making processes and troubleshooting by the technical bureaucrats prevailed over political considerations.

Conclusions

The FTLRP has not been a straightforward affair and has been contested on the ground in terms of land allocations. The narrow analytical focus on cronyism and benefits accruing to the elites and former ruling party leaders and supporters has clouded a much deeper analysis of land allocations. The FTLRP broadly benefited the masses and showed progress in terms of the numbers of people moved into the resettlement areas. Analysis also shows that, rather than just the poor, those interested in commercial farming, and who had resources, have also benefited, which means the broadening of benefits as a result of the FTLRP. To sum up, the key question is how to interpret the role of the elites, the politicians and their protégés? Can the whole FTLRP be condemned entirely because of the few 'bad apples in the basket'?

Nationally, approximately 400 individuals on fewer than 2 million ha of the 10.4 million ha that the government acquired have been the focus of attention in terms of: a) selecting choice farms; b) multiple ownership; c) pirating the land farms; and d) pillaging infrastructure. Is it justifiable to de-legitimise the whole programme based on the behaviour of relatively few people? While morally it may be justifiable, there is a need for more careful examination of the majority of beneficiaries who are now on quality land, with a potential to move agriculture forward. At the same time, from a political as well as a moral standpoint, there is a need to resolve the issue of multiple land ownership by the elites so as to fulfil the social equity objectives of the programme, but also to address the programme's ethics. The equity issue should not just be about white versus black land ownership, but should be racially blind and apply to every Zimbabwean. On the face of it, therefore, social equity seems to have been undermined by the intensity of the accumulation tendencies of the elites, many of whom are embedded in ZANU-PF. The FTLRP allocations hide incipient self-centred interests, particularly on the part of those with security and higher political leadership positions who tended to receive most of the well-endowed land allocations.

The land reform programme has a mixture of beneficiaries, from the poor to the better off in society. Within these categories are found wealthy men and women, youths, experienced and qualified people in agriculture, and some without any agricultural skills or experience. The new resettled areas have a wider class mix than was the case under the former agrarian structure. The following observations may be made:

- First, although ZANU-PF had the largest say in the land allocation process, some opposition members smuggled themselves on to the beneficiary lists and duly benefited. The fact that the opposition won some constituencies covering the resettled areas, and gained a significant number of votes even where they lost to ZANU-PF in the elections in 2000, 2002, 2005 and 2008, serves to demonstrate the range of political views among those who benefited from land allocation. There were also incidences where the government listed some prominent opposition officials as beneficiaries in the public media, with the Reserve Bank of Zimbabwe placing adverts showing that opposition officials were also beneficiaries of the mechanisation programme it was funding. On the other hand, although it cannot be contested that the opposition did benefit, the scale of the benefits certainly can be contested, as (apart from those who were splashed in the media) fewer of those who declared themselves to belong to opposition parties obtained land.
- Second was that people's choice of political party affiliation changes all the

time, depending on current preferences. Therefore, some of the beneficiaries could have changed party affiliation over time, and could have used the ZANU-PF platform for benefiting from the land reform programme without necessarily remaining members of ZANU-PF. The fact that some beneficiaries participated in ZANU-PF activities did not seem to be reflected in voting outcomes, as ZANU-PF, though winning the popular vote, lost control of parliament and came second in the first round of presidential elections in 2008. The voting data are even more telling at local level, where ZANU-PF performed poorly in resettled areas.

- Third, even when an assumption is made that all the beneficiaries were ZANU-PF supporters, the argument is difficult to sustain given that such supporters would simply have ignored 'formality' and opted for continued *jambanja* as the 'special party people'. The beneficiaries were opting for orderliness in allocation, which was the preference of the opposition. The fact that time, energy, effort and resources were needed to make an application suggests the strong desire for land beyond the politics of it. One could argue that applications were a response to political pressure, but no one was forced to apply or forced to invade farmland. The fact that 74.6 per cent of the beneficiaries made applications to some administrative or local authority – and in some cases political party – shows their willingness to follow some formal procedure in acquiring the land. True, some areas in which applications were made were more political than others, but this does not contradict the fact that there was a meaningful demand for land.
- Fourth, although civil servants were said to be some of the key beneficiaries of the land allocation, there is very little analysis of this group. The fact that many of them were said to be associated with the opposition because of their organic links with urban people gives substance to the argument that the opposition members also benefited from land allocation. However, on the farms, they obviously entered through the veil of ZANU-PF, some of them to the extent of chanting party slogans, although this is not allowed by the Public Services Commission.

In conclusion, it can be said that there was a broadening of claims to the state. Although there were elements of claiming political affiliation, this was clearly a way in which individuals were negotiating access and their stay on the allocated land. In terms of allocations and benefits, both the rich and the poor were therefore vociferous in proving their party allegiance at the outset of the land reform programme. However, staying on allocated land was not determined by negotiation alone. In fact, those allocated land had to demonstrate that they were working at farming, hence the state invoked the land audit as a 'stick' to get the farmers to use the land, which had mixed success. Therefore, land allocation policy and practices can be seen as ordered chaos in which there was an attempt by some actors to control the process. This was because the chaos was contributing to the de-legitimisation of the programme as a whole. Yet, at some level, the government was doing all it could to resolve problems with the land allocations. However, matters of self-interest, especially when it came to the 'one person one farm' policy, tended to affect policy implementation, resulting in cases of multiple farm ownership that the government struggled to resolve. Also, there are still perceptions and realities that many people who should have benefited from the land allocations did not; a land audit was then required to address some of these anomalies.

4 | Juggling land ownership rights in uncertain times

Introduction

The Fast Track Farms (FTFs) are emerging as new sites of struggle in the development trajectory of Zimbabwe, not least because of the unfinished business of land and agrarian reform, but more generally due to the uncertainty that surrounds land reform itself under the banner of the Fast Track Land Reform Programme (FTLRP). This chapter seeks to explain tenure within the peculiarities and character of the current agrarian framework of Zimbabwe. Tenure has become the cause of struggle between multiple groups at local and national level, all of whom are seeking to find answers to why land reform seems not to be meeting expectations. Given the economic decline and increasing levels of food insecurity, it is necessary to establish how tenure conspires with other factors (see Chapter 5) to limit the new farmers from fully utilising their land.

Tenure security has generated intense arguments. It is natural, after a public reform programme that saw violence as the driving force, that beneficiaries would seek tenure security to protect their rights. It follows that preference for a particular form of tenure is influenced by the context, not by the strength or weakness of any specific model. In the case of the FTFs, the political context of land takeover by the government had the effect of removing any trust in matters relating to property rights on the part of the landowner, especially on the FTFs. Furthermore, the sidelining of the judiciary in land matters, through Constitutional Amendment No. 17 on 14 September 2005, confirmed in the eyes of settlers that that notion of trust had broken down, even though the state had political objectives that seemed to be protecting the beneficiaries themselves. Former landowners in particular had no satisfaction on land matters from the courts; this was a lesson to the new beneficiaries, who realised that they could be treated in the same way. Observing how former landowners were being treated, and noting the lack of commitment to legal reforms for clarifying tenure, the new land beneficiaries were prompted to seek tenure that they viewed as secure. Land beneficiaries, therefore, see freehold title deeds, if only as a transitional measure, as providing such tenure security.

However, in Zimbabwe in general, markets influence ownership of land in very specific ways: demand and supply determine land transactions outside public lands (public lands, which now include the FTFs, are under state con-

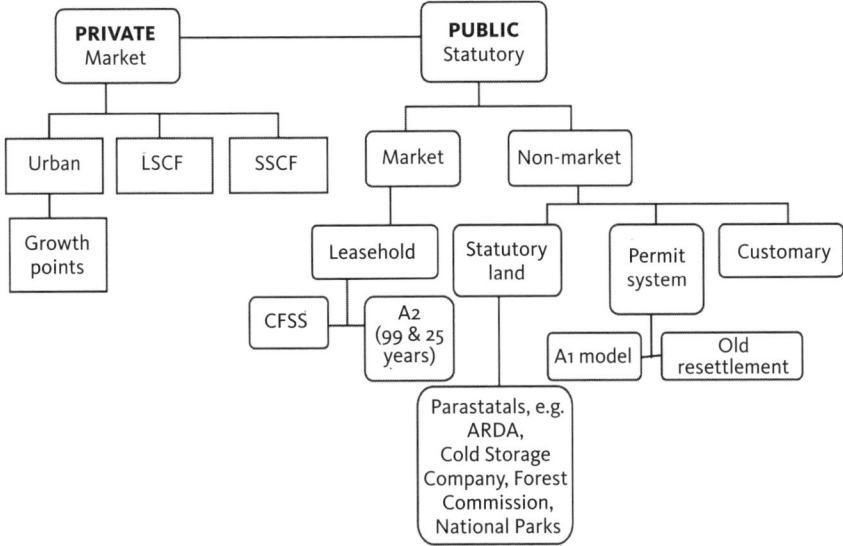

4.1 Forms of tenure with legal and administrative recognition in Zimbabwe (*source*: Based on information in various government policy documents)

trol). The FTLRP did not entirely manipulate the land markets, but rather reduced the area of land that could be traded by individuals. Government controls much of the commercial agricultural lands while users currently retain use rights. At this stage, appropriate elements of tenure security are being negotiated, with the government inclined towards a preference for leaseholds on acquired and transferred land. In general in Zimbabwe, the dominant types of tenure are: freehold titled lands, land under leasehold, land held under customary tenure, and state-owned land allocated through leasehold or permits (see Figure 4.1).

The 'customary' system of land tenure usually applies to land held under the jurisdiction of traditional leaders, who then play a role in the management of such land. In dispute is what form of tenure should apply in Zimbabwe to the large-scale commercial farms (LSCFs) following their acquisition and redistribution, and how that can provide long-term security. It is a fact that the FTLRP altered agricultural land property relations by extending state land ownership, allowing permits and leaseholds, while substantially reducing freehold tenure. In some cases, the state has let the administrative offer letter act as an acknowledgement of access to land, but not necessarily of its ownership. The two approaches that have dominated the debate on the future of acquired land concern the relative desirability of freehold titles and leaseholds.

The government formalised 99-year and 25-year leases for all acquired state land. Government argued that: '... although there seems to be constringent measures in the 99-year lease agreement, they are justified to ensure that land does not go back to the hands of the few advantaged people at the expense of the rest and at the same time ensure productivity' (MLRR, 2009: 36). Yet farmers on the ground face uncertainty, as a story in *Newsday* regarding the plight of new farmers shows:

> Douglas Mhembere, a War Veteran, has a small holding outside Harare that comprises 160 hectares on which he farms cattle and tobacco. He has 60 labourers and their families living on the farm. He had a successful harvest and hopes his next crop, which has just been planted, will be every bit as profitable. 'What I did was, I just said "I must just go onto the land and get on my own,"' he told ABC News recently. Mhembere says that decision has helped change his life. But in a country where land title is nowhere near decided, one major issue still hangs over Mhembere's head. He has no papers for his land, and as a result no way to borrow money from any bank to improve his farm. Because he has no official lease, Mhembere is like a squatter and has no legal rights to the land. 'That is the thing. I don't have the papers,' he said. That remains the situation across the whole of Zimbabwe for all farmers on seized land.[1]

The leaseholders have received a muted response, if not downright rejection, from financial providers including banks because of the inadequacies of leaseholds as collateral value. In addition, the government has refused to concede transfer rights to any other party, including the banks. Yet, the banks argue that it is important for them to be able to transfer land from non-performers in cases where the users fail in their farming enterprise and therefore the bank fails to recoup its investments; those investments are funds deposited by private individuals. In any case, there is a view that the state wields too much power in the leaseholds, which in effect means that leasehold land is state property. Such state ownership creates uncertainty in the sense that government can politically shield poor performers, making it difficult for financial institutions to recover their depositors' money.

Confidence in the current form of leasehold tenure, among the new and 'old' commercial farmers as well as among financiers, is almost non-existent. In general, those pushing for the bankability of the leaseholds have tended to focus on providing 'security' to agricultural financiers for agricultural lending and to enhance contract farming (ibid.). Nevertheless, there is a real fear of land reform reversal if total ownership is provided through freehold title deeds. Hidden behind this argument is also the fear felt by competing political parties of losing political control. Consequently, a range of reasons have been given against issuing title deeds, such as the worry that land sales could contribute to destitution of the poor as they sell land to the cash rich, who are a particular class of former commercial farmer, both black and white. The issue of land sales by the poor seems to be a hidden political pretext for not giving freehold tenure to new beneficiaries. In the current lexicon, this would fit into what is described as the 'reversal of the land reform programme' (GPA, 2008).

At the same time, the new land beneficiaries can be seen as insecure, in that they are exposed to the threat of eviction by the state or by the elites (Berry, 1993). In addition, the public uncertainty about the 'completeness' of the acquisitions and the continued 'farm disruptions' or 'invasions' reported in the media from time to time serve to weaken the 'current' ownership arrangements. This is because there are former landowners still fighting in the courts, in Zimbabwe and elsewhere, over their land rights. Some are fighting for a return of their land; the majority, however, would like compensation for the loss of their farms, both for the land and for the improvements made to it. Pronouncements to the effect that acquired commercial land cannot be contested in the courts, or that the government will not pay for land, have not closed the chapter on land litigation. Such legal contests, profiled in national and international media and via a range of other platforms, create uncertainty among the land beneficiaries in particular.

However, the new land beneficiaries seek freehold titles mainly because of the history of such ownership in the LSCF sector. It is a proven form of tenure, and was perhaps a key element underpinning the success of the white commercial farmers. The freehold title deeds to some extent facilitated the bankability of land, which then created a land market in which, for the most part, a few white farmers participated. For the majority, freehold title to land before and after independence in 1980 was symbolic of their subjugation and marginalisation and was a contributor to poverty and weakened democratic rights. For close to a century, the majority were not free to exercise their land rights in the market of their country of birth. This then created the basis for the FTLRP, driven largely by politics.

Land tenure as a political tool

Land is a resource that elicits power struggles among many groups of people. Such struggles can be seen through physical scuffles and intense negotiation. However, there is also the possibility of compromise, especially when such land struggles damage the economy and people's livelihoods. People all over the world, throughout history, have had to decide who could use which resources, when, where and how – land not being the least of them. The resulting rules, created by people, usually reflect an attempt to manage land and natural resources through institutional arrangements (North, 1990; Ostrom, 1990; 1992; Nemarundwe, 2003). Most studies on tenure (Roth and Bruce, 1994; Cheater, 1984; 1990; Platteau, 1996; Migot-Adholla and Bruce, 1994; Okoth-Ogendo, 2000; 2007) refer to a bundle of concepts related to space, size, composition, interactions, interests and objectives. Much of this literature sees 'community' in one or more of three ways: as a spatial unit, as a social structure, and as a set of shared norms. These three ideas form the basis on which most of the advocacy around tenure in the FTF community rests. However, these concepts fail to explain the cause of these features or to articulate their effect on land tenure security on the FTFs. They offer, therefore, a weak foundation upon which to base policy.

In Zimbabwe, the state and its local protégés (War Veterans, the then ruling party authorities and technical bureaucrats) have retained control over what happens on the FTFs. However, the activities of extra-legal bodies have had the effect of inhibiting the full functions of state institutions and even the development of farmer-based institutions at scheme level. These extra-territorial and extra-legal structures tended to override government institutions and personnel in their work. This means that the ability of government officials to provide technically sound advice, extension services and the regulation of land rights was curtailed, and there was nowhere to turn to for recourse, as the top levels of leadership in government, who were also politicians, undermined their officials' effectiveness.

In the conceptualisation of the A1 farms, the community was viewed as a unified, organic whole. Yet clearly questions remained about the attendant differences between beneficiaries and how these differences affect production outcomes, local politics, and strategic interactions within participating institutions within that community. Nobody saw the possibility of layered alliances that could span multiple levels, including that of politics. The fact that formal powers for allocating land were vested in land committees created an extra-legal state structure, powerful in defining how, by whom and for what purpose A1 lands could be used. This was irrespective of the offer letter, which was given to the land beneficiary as evidence of allocation by the administrative authorities.[2] In a way, the administrative offer letter had no real validity in proving personal ownership, or preventing interference with that ownership.

Yet it would seem that the government deliberately reformed its own institutions (be they Agritex, the Grain Marketing Board, or departments based at district level) and in essence mainstreamed them into political structures, although this was illegal according to government regulations. To some extent, government saw its own structures as a hindrance to the reform process (Chaumba et al., 2003b). By not specifying tenure, it seems that the government created a means of controlling people, while at the same time keeping government bureaucracy at arm's length from interfering with what went on at farm level. Against this background, the offer letter, which the state handed out to potential beneficiaries, was an important weapon of control yet it was the only available official signature to prove 'ownership' of allocated land. At the same time, in tying the issue of agricultural loans and inputs to the offer letter until 2008, the government not only managed to influence who got what state resources, but also extended its control of farmers and people on the

FTFs. In this way, the status of land ownership and rights ascribed by the offer letter remained hidden and unclear in political terms for a long time.

Continuities in state tenure policy In the policy-making arena, various stakeholders are in a constant state of negotiation, compromise and trade-offs to satisfy multiple and often conflicting objectives. As a result, implicitly or explicitly, land tenure policies express political choices and the distribution of power between the state, its citizens and local systems of authority. Government can thus enhance security or undermine it, depending on circumstances.[3] This study was concerned with how the competing forces were coalescing in order to manage state-acquired land. Much has been written about the perverse legal insecurity of settlers in the resettlement schemes established between 1980 and 1997 (Moyo, 1995a; Tshuma, 1997; Matondi, 2001; Dekker and Kinsey, 2011), and many commentators have pointed to the failure of policies designating precise land ownership arrangements in both communal and resettlement areas (Matondi, 2001; 2008a).

The FTLRP reflects certain policy continuities of the state; these may be seen as self-serving for those individuals running the state at any given point in time and they arise from an unwillingness to clarify land ownership in resettlement areas which goes back to independence in 1980 (ODA, 1988; 1996). Communal areas remain in the trusteeship of the presidium, with local institutions retaining management and administrative rights over the land and people. Clearly, in all instances where the state has sought to clarify tenure through the offer letter, the 99-year leases and the permit systems, it has been extremely cautious about specifying land ownership conditions that seem to imply that it is giving up its own rights by strengthening the rights of the individual. In general, the state has tried to match its benevolence (i.e. the free issuing of land and inputs) with control. During the 'Rhodesian' period, this control, and lack of development, of the majority black people was exercised by strengthening the asset base of the minority – and that asset base was land. However, after 2000, a similar situation was created. What changed significantly were the scale, breadth and range of the control, and the fact that land was a key resource for distribution.

The Rhodesian state (pre-independence Zimbabwe), however, gave land ownership to the white landed settlers through the issuing of freehold title deeds. The land ownership arrangements, based on freehold title deeds and long-term leasehold under the Commercial Farm Settlement Scheme (CFSS), provided sufficient confidence to the farmers to enable them to make agricultural investments that were the envy of Africa. But it should not be forgotten that these settlers came to Zimbabwe thanks to a law that allowed freehold tenure, protected them extremely well, and gave them absolute ownership of land and the resources on it (Shivji et al., 1998). Such assurance of property rights in law, defended by the courts and by security agents, had the effect of releasing for white settlers economic opportunities beyond farming (Rukuni et al., 2006). Therefore the colonial state created formulated laws and institutions that were to defend this form of tenure for nearly 100 years.

The nature of rights obtained through state benevolence In the FTLRP, beneficiaries are highly suspicious of the state. This is because the state appears to have been benevolent through facilitating their access to land, but, ironically, at times it turned against its own beneficiaries because it was not sure about their political allegiance. To a large extent, the majority of the new farmers have been in limbo as to whether or not to commit resources for long-term investment. They have consistently bemoaned the lack of resources and poor government planning from year to year, as well as 'illegal economic sanctions', to account for poor production. Behind their hesitance to invest lies what they see as the state controlling what goes on on farms 'through the back door' by not clarifying tenure. However, by not using their land to its maximum potential, they have strategically maintained pressure on the government to deal with tenure issues; at the same time, this strategy has been used by farmers in order to unlock public funding for agriculture.

Some new farmers have utilised government indecisiveness on the tenure issue to pretend to occupy or to utilise land while they assess the government's intentions on ownership rights. Government threats to withdraw support to A2 farmers have never been taken seriously by the farmers, as they knew that the government needed them on the farms in large numbers during the initial stage of the FTLRP and up to 2008. At the same time, for various reasons including recurring droughts, 'illegal economic sanctions' and what others have described as economic sabotage (Moyo and Murisa, 2008), the state also had a national obligation to support agriculture, including the new farmers. The new farmers, however, clutched at these reasons to justify land underutilisation in what can be described as a cyclical 'blame game'.

However, history has shown that, in general, smallholder farmers by virtue of their numbers can politically manipulate the state machinery to shape redistributive policies, just as the larger farmers fight to preserve their privileges. All the same, the small farmers have been unable to persuade the state to provide them with the forms of tenure they would like. Across the country, different stakeholders – including financial institutions – have argued for clarity on land tenure as a basis for supporting agriculture on the FTFs with lines of credit. However, apart from condemning financial institutions, the government has shown little interest in tenure reform beyond defending the leasehold systems that it prefers for FTFs. In fact, the state has raised concerns of tenure only in the context of protecting settlers and not as an incentive to enable land beneficiaries to fully utilise their land.

When one examines the negotiations over the right to control land and the shifting relationships of the different political and social actors, a change in the behaviour of the state towards the new farmers can be noted. These relationships play out within the centre and at the periphery of the internal politics of the powerful former ruling party. As farmers manipulate these relationships, they are acutely aware that government needs them on the land in a symbolic sense as well as in their role of producers. Before 2008, the government felt obliged to provide subsidies to the impatient farmers and placed itself in an unenviable relationship with the new settlers, who expected government to be a provider of agricultural support. The subsidies and favours to the new farmers ranged from the provision of free inputs (seeds and fertilisers) and access to very cheap fuel and electricity and to equipment such as tractors, harvesters and ploughs, to the favourable pricing of agricultural produce. This drained government finances because the farmers in their turn were not producing enough, not just to pay back some of the loans, but to feed the nation and generate income for the country as expected by the government. In general, there was very little to show in terms of stabilised food production, employment creation or foreign currency generation in return for the fiscal investment.

However, new farmers, while enjoying some level of state protection, still question their relationship with the state. While feeling some sense of enfranchisement through the FTLRP, they are worried by the short but violent history of takeovers of the farms they now occupy. Some in the A1 scheme believe the government is not helping them adequately to be successful farmers. They also find government policies to be ineffective, inefficient or otherwise problematic. However, relationships between the state and the new farmers should not be viewed in overly combative terms, because quite often one or the other side seeks and finds ways to resolve contentious issues. Often, the state may dominate, with the willing acquiescence of the new and grateful settlers. Similarly, new farmers may assert their claims in terms of non-negotiable demands, which they stick to, such as refusing to move when ordered to do so. This tends to start a protracted tussle over land in the newly resettled areas. All the same, the state and settlers are 'friends', so to speak – but for how long is anybody's guess.

Manoeuvring weak tenure policies Poor people and shrewd entrepreneurs have attempted to manoeuvre and circumvent the unfavourable land tenure policies in order to secure access for themselves. There are various ways in which they do this: through simulating use, demonstrating social compliance to the benefactor, negotiating with the state for space to continue operating, undertaking duties beyond their mandate to 'please' the state, simply abandoning the FTFs, and, lastly, through direct opposition to state directives. Settlers are not ineffectual, and they juggle politics because they know the weaknesses of the state in managing the land at local level. Therefore, the apparent power of the state at national level might not extend to the local level, where it may be weaker with regards to land matters than assumed. The state perpetually tries to reassure new settlers that they are there to stay as the legitimate claimants of the land, i.e. that the land reform is irreversible (GPA, 2008). In Mazowe, the research team witnessed several farmer field days, where government officials were at pains to reassure the farmers that no one would remove them.

A covenant seems to have emerged between new settlers and the government, but with clear indications that the government needs the settlers more than the settlers need government. Beneficiaries are neither weak nor passive; they are able to define their room for manoeuvre when necessary and to challenge the monopolisation of power by political elites (Scott, 1985). Thus, the A1 farmers, weak as they may appear, have weapons that they use to mould authority within certain limits. It may be that the new farmers are in fact holding the state to ransom and managing to get the concessions that they need.

Sources of tenure insecurity Threats of their removal by government and the continued land audits (PoZ, 2003; 2006; Utete, 2003a; MLRR, 2009; MLRR and SIRDC, 2006; 2007; 2008; Buka, 2002) – backed mostly by negative commentaries from a range of analysts, bureaucrats, politicians at local and national levels, traditional leaders, development agencies and the media (the 'state watchers') – have created suspicion and hence insecurity for the new settlers. This is in addition to the actual removals of new farmers by the state, local committees, and at times by powerful people. Indeed, in Mazowe, local farmers are increasingly averse to talking about land ownership issues and they suspect researchers visiting them, fearing that they are part of a 'state monitoring system' or a way for the state to identify poor-performing farmers for listing for eviction. Some of the farmers were extremely frustrated and agitated with the land audits, and were beginning to question the motives of the state. Clearly, such threats create a lack of confidence among farmers, so that they hesitate to invest in the new farms (Moyo, 2008). The 'state watchers' identified above continue to question the capability of the new farmers to produce on the land, while making no effort towards rebuilding that capability.

The studies in Mazowe are beginning to show that insecurity is not the result of a lack of legal land ownership, but rather reflects the inadequacy of dispute resolution and the power exercised by state bodies. It is important to establish how the local community-arranged security strategies accord with the social engineering of the state. This chapter describes the essential elements of the socio-political order in the newly resettled areas, and the forces to which it is responding (see Chapter 8). New studies are beginning to show that the social order that minimised thefts and personal insecurity before the replacement of former white owners has broken down (Matondi, 2005; 2011a; Sukume, 2005). By 2007, major problems of personal insecurity underpinned by continued threats of evictions and actual state repossession of some plots made new settlers reluctant to commit to living in the newly resettled areas. Land audits have only had the effect of maintaining an environment of threat, and have not been followed up by practical action, a situation that has contributed to land underutilisation.

The security problems of land management mirror the unfinished nature of the land reform programme and are the source of agricultural insecurity. The problems are a consequence of the porous land tenure system in the new farming areas and take the form of misallocations of plots, planning difficulties, lack of access to infrastructure, boundary disagreements, thefts, unwillingness to share resources (irrigation equipment, barns, milking parlours, etc.), illegal gold mining, illegal cutting down of trees, poor road networking and blockage of roads. These are some of the practical challenges that new farmers face on the FTFs. The beneficiaries, when faced with all of this, question whether it is worth struggling – literally alone – on the FTFs.

The offer letter for land and its meaning for new farmers in Mazowe District

When people moved to the farms, the last thing they thought about was how ownership was to be expressed. However, as they settled legally and illegally, they made an attempt to get papers (offer letters from the government) in order to claim a stake. Others, when they were on the farms, realised that issues of residential, rather than just land, occupancy (especially of farmhouses and compounds) could have immense significance, determining even their sense of existence as new farmers. This forced them to seek the paperwork (again, offer letters) to confirm their entitlement to both land and fixed infrastructure. One farmer compared it to acquiring a house in town or a car, saying that registration and getting papers are as critical as a signature to denote ownership. Another farmer referred to the offer letter as being like 'the mark on the shoulder left after the immunisation of a child, which is permanent' – a good illustration of their views concerning the strength of ownership conferred by the offer letter. In other words, these farmers view the offer letter as a 'true mark of ownership'.

In the Ruzivo 2007 survey, the majority of the A1 and A2 farmers in Mazowe District indicated that they were in possession of an offer letter (Table 4.1). There are, however, a few farmers who admitted that they did not have offer letters, although the proportion seems to be higher among the A2 farmers. It is difficult to establish why these were settled without offer letters, because even those who got land through *jambanja* eventually got offer letters. The only interpretation of these figures would be that such farmers are probably

TABLE 4.1 Possession of an offer letter by the land beneficiary

| Possession of offer letter | Type of scheme | | | | Ruzivo 2007 survey total | | MLRR/SIRDC 2006 land audit total | |
| | A1 | | A2 | | | | | |
	No.	%	No.	%	No.	%	No.	%
Yes	338	99.41	182	92.39	520	96.83	701	80.76
No	2	0.59	15	7.61	17	3.17	167	19.24
Total	340	100	197	100	537	100	868	100
Not answered	1	0.29	0	0.00	1	0.19	–	–
Grand total	341	–	197	–	538	–	–	–

Source: Ruzivo survey, 2007; Ministry of Lands and Rural Resettlement (MLRR) and the Scientific and Industrial Research and Development Centre (SIRDC) land audit, 2006.

Box 4.1 Farmers' views at Barwick and Wychwood as to the meaning of an offer letter

What is an offer letter?

A letter which is not permanent which shows that you can be chased away any time.

It shows that you are legally allowed to farm at that plot.

It is a letter of claim to that piece of land.

It is a permit that allows me to claim that land.

It is legal, but I cannot sell, it can be withdrawn any time and I can't subdivide and sell.

What are the provisions of the offer letter?

One cannot sell the plot.

One cannot construct permanent structures (similar to the white farmers' buildings).

Allows me to do what I want but I can't sell.

You can borrow with it.

---

settled illegally, or had merely moved into the resettlement areas late, since earlier discussions revealed that movement into the resettlement areas has continued to the present day.

In the focus group discussions (FGDs), the farmers pointed out that they were not yet certain about the permanence of their stay in the resettlement areas. The fact that they have not been given lease agreements does not give them much hope. Yet, the offer letter was characterised as quite helpful when it comes to accessing inputs (fuel, loans, etc.), especially from the Grain Marketing Board (GMB). It also acted as a means of protection against farm invaders and proof of residence to the police, given that various people on the FTFs were alleged to be thieves. It was difficult, in the initial stages of the programme, to know who was who on the FTFs, so the offer letter was a sort of identity document, as well as proof of residence and legitimacy for staying in the area.

One complexity arose from the differences in how beneficiaries interpreted the provisions of the offer letter and any other enclosed documents. Some farmers had problems with understanding what they could and could not do with their land in relation to long-term development. This became more of an institutional problem, as it related to the bundle of rights that the possession documents specified. There is evidence for this in the wide differences in the ways in which farmers have interpreted their rights in an already poorly defined tenure system. The system is not clear about what farmers are entitled to do. Many farmers felt that the offer letter was not ideal. They considered that the offer letter was 'not a certificate' but was like a 'duplicate or photocopy of a promised original document', which is not secure and can be withdrawn at any time. It was referred to as a temporary document. They compared it to title deeds, which they said the private banks were accepting as collateral for loans, while the offer letter was only acceptable to government-linked financial institutions such as Agribank. The farmers pointed out that big commercial banks aligned to government, such as the Commercial Bank of Zimbabwe, accepted the offer letter of 'big shots', mostly on the A2 schemes.

The farmers were also doubly worried by the fact that an offer letter contains a section that specifies that it can be withdrawn. This meant that, as a risk management measure, key investments were made only in temporary fixed assets, such as shelters made of poles and dagga (a mixture of termite soil and cattle dung) and pit latrines. Farmers said they would only build permanent structures after the lease agreements were issued. For instance, at Ballyhooly, alongside the Chiweshe communal lands, settled under the A1 model in 2002, most of the settlers were from the communal areas bordering the farm. Given the proximity of the new settlers to their communal homes, they have not bothered to build permanent structures. However, there were four settlers who felt that they needed to develop new homes, and they have built houses of brick under thatch and asbestos, despite the perceived risks. The majority still squat in the farm compound houses because of the time it takes to travel to and from their communal homes, which they would rather use for farming activities. However, in the offer letters for land for both A1 and A2 schemes, it is clearly stated that the government has no obligation to pay compensation for either land or improvements, even to new settlers who may have invested in the new land.

Threats faced by land beneficiaries as a source of insecurity in Mazowe District

The issue of settler eviction haunts new settlers, yet it has historical roots in Zimbabwe, where squatter eviction has long been practised. The net result is that land resettlement in Mazowe brought anxiety to people already struggling to cope with economic instability and decline at the time of the survey in 2007. Such anxiety increased their efforts to secure their own claims to land by invoking or strengthening their ties to land management patrons in the form of extra-legal land committees. To some extent, the protracted litigation since 2000 has paradoxically created an almost chronic condition of uncertainty over land ownership. The multiple contestants for the land in Mazowe made it very difficult to stabilise the FTF areas. Some people competed with institutions, while others used the institutions to get state resources and land. The contestants have had many opportunities to revise their strategies and to learn from their experience how best to manipulate the land management system through circumvention and deliberately creating conflicts as part of securing claims.

The proximity of Mazowe to urban areas such as Harare and Bindura increased the farmers' vulnerability. However, it also gave them room to manoeuvre in terms of land rights. The farmers saw that they had the opportunity to retreat to their urban bases in order to secure jobs in case of problems with land rights. Thus, urban space and formal jobs (mainly civil service jobs) provided an important launch pad to deal with the risks associated with land. Yet the threats were also multiple. For instance, in an effort to boost the economy, the state has been identifying and taking over land for its own projects. The proximity of Mazowe to Harare makes it an attractive choice for locating such state projects. These, being national in character and said to bring public benefits, are considered strategic, and so override any claims to land by the settlers. Such projects are another source of insecurity, because no one knows when the state may want to take land for such a purpose.

At Mugutu Farm, in line with the 'Look East' policy (FES, 2004), the local authorities, together with the district and provincial land identification committees, recommended the establishment of a project run by a Chinese company (Regstar Investments) that involved brick-moulding on subdivisions 17 and 19 (MLRR and SIRDC, 2007). As a result, an A1 farmer who has a plot next to the brick-making premises has had serious problems. He pointed out that he was allocated his land by the District Land Committee (DLC), but there is some conflict with the Chinese company. The problem began when the Chinese complained to the provincial office that the farmer's crops would obstruct their clients (as there is a main highway close to the farms). The A1 farmer was then ordered by the DLC to stop any farming activities on that plot. He was confused because the same authorities that had given him the plot were now the ones telling him to stop farming. He added that the DLC promised to relocate him to another plot and to refund him for the costs incurred during land preparations, but this has not happened.

While the surveys discovered fewer incidences of threats of evictions, the MLRR and SIRDC (ibid.) audit shows many cases of actual eviction at the behest of the DLC, which took the right to re-organise farmers to be part of the planning process. In the sample survey, 6.3 per cent (n=282) reported threats, while in the A2 scheme 4.1 per cent (n=145) did so. It should be noted that the reporting of threats of eviction was not easy, as it jeopardised the chance of getting land in those cases where individuals were offered alternative land. In fact, on the questionnaire survey, more than one in five of the farmers did not respond to this question. Many regarded the question as highly sensitive and feared victimisation if the people who may have tried to evict them possessed some degree of power in the political arena – or were in the army or police. All the same, those who responded to this question pointed out that 'powerful people and politicians' were the culprits behind the attempted evictions. Given that the resettled areas are essentially communities in transition, respondents are reluctant to answer questions about conflict.

While it would seem that the majority of farmers in both schemes did not face eviction of any sort, there were murmurs of discontent expressed in FGDs. In informal discussions with farmers and officials, the issue of the eviction of A1 farmers seems to have been a highly sensitive one. It was an issue with political dimensions, to the extent that some of the officials tried with limited success to defend the policies concerning A1 settlement. However, it was the attempt to evict those said not to be using their plots which was a sore point, although the percentage of those evicted on the basis of non-farming was low, because, in general, the government wanted to give new farmers the chance to prove themselves, and there was no set period for assessing such performance.

A very disturbing trend was that some of the powerful new settlers who had displaced the A1 farmers were the very ones who clamoured most for freehold title. At the same time, despite getting land supposedly thanks to the criteria of resource repossession, they were always at the forefront for getting free inputs. It would seem that the powerful are in the process of dishonestly robbing the A1 farmers by manipulating the DLC. In addition, they rob the poor not just of land but also of the means of production. Nevertheless, some of the A1 farmers who still remain have been lucky because they have become stronger and are fighting for laws to legitimise their situation. In addition, they have organised a whole system with which to defend themselves, both from the demands of the state and from those who would want to replace them by force. However, the powerful owners are also moving towards a more secure hold over property, through the 99-year lease; these leases are granted to the most powerful owners first, and it does not look as if they will be provided to A1 farmers in the future.

Conflicts and insecurities on the farms in Mazowe Land conflicts seem to be the norm rather than the exception in Mazowe District. The expectation was that over time such conflicts would decrease, as settlements got organised and took root. However, this seems not to be the case in this highly contested district (Matondi, 2005). In fact, conflicts remain unresolved, creating uncertainty among the farmers. The new settlers have lost confidence in the state institutions to resolve these situations; opposing settlers were asked by government to pay for conflict resolution services from Agritex in 2007. In addition, the person who lodged the complaint had to visit the offices of Agritex as well as provide transport for the officer to visit the farm. Ostensibly this was because the department felt that some of the conflicts were too minor for the government to deploy resources to resolve them; in fact, the department had no funding and could not even provide stationery to document conflict cases. However, the message given to farmers is that the state is abdicating its responsibility where conflict resolution is concerned.

For the beneficiaries, the numerous conflicts have led them to question whether it was worth coming to the FTFs in the first place. This is because the conflicts in Mazowe – as in other districts where they relate to land – are too numerous and seem to change in form over time, with no indication of their eventual resolution. One woman beneficiary in the A2 scheme decided to call it quits and left for Canada without informing anybody, because of the incessant conflicts with farmworkers and peer settlers, and the lack of adequate support for her farming activities. Some conflicts were lodged with the courts, as new settlers made claims and counter-claims against each other. For instance, a group of A2 settlers whose land was invaded by a powerful A2 settler lodged a court application. Another conflict arose at Lowdale, where it seems that the white farmer and the police joined forces to evict the A1 settlers of the Hwata clan. The Hwata clan (27 families) is claiming the land, since there are traditional shrines at Shavaunzi Mountains. This conflict has dragged on since the onset of the land reforms, with both parties determined to stay on the land.

A major source of conflict relates to the double allocation of land, i.e. the same piece of land allocated to two (or more) people. There were people who manipulated the system to be allocated land very late in the programme. These were seen as the worst predators as they tried to force their way into the resettlement programme; they were described as *'vana mucheka dzafa'* (predators who eat what they did not hunt, at the expense of the bona fide hunter). They tend to be aggressive, to the extent of wanting to prejudice the claims of the current owners who have invested in the land and now regard the FTFs as their rightful property. In these cases, they would get official offer letters when the settler on the ground already had an offer letter. Double allocations arose from deficiencies in the government's administrative land capacity management to detect such cases.

The boundaries of the allocated plots should ideally provide a basis for clarity on the piece of land allocated to an individual and should not be a source of conflict. However, the plots in Mazowe were demarcated by technical officers on maps and with pegging carried out using some form of survey, but maps do not give all the relevant detail. It would also appear that, at farm level in Mazowe, the driving force behind boundary conflicts is the issue of land scarcity, because the government wants to put as many people as possible on the land it has acquired compulsorily. Settlers noted that conflicts over boundaries were caused by inadequate land, jealousy, poor demarcation and so on. If a plot owner sees that their neighbour is underutilising land, the temptation to encroach on to that land is very great. Such tendencies are exacerbated when the land differs in quality among the plot holders in terms of its usability (i.e. arable, cleared of stumps), its potential for irrigation, and its proximity to Chiweshe communal areas, where there is a large population wanting to benefit from land allocations. It is one thing to demarcate boundaries for resource ownership and quite another to convince different land claimants to respect such boundaries. The conflicts in Mazowe District thus mostly relate to the meanings of boundaries, and result in a tendency to individualise landholdings and claims.

What can be concluded from all the cases that relate to boundary problems in Mazowe District is that the resettlement areas are unstable in many ways. This instability makes it very difficult to have a predictable system upon which to plan for land use and targeted production levels. Clearly, land rights only make sense when there is a proper survey and demarcation in the new areas, and individuals have the necessary means to preserve their land rights. Title to land is secure only to the extent that the tools that enforce the title are secure – and in this case that the government's offer of land will not be challenged. Ordinary individual new owners could band together to hold and defend land, but this has not been possible in the government-controlled resettled areas of Mazowe.

Competing classes and tenure implications The resettlement areas are slowly becoming territories for the survival of the fittest. The A1 farmers indicated that A2 farmers behave like white people (*varungu*), in that they claim to have nothing to do with tradition, culture or even the village headmen. However, there are some big A2 owners who cut deals with the village leaders because they have the money to buy their support. When it comes to infrastructure shared with the A1 farmers, it is they who decide the terms of sharing and when this has to happen. The A2 farmers also tend to monopolise the extension services. This is because they provide the extension officers with accommodation, transport, and sometimes food. The A1 farmers have consequently concluded that state support depends on whether one has money or not. Usually those without money lose out because, as one settler put it '*muso wako kana usingazorwe mafuta hauzivikanwi*' (if you are not well off no one looks after your interests). Another settler concluded that: 'We are competing with those who have "*mota dzine mhopo pamusana*"' (the wealthy with 4x4 vehicles).

However, some beneficiaries have become successful farmers, despite the odds they have faced as they have established themselves on the farms. The new, successful A2 farmers appear to be aloof – the new 'white men' (*varungu*), as they are called by their workers and the people they deal with in the resettled areas – and are in a perpetual state of owing their government benefactors. Many of the field days organised by Agritex are held at their farms, ostensibly to demonstrate how they have 'done better' than the previous white owners. At one field day attended by the author, with over 1,000 guests, the proud owner demonstrated the level of pedigree of his livestock herd, the levels of farm organisation and management, the income realised, the export-oriented nature of his citrus production, and the fact that, whereas the previous owners had two guards, he now employs 18 because of too much larceny at his farm. This claim of success is based on superficial comparisons, given that the farming models of the FTLRP are different from those practised by the former owners. In any case, the FTFs are existing in a different context, with different kinds of support (generally on the weak side), and poor land rights (except for some).

At one FGD (26 June 2007), there was a heated debate among the A1 partici-pants about what issues to put forward for discussion. One issue that arose was about a tractor that had been donated but was taken from the rest of the farmers by a big, elite A2 farmer. The FGD participants were apparently divided over this, with some enjoying good relations with the A2 elite farmer and others not. One farmer then stood up and said: '*Varume hatitaurei chokwadi, kwete kutsvaga zita rakanaka*' (Gentlemen, let us say the truth and not look for a good name for ourselves). It became apparent that the settlers were uneasy because the big A2 farmer they shared land with was making concerted moves to have them evicted. The A2 farmer felt that the land he had was inadequate for his agricultural plans, and was furiously trying to convince the authorities to move the A1 farmers elsewhere. A participant then retorted: '*Takachonjomara papurazi pano, hatisati tagara*' (We are squatting at this farm because of the threats made by the big A2).

Many A1 farmers accuse extension workers as behaving like personal workers for the big A2 farmers. At one scheme in 2007, farmers raised cash contributions that were given to the extension officer for diesel, but the diesel was never delivered. The fuel tanks left by the former owner are on the A2 plot, but are supposed to be shared. The extension officer, who is supposed to manage the issuing of the diesel, was accused of behaving like a fuel attendant for the big A2 farmer by denying A1 access to diesel on flimsy grounds.

Leaving the Fast Track Farms

Given the euphoria over the land resettlement programme, many of the new settlers are suddenly discovering that farming is a 'no joke business' that requires serious commitment and resources. The adage that 'agriculture is a way of life' is only partly true. In Mazowe, there was a lot of movement at the onset of the FTLRP, to the extent that it was difficult to tell whether such movement was due to the beneficiaries opting out of resettlement or relocating to new properties because of the planning processes, or whether they were simply choosing better plots than those they were allocated. Some people simply found it tough and left the FTFs, with others pointing to the weakness of land rights as a key factor affecting their desire to go. Some farmers who have no confidence in their tenure status:

- have never attempted to take the land they applied for;
- are abandoning A2 land so as to move on to an A1 farm that seems to offer group security, sometimes based on kinship;
- are returning to communal areas, especially in circumstances where they have failed to produce for a number of years;
- are illegally renting out their land; or
- play a type of balancing act depending on their resources during any one season, thus spending one year in and the next out of farming, creating a situation of use and underuse of land.

In Mazowe there was a movement of people across different schemes and tenure regimes, which included land being abandoned by new farmers for various reasons. This abandonment has taken place in different geographical areas and for a variety of reasons (see Box 4.2). Poor and contested land rights have resulted in poor performance among the farmers in the new resettlement areas, which in turn has led to resettlement 'exit'. This has been more pronounced among new settlers who are formally employed but are low earners in their off-farm jobs. After weighing up the economic opportunities of farming, some have first scaled down their activities and then, if opportunities have not improved, eventually have abandoned their farms.

Exiting from the FTFs can be categorised as voluntary and involuntary. The *voluntary exit* can be attributed to: land being of an inappropriate type for the desired enterprise; relocation to better and bigger areas of land; or moving back to one's place of birth to enhance kinship security. The *involuntary exiting* is due to: lack of resources; poor farming knowledge; conflicts with other settlers; and eviction by others. Some politically powerful A2 farmers are known to be perennial occupiers of farms, taking them because they want to 'harvest where they did not sow'. Clearly, eight years after the programme commenced, one would have expected some semblance of social and institutional order on the farms. However, conflicts continued to be rife, with thefts, boundary disputes, fights over equipment, farmers cultivating already cropped areas as they fight for the same pieces of land, and disputes over offer letters given for the same plot. These factors all contribute to the settler's decision on whether to stay or not.

In Mazowe there were instances where beneficiaries originally allocated A2 plots had moved to A1 plots to accommodate those resources that they could mobilise. Some had moved away from soils they regarded as poor for crop production; in most cases these were on land that had been exhausted by many decades of tobacco production in the Mvurwi Intensive Conservation Area (ICA). Others were seeking land with a better water supply. Yet others

---

Box 4.2 Patterns in 'exiting' the settlements in Mazowe District

Movement from A2 to A1: This can be either voluntary or involuntary. Some A2 farmers leave for an A1 farm because of a lack of farming resources or having been too ambitious at the initiation of the programme, and, rather than abandoning farming, they voluntarily leave for a smaller A1 plot that they can manage with the resources available. It is involuntary where new farmers are forced to leave the A2 farms because of a lack of access to resources and they would not have left farms if there had been adequate resources.

Movement from A1 to a communal area: Most settlers in these cases are disillusioned with the land reform programme and move back to the communal areas. The promises of inputs and agricultural support have not been fulfilled, security of tenure is not guaranteed, and most have had poor harvests since settling on the farms.

Moving from A2 to a formal job in town: This group includes new farmers who applied for land yet held formal jobs in industry. For these farmers, working the land was to be a pastime and not their core source of livelihood. However, the weekend part-time exercise proved to be too costly and imposed time and other demands against a background of weak land rights. They therefore decided to concentrate on their core business outside farming.

Oscillation between A1 and a communal area: The farmers who responded to the study were not keen to mention that they were maintaining two homesteads. This is because they thought the research exercise was part of an audit by the government. They were afraid that their land would be taken away from them if they indicated that they were still maintaining homesteads in their original communal areas. It could, however, be inferred that most still maintained their original homesteads because, if they are claiming to be making a lot of money and building new houses, then they are investing in their original homesteads and not on the FTFs.

---

preferred land suitable for livestock production (Barwick ICA) on the basis that pastoralism requires fewer immovable assets, and if the land is grabbed by someone else, one can simply move the livestock away and there are minimal losses. Beneficiaries who initially took land adjacent to main roads are now reluctant to take up such land because of the fear of 'nefarious highway visitors' on the prowl for the best farms.

Box 4.3 The process of abandoning the resettlement areas in Mazowe District

Abandonment of resettlement: This refers to farmers from both the A1 and A2 schemes who have completely abandoned the resettlement areas voluntarily and usually without telling anybody. They have been frustrated by the lack of cash to finance their farming ventures. Resources have been inadequate and government support has not been forthcoming, leading to poor performance, which in turn has led some to quit their plots. In most instances individuals in this group do not announce their departure but simply leave. This accounts for most of the plots where respondents said they did not know the whereabouts of the former occupiers.

New farmers with second thoughts but hanging on: These are new farmers who are unsure about utilising their plots, and are simply living from day to day. They have realised the pitfalls in agriculture and are weighing their options as to whether to leave or to stay. They have experienced the problems facing land reform, and have realised that they lack the capacity to produce, but in most instances are unwilling to come out in the open and admit this.

Leaving plots with somebody: These farmers have found it hard but do not want to lose the land because they hope that agriculture will be better one day. They leave the land with friends or relatives, or rent it out to others.

Surrendering land to the authorities: There are a few instances in which new farmers formally surrender plots; usually this is when they move to a new scheme.

The abandonment of settlements in Mazowe was not confined to either A1 or A2 farmers. Both sets of farmers have to manage a high level of political risk, and they take pragmatic decisions to secure their own livelihoods either by 'playing the game' or by leaving. Thus migration in Mazowe, forced or voluntary, occurs within a system that is largely unstable and still re-establishing itself following the massive changes wrought by the FTLRP. The majority of settlers are ordinary people trying to find opportunities for livelihoods for themselves and their families. Some chose resettlement out of desperation, because they did not have any other source of livelihood. Some have invested time, effort and resources into farming and cannot leave lightly. For others, participating in land reform was just an experiment, and they have abandoned the land for some other livelihood option (see Box 4.3).

Strategies for obtaining and maintaining rights to the land

Split land use as a tenure bidding strategy in the context of decongestion objectives A key phenomenon that is emerging is the maintenance of split households as a risk mitigation mechanism. This is a method by which A1 farmers in particular protect their land rights through maintaining their communal home as a fallback option. This is done directly, through continued use of land in the communal areas, or indirectly through leaving family members to use the land and other property so that, in the event of eviction, they will still possess their communal land. A discussion at Davaar Farm showed that most of the participants still maintain their communal homes. Some left the land in the hands of relatives or children so as to safeguard their claims in case they are evicted from the FTFs. The farmers strongly argued that they would give up their communal homes only if they were given title deeds to their new land. The FGD respondents were also asked to indicate whether they were still farming on the plots they had before resettlement, and, as indicated in Table 4.2, almost one in five for both the A1 and A2 schemes indicated that they were still farming on their original plots. The proportion is slightly higher among the A2 farmers.

TABLE 4.2 Are land reform beneficiaries still farming on their original plot?

| Responses | Type of scheme | | | | Total | |
| | A1 | | A2 | | | |
	No.	%	No.	%	No.	%
Yes	54	16.87	42	23.20	96	19.16
No	266	83.13	139	76.80	405	80.84
Total	320	100	181	100	501	100
Not answered	21	6.15	17	8.59	38	7.05
Grand total	341	–	198	–	539	–

Source: Ruzivo survey, 2007.

The split household phenomenon has a gender dimension as well. New farmers have invested significantly in new marital and cohabitation relationships in order to manage split households. This is very common with men who originally participated in the *jambanja* on farms and subsequently established new households. In an era of HIV and AIDS, this has created real problems on the newly resettled farms; there are reports of infections and cases of death attributed to the disease (Magaramombe and Chiweshe, 2008). The issue of land rights for the new settlers and the gender equity issues have implications for systems of inheritance in the event of the death of a plot holder. As men in A1 schemes create and re-create new households in a context of seemingly limited land still under the control of the state, there are several tenure questions that need to be addressed from a gender equity perspective.

At one FGD (16 June 2007), a participant argued that an African never severs his/her roots, and therefore links with communal areas must continue because they are the home of relatives and the blood of the ancestors and maintenance of the lineage (*rukuvhute rwedzinza*). Yet, others felt that such links are mainly determined by distance; Chiweshe communal lands are near, allowing new farmers on FTFs to maintain dual homesteads, and therefore continued access to their ancestors.

Men justified the 'new' families they created on the basis that a man 'wherever he is must develop a lineage [*dzinza*] through procreation' (FGD, 16 June 2007). Clearly, traditional systems were being re-enacted, but they have become a source of more serious problems in the division of land between men, women and children, while benefits accruing from that land (income and produce) have ruptured some families.

A key indicator of uncertainty is reflected in the response to a question about where the dead should be buried. One of the assumptions proposed was that, when the settlers bury their relatives on the FTFs, this would strengthen their land rights based on the concept of *rukuvhute rwedzinza*. The majority of new farmers still felt that they would bury their relatives in the communal areas for cultural reasons. This was because the majority Shona people have a belief in the reincarnation of the body, and hence bury their dead within family cemeteries. At Fairview there is a cemetery at the farm used to bury farmworkers, but the new farmers have shunned it, and say they cannot mix their dead with people of foreign origin (meaning farmworkers or white farmers). There was only one case of a farmer's grandchild who was buried in the farm cemetery.

In the fields of geography, political economy and sociology, the objective of the state was seen as being influenced by the need to reduce pressure on communal land through a process largely referred to as 'decongestion'. This is defined as the process of removing people from areas of habitation where overcrowding affects their day-to-day management of natural resources and farming, to areas where there is a sparser population and better quality land, so that people can farm more easily and have fodder for their animals. This definition fits the government of Zimbabwe's aim of decongesting overcrowded communal areas with minimal grazing lands; farmers in these areas produce little food, as the soil is not fertile enough. The decongestion concept has to be understood within the context of the history of land issues in Zimbabwe, a history in which black people were moved from their homes to pave the way for white commercial farmers. This historical view influences the discourse on land and decongestion, and helps in understanding Zimbabwe's political approach to land and agriculture.

The issue of decongestion in communal areas such as Chiweshe remains controversial in Mazowe District. In informal interviews, some people expressed the view that there was no significant communal area decongestion, because it was believed that most of the farms were allocated to people from urban areas such as Harare and small towns such as Bindura, Concession or Glendale (see Chapter 3). The 2004 survey established that there were 136 traditional leaders in the Chiweshe communal area, and chiefs in particular who moved to the FTFs were said to be representing the people from the original villages they came from. This means that people who moved to the resettlement areas still had links to their relatives from their communal areas. The links that exist take many forms, but tend to follow customary social patterns and relationships. Many of the new farmers indicated that they miss their relatives, friends, acquaintances and so on, but felt that developing the resettlement areas was a job that needed to be done. They indicated their irritation with the lack of social services and a predictable livelihood, but that did not outweigh the fact that they are on better land and have done reasonably well in some good seasons.

The fields and homesteads left behind by the people who moved to the resettlement areas are still used for subsistence and cash farming of conventional crops such as maize. This matches the new land uses on the FTFs, which combine cash crop farming and subsistence production. The 2004 survey (n=251), established that in both the A1 and A2 farms, many of those originating from rural areas still had relatives in their places of origin. Some 45 per cent of the respondents in A1 settlements indicated that there was no linkage, and 29 per cent in the A2 settlements said the same. Just over 44 per cent of A1 respondents reported that they still had links with their communal area, and a total of 49 per cent indicated that there was someone still in residence at their place of origin. The 2007 survey showed that at least 7 per cent (n=539) had left their homesteads occupied by children, 4 per cent had no one in occupation, 26 per cent had relatives in occupation and 2 per cent still occupied their own homesteads. Again, this shows that many of those who left for the resettlement areas were unsure of their future within this scheme and so did not want to give up their homes.

The fact that in 2004 at least 38 per cent indicated that the residents on their homesteads were relatives, without specifying who these relatives were or the nature of their relationships, confirmed the split phenomenon. For those who did specify, 15 per cent indicated that their parents were still at their place of origin. Given that the average age of those who obtained land is 46 years, this means that the remaining parents are elderly and largely incapacitated to continuously use the land productively. In this way, the new settlers still retain their right to use the land in the communal area, and can do so for both commercial and social welfare reasons – as they look after their parents. It seems from the evidence that there was no significant decongestion in the places from which respondents originated.

Research is needed to establish the agrarian structure in the communal areas in terms of types of land use,[4] land use intensity and land sizes following the FTLRP. Most of the old homes in communal areas have been reduced to *matongo* (abandoned homes) with no one looking after them. The phenomenon of *matongo* in communal areas will need thorough investigation, for it may reflect the demise of families through natural processes and abandonment through migration to other areas, both urban and rural (including to FTFs). A survey will need to establish when people left, and will also need to ask the beneficiaries on FTFs where they came from. Through this approach, the level of decongestion may be established.

In summary, most of the beneficiaries did not give up their ownership of land in the communal areas, mainly because they were not certain of security of tenure within the resettlement areas. This has implications for agriculture in that farmers now have dual demands for inputs and labour in both the communal areas and resettlement areas. However, some new A2 farmers think that split ownership of land is something to celebrate, noting that it is rare in the world for an individual to own three properties: one in a newly resettled area, one bought in the urban area with title deeds, and the third being communal area property that is a natural right allocated by traditional leaders and/or by the head of the family. While the properties in the communal and urban areas have some form of tenure security, this cannot be said of the FTFs where security is based on some vague proof of production, a temporary offer letter, and some form of patronage depending on acquiescence to the benefactor – in this case the state, the ruling party or their administrative appendages such as the land committees.

Simulating land use as a strategy for retaining rights Since the beginning of the land reform programme in the 1980s, a dominant strategy used by white large-scale farmers was to convert arable land to other uses, including wildlife protection, in what the government saw as a ploy to protect their land from designation for compulsory acquisition (Moyo, 2000b). This happened within the context of a lack of agreement about what would constitute acceptable land use in terms of economic return, when wildlife and eco-tourism were apparently providing a better economic return than crop production. While in the past this was less important as a national issue, given the abundance of food and export crops at the time, it is now a key issue in the context of the crisis that agriculture faces. During the FTLRP, beneficiaries had to face a situation in which they were forced to put a certain amount of land under food production for patriotic reasons, not least because they were under a form of state tenancy. Some new farmers produced maize and wheat solely for marketing to the GMB, simply because they feared that if they did not do this they would face eviction, or would be labelled unpatriotic.

In addition, there are many cases of 'pretend' land use, when in fact nothing was happening on the land. Settlers developed complex methods for evading the auditing of activities at the plot level. An example of simulated land use is the burning of maize stalks so that no one would know whether or not the land had been ploughed in the previous season. In the Barwick ICA, farmers said that cattle were rented during land audits so that settlers could be seen to be using the land. Some of the land use simulation was in the form of planting unviable crops or crops regarded as not strategic (meaning crops on which the government does not impose price controls) such as millets on land that could be better used for maize. Taken together with the government's weak monitoring capacity, this has meant that some farmers have got away with doing nothing, unnoticed for a long time. The most important question is: what is the minimum expectation when someone is resettled? Is this expectation judged in terms of output or by income, or just survival through farming? Certain benchmarks have to be set to measure the expectations for resettled new farmers.

In general, new farmers are attempting to juggle production in both communal and resettlement areas. A few with resources are capable of managing such production, but the majority tend to under-invest in inputs on both properties so that the yield levels for crops tend to be lower. Had such resources been strategically invested in one property, this could have improved production. However, a new and positive phenomenon is that new farmers are using resettled areas as commercial areas for making money, and the money is eventually invested in communal areas in the form of home improvements and the acquisition of household assets. There is no doubt that those farmers who have worked hard have improved their standard of living: previously they did not own property, or owned only a limited amount.

Weekending with a national resource The new settlers have also come to see land as providing extra opportunities, and therefore try to combine an off-farm job with farming so as not to let go of farming as a negotiating tool for their stay on farms. The phenomenon of 'weekend' and 'phone' farming has thus become embedded in Zimbabwean lifestyles. In this scenario, settlers in Mazowe troop in, using various forms of transport, to the farms on Fridays and are back in the urban areas by Sunday evenings. In other words, unlike the former white owners, they are not usually physically resident on the farms, but use farms as a weekend outing that becomes the 'amusement talk in offices on Monday mornings' (key informant interviews, 5 June 2007). Another telling joke that was associated with civil servants during the height of the land transfers (and the apparently personal search for land) was the 'jacket phenomenon'. It was said that civil servants were notorious for leaving their 'jackets on the chair in the office and spending most of their time at the farm (or searching for one). The jacket left in the office is "evidence" of presence (and doing work). In this case they pretend to be doing their civil service job.'[5]

A range of explanations account for the jacket phenomenon and also apply to weekend or phone farming, which was carried out by most beneficiaries, especially in the first five years of the FTLRP. For some, the appeal of good living in the urban areas (electricity, piped water, entertainment, etc.) is too strong for them physically to relocate to remote and harsh FTFs. For others, the uncertainty of land reform means that they make rational social and economic judgements about keeping their jobs and farming from a distance. This has tended to make civil servants and similar beneficiaries unproductive because they are engaged in too many income-generating activities, with very little success in any of their undertakings. Somewhere and somehow, the public is short-changed, because there is no efficiency or effectiveness either way – in farming or in the civil service.

In fact, the settlers deliberately ventured into weekend farming knowing that there was little that the government could do. This was at a time when the settlers felt that they were helping government by threatening the white farmers who remained on the land. In the process, the beneficiaries were placing the government in perpetual bondage to them. Therefore, it can be argued that the new farmers are not entirely weak or passive, because they also define boundaries with politicians through manoeuvring encounters at different times, depending on the politics at play.

Audacious investment in assets as a tenure bidding strategy New farmers are showing some resilience as they stabilise on the farms. In some cases, they have shown outright defiance of the authorities. Cases of attempted eviction have been met with resistance as the new settlers ignore the recommendations of the DLC. At times, beneficiaries have taken government and the DLC to court to stay on the allocated properties. In some cases, they simply refuse to move away. The authorities have used the bait of alternative land to convince those recommended for reallocation that they should move. At Berea Farm, a farmer who settled in 2003 and did not have an offer letter went on to build a two-roomed brick-under-asbestos house, plus a hut and a toilet. A new person was then offered the same plot, but the DLC recommended that the offer letter should be applied to another plot for the new person.

It would seem that the settlers have suddenly discovered that one way of securing tenure is to develop the plot by establishing physical infrastructure, even in the absence of an offer letter. Farmers at the Berea settlement seem to be colluding to venture into such investments. For instance, another farmer did not have an offer letter, yet built a big house and installed electricity. In recognition of the vast improvements made, the DLC decided to offer him the plot. However, the DLC was worried by this development, where plot owners rushed into making investments in physical infrastructure so as to secure their tenure. A key concern was that such illegal investments have the potential to make administrative problems for the DLC. This was because, given the fast pace of change, the land authorities were not in a position to know what was happening on the ground. Individuals took advantage of this monitoring incapacity to make investments that were not allowed, and then colluded with the scheme-level committee for support in claiming the land, which they were occupying illegally.

The precedent set by the DLC was that it could issue an ex post facto offer letter. In another case, two beneficiaries at Bain Farm, Mr B and Mr C, were initially allocated subdivisions 8 and 6 respectively. However, the farm was re-planned and everyone except Mr C had their land consolidated into bigger and more viable units. Mr B consolidated his plot 8 with the neighbouring plot 7. Incensed by his failure to get more land as well, Mr C went into plot 7 and built a huge storage shed and four three-roomed compound houses. He then erected a fence around the properties that he had built. This prompted a very bitter dispute between Mr B and Mr C. The National Land Inspectorate visited the farm several times but no amicable solution was found. The DLC recommended re-planning of the subdivisions to allow Mr C to have the piece of land on which he had built the structures. It was also recommended that he should compensate Mr B with an equivalent piece of land from his plot 6.

Therefore, new farmers, especially those without offer letters or 'extra' resources, use investment as a weapon to stay on the farms. In some cases, those without offer letters invest in assets and fully utilise their illegal plots, and then approach the government through the land committees, arguing that they deserve the land because they are productive and have made investments to that end. Sometimes the settlers receive their offer letters, but at other times they lose out when plots are allocated to other beneficiaries. This tends to create conflict, and can result in land committees being accused of corruption.

The poor's political arsenal for obtaining abstract land rights The state display of power nationally may not be supported by actions on the ground. The new farmers have at times responded in their own ways to insecurity. FTF actors weave innumerable relationships among themselves, and plot against the state in a very calculating manner, pressuring the state but also working with it. In Mazowe there were forms of resistance that required little or no co-ordination. In fact, to reclaim their space, settlers made use of implicit understandings and informal networks to avoid confronting the state directly.

Yet through disengagement by evading ZANU-PF meetings or voting for the opposition in secret ballots in Mazowe in 2008, they were showing a deepening crisis of confidence towards the state and their own party (see Chapter 3). Although political action could be described as voluntary, in Mazowe, once settlers noted signs of the state not delivering, they opted for change despite the benevolence the state had shown by giving them land. The choice to engage or disengage in political action may not be done openly at an individual level, but certainly as a 'block' they demonstrated that, although they benefited from the land, they cannot be taken for granted. Thus, if the settlers decide to organise, power can be aggregated beyond the reach of the state and be used as a counterbalance to excessive political centralisation. The weak have weapons with which they can challenge the elites, define their own spaces within which they can manoeuvre, and mould authority within the limits of their abilities. In the FGDs, the beneficiaries were literally using 'weapons of the weak' in the form of passive resistance to the distorted forms of tenure on FTFs. These were the ways in which they responded:

- First, they used the political argument that, without them, there is no land reform to speak of. When asked if they feared eviction by government in the future, the new settlers did not think that this was possible. Inasmuch as land was about production, it was also about people who claimed: 'We *are* government, so how can government remove itself?' They noted that the reason why they were getting preference in terms of subsidies was simply because they 'were government', and would do all they could to make agriculture a success and pay back the government that believed in them.
- Second, the land occupations were the greatest weapon that the new settlers could use against the state. They claimed that they were at the forefront of making land reform a reality, so issues to do with ownership were secondary to access. In fact, '*as* government', the settlers believed that *jambanja* provided them with a tool to negotiate *with* government. This was because government was forced to acquire the land and formally settle the people. The result of *jambanja* was that there were more people on the FTFs, which meant that government could not easily evict them, as this would create a political crisis. The new beneficiaries noted that the government was not hard on them, but seemed to do what it could to encourage them to stay on the land, which validated their occupancy. For instance, the settlers would not be reprimanded for 'truancy' or just 'being naughty': there were cases of known vandalism of property, attacks on animals and thefts that went unpunished.
- Third, the settlers went on to the FTFs without tools for working the land. It is for this reason that the government tried to take responsibility for the provision of inputs (seeds, fertilisers, fuel, implements) and working

capital as well as mechanisation. In many cases, the government money was inadequate to meet the promised subsidies to the new farmers, as demand far outstripped supply. The new farmers in the FGDs pointed out that the provision of inputs (inadequate as it was) showed that they were indispensable, as the government needed them on the farms. If government had not supported them in this way at the beginning of the FTLRP, many of the beneficiaries would have literally 'walked away' from the FTFs. However, the government then went on to provide subsidies to the new farmers, even when it was clear that they were defaulting year after year. In some cases, fuel and other agricultural inputs were diverted by farmers to the black market, without any form of sanction on such farmers. In fact, 'the abnormal became normal' during the FTLRP, as the new farmers asserted their new-found rights on the FTFs.

However, state–settler relations were not overtly combative. The settlers would listen to 'their' government on many matters to do with land reform, and at times would even agree to be moved from one farm to another, because the government was 're-planning the schemes'. At times, therefore, there was social (read political) compliance, and benefits could be negotiated, because there was a belief that everything that was being done by the government was in the best interests of the settlers and the nation. In this regard, the settlers also established a strong relationship with the civil servants, who had also become farmers, albeit on a part-time basis. Thus the civil servants joined with the farmers to defend their land rights. In the process, some civil servants manipulated the policy for self-interest, although there were others who fought for justice and fairness in policy-making. The majority of those who colluded for their own gain were arraigned before the courts on allegations of 'defeating the objectives of the land reform programme'.

State weapons for controlling the new settlers

In any discussion of land ownership policy, a key question is: where must the rights of government end and those of settlers begin? This is a fine line to tread, as in the case of tenure on the FTFs. The state has not been over-ridden by the settlers as it also has weapons to keep them under control. The main problem is that at times the government exhibits uncertainty, which the beneficiaries then interpret as meaning that it has no confidence in itself and that it might reverse the FTLRP. As a result, in the media the government has been perpetually (if not desperately) at pains to reassure settlers that land reform is irreversible and that no one will be displaced.

Yet on the ground there are certainly cases where the new settlers have been removed for various reasons. The state has instituted legal and constitutional changes to reassure settlers that they are on the farms for ever, but under conditions and on terms defined by the state itself. The fear of removal is particularly telling, given that the political parties agreed to include a provision about the irreversibility of the land reform programme in the Global Political Agreement of 2008. Such pronouncements have the effect of creating uncertainty among the land beneficiaries, who may view the state as weak compared with the former landowners, who are still fighting to get their land back or to obtain compensation for it. One participant in an FGD noted that: 'It is as if the government is in doubt about the longevity of the resettlement.'

At the same time, all this uncertainty has the effect of keeping the settlers subservient to the state. This means that the new settlers have to do what the government wants, including allowing the government to define what type of rights they deserve, without having any input into the policy discussions. Some officials in government argue that 'government gave the settlers free land, so there is no need to give them any rights, because doing so will mean loss of control by the state' (key informant interview, July 2009). In addition, the government strongly believes that it alone is the best defender of the farmers, because giving them rights, especially the right to transfer land, will result in land reverting to the former landowners. In one FGD, it was pointed out that this 'would embarrass the president, who made the land reform programme possible' (key informant interview, July 2009).

The delay in the issuance of land permits and leases with adequate legal status to the newly created farms creates insecurity. The new farmers would prefer secure tenure because it would represent the final conferment of land rights. At the same time, a major obstacle is that the new farmers are aware that most former landowners who lost land and property have largely not been compensated because the government has no money. The escalation of litigation by the former landowners in the regional and international courts clearly means that the legality of the land transfers and compensation for acquired farms are still being contested. The international community has also been unwilling to fund the resettlement programme.

Although it provided the new farmers with subsidies as a means of control, the government exploited the sense of obligation of the beneficiaries who received almost free handouts. The settlers felt obliged to defend the government, because it was a provider at a time when the international community was unwilling to help farmers on resettled land. The government also used the weapon of technical control, through targeting some farms for survey and demarcation. 'Re-planning' to create order became a tool that intimidated the new farmers, who then felt they had to do all they could to support the government. In this context, threats of re-planning were enough to keep the beneficiaries in check as well as ensuring that they complied with any government directive. In addition to threats of re-planning, there were the land audits, which the government said it intended to carry out so as to identify and remove the unproductive and those underutilising land, as well as multiple farm owners. The government carried out few audits, particularly on the A2 farmers. However, even the outcomes of such audits were not taken to their logical conclusion, nor were the findings ever implemented to help the agricultural sector, yet the government continued to invoke them once in a while to keep the beneficiaries on their 'political' toes.

The government also depended on its protégés (War Veterans and party functionaries) on the ground to keep settlers in check. To test the loyalty of the new settlers, the former ruling party would ask for regular donations to fund national activities such as independence celebrations, heroes' holidays, condolences when prominent party members died, and events such as the birthday celebrations of their leader. Beneficiaries were required to provide donations in cash or kind (produce) for such occasions. Failure was regarded as being 'anti-party' and therefore undeserving of allocated land. In some cases, new farmers were not evicted directly, but the resulting social conditions made it difficult for them to integrate with others or to access some of the state resources for farming. The government also elevated traditional leaders to play a similar role in the resettlement areas. The chiefs in particular were given whole farms and were encouraged to oversee the people on the FTFs. Village heads were nominated to help the chiefs in 'looking after the people', especially the A1 farmers.

At the national level, the ZANU-PF government used the public media as a weapon to keep the settlers under control. They regularly reported stories about former white farmers moving back to reclaim their farms illegally. In 2008, this was used as an election gimmick: ZANU-PF and the public media made allegations that the former white farmers had moved back to strategic FTF areas in anticipation of a win by the MDC, whereupon they would force the new farmers off the land. Following the elections in 2008 and the stabilisation of the economy, there has been no evidence of sustained attempts of re-entry on to farms, apart from the usual litigations by the former landowners recorded in the courts from time to time. The use of the public media was intended to exploit the emotions of the settlers to defend the FTLRP and thus help the ruling party, and, in the process, help themselves as beneficiaries.

In general, the government has used 'lack of trust' as a way of keeping the new settlers in check, because they did not know each other before they settled on new land and in new communities. In fact, the collective organisation of settlers tended to occur within the political circles of their party, which was what got them on to the FTFs. The state then used the political party structures to control people who had no social links to each other; this weakened their tenure rights and their sense of collective action against any provisions they felt impinged on their rights. The collective voice of the farmers that could have come through farmers' unions was not audible in the highly politicised spaces of the FTFs. Yet, this discourse may be countered by the realities on the ground, where beneficiaries and actors moulded information and studied the characters and reactions of politicians. More often than not, the politicians were trying to cleverly manage people by changing the timing and nature of 'land policies' to fit their political agenda. For instance, the government would announce that all land was acquired, but immediately counter that land under bilateral agreements was spared from acquisition. While this could have confused the 'invaders' of such properties, it also allowed them leeway to negotiate for the allocation of land that was *not* under any such agreement. Using such tactics meant that the beneficiaries were able to create their own space – a space that would be difficult for the state to influence without causing political problems for itself, but also one with the potential to initiate a wave of upheaval on land matters.

Tenure security preference of the beneficiaries

Land tenure is not a static concept and is influenced by society and policies that are put in place over time. In this context, the tenure issues in the FTLRP reflect the radical changes that have taken place with regards to an important resource in Zimbabwean society. In general, there is no single type of tenure that is right or wrong on an international level, only forms of tenure that are viewed by society as working to its advantage. Designing or imposing a certain kind of land tenure system will not resolve all land-related problems. Instead, society must weigh the advantages and limitations of each tenure regime. However, farmers have certain tenure preferences they demonstrated through their actions and their statements. In political circles, freehold title deeds are feared as they have the potential to allow the former white commercial farmers to buy back some of the land and thereby reverse the redistribution of land that was achieved over the past decade (this is seen as whites regaining land by the back door). In addition, the fear of land re-concentration among the rich emerges from the fact that the majority poor depend on land for their economic survival. In government tenure policy, rental and joint venture arrangements are prohibited, as they are thought to encourage the use of A2 beneficiaries as a 'front' for white farmer operations.

In Shamva, the majority of the A2 farmers (65 per cent) expressed confidence in investing in the land under the provision of the offer letter. On the other hand, in Mangwe District the 99-year leases were preferred since offer letters did not define the landholding. The farmers argued that the offer letter does not provide security to invest in the land, and pointed out that if they had 99-year leases they could mobilise resources and construct a dam because they will hold the land for the long term. The economic problems had restricted the ability of farmers to invest, and this happened at a time when capital investments in agriculture were on the wane. In Mazowe District, the majority

(55.2 per cent of A1 and 51.4 per cent of A2) of the respondents preferred title deeds and 47 per cent of A2 farmers wanted leases. The farmers were choosing what they thought were secure types of ownership that would provide them with security and the ability to use land as collateral.

The points raised by settlers make reasonable sense, given the status of some of the acquired infrastructure today. Spending so much time in the resettlement areas enabled us to get a first-hand impression of how the 'inherited' infrastructures are being used and managed. Some of the farmhouses visited are in a state of disrepair. Some of the problems include the removal of fittings, firewood cooking inside the houses, using finely cut planks for firewood, garbage not being removed, livestock (goats) kept inside the houses, and many other activities that waste the advantages of such structures. When asked why they were doing this, the users of the houses simply retorted that 'such is the situation when ownership is not defined'. They care little for the property because it belongs to the state, which is not a person but an abstract system, and therefore meaningless as an owner. In effect, there is no owner in their view. The settlers therefore showed that, without clearly defined regulations, a major casualty of the FTLRP is the impressive housing infrastructure that former white farmers had constructed in the rural areas at great cost.

Conclusions

The study of land rights in Mazowe District provides a microcosm and manifestation of the problems that the FTLRP faces in Zimbabwe. The fundamental issues with regard to giving out land and what mechanisms are required to transform settlers into real farmers have not been properly addressed. Evidence from Mazowe District has shown that the assumption that the land reform problems have been resolved is still not supported by the realities on the ground. There are numerous conflicts over land, with allocated farms facing threats of takeover by 'new' applicants either wishing to locate themselves on the best possible land, or simply corruptly wanting to enter the programme late. The fact that some seek to get land 'by hook or by crook' and at times influence the re-planning of farms from A1 to A2, leading to the eviction of other settlers, makes the new farms places where the rule of 'survival of the fittest' holds sway, and women and the politically weak are always under threat. A significant change in Mazowe was the deliberate policy to increase the number of A2 farms, which meant the re-planning and reallocation of some plots and the movement of people who would have been on the land for two or three farming seasons. However, it was not so much this change of policy that was remarkable but rather the debate around it.

The narrowness of the land rights discourse is illustrated by the manner in which the government seems to be cornered by the new beneficiaries, who are watching for what the government will eventually do with their deserved rights.

A series of government announcements on tenure (the so-called 'bankability' of land) have been ignored by some banks, and the leaseholds have remained the corridor talk in government, which is not helping the new farmer wanting to get on with the business of farming. However, others, oblivious to this fact, have just got on with using the land they have obtained, relying purely on their own effort. The survey demonstrated that the new settlers mostly want freehold title deeds, despite there being opinions against this expressed by some politicians and academics. Something that for the beneficiary is a straightforward practical matter in an otherwise uncertain environment has been politicised and theorised at the expense of the farmer seeking security in order to obtain the resources necessary for farming.

The government's preference is for leaseholds, but these are being unceremoniously foisted on the new farmers without any consultation and with noisy arguments about their being as 'good as freehold title deeds'. It is now over ten years since the FTLRP commenced and five years since government started developing the leasehold documents that were launched with pomp and ceremony in 2006. Yet despite their political support, they remain mistrusted not only by financial institutions but also by farmers, even by some who have had them for several farming seasons. It is surprising that such a critical issue would have run its course without a more robust debate, but, as it turned out, any debate was between the same old players in Harare, not out on the farms. Again, one notices a clever tactic to put forward a position of self-interest as government policy.

What happened with regard to land distribution also happened with respect to the realities of production. There is no predictability with respect to land use and production in the newly resettled areas. The real needs of farming mean that hanging on to claimed land (however large the area of that land) has no value without access to water, agricultural inputs, credit and markets. New settlers are trying to juggle these elements, as well as their livelihoods, while holding on to the land and pretending to use it, maintaining as many sources of income as they can, including formal jobs as well as multiple farms and homes. Not all is doom and gloom, however, as some new settlers are doing well – not least because of the investments that they have made on the land. In determining why these settlers are doing well despite the odds, it was noted that they show remarkable resilience and a nuanced way of dealing with tenure uncertainty. Strategies include installing new infrastructure, production for export, value addition and so on, all stemming from the desire to prove to the authorities, and/or for their own personal livelihood, that they can produce more than the previous owners. Nonetheless, the successes achieved by these few settlers are too small to contribute to the agricultural recovery of the nation. The sum total of problems that tenure uncertainty elicits is so overwhelming that, with current trends of production in strategic districts such as Mazowe, agriculture will just trudge slowly forward in the short or even medium term.

This analysis exposes a disturbing trend in emerging land rights. While the FTLRP itself had problems from a number of perspectives, it compounded these by continuing with the same dogmatism. The debate on resettlement stability has been limited yet is still very fanatical compared with the discussion of issues such as farmworkers, gender, security, etc., which are easier to articulate because they speak to popular sentiment. The reality is that there was a confusing interaction of people and policy, as well as uncertainty and trepidation, and these factors affected whatever commitment to address the inequities politicians may have had. On a more theoretical level, such developments should not be a surprise, at least to the adherents of the school of 'policy as a process'. Since tangible policy statements and implementation guidelines on the FTLRP have been lacking, and the policy process was much more 'fuzzy' than a sequential structure of formulation and implementation, a different approach is required in order to understand the process and outcome and what is needed for the country to move on and to stabilise land rights.

5 | Complexities in understanding agricultural production outcomes[1]

Introduction

The implementation of the Fast Track Land Reform Programme (FTLRP) was characterised by severe disputes that affected agriculture in its broadest sense, with production being the major casualty of the land transfers (Marongwe, 2003; Rukuni et al., 2006; 2009; Zikhali, 2008). Yet much wider contextual issues contributed to agricultural decline, not merely land reform. Given that land and agrarian reform as both concepts and processes have a logical symbiosis with agriculture, it is necessary to establish agricultural performance during and after the land transfers. This chapter focuses on assessing agricultural performance in the post-2000 resettlement schemes, and how this was influenced by policies, institutions and processes, climatic conditions, farm type, use of inherited infrastructure, class of farmers and their background, and differential access to farming resources.

Agricultural performance declined significantly on the former large-scale commercial farms (LSCFs) after the start of the FTLRP (RBZ, 2005; Richardson, 2005; Moyo, 2011a; 2011b). The majority of the beneficiaries of the FTLRP have not yet reached the expected production levels,[2] citing challenges of access to seed, fertilisers, chemicals, equipment, support services and output markets. However, as this chapter shows, the implementation of the FTLRP has thrown up important ideological differences and contradictions with regard to exactly what is required to get back to the agricultural production levels of the mid-1980s to the mid-1990s. Key questions relate to the definition, character and objectives of agricultural policy, the type and quality of institutions to facilitate implementation of the policy and strategies, and the quantity and quality of other production resources required to meet the demand of those settled under the FTLRP. It also questions the application of pre-FTLRP production models in a changed socio-economic environment that requires new and innovative solutions.

Definition and character of agrarian transformation

To reinforce its land transfers, the Government of Zimbabwe (GoZ) launched a massive farmer support programme. This programme, unprecedented in the history of Zimbabwe's agriculture, ran from 2001/02 to 2007/08. However, performance assessments suggest that agriculture has underperformed at the national level. Production trends outlined in Table 5.1 show that production figures have largely remained at their lowest level; some commodities, such as maize and tobacco, have started to increase marginally, but the figures are certainly not comparable to the situation before the FTLRP in 2000.

There are strongly opposing views as to the factors that account for such performance. One group of writers (Sadomba, 2008; Moyo and Murisa, 2008; Moyo and Yeros 2007b) argues that poor performance was largely due to the sabotage of the programme by the white farmers (and a mostly white-controlled industrial sector), as well as to restrictive measures and/or sanctions imposed by the international community, especially on balance-of-payments support that affected the economy in general. On the other hand, another group of writers (Raftopoulos, 2003; Madhuku, 2004; Hellum and Derman, 2004; Hammar et al., 2003; Alexander, 2006) argues that it was a disabling environment permeated by human rights abuses and violence that undermined the FTLRP and accounted for the decline, and that the use of violence and the forceful takeover of land had the effect of undermining property rights, leading to underinvestment in agriculture (Richardson, 2004; 2005). Other writers (Selby, 2006; Matondi, 2008a; and, in part, Scoones et al., 2010) believe that agricultural decline could be the result of a combination of the factors cited in these opposing views, together with the speed with which the programme was implemented. A range of elements conspired to lower production levels; these related to the inability to speedily address the agricultural skills gap, unfavourable weather, numerous conflicts and litigations, and the broader economic environment that failed to make farmers fully commit themselves to farming, in addition to weak support institutions.

Zimbabwe's agriculture today reflects the outcomes of the radical land transfers of the FTLRP in terms of the transformation of landholding structures and property rights. New social relationships have also emerged with reference to production (Murisa, 2007) as well as new communities and new agricultural practices (Munyuki-Hungwe, 2008; 2011). A1 and A2 farmers exist side by side, together with a few former large-scale white owners (around 300 as of 2011) who retained their farms, exchanging knowledge and assistance and sharing resources. The production relations evident at the local level encompass a mixture of farmers of different classes, genders, financial means and interests. There is also a mixture of new and old institutions, all attempting to find space within the new agrarian system and relationships. Agricultural labour relations and conditions are also different from what they were in the past, as ex-farmworkers either face difficulties or have been 'liberated' from the shackles of what Rutherford (2001) described as 'domestic government' run by the previous white farmers. Former farmworkers are rediscovering their worth and the true value of their labour, meaning that they can now resist providing that labour to those who cannot pay adequately. Commerce

TABLE 5.1 National productivity trends, 1980–2009 ('000s)

Year	Maize Area (ha)	Maize Production (t)	Wheat Area (ha)	Wheat Production (t)	Cotton Area (ha)	Cotton Production (t)	Tobacco Area (ha)	Tobacco Production (t)
2000	1,374	1,328	42,551	229,775	415,000	353,000	85,000	236,000
2001	1,240	1,620	37,269	197,526	397,000	333,000	76,000	202,000
2002	1,328	1,526	39,000	195,000	229,000	195,000	71,000	166,000
2003	1,352	605	40,809	122,427	282,000	240,000	54,000	82,000
2004	1,494	1,059	70,585	247,924	389,000	331,000	41,000	65,000
2005	1,730	1,686	65,454	229,089	350,000	196,000	56,000	75,000
2006	1,712	915	67,201	241,924	300,000	258,000	27,000	55,000
2007	1,446	1,485	49,707	149,110	354,000	297,000	53,000	79,000
2008	1,722	953	10,300	31,000	431,000	224,000	62,000	68,000
2009	1,507	471	18,201	36,400	338,000	247,000	48,000	64,000
2010	1,803	1,243	15,000	30,000	261,000	172,000	67,000	93,000

Source: FAO/WFP, 2009 and 2010.

and industry have also had to adapt to the changed agricultural production base through new forms of internal financing of production as well as wider agro-industrial production relations.

The emerging agricultural production techniques and systems, including the adaptation of old resettlement models into the new A1 and A2 schemes, have resulted in new terminologies being coined alongside the FTLRP. New farmers have been caricatured in various ways as the architects of the decline of agriculture. Farmers have been criticised for poor land utilisation, with people commenting that, for example, new farmers are involved in '*kurima sorabeans*' (meaning 'farming grass', although in this phrase grass is replaced by soya).[3] In some instances, new farmers were caricatured by those in communal areas as '*vana Museyamwa*' (a term derived from the eland totem and humorously used to depict some inefficient black businessmen) who could not pay farmworkers, unlike the former white large-scale farmers (feedback meeting, Chiweshe communal lands, 24 April 2009). However, others acquired new titles such as 'boss Johns' or '*murungu wenyu*' (a black person described as the new white man) because of their production prowess, or simply because they were the new farmers and were in the process of exerting authority.

In examining the above, various writers at the national level have presented a rather abysmal picture of Zimbabwe's experiences of the structural changes in land ownership (Moyo and Yeros, 2005b). The farmers are said to be nothing more than phone farmers, accused of looting state resources as well as the infrastructure of the former owners, of being too dependent on the state or too political (Derman, 2006; Alexander, 2006). In general, the changed agricultural landscape of Zimbabwe provides an interesting case study in terms of a radical programme that has totally transformed Zimbabwe's agriculture and the life of women, men and youths in the country in different ways. In the research results feedback meeting carried out by Ruzivo (Moyo et al., 2009), new farmers were realistic about their circumstances; they never expected to be 'super producers' within a short period of time, as pointed out by the head of a government department in Bindura (key informant interview, March 2008).

In Mazowe, participants in the results feedback meetings (January to March 2009) conceded that productivity on the newly resettled farms was way below that of the previous white commercial farmers. Some land beneficiaries were suffering from hunger. Sometimes, new farmers in A1 schemes had had to get food from the Chiweshe communal areas because of a combination of unfavourable weather and a lack of inputs and tillage services at a time when they were settling on their new plots. In a way, some relationships have been strengthened between communal and resettled farmers because of food remittances. In addition, since the new farmers have increased their production, they in turn have been able to provide food to people in Chiweshe communal areas, given the phenomenon of split households described in Chapter 4. There was no clearly defined route for the food remittances, as both communal people and resettled farmers claimed to be assisting the other.

While the land accessed by the farmers has the potential for increased agricultural productivity, the major constraints cited include poor farmer selection leading to unskilled farmers owning the land, poorly targeted subsidies, unfavourable weather patterns, inaccessibility to new technologies, weak farmer organisation, poor marketing strategies, chronic shortages of inputs, inadequate land rights, and political instability contributing to a lack of confidence and international isolation.[4] The reality is that current agricultural production is being influenced by many factors. At the local level (Mazowe, Shamva and Mangwe Districts), this complexity of issues is being discussed and the different factors that have contributed to the decline in agricultural performance identified.

Retrospective analysis: trends or discontinuities?

It is becoming evident that if sustainable agriculture is to be achieved in the short term, the different forms of smallholder agriculture – in communal areas, the old resettlement scheme farms, the A1 and A2 farms, and the remaining large white-owned farms – should have a symbiotic relationship. The aim of agricultural policy is to ensure that land should not only provide livelihoods for people, but also contribute to foreign exchange, employment, food, agriculture-related raw materials and markets and produce a surplus for investment. While the contribution of smallholder agriculture to the economy has fallen in many industrialised countries, Zimbabwe has tended to anchor its economy in this sector. Agriculture today has become a hot topic for international development (Matondi et al., 2011) and a gamut of international players (both private and public) are interested in Africa's land resources for a range of reasons. Yet, in the national context, land is something that embodies the rediscovery of agriculture as a key security issue, and therefore it stands at the heart of sovereignty.

In the case of Zimbabwe, agricultural support has been pivotal. Government budgetary support to agriculture was enormous during the FTLRP and continued on this trajectory, with government and donors budgeting US $1.9 billion for agriculture from 2009 to 2011, which meant that spending on agriculture grew to around 13 per cent of gross domestic product.[5] However, this amount invested over three years was more or less equivalent to commercial lending to agriculture in just one year before 2000. According to John Robertson, quoted by Mutenga (2011),[6] commercial lending to agriculture was US $1.87 billion in 2000,excluding government programmes based on subsidies and donor resources provided to vulnerable groups. Yet, during the FTLRP, the generous support had a muted and mixed impact. A calculated strategy to reduce the role of the state in agricultural matters following the formation of the Global Political Agreement (GPA) faced resistance from those who viewed such a reduction as reversing the gains of the agrarian revolution, and hence the ongoing liberation struggle centred on land. This is the context in which the performance of agriculture will need to be understood in the transitional period of the Inclusive Government.

Zimbabwe has broken generations of large-scale land ownership. While the commercial agricultural sector had a clear economic grounding, it failed the test of time in terms of its social and political legitimacy, given that the majority of the black people were not fully part of it (Utete, 2003b; Tshuma, 1997; Rukuni, 1994a; Rukuni and Eicher, 1994). Yet, in trying to reconcile what was a racially based dual economy, land reform took a violent path that seemed to negate its legitimacy (Moyo, 2001; Yeros, 2003; Sachikonye, 2004). The tortuous first ten years of the FTLRP suggest that there are numerous roadblocks on the way to a more efficient reallocation of land for sustained agricultural production. Many of the beneficiaries on the land, especially the A2 resettlement farmers, seem to be playing a 'waiting game', while A1 farmers have moved towards using the land and improving production. The question is: why are the better-resourced beneficiaries ambivalent about investing in agriculture compared with farmers regarded as poorly resourced? Does it follow that the poor beneficiaries are willing to take greater risks than their better-resourced counterparts? Alternatively, is it desperation on the part of the poor that encourages them to produce and to live from day to day in order to feed their families?

Government at the central level sought to be the champion of the land transfer programme, leaving beneficiaries as the followers of state directives. The problem then transmuted at the local level, where beneficiaries waited for the state to drive agriculture. Local producers were subordinated to supra-local authorities for access to resources for production, with politicians at times trying to be technical extension officers determining what farmers should produce and in what quantities, under operations some termed 'command' agriculture. The intervention of the state from above was by arbitrary imposition rather than by invitation. In this context, the question that lingers is whether the methods of land reform have been counterproductive in a country that started with significant land insecurity and skewed land ownership with racial undertones. Understanding agriculture, therefore, requires careful analysis of the behaviour of the state (and its politics) in relation to the producer (the beneficiary of the land transfers). It also requires a deeper analysis of the context of land transfers and how beneficiaries and institutions underpinning agriculture reacted at the local level.

In Zimbabwe's new resettlement areas, the main question is: what are the circumstances that determined a slower than expected response to government-supported agriculture on the part of the land beneficiaries? Various hypotheses have been advanced as to the reasons for the half-hearted responses that are reflected in declining production. Given the progressive weakening of the national economy, one can be persuaded to believe that a huge vacuum was created in the provision of agricultural services and inputs. Yet there were some strong forces that actually worked *against* agriculture (Rukuni et al., 2006; 2009). Retrospective analysis at the local level can provide answers to some of the questions about how the state replaced the private sector with regards to the supply of services and inputs, inadvertently creating a dependency syndrome at a time when the state was failing to control the economy. At the outset, the theory was that the land transfers were to be supported by minimum essential services (GoZ, 2001); however, on implementation, this policy provision was set aside as the government opted to speedily conclude the agrarian reform programme, without the provision of key services. The support provided by the state in the years following the FTLRP was an effort to plug the gap that in the past, and under normal circumstances, would have been filled by the private sector. As a result, the government policies, institutions and processes that were used to fill this gap have been unable to sustain the services required, as they were never really designed for agricultural service provision.

Crop production

Cereal production in Mazowe, Shamva and Mangwe Districts In Mazowe and Shamva, the main crops grown are maize, tobacco, wheat, soya beans and various types of horticultural produce, including citrus. In Mazowe, maize is the dominant crop and grown by the majority of A1, A2 and communal farmers. About 38,000 ha were planted under maize in the 2003/04 season in all the sectors. The communal sector contributed much of the area, with the least amount of area contributed by the LSCF sector that was untouched by the reforms. In terms of production, the communal farmers contributed 70 per cent to total maize produced in the district; this is typical of national trends, where on average communal farmers contribute between 60 and 70 per cent of the maize produced in the country.

The 2004 Ruzivo Trust survey in Mazowe reflects a similar pattern: crop production in new resettlement areas is skewed towards commercial maize (31.7 per cent). Table 5.2 shows the large disparities between area and production targets and the actual production attained in the 2003/04 season for cereals. Clearly, communal areas (with over 75,000 tonnes) demonstrated the competence of this sector in maize production. However, the combined total was far from achieving the district potential of 355,000 tonnes, which this district produced before the FTLRP in 2000.

In Shamva District, maize was the most important crop, taking up some 71 per cent of the cropped area in 2005, and was grown by almost all farmers in the district. In the 2004/05 agricultural season, the total maize produced

TABLE 5.2 Cereal production patterns in Mazowe District in the 2003/04 season

| Crop | A1 | | A2 | | Communal | | LSCFs | | Total | | District potentials determined by Agritex | |
	Area (ha)	Production (t)	Area (ha)	Production (t)	Area (ha)	Production (t)	Area (ha)	Production (t)	Area (ha)	Production (t)	Area (ha)	Production (t)
Maize	2,680	6,578	5,040	17,956	28,325	75,245	2,000	8,000	38,045	107,779	80,000	355,000
Wheat	213	828	1,638	4,239	1	3	7,500	22,500	9,352	27,570	45,000	180,000
Sorghum	28	47	384	923	259	173	26	104	697	1,247	5,100	15,000
Rapoko	4	8	5	13	41	12	–	–	50	33	–	–
Mhunga	–	–	–	–	43	13	–	–	43	13	–	–
Total	2,925	7,461	7,067	23,131	28,669	75,446	9,526	30,604	48,187	136,642	130,100	550,000

Source: Agritex, 2004.

TABLE 5.3 Sectoral distribution of maize production in Shamva District

Sector	Total number of farmers	Farmers growing maize	Area under maize crop (ha)	Total maize production (t)	Yield (t/ha) of maize	% of total maize production
All sectors	15,635	15,632	21,974.90	29,768.20	1.4	100
Communal	11,606	11,603	11,283.00	11,996.90	1.1	40
Old Resettlement	1,406	1,406	6,274.00	8,365.20	1.3	28
A1	1,737	1,737	3,102.85	7,725.65	2.5	26
A2	92	92	521.00	1,680.50	3.2	6

Source: Agritex, 2004.

in communal areas, Old Resettlement Areas (ORAs) and the Fast Track Farms (FTFs) was about 30,000 tonnes. Communal farmers contributed 40 per cent, followed by the Old Resettlement Areas (28 per cent), A1 schemes (26 per cent) and A2 farmers (6 per cent) (see Table 5.3).

Maize production in Mangwe was key despite the unsuitable climatic conditions in the district for the production of the crop. On average, the A1 farmers cultivated less than 2 ha of maize and they averaged yields of less than 0.5 tonnes per ha.[8] In Mazowe, the average maize yield in the 2003/04 season for communal lands was 2.65 and for A1 farmers it was 2.45 tonnes per ha. The A2 farmers averaged 3.56 tonnes per ha, which is close to the 4 tonnes per ha produced by the remaining white commercial farmers. For Shamva District, maize yields in the A1 farming sector at 2.5 tonnes per ha were marginally higher than in the communal sector.

In the ORAs, yields averaged between 1 and 1.5 tonnes per ha, with 1 to 4.6 tonnes per ha under irrigation in the A1 areas. However, it has been noted (Sukume, 2005) that these yields were far below the potential for dry land production, known to be between 3.5 and 4 tonnes per ha. The extension worker assessments indicated significant contributions by the newly settled farmers, considering their small number compared with communal farmers or old resettlement farmers (Pazvakavambwa and Hakutangwi, 2006). The assessments showed significant variability between sectors and locations: productivity ranged from 0.5 to 1 tonne per ha in the communal areas. There is not much difference geographically between Mazowe and Shamva – the agro-ecological conditions are more or less the same. One observation was that, for Mazowe and Shamva, yields may be higher than the national averages, but they are barely half the potential yields for the district.

However, the number of farmers growing maize decreased between the 2004/05 season and the 2009/10 season, at which point overall national maize production started to rise following the formation of the Inclusive Government. Maize is a staple food in the country, and despite the unfavourable weather conditions for growth of the crop, farmers still allocate some area to maize each season. The land allocated to crops in general was low in Mangwe compared with Mazowe or Shamva, given the growing conditions, even for crops that ordinarily do well in this district such as sorghum. The low yields in Mangwe District have been attributed to poor soils, unreliable rainfall and poor agronomic practices, especially late planting and low chemical fertiliser application (both compound D and ammonium nitrate). The yields for sorghum were very low and continued to decline, as the government did not prioritise sorghum seed in the same way they did for maize.

Oil crop production in Mazowe and Shamva Districts Cotton is grown mostly in Mazowe and Shamva. However, in all the districts production has been considerably below the potential level. In Mazowe District the area planted to cotton in 2003/04 was only about 15 per cent of the target set by government, while production was only 13 per cent of the potential (see Table 5.4). Production of groundnuts in the districts has also been well below potential levels. One cash crop that was widely grown in all sectors was sugar beans, which showed an upward trend in terms of production outputs. The total production of sugar beans from the four farm sectors reached 66 per cent of the production potential.

The 2005 Shamva District report (Sukume, 2005) also shows that soybean was a relatively new crop to smallholder farmers during the early years of the FTLRP, explaining the small amount of land allocated to it. However, soybean production seemed quickly to gain popularity among the resettled farmers in Shamva because they contributed more than 80 per cent of district production during the 2003/04 season. In the 2003/04 season, A1 farmers in Mazowe District out-performed all other sectors with a yield of 2.9 tonnes per ha for soybeans. The A2 farmers' average yield was 2.1 tonnes per ha while that of LSCFs was 2 tonnes and communal farmers produced 0.6 tonnes. This contradicts the widespread conviction that A1 production is identical to communal area production. In addition, in general the achieved productivity levels are above the national average, projected at 1.7 tonnes per ha for the first five years after 2000.

Tobacco and paprika production in Mazowe District Tobacco is grown by 6 per cent of all the sampled farmers in Mazowe District, and yields were generally low because the farmers were relying on rain-fed production systems for this crop, which usually only does well under irrigation.[9] The yields averaged less than 1,000 kg per ha on most farms. For the 2003/04 season in Mazowe District, paprika production was about 50 per cent of the production potential. The average yield was only 580 kg per ha (see Table 5.5).

Crop production challenges The quantity and quality of crop production based on area, yields and outputs were influenced by a range of complex factors. At the level of the farmer, many on the FTFs started by producing familiar crops based on familiar production practices. More often than not, this entailed producing those crops that they were used to (A1 farmers), while the A2 farmers sought knowledge from the remaining ex-farmworkers and various sources of information, effectively using government extension agencies to explore what they could do. Some A2 farms inherited infrastructure and machinery from the ex-farmers of which they did not know the purpose or use. On some farms the equipment was left to deteriorate, while on others it was stripped for parts or sold. This significantly reduced the farmers' ability to use the land.

In some cases, resettled farmers were overwhelmed by the land and resources

TABLE 5.4 Production of oil-yielding crops in Mazowe District in the 2003/04 season

Crop	A1 Area (ha)	A1 Production (t)	A2 Area (ha)	A2 Production (t)	Communal Area (ha)	Communal Production (t)	LSCFs Area (ha)	LSCFs Production (t)	Total Area (ha)	Total Production (t)	District potentials determined by Agritex Area (ha)	District potentials determined by Agritex Production (t)
Soybean	1,260	3,593	2,342	4,979	1,819	1,128	1,000	2,000	6,421	11,700	12,000	21,500
Cotton	139	139	275	281	646	680	34	41	1,094	1,141	7,300	9,000
Sugar bean	105	153	626	830	438	163	2,000	3,000	3,169	4,146	4,530	6,260
Sunflower	9	9	8	18	165	94	5	3	187	124	530	1,042
Groundnut	10	7	222	400	25	13	–	–	257	420	2,330	1,210
Total	1,523	3,901	3,473	6,508	3,093	2,078	3,039	5,044	11,128	17,531	26,690	39,012

Source: Agritex, 2004.

TABLE 5.5 Production of tobacco and paprika in Mazowe District in the 2003/04 season

Crop	A1 Area (ha)	A1 Production (t)	A2 Area (ha)	A2 Production (t)	Communal Area (ha)	Communal Production (t)	LSCFs Area (ha)	LSCFs Production (t)	Total Area (ha)	Total Production (t)	District potentials Area (ha)	District potentials Production (t)
SoPaprika	21	13	6	36	292	138	–	–	319	187	250	368
Virginia tobacco	182	207	377	718	693	743	60	96	1,312	1,764	9,700	17,000
Barley tobacco	40	56	150	240	691	346	6	10	887	652	1,600	1,750
Total	243	276	533	994	1,676	1,227	66	106	2,518	2,603	11,550	19,118

Source: Agritex, 2004.

they received. A1 farmers indicated that there was an informal understanding that they should grow maize and not other cash crops. At Hamilton Farm, the farmers claimed that a government official told them to grow only maize and feed the nation (Sukume, 2005). Some A1 farmers, new to the commercial farm environment, were using their land productively, achieving more than twice the national average yields in cotton, maize and tobacco (Shamva survey, 2004/05). However, half of the A2 farmers had cropped less than half of the arable portions of their land in the 2003/04 cropping season. Productivity was quite high by prevailing national standards. Since there was overcrowding on the communal areas and farmers did not have land to rear cattle, accessing land in the settlement schemes provided the settlers with enough grazing and they had the potential to rear cattle for commercial purposes (Mangwe survey, 2007).

Prior to 2000, the majority of commercial farms (80 per cent) in Mazowe carried out agriculture throughout the year with the use of irrigation. By 2004 the Ruzivo survey showed that 41 per cent (175,375 ha) of farm area was under irrigation. Water resources were mainly from dams and the perennial rivers and streams. Thus, even during years of erratic rainfall, crop yields were impressive, as the infrastructure was still in a state that farmers could use. However, by 2007, the Ruzivo survey found that in Mazowe only 12 per cent of farmers (n=520) were using irrigation, while the remaining relied entirely on rain-fed agriculture. There was a significant decline in irrigation activities over the years, which seems to imply the inability of new farmers to continue to utilise the irrigation infrastructure they inherited from the former landowners. Where irrigation was being practised, a number of detractive issues were observed. These included dysfunctional irrigation committees, poor collection of levies, poor yields under irrigation, inefficient use of water and poor timing of planting; all of these factors contributed to low production. Some equipment was being put to personal use by some farmers and there was political interference regarding access to inputs, equipment and water.

Almost all farms inherited some irrigation equipment from the previous commercial farmers, although some of this equipment was vandalised during the resettlement programme. More than three-quarters of the respondents (76.3 per cent) mentioned that water was available for irrigation and only 16 per cent claimed to have no irrigation source available to them.

In terms of technology, the A1 farmers had specific challenges they faced relating to tillage units to plough the land. Whereas most beneficiaries who were settled soon after independence lacked the requisite productive resources, results of this survey seem to indicate that the majority who benefited in the FTLRP have most of the essential mechanical and draught resources. More than 80 per cent in Shamva, for instance, had cattle and a plough, the key tillage resources to engage in at least some minimum cultivation. Less

TABLE 5.6 Number of livestock by sector in Shamva District in 2005

Livestock	Shamva					Mazowe			
	Communal	Old Resettlement	A1	A2	Total	Communal	A1	A2	Total
Cattle	24,145	6,490	7,153	534	38,322	68,626	2,095	7,455	78,176
Sheep	1,487	442	623	105	2,657	413	309	205	927
Goats	14,891	1,310	2,681	442	19,324	22,838	511	567	23,916
Donkeys	288	19	126	0	433	386	23	2	411
Pigs	191	41	34	0	266	–	–	–	–
Rabbits	–	–	–	–	–	–	–	140	140

Source: Livestock data in Agritex files for 2004 (Matondi, 2004; Sukume, 2005).

than 50 per cent of the farmers, however, tended to own other assets. This can be limiting, especially if farmers are to fully develop the complete 6-ha extent of their plots. For that, farmers would need planters to reduce the effort needed for planting and cultivators to lessen the burden of weeding, among other ox-drawn implements. The high demand for District Development Fund (DDF) tractor units expressed by A1 farmers tends to show that current asset configurations are not adequate for them to fully utilise their 6-ha plots.

However, a series of problems were also noted that were beyond the control of the farmer. These problems included the unavailability of inputs country-wide, the lack of machinery and poor skills. First, as far as inputs were concerned, they were available outside the appropriate planting times, meaning that farmers used the inputs purely for the sake of 'simulating' land use (see Chapter 4). The second problem related to the fact that some farmers had little or no equipment to use for crop production. Hoes were not suitable for commercial farming, especially on the deep, hard, red soils and with the increased land area; tractors were required. Some farmers resorted to using cattle not just for draught power but also for transport and for threshing wheat, given the serious shortage of combine harvesters in the first three to four years. Farmers quickly learned to be pragmatic, given that any delays, for example in harvesting wheat, had serious consequences for their profit margins. Third, a key problem noted later on in this chapter was simply that the new settlers' skills were inadequate for successful farming; one or two seasons of failure demotivated the new farmers, some of whom left unceremoniously without telling anyone, while others surrendered their plots to the responsible authorities.

Livestock production

Livestock patterns in Mazowe, Mangwe and Shamva Districts Cattle ownership in the resettled areas has been on the increase for several reasons: the movement of cattle from communal to resettlement areas as farmers have settled there; the adoption (or buying) of cattle left by the previous owners, especially by the A2 farmers; the acquisition of livestock following the modest sale of produce; commencement of breeding by cattle farmers to increase and sustain all livestock, but particularly cattle. However, the largest growth has been witnessed in the poultry sector, especially in the blocks of properties surrounding Harare in Mazowe District; these were traditionally known for their small-scale intensive farming, of which poultry was a key activity. Many households in resettlement areas and communal areas own some type of livestock. There are high numbers of beef cattle, followed by goats in both the A1 and A2 schemes. Trends in livestock ownership are showing similarities, but cattle on A1 farms are increasing in number faster than on A2 farms. This situation reflects national trends, with the bulk of the beef herd in the communal sector (see Table 5.6).

Cattle in particular were highly valued, with many A1 farmers regarding the acquisition of livestock as a high achievement following their allocation of land and first production and sale of their crops. Clearly, issues of cattle accumulation versus sustainable production and use (or seeing cattle as a business) will need to feature prominently in the future. Yet livestock demonstrate a multiplicity of functions; they also provide a range of products and services, including meat and milk for households, transport and draught power, and can be a source of cash income that is often invested in crop production. Farmers indicated that they also use their livestock as a hedge against risks (such as inflation and insecure tenure), as a buffer during years of food shortages, and for meeting social and religious obligations. In Mangwe, the farmers complained that during the era of subsidies the government input support programmes provided inputs such as fertilisers, boom sprays, maize and sorghum seeds and tillage equipment for crop production, but there was a visible lack of government support for livestock projects.

Livestock practices and challenges In both the A1 and A2 models, livestock numbers are nominally increasing through reproduction within owned herds rather than through purchases. However, the destruction of boundary fences is the major cause of livestock losses. A large number of paddocks have been destroyed and continuous grazing is taking place with no rotation, similar to practices in communal grazing. A large number of schemes have fewer than five functional paddocks per homestead. Massive vandalism of paddock fences occurred during the first few years of the land reform programme, and some 92.5 per cent of the respondents indicated that no new paddocks had been constructed after settlement. The result is that livestock management on the FTFs is a huge challenge given the lack of essential resources such as paddocks, dip tanks and veterinary medication. A large number of the settlements did not have functional dip tanks, although most settlements have at least one tank. Most of these dip tanks are poorly maintained and the supply of dipping chemicals is inconsistent. The government failed to provide dipping chemicals through its Veterinary Services Department until 2008, when the economy was liberalised.

For the dairy sector, the majority did not find any existing dairy parlours, nor have they invested in new parlours. Other key requirements such as weigh bridges, cattle races or crushes, feeding pens, small stock pens, feed sheds and food mixers were not available. Yet the limited infrastructure that was available was either underutilised or vandalised, with accusations being made that the farmers who were forced off the land had been responsible for this. In some cases, the infrastructure was neglected due to lack of knowledge about how to use it.

As Zimbabwe implemented its land reform programme, the government failed to put in place robust livestock management systems as the economy and agriculture went through radical change. In fact, significant numbers of cattle were lost due to common livestock diseases that could have been contained in the past. In Mangwe, at least 44 per cent (n=791) of the farmers lost an average of three cattle annually. While farmers suspected that diseases were killing their animals, some 25.6 per cent (n=792) indicated that they did not know what the diseases were. Some referred to black leg as being a major culprit in animal death. This disease can be vaccinated against, yet in 2008 the vaccine was scarce in the country. The problems of foreign currency limited the possibility of importing the vaccine from South Africa, Botswana and Namibia.

Zimbabwe was suspended from the European Union beef market in early 2000 because of its failure to control foot and mouth disease. The loss of the 9,100-tonne beef quota has had far-reaching effects in the livestock industry and the economy in general through loss of foreign currency. The disruption of livestock management systems due to the removal of fencing (and rusting fencing because of underinvestment) ultimately facilitated the spread of vector disease. While the government moved people (and animals), there were no rigorous measures put in place to ensure animal health.

There was very little effort by government to assist farmers in building their beef herds. In 2004, government made available about US $61 million for building the beef herd through short-term loans. In Mazowe District, 105 farmers benefited from the scheme, with each farmer getting an average of four heifers – a low number for triggering livestock transformation and contributing to positive economic development in the district. On the other hand, the lack of availability of cattle for sale was a major problem during the 2000–08 period, as many people were holding on to livestock such as cattle as a hedge against rising inflation. So widespread was this practice that even those people not fully involved in beef production used cattle as a way to insure against inflation.

First, the problems relating to livestock start at the policy level. There is no robust livestock policy and livestock issues seem to have been subsumed into agriculture in general, which traditionally is strongly weighted towards crops. Despite some attempts at institutional reform through founding the Department of Livestock Production and Development, as well as strengthening the Veterinary Services Department, livestock tends to be subservient to crops. Second, the livestock management institutions in government face collapse. Experienced livestock specialists have left government for neighbouring countries because of the poor conditions of service. There is no institutional memory, and so the government is continually starting afresh. Third, implementation of the FTLRP was seriously handicapped by a lack of resources, and the government unleashed people on to commercial livestock farms without adequate preparation. Thus, their attempts at communal-type livestock production systems on commercial farms have been fraught with problems that are undermining the sector.

The complex factors at play in agricultural production

The state has been dominant in supporting production based on the massive subsidies it provided to a form of agriculture that was biased towards the FTFs. Some A2 farmers reported their attempts to regulate their crop production by complying with the directives to produce maize and wheat, as these are crops required by government for food security. For this reason, FTF farmers deliver maize to the Grain Marketing Board (GMB) to demonstrate land utilisation (Shamva survey, 2004). In Shamva District, the A2 farmers mortgaged non-farm assets in order to support agricultural production on the allocated land, as a basis for defending porous land rights. In Mazowe, farmers constructed gardens and kept chickens to show a semblance of agricultural activity. In a similar vein they brought cattle and goats on to the farm, sold some maize to the GMB, or sold some livestock. All these activities were carried out at a minimum level, as a basis for defending the acquired land rights.

Existing agricultural markets found it difficult to understand the new farmers, as many of them had no track record in farming. Banks were unwilling to lend to 'commercial' farmers who had no relevant records, because the level of trust had not yet been established. There were also issues that some of the A2 farmers were urban people who reinvested their farm proceeds (including subsidies) in urban ventures, including the fuelling of the parallel money market until 2008, and some used the subsidies to build houses in urban areas. The currency mismatches between the Zimbabwean dollar and foreign currencies made it lucrative to benefit from public subsidies that were to be repaid seasonally at ridiculous amounts, as otherwise the money would have been eroded by inflation. At the same time, the A2 farmers used farm managers to play a 'holding' role as they assessed the situation with respect to land rights. This largely resulted in much of the land being underutilised to some extent; for example, production areas were reduced, or unviable crops were planted to give a semblance of land use. In an interview (22 June 2010), a provincial Agritex official decried the situation where a person holds 100 ha and only utilises 10 ha or less each year in the A2 scheme.

Farming is proving that hanging on to claimed land is meaningless without access to water, agricultural inputs, credit and markets. New settlers are trying to juggle their land claims as well as their livelihoods by pretending to use the land, maintaining many sources of livelihood and income (including formal jobs), and keeping multiple farms and homes.

Farmers also faced specific difficulties in the production of maize. For instance, an Agritex official (key informant interview, 21 June 2007) noted that, had the remaining white farmers exerted themselves, production of maize could have been higher. To him all farming systems (large and small) worked in a complementary fashion, with the farmers supported by the agro-industrial sector, specific commercial financing and marketing arrangements. It was clear that the disruption of one sector had ripple effects, and that this accounted for the declining production performance of the communal sector, which should have done better in the production of commodities such as cotton and maize. However, the remaining white farmers faced a myriad of challenges, the greatest being the threat of invasions, which meant that they chose to operate below their capability since they felt insecure. In addition, many of the farmers were overburdened by borrowings and disadvantaged by the use of their equipment by people with influence, who in turn guaranteed them security of tenure. Under the circumstances, they could not have achieved an optimal level of production.

The effect of post-2000 input arrangements Whereas the focus has been on the process of land reform during the agricultural production crisis of recent years, the role of access to agricultural inputs, especially fertilisers, has not been fully recognised. Distribution of fertiliser has been drastically transformed since the beginning of the FTLRP, as government took over fertiliser from the key producers for its own programmes. The reintroduction by government of price controls during the first five years of the FTLRP was a significant move in determining the production and distribution of inputs in the entire agricultural sector. Through parastatals, the government used subsidised input credits and price controls to benefit farmers with sub-economic fertiliser prices. However, the manufacturers were clearly unhappy about this and significantly reduced their output, leading almost to the shutting down of their capacity to produce fertiliser. The problem in the industry was compounded by the emergence of the black market. Allegations surfaced that much of the subsidized fertiliser was being directed away from the farms and to urban black markets, resulting in exorbitant prices. All these factors led to shortages of fertiliser in the formal markets and the growth of a black market where prices were at least twice the official prices.

The strategy regarding the provision of agricultural inputs after 2000 was fraught with problems. The wide range of programmes initiated by government to support the agricultural sector directly and indirectly involved an assortment of institutions and organisations in the input supply chain. Despite these arrangements, the late disbursement of inadequate input packages was a key factor that contributed to low levels of agricultural production. The institutions and organisations concerned included government departments, parastatals, private companies and banks, the army, and some non-governmental organisations (NGOs). These various players had different levels of power, expertise and interests, and the result was that many farmers accessed inputs from the black market, having no other source.

A major problem up until 2008 was the pricing of agricultural commodities. The pricing system assumed that all farmers were getting subsidised inputs through government agencies such as the GMB and Agricultural Bank of Zimbabwe (Agribank), so the pricing formulae reflected the subsidised input costs. However, farmers ended up being disadvantaged as they received very low prices for the controlled commodities that they produced. This practice resulted in serious viability problems for the majority of farmers because many were not able to access the subsidised inputs.[10] Empirical evidence from Mazowe, Mangwe and Shamva demonstrates that most farmers in these districts faced difficulties in accessing inputs.

The government sought to address the short-term problems in the production chain, putting the focus largely on inputs (seeds and fertilisers) and, to a smaller extent, on services. In Mazowe District, 31.6 per cent of the farmers (n=251) cited the high prices of inputs as a major hindrance in production. They indicated that, in the 2004/05 season, Mazowe District was seriously undersupplied with seeds and fertilisers. In terms of seeds, there was a shortfall of more than 1,500 of the 1,900 tonnes required. The story was the same for fertilisers, with no supply of ammonium.

The farmers relied heavily on the government for external support for inputs. They were not self-reliant, and from focus group discussions (FGDs) it was obvious that they expected the government to cater for their production needs. For example, about 77.4 per cent of farmers from the Mazowe survey received assistance in the form of fuel, draught power and inputs from government. Farmers in Mangwe regarded new farms as requiring direct government support because individual farmers, coming mostly from economically challenged households, could not invest on their own. The rapid pace of resettlement also affected the ability of families to mobilise resources, even if they had the means and the will to do so. To its credit, the new government in 2009 introduced a range of policy measures, such as multiple currencies, that enabled farmers to purchase seed and fertilisers on the open market. The reduction of the government subsidies forced farmers to buy farming inputs from within and outside the country, giving them much greater flexibility. This allowed farmers to increase the area under production and to plant several crops, although yields still remained low, which largely accounted for the unimpressive production output figures.

Financing contradictions As government implemented the land transfers, a huge vacuum occurred in the financing of agriculture. From 2000 onwards, the government financed most agricultural activities, creating a huge portfolio of state subsidies spread across all the farming areas, but specifically for the new

Donors	Open market	Government			2000
Donors	Open market	Government			2001/02
Donors	Open market	Government	PSF (RBZ)		2004
Donors	Open market	Government	ASPEF (RBZ)		2005
Donors	Open market	Government	RBZ – MECH	MAGUTA	2006/07
Donors	Open market	Government	RBZ – MECH	MAGUTA + SADC	CHAMPION	2008
Donors	Open market	Government	Presidential inputs	2009/10

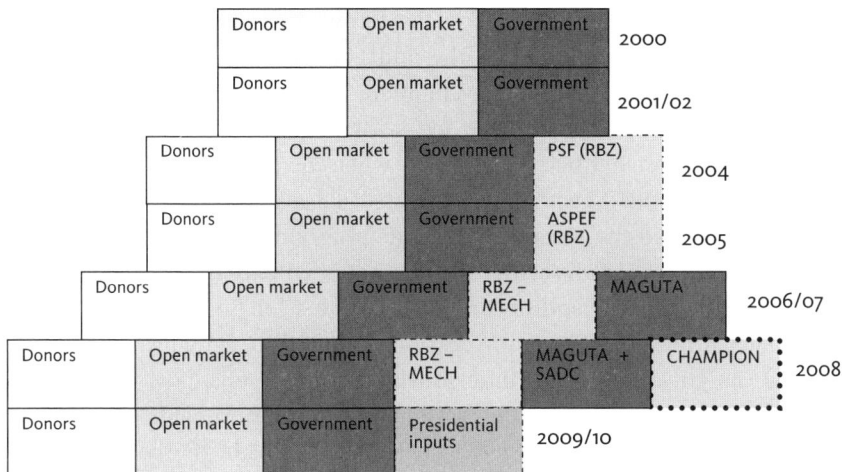

5.1 Changing agricultural financing arrangements during the FTLRP (*source*: author)

resettlement areas. This resulted in the introduction of programmes such as the Government Input Scheme, the Agricultural Sector Productivity Enhancement Facility (ASPEF), Operation *Maguta* (well fed)[11] and the Champion Farmer Programme (CFP). In Mazowe, at a feedback meeting in Chiweshe communal land on 24 April 2009, the respondents were asked their understanding of *Maguta* and they stated: '*chirongwa chehurumende chokubvisa rubatsiro kumaruwa vachiisa kumapurazi*' (a government programme designed to siphon support from communal areas to resettlement areas). One young man suggested that the government only helps resettled farmers because '*ndiko kwavari kurimawo*' (that's where they are farming as well). In these schemes, the government bought the inputs (seed, fertilisers, fuel and equipment) and gave them to the farmers. These programmes changed names seasonally, but the premise remained the same. The government continued to put money into agricultural production, with very little success.

The national financing arrangements for agriculture were quite striking, as shown in Figure 5.1. Until 2000, the government had traditionally provided subsidies to a limited extent, usually in drought years and with the assistance of donors, while the open markets dominated financing arrangements for farmers. The entry of the Reserve Bank of Zimbabwe into agriculture followed the appointment of Dr Gideon Gono as governor of the bank in 2003; this changed the face of economic financing, specifically that of agriculture. A broad range of fiscal interventions was introduced, particularly in the agricultural sector, to support the significant policy shift that came with the FTLRP.

As can be seen from Figure 5.1, Dr Gono had an immediate impact through the introduction of the Productive Sector Facility (PSF), which was to be enhanced with the ASPEF; this made the farmers very happy. The PSF and ASPEF were to be broadened with the addition of *Maguta*, followed by the CFP. Even the Southern African Development Community (SADC) was to be included: it was to contribute some 300 million rand (approximately US $36 million), mostly from South Africa at a time when the political parties were also negotiating. Subsequently, with the drying up of these government facilities, the president introduced the presidential inputs programme, which on the whole has benefited farmers in all sectors and has not been biased towards the FTFs. However, many today depend on the open markets for financing agriculture, a situation that has coincided with, and is connected to, agricultural recovery.

Should the government not have provided for the subsidies? The answer is complex, given that in any one season there are households (vulnerable, poor or old) who should be targeted for subsidies, yet in the context of the FTLRP they were *not* targeted. The financing, acquisition and distribution of agricultural inputs through government programmes were too open to abuse, in a situation where demand for inputs far outstripped supply.

Farmers in Mazowe, Mangwe and Shamva could have accessed any of the funding provided by government through these schemes. Evidence from Shamva reflects that the majority (75 per cent) of farmers depended on their own money (the open market) to finance fertiliser acquisition, with very few depending on Agribank loans, loans from neighbours or remittances from working relatives. Most A2 farmers have found it difficult to acquire farming equipment and inputs. Some of them, especially civil servants, own houses and cars in the urban areas, but they are reluctant to use these properties as collateral for loans due to tenure insecurity (Mazowe survey, 2007). The inability or reluctance to use personal property as collateral handicapped the farmers from sourcing alternative finance from the open market. Relying solely on government to fund everything, in a situation where demand was high and the production of inputs limited, created serious limitations on the farmers' ability to produce. The post-2000 financial arrangements were, therefore, grossly inadequate to encourage agricultural production in the resettlement areas, especially given that the majority of the farmers were coming from a resource-poor background. At the same time, private financial institutions failed to play a significant role for five reasons:

- Many were muscled out by the government inputs programme.
- They felt that it did not make sense to finance agriculture without collateral.
- Many were linked to international (western) institutions that were opposed to funding farmers on contested land.
- The farmers were transient, so the financial institutions had no capacity to keep track of them.
- The high inflation destroyed any pretence of financial support to agriculture.

The financing of input acquisition has been compounding the difficulties faced by A1 farmers. The controlled markets for grain have been paying farmers too late, and, even after the formation of the Inclusive Government, the government has been unable to pay the guaranteed prices, despite the farmers having delivered the grain. Thus farmers have little of their own resources to fall back on when in need. In addition, this exposes farmers to late season price hikes when buying inputs, further limiting their ability to acquire the right amount of inputs for their production processes.

Extension challenges The FTLRP created a new dimension of extension needs. The process of selecting beneficiaries for A1 resettlement had no established criteria specifying farming knowledge or skills. The majority of the settlers had no proven skills in agricultural production. For the A2 settlers, the application forms used had a section covering the applicant's qualifications and experience in agricultural production, but, even here, the applicant's farming experience may not have been considered in the selection because the process became open to anyone. In fact, many people ended up using the political route to access the land, which meant that the technical criteria were ignored. This resulted in settling farmers on commercial agricultural land who had no agricultural training or practical experience, which demonstrates the enormity and uniqueness of the extension problem in the post-2000 resettlement areas. However, alongside the increased demand for extension services from 2000, the capacity to provide those services deteriorated.

According to Pazvakavambwa and Hakutangwi (2006), the ratio in the country of extension workers to farmers had worsened to 1:800 in the rural and resettled areas, which was way below the official ratio of 1:250. This statistic clearly indicates that the quality of services given to farmers greatly deteriorated. Agritex personnel on the ground pointed out that the following ratios – 1:150 for A1, 1:50 for small A2, 1:30 for medium A2, 1:10 for large A2 and 1:30 for communal – were ideal for providing the quality of service that could lead to increased productivity and transform rural areas. On average, one extension worker can serve up to seven farms with an average of 60 farmers each, which translates into about 420 A1 farmers. In 2004, Agritex in Mazowe was supposed to have at least four extension workers serving one working area (in the resettlement areas) or serving one ward (in the case of communal areas). That requirement for four extension workers per working area was not met; it would have required a lot of investment from government and other sources, and this was not available.

In 2004, there were 37 extension workers in Mazowe District, against a requirement of 116. The extension workers who provide basic training in farming are pivotal in land reform. The challenges faced by Agritex included not only a lack of experienced officers to meet the increased demands of new farmers, but also a lack of transport that restricted staff mobility, the shortage of funds to train new staff, and a lack of accommodation in the resettlement areas. In Mazowe, the frequency of extension worker visits to farms varied from ward to ward. In the 2004 survey, at least 69 of the respondents said that they were visited often, while 38 indicated that they were visited once a month. The frequency of the visits reflects the capacity of Agritex to deliver, as the few officers available tended to cover large geographical areas. In order to increase the frequency of extension worker visits, the ideal situation would be to have the extension workers residing in the areas they cover. However, this is usually not the case as there is a shortage of accommodation on the farms. The new settlers refused to provide housing for government extension staff.

In Shamva, the survey showed that the fears about poor provision of extension services in the A1 areas were well founded. Of the sampled farmers (n=128), 20 per cent reported that there was no extension worker providing services within the scheme. The majority of those indicating the availability of extension services claimed that contact with extension workers was too infrequent; 53 per cent of such farmers reported that contact was 'once a year', 'once a month', 'infrequent' or 'not at all'. Some NGOs and private companies stepped in by providing extension workers in the worst affected areas. Of the sampled farmers in Shamva District, 38 per cent reported that they received extension messages from private and NGO organisations. However, farmers pointed out that such services tended to be specific to certain enterprises and did not cover the broad range of needs.

Young and poorly trained extension officers, of them aged in their twenties, had to attend to largely elderly A1 and A2 farmers with different needs. In addition, in most cases the training received by the extension officers did not match the requirements and demands of some of the new, sophisticated A2 farmers. These farmers were highly literate, some educated to university level, with regular access to multiple knowledge sources on the Internet and through the media, and who could carry out research on specific issues. In most cases the extension workers did not know much and were challenged by the new farmers, or regarded as not useful. However, the farmers still needed the workers to visit them, and Internet-based knowledge is not always easily translated into solving a practical farm problem. Despite their workloads, extension officers were given added responsibilities to co-ordinate fuel supplies, carry out land demarcation, mediate in conflicts over boundaries, and so on. The activities that they had to carry out in the field and at their offices were overwhelming for a small complement of staff, often without experience in their additional duties.

According to the research findings at site level, the majority of farmers (93 per cent) viewed public extension messages to be useful to their production decisions. Such a high statistic is indicative of the fact that farmers realised the importance of extension services for the success of their enterprises. Farmers at the site level agreed that extension services should be improved, and made suggestions that centred around increasing contact with farmers as well as improving the quality of services (Matondi, 2005). Farmers suggested that extension officers should be provided with transport so that they can easily access the remote areas that are usually ignored due to the lack of transport.

Labour issues The FTFs have access to a wide range of labour in terms of type, experience, gender and technical capacity. In the majority of cases, the new farmers were drawing labour from the ex-farmworkers, even though additional numbers had been drawn from new farmworkers brought by the new farmers. The survey in Mazowe reflected that a high proportion of the plot holders who employed managers were non-resident, although there were some resident plot holders who also employed managers. Managers can be employed for two main reasons: the landholder either is not available to do the farm work, or does not have the necessary agricultural skills and knowledge. However, there is a data gap in determining why farmers who reside permanently on their plots employ farm managers. A closer analysis of A1 and A2 models indicates that 80 per cent of A1 farmers did not employ farm managers, while this was the case for about 40 per cent of A2 farmers. This further explains why there was a large percentage of A2 farmers who were part-time compared with A1 farmers. In addition, the *type* of manager employed is significant. In Mazowe (n=261), some 49 per cent of the A2 farmers employed managers who did not have any qualifications, while 27 per cent employed managers with an agricultural certificate.

One striking feature of these statistics is the high level of employment of managers who have no training in agriculture. This can be attributed to three factors that need verification. First, the size of the farm operations may have limited farm income, and therefore the farm proprietor could afford to employ only an untrained manager. Second, the competition for access to qualified managers could have been high, meaning that the proprietor had to meet market wage rates in a sector that was not paying well when the outputs were sold, for example when the controls in commercial maize marketing meant that there was a ceiling in terms of what the farmers could get, depending on yields and volumes of output. Third, many of the previous farm managers were beneficiaries of the land reform, and hence became landowners rather than electing to continue managing farms for other people.

The data clearly show that, as farm size increased, plot holders were much more likely to hire a farm manager. In Shamva District, the survey showed that a significant proportion of farmers were hiring permanent labour in the newly resettled areas, mainly to solve problems of weeding (mentioned by 54 per cent of respondents), harvesting (38 per cent) and livestock herding (27 per cent). Of the 128 sampled farmers, 24 (or 19 per cent) employ permanent farmworkers, with an average of 4.6 workers each. This translates to about 0.85 permanent workers per resettled farmer. Given that each farmer on the A1 scheme has on average 12 ha of arable land, this in turn translates into 1.4 permanent workers per 10 arable ha – a substantial employment rate. Given the poor tenure situation of former farmworkers, concern has been raised about the possibility of exploitation by resettled farmers. In Shamva, there was generally no evidence of exploitation. The 2004 survey showed that A1 farmers on average adhered to the stipulated wage guidelines provided by government.

The LSCF sector before 2000 was known for its complex labour supply and management system. Despite generally poor farmworker conditions of service in Mazowe – and in Zimbabwe in general – there was an effective and efficient system for mobilising labour who were resident on the farms and worked the land. The system was based on labour retention, mobilisation of farmworkers, and negotiation for sustainable remuneration. Late in the 1990s there was growing farmworker representation with respect to rights and conditions of service. This saw some improvements in the livelihoods of some farmworkers. However, the question of labour supply on the new farms has been the subject of varied interpretations and assumptions. New farmers have complained to political authorities that ex-farmworkers have been reluctant to work for them because they owe allegiance to the former landowners (MLRR, 2009). Yet, on the ground, ex-farmworkers have found the new landowners contemptuous of them as workers, and felt looked down upon and regarded as renegade members of the opposition. While relations between new landowners and ex-farmworkers are slowly improving as the irreversibility of the land reform sinks in, there is a need for a clear agricultural labour policy underpinned by an effective institutional framework where wages are determined and labour disputes resolved.

In Mazowe, farmworkers regarded the new farmers as completely un-equipped because of their lack of organisational skills for commercial farming. For instance, in the FDGs (Mazowe, June 2007), farmworkers noted that at times they shouldered the responsibility of decision-making for their new employers, who had no idea about farming. They complained of the 'stubborn' new farmer bent on asserting their authority over them, rather than accepting that they had no idea about farming. In Ward 14, a new farmer was insisting on putting wheat on the land in August, instead of the traditional May/June. The new farmers, due to 'ignorance', would go against the technical advice of the extension workers or the advice from the farmworkers with experience. Many did not differentiate between the power of taking over the land and the knowledge needed to run a farm on a professional basis, where specific technical expertise was required to produce crops. Cases of the wrong types of fertilisers being applied at the wrong times were also noted, with farmers

Box 5.1 The plight of farmworkers due to HIV- and AIDS-related problems

The participants pointed out that three plot holders had died of AIDS. It was also noted that most of the workers are dying of AIDS-related illness due to promiscuity, because most of them engage in risky behaviours such as having multiple sexual partners. They pointed out that the HIV and AIDS pandemic is affecting agricultural production at Fairview Farm. The plot of one farmer who had died of AIDS was inherited by a very young son who is not interested in farming. Another plot now belongs to a widow who is terminally ill and is no longer actively involved in farming due to compromised health. There is also another plot holder who is terminally ill and his wife cannot actively engage in farming because she needs to look after her ill husband and all the family responsibilities. Awareness campaigns about HIV and AIDS are being carried out at the scheme in churches and at ward meetings. The scheme members are supporting the widow of the late farmer by providing free tillage and planting. They also sourced outside help from the District Aids Action Committee in Concession and they were given a kit for home-based care.

Source: FGD, Fairview Farm, 7 July 2007.

suffering losses that could have been avoided had they given the professional farmworkers and advisers the scope to play their part.

The farmers in Mazowe face significant labour shortages in the new farming areas, especially during peak farming operations such as planting, weeding and harvesting. Some farmworkers were allocated pieces of land and have been sufficiently economically empowered so as not to need to work on other people's farms. In addition, much of the labour has been absorbed by the mining sector. However, ex-farmworkers' continued stay in farming zones (i.e. residential areas) is a cause for concern to the beneficiaries, as they have accused ex-farmworkers of using electricity and water without paying bills. Other allegations included theft, vandalism of property, and indiscriminate cutting down of plants. Most of the beneficiaries lack the skills for labour mobilisation, and therefore there are poor relations and animosity between farmworkers and newly resettled farmers, creating conditions of mistrust.

Commercial agriculture requires labour, yet much of the experienced labour has been lost to the informal sector, such as cross-border trade, local buying and selling of second-hand goods, working as gardeners in urban areas or in artisanal activities, migration outside the country, gold panning, etc. At the same time, HIV and AIDS severely disrupted the labour market;

institutional interventions were limited by weak government health services in the resettlement areas at a time when donors were unwilling to provide resources to NGOs to continue health-related work. The disruption of health delivery systems on farms due to the land reform programme meant that farmworkers were increasingly exposed to the disease. Box 5.1 shows some of the evidence of the impact of the disease and the institutional responses. Studies by Ruzivo Trust in communal areas showed declining incidences of bedridden cases (Matondi, 2011b), yet on the FTFs there were still challenges because access is severely limited (Mufandaedza and Matondi, 2008; Magaramombe and Chiweshe, 2008).

In Mazowe, many of the new farmers came with their own labour force, mostly experienced in communal farming. However, commercial farming requires a balanced workforce of trained and untrained workers for it to succeed. The lack of training and background in agriculture has seen some of the new farmers compromising on some key farming decisions. The employment of casual workers in the district tended to be the norm. There were a few farmers who employed more than 100 casual workers, and the A2 model tended to absorb more casuals than the A1 model. The majority of farms employed six to ten casual workers, with the next largest proportion employing one to five. It is important to note that the employment of casual workers increased in the peri-urban model. This is typical, as the peri-urban farmers rely on casual workers, most of whom were farmworkers prior to the FTLRP. The distribution of casual workers also showed interesting patterns compared with permanent workers. For permanent workers, there were no significant distributional tendencies, whereas most of the respondents who obtained casual workers were concentrated in wards that were urban-based or close to the Chiweshe communal areas.

In Shamva, there was a significant utilisation of permanent labour on A1 farms, but the survey showed that reliance on casual labour was even more significant. Of the sampled farmers, 57 per cent indicated that they hired casual labour during the 2003/04 season, with an average of close to four casual labourers per farm. There is potential for the hiring of casual labour to increase even further, as only 30 per cent of those who did not hire casual labour had sufficient labour for their farm needs, and the remaining farmers indicated that they would have hired labour had they had adequate financial resources. Generally, the sampled farmers indicated that getting farm labour was relatively manageable. The majority (77 per cent) of those who experienced difficulties in getting labour indicated that this was due to the traditional suppliers of labour (former farmworkers and poor communal and resettled farmers) turning to other, more lucrative, income-generating activities such as gold panning and their own agricultural production. The rest (23 per cent) listed demand-related constraints, such as the remaining white farmers outcompeting A1 farmers and too many farmers chasing a fixed number of workers – factors that were causing wages to rise to excessive levels.

Ambiguous market structures and channels Farmers face a range of complex market-related challenges beyond their control. For the A2 schemes, as a commercial model, the farmers require functional commercial markets to access lines of credit. These were inadequate during most of the decade of the FTLRP. The growth of the commercial sector was clearly inhibited because of the assumed destruction of the agricultural producer base. However, the commercial financial market sector never attempted to reform to respond to the realities of a new agrarian base. Misgivings over issues to do with transfer in the current leaseholds meant that the prospects of private sector investments in A2 farms were limited. This affected the ability of the new farmers to raise non-government resources to produce, and therefore to meet market demands and expectations.

After 2000, many farmers found it very difficult to recover production costs while the government determined prices, especially the newly resettled farmers who mainly produced state-controlled commodities. The reintroduction of market controls by the government also excluded the participation of the private sector in the marketing of maize, grain and wheat. At the same time, the state's involvement in determining the prices paid to producers for agricultural commodities made it very difficult to link production to markets. Tobacco and cotton had been traded through predetermined channels, mainly because there are very few buyers. In such circumstances it was very easy for buyers to collude and agree on one price in order to influence policy at the expense of the producers.[12] Producers of tobacco and cotton have had to withhold their produce, requesting higher prices from the buyers. While locally consumed fruits and vegetables were marketed freely through a number of channels, produce targeted for the export markets was also government-controlled, in the sense that 50 per cent of the foreign currency earned was exchanged at an exchange rate determined by government.[13]

In Mangwe District, agricultural produce, which includes mainly livestock and a few field crops, was largely sold in small, local, community markets. This was because the amount of produce did not make it economically viable to invest in transport to reach better markets (Matondi et al., 2008). Local trading was, however, based on negotiation between the buyer and the seller. Middlemen often took advantage of the local trading of farm produce, offering commodities such as soap, salt and clothing in exchange for grain. Private buyers played a prominent role in the marketing of produce because the prices offered by the GMB were below an economic level. The producers were still often exploited by private buyers, especially after the deregulation of the markets. Yet, although farmers noted the exploitative relationships with private buyers, they still dealt with them because they were a source of immediate cash, unlike the government, whose promises to pay were not fulfilled. More often than not, they tended to be proactive and come to the producer, with cash and transport, while the public GMB waited at its depots, did not provide transport, and often did not have the cash to pay the producer on the spot. Given the hyperinflationary environment that prevailed, farmers preferred cash to cheques because the withdrawal limits at the banks were controlled and too low. This made private buyers more economically desirable.

However, evidence from Mazowe indicates that farmers were 'chickening out' of private company contracts because of the stringent requirements, and instead were opting for government-based contracts that were more relaxed and could easily be flouted. This issue related to contractual arrangements and whether there were rules and regulations to deal with defaulters in government contracts. There seems to have been a lack of transparency and issues of principal–agent relationships, where politicians have the power to forgive defaulters on government contracts. One farmer at an FGD noted that the government seemed to do this in anticipation of votes and political support. Other reasons why contract farming was on the decline, especially on the private side, surround issues of land tenure and security and the risks associated with entering into a relatively long-term agreement under uncertain land ownership conditions. Selling produce outside contractual arrangements was also a key problem, as farmers opted for the open market where there are normally private companies and individuals offering higher prices. While contract farming offered a framework of market guarantees for producers, this proved to be an implicit tax on farmers in a hyperinflationary environment, with the benefits accruing to the merchants, not the farmers. The merchants managed to manipulate producers and maintain low prices for outputs, while some of these implicit taxes on farmers resulted in side marketing and price wars, for example in the cotton sector.

Conclusions

This chapter has shown that in general the FTFs have been performing well below their agricultural potential in all the districts. In some cases less than 30 per cent of the potential has been achieved due to a complex combination of domestic and external, on- and off-farm, micro and macro factors, land transfers, the agro-industry and the wider economy. For most of the years of the FTLRP, the government failed to plan adequately for any agricultural season. Many of the policies pursued by government for providing subsidies almost every year created a syndrome of dependency. When the government undertook to provide inputs for six years from 2001, they little realised that they were taking initiative away from the farmers. From then on, farmers increasingly depended on and expected government to provide them with inputs. Yet, although the government was unable to fully meet these demands, it worsened the situation by crowding out farmers and retail outlets by continuing to source and provide inputs to farmers. By commandeering all the available inputs for the government programme, it left only one source available. The government would have been more successful if a percentage of available inputs had been allowed into retail outlets. If this had been done, those farmers with resources would have been able to purchase their input requirements and the situation, in terms of access to inputs, would have been a lot better.

Communities in resettled areas, by the middle of the last decade, began to realise that government had played its part and it was now up to the farmer to produce on the land. Since 2008, there has been an increased level of farmer-led activities on FTFs, such as the revival of farmer field days and district agricultural shows, and farmers sourcing their own training as collective bodies. The willingness to pay for extension services has demonstrated that a revolution is taking place in the farmer's mindset; farmers are now willing to cover their own costs rather than rely on free extension services. In fact, some of the community members in Mazowe District started a campaign drive, with one farmer at a field day on his farm (20 February 2009) making a speech that pointed out that 'farming is supposed to be about making profits'. By the time of the formation of the Inclusive Government, a real transformation was occurring on the FTFs in Mazowe District. While a mindset that had been shaped by the FTLRP could still be found in FTF communities, there was evident change. The research results feedback meetings from January to March 2009 showed that political sloganeering had stopped or was at a very low level on A1 farms such as Longcroft. The use of symbols denoting political party support, such as the lifting of the fist (ZANU-PF), and the condemnation of opposition parties were replaced by development sloganeering, such as 'forward with farming' (*pamberi nekurima*) and 'down with the lazy' (*pasi nevane nungo*).

However, there is no question that the broader context has affected the farmers in many ways, simply because markets for both inputs and outputs collapsed or operated very minimally, with the government calling the shots in every aspect of agriculture. There was very little space for the private sector or the farmer to be innovative or to take equal responsibility for getting agriculture moving. It is this scenario that land policy should address, based on lessons from the field in the farming areas. Lessons will also need to be drawn from international experiences and, just as importantly, from Zimbabwe's own history, because the country has examples from the past that show what worked and what did not. Work on land policy is now possible, given that agriculture has shown signs of recovery as a result of the macro-economic policy shifts towards the markets in 2008 and the reduction of the fiscal activities of the state.

The field evidence shows that Zimbabwe's new agrarian structure has unexplored potential, which can be realised as the economy stabilises. The question of concern is how to generate agricultural growth within a context of an increased number of farmers with limited farming knowledge and skills, inefficient and high-cost inputs, poor trading performance for outputs, insufficient investment by the private sector, high-cost or non-existent rural capital markets, and many other problems. The recommendation is that increased agricultural productivity, the basic engine of agricultural growth, should be revived, based on an appropriate incentive environment in which the farmer can invest if agriculture provides good economic returns. However, this depends on better relative prices obtained by farmers, which in turn depends on more efficient marketing and better access to agricultural finance. Thus, there are three functional areas critical to agricultural growth within which institutional and organisational reform will play a part: technical change and productivity, market efficiency, and financial services. In addition, there are questions about how to organise an efficient flow of support services (by public, private and community-based institutions) within each of these areas, and then about how to provide the three functions in a way that motivates sustained investment by farmers in their own improved productivity. Above all, the state must provide an enabling environment through the provision of clear policies, strategies and enforceable legal frameworks to support innovation by all the stakeholders in the agricultural sector.

6 | Access to services and farm-level investments on Fast Track Farms[1]

Introduction

The scenic drive from Harare to Bindura used to be a thrilling weekend activity for most 'Hararians' prior to 2000, as they enjoyed the spectacle of farming as seen through lands with impressive crops (maize, cotton, wheat – depending on the time of the year) citrus and livestock. Behind the rows of neatly cropped fields and farm layouts was the 'engine' of the farm's organisation, run by resident farm owners and workers. The impressive physical layouts exhibited by such cropped farms were the result of decades of effort and hard work on the land, as well as systematic investment and support by government and the private sector in the colonial and post-colonial periods. In the first years of the Fast Track Land Reform Programme (FTLRP), the roads leading out of Harare changed. Depending on the time of year, it was not surprising to see much of the land under veldt fire, or overgrown with thick grass, or dotted with some form of pole and dagga huts. However, over the past decade, since the 'new' farmers first settled, meaningful farm investments have eluded the commercial farming areas. While many black people have moved into commercial farming areas, there has been a significant decline in agricultural production and many lost opportunities.

Despite the visible underinvestment, there are a few new farmers who have done their best to invest in agriculture under inordinately difficult circumstances. Clearly, agriculture is now on a path of recovery, but it still requires broader and deeper farmer-focused investments to grow and be self-sustaining. The farming arrangements of the A1 and A2 farmers show serious levels of underinvestment compared with the situation prior to the reforms, and compared with the way of life of the former landowners. When the available resources are considered, especially those provided to the A2 farmers (see Chapter 5), one notices a serious mismatch between such resources and the outputs and lifestyles of the new farmers.

The A1 farmers presented the greatest scope for driving agriculture forward, as can be seen in a variety of studies (Moyo et al., 2009; Marongwe, 2008; Scoones et al., 2010). Investing in people as well as in agricultural hardware is a central issue of the agrarian reforms and is key if those reforms are to move forward. The importance of agriculture and land reform does not just lie in neatly cropped fields; it lies in the end product – food, agricultural products, employment and foreign currency, as well as a generation of people with better standards of living. Therefore investment is central to defining what agriculture means, and what it has to achieve through the reforms and restructuring.

The last ten years of the FTLRP have seen a significant level of disinvestment due to the conflicts that have characterised the programme. There is no doubt that productive infrastructure on the farms, as well as social infrastructure, deteriorated during the height of the acquisition and allocation of land (Marongwe, 2008; Sukume, 2005; Matondi, 2005). A number of reasons account for such deterioration, primarily the conflicts surrounding assets and the fact that the quick forced removal of former owners meant that there was very little time for the handover/takeover of assets. There were allegations of asset stripping by former landowners (Taylor, 2002; Scoones et al., 2010; Moyo, 2008), while some assets were lost during the process of relocation. In large part, the non-existence of policy guidelines – until the formulation of a legal instrument enacted in 2004, the Acquisition of Farm Equipment or Material Act (Chapter 18: 23) – explains the significant asset stripping that went on in the farms in the early period of the FTLRP.

It was perhaps from 2004 onwards that the new farmers (after a few years on their allocated land) began to gain confidence and commenced building capital and a semblance of security in the new farms. Initially, the new farmers avoided huge capital outlays because of the uncertainty of their position. In fact, they first sought to amass (and secure) the equipment of the previous owners. However, in places such as Mazowe, one can identify increases in new housing and the acquisition of farm implements as some of the key investments by new farmers. Such capital investment took place not only at farm level but also at the community level, as proceeds from farming were channelled to public infrastructure such as schools. Given the differences emerging from studies into the status of assets (Moyo, 2008; Scoones et al., 2010), the research sought to establish what investments had been made in Mazowe and Mangwe Districts in the last ten years.

While government moved in to assist farmers with raising their production levels, many private sector companies (including banks) and development agencies shied away from investing capital in the Fast Track Farms (FTFs), ostensibly due to the farms' status as 'contested lands'. In fact, some went to the extent of dissuading those who may have wanted to put resources into the FTFs from doing so, citing a range of economic measures against the Government of Zimbabwe (GoZ), and against the FTF areas in particular. It does not follow, however, that the development agencies invested in the land that was not 'contested'; rather, they focused their resources on humanitarian assistance instead of directing money to long-term investments in irrigation and other productive infrastructure in communal areas which were not contested farms. There is a view that, although humanitarian assistance saved the lives of many people, this was at the expense of long-term investment. In many meetings attended by the author on land and agricultural matters, a strong belief was expressed by government that if such humanitarian funding had been invested in agricultural development, perhaps Zimbabwe would not have needed humanitarian assistance in the first place (meetings with officials in donor organisations and government, October to November 2010). Thus, money directed to humanitarian assistance has to be seen within the context of politics, and its international dimension based on the political questions relating to Zimbabwe at the time; in addition, it is also important to consider it within the context of the effect it has had of stalling investment in agriculture following the land reform programme.

The result was that government was left to shoulder the burden of getting agriculture moving alone,[2] and therefore, as resources were limited, much of its capital was allocated to short-term seasonal production support in the form of inputs (seeds, fertilisers, fuel and tillage). In some cases, the government, through the Ministries of Health and Education, promoted the revival of satellite clinics and schools on the FTFs (explained later in this chapter) as a developmental and social responsibility measure. However, investments in agricultural communities have largely been at a minimal level, and perhaps are insufficient to drive the sector to meet the country's food, product, employment and foreign currency requirements. While some authors (Scoones et al., 2010) believe that significant investments have happened, this chapter shows that there is a need for an in-depth and wide-ranging analysis of the quantity, quality, relevance and sustainability of the types of investment as a basis for determining investment needed in the future.

Typical 'productive farm investments' prior to the Fast Track Land Reform Programme

The newly resettled farmers inherited various assets from the displaced white farmers. On-farm assets prior to the FTLRP included movable and immovable assets used to produce agricultural commodities, and those used to derive a livelihood. Technology, along with the research and development behind it, was a key investment area by government. However, at the level of the farmer, assets and infrastructure, including their maintenance, were key in conducting the farming business (Moyo, 2008). Such assets can be divided into the following categories:

- *cropping assets:* fixed (horticultural produce grading sheds, irrigation systems, greenhouses, engines, water reservoirs, dams, drying rooms, storage tanks, cold rooms) and movable (centre pivots, portable water carriers, tractors, cars, lorries, combine harvesters and accessories);

- *livestock assets:* fixed (sheds, barns, paddocks, internal [paddock] fencing, milking parlours, chicken runs, pigsties) and movable (livestock, spray races);
- *social services:* fixed (living quarters such as farmhouses, farm stores) and movable (cars, etc.); and
- *general farm assets:* drier and grading complexes, grinding mills, silos, fuel tanks, storerooms, external farm perimeter fencing.

The public and private sectors as sources of agricultural investment The colonial government promoted agricultural research biased towards maize, tobacco and beef cattle because of the strategic importance of these commodities in the economic chain and for consumers, both domestic and international. This resulted in intense investment in the area of research, and the establishment of other research stations that focused on other crops and livestock, such as Blackfordby in Mazowe, Henderson Research Institute in Mazowe, Mlezu College in Midlands and Rio Tinto Agricultural College in Kadoma (Mutangadura, 1997). These institutions provided the white farmers with information and knowledge that made farming a success. One of the milestones of the research was the breeding of local maize hybrids that resulted in Southern Rhodesia (now Zimbabwe) becoming the second country after the United States of America to market certified hybrid maize seed in 1949 (Rukuni et al., 2006). There were also government subsidies for the building of agricultural assets; for example, support was given to the white farmers to build soil and conservation works, which saw the building of 5,022 dams (Rukuni and Eicher, 1994).

The independent government also put in place subsidies that enhanced agricultural productivity. Such support was provided through research, extension and infrastructure development by government. For instance, the District Development Fund (DDF) operated at the district level and worked in tandem with the Rural District Councils (RDCs) on the construction and maintenance of secondary roads. In some cases, farmers would use their own resources to assist in the maintenance of roads in the large-scale commercial farming areas, which meant that these areas had fairly well maintained secondary roads. Before the merger of the District Councils (which represented communal areas) and Rural Councils (representing commercial farming areas) in 1988, funds for infrastructure development were provided through taxing landowners and local vehicles. In addition, the government also provided grants to both types of council.

Before the FTLRP, white farmers had a comprehensive telephone network based on a national exchange located in Mazowe District that allowed them to connect internationally and access markets, information and knowledge, finance, inputs and technologies. During the land occupations, a lot of vandalism occurred; this led to the destruction of telecommunication infrastructure.

However, massive investments in telecommunications through cell-phone networks have revived the sector, allowing most farming areas to be connected by phone. Given the reduction in the costs of information communication technology, hardware and service charges, there is a sound basis for using telecommunications for the dissemination of agricultural information.

Compensation issues for land and assets The government acknowledges that the former landowners made significant investment in commercial agriculture and will need to be paid for their effort. This has been a consistent message since the insertion of a provision that government would pay for any improvements on acquired land in the draft (rejected) constitution in 2000; this principle has been restated in amendments to the constitution made in 2000 and in 2005, as well as in provisions provided for in the Global Political Agreement (GPA) of 2008. Unfortunately, such a commitment has not been matched with action, given that the government had no resources to pay compensation, especially as it became fiscally stretched with an economy run mostly on domestic finances. In fact, by 2009, only 297 out of the 2,721 farmers who had been transferred on to state land had been paid compensation. However, 900 farms had been valued for compensation purposes by that time. Former commercial farmers in Mazowe have not received compensation, nor have white landowners in other districts.

However, the issue of compensation is complex and reflects divergent political views. This starts right at the fundamental level of the valuation of improvements made to properties. Rukuni et al. (2009) noted that the figures provided by the key actors for land and past investment compensation were unrealistic (relative to the Zimbabwean economy and the total agricultural assets the country holds). For instance, the Commercial Farmers' Union (CFU) is said to have suggested various compensation figures of between US $5 billion and $15 billion.[3] The *Daily News* (2003) reported that, according to the CFU, farm equipment alone worth 75 billion Zimbabwean dollars (US $1 billion) had been looted or destroyed on commercial farms since the beginning of the land reform programme in 2000.[4] The government estimated a total figure for compensating farmers at US $6.314 billion. This figure was arrived at by using an average figure of US $1 million per farm, which covered both land and improvements, multiplied by the number of gazetted farms, which stood at 6,314 (MLRR, 2009). The white farmers' group Justice for Agriculture (JAG) in its proposed lawsuit claimed that the government was supposed to pay an estimated US $7 billion compensation (in 2003) for land and improvements on all acquired farms (Rukuni et al. 2009); this figure included values for both land and improvements and for loss of income due to disruptions on farms.

In informal discussions with the author, donors pointed out that if ex-commercial farmers got anything close to US $3 billion they would be very lucky. This was because there was a need for an analysis of the proportionality of compensation relative to the wider economy and wider needs of the country. Zimbabwe's total economic output (gross domestic product [GDP]) by 2009 was not much more than US $3 billion, with liabilities in terms of debt and arrears of over US $7 billion. As the country's liabilities were already more than double its GDP, the billions of US dollars in compensation were unrealistic (interview with an official working for a donor agency, March 2010). In addition, subsidies, which were derived from all Zimbabwean taxpayers, went into commercial agriculture and significantly benefited the former landowners for any improvements that they made, so the value of these should also be taken into account. However, isolating those subsidies from the actual effort of the landowners is not easy, which means that all affected parties have to sit down and negotiate on the actual compensation that will need to be provided to the former owners, and also to the farmworkers.

According to farmers in Mazowe, new landowners were also waiting to see what the government would do on compensation issues, given the past government subsidies (focus group discussions [FGDs], June 2007). The argument was that if the government was prepared to pay the former owners compensation, then public subsidies to new farmers should continue, given that commercial agriculture was heavily subsidised in the past. Some felt that the compensation issue was a matter for government and the former landowners, and it had nothing to do with them; they were simply happy to be on the land. However, there were also strong views that payment for the past investments in infrastructure should be made so that the 'court issues' could come to a halt, as these were a major hindrance to the growth of assets and related production on the farms. Others were of the opinion that those who took the personal effects of former owners will need to pay for them or give them back, because it was 'uncultured' to take the personal property (goods for domestic use) of other people.

At the same time, some noted that it is difficult to account for the assets, given the *jambanja* and the rapid flight from some farms by landowners, some of whom left their farms to be taken care of by managers. The caretaker managers were accused by the new farmers of looting the properties, while others place the blame squarely on the new farmers. There was also a view that compensation for fixed infrastructure could be paid despite years of deterioration. Some exiting farmers who had ample time managed to develop registers of their assets; less fortunate farmers were unable to do this, as the rapid farm invasions did not leave them time to account for everything. Some have maintained the farm records that they kept and are using these as a basis for their case for compensation for improvements, as agreed to by government. However, the value of any compensation is contested in terms of: a) discounting for government (i.e. taxpayer) support, before and after independence; and b) the actual valuation of the assets then and now, taking into account wear and tear. These are issues that require some negotiation at a political level based on the calculations that the different land and property valuers (for the former landowners or for the government) have come up with.

Typical farmer-led 'public' social investments prior to fast track

The previous farm owners invested heavily in social service infrastructures that were significant in keeping farmworkers captive as workers. In fact, the children of farmworkers accessed basic education that locked them into the social culture of the farming compounds, where education was not regarded as a priority. This was at a time when there were few opportunities outside the farms. However, although these social infrastructures were important, they tended to keep farmworkers isolated from the wider society, and produced children whose ambition was often to become farmworkers themselves.

In this concept of 'captivity', a key intervention was the establishment of farm stores operated by the former landowners. These farm stores were known to have been a means of tying farmworkers to specific farms and farmers. One way in which the former owners did this was through providing credit at the local farm store, in a process described as *'nyora kumusana'* (writing on the back). This means that groceries would be provided as a loan, and the store would then charge the value to each worker at the end of the month (FGDs with serving and ex-farmworkers, June 2007). The farmworkers got access to groceries and other household goods on credit. Given their very low salaries, the farmworkers became perpetually indebted to the landowner. This was because, by the end of the month, they did not have any disposable cash, and they had to borrow goods again the following month. This had the knock-on effect of tying them to the landowner as a source of labour on an almost permanent basis. The farm owners also made it difficult for farmworkers to move from one farm to another or to escape an almost slave-like life on the farms. This is what Rutherford (2001) described as 'domestic government'.

Yet, at the same time, the owners also played at philanthropy, providing services such as clinics, schools, access to transport and sports sponsorship. At a strategic level, the farmer wanted the farmworker tied to the farm – socially, economically and for reasons of governance – through these minimal social investments. This was strikingly described by one War Veteran as: 'not making you rich and neither poor, but somewhere closer to the poor and tying you to the farm owner' (key informant interview, 3 June 2004). The farm owner built on this with exclusive farm-compound social activities. One example was allowing public places for beer drinking; another was the promotion of imported cultural activities (Nyau dances of Malawian origin), that became specific to commercial farms. Such cultural fortification strategies provided the farmworkers with a unique social space, tending to isolate them from the common Zimbabwean rural or urban space. Such a strategy was also replicated in the mining areas. The effect was that when *jambanja* visited the farms, it was convenient to regard most of the farmworkers as alien. Yet the War Veteran (key informant interview, 3 June 2004) described this as:

> well calculated to keep farmworkers within sight, but also 'far away' in a literal sense. The ex-farmworkers never bothered to look at the life of the 'boss', living in a large farmhouse with all the paraphernalia of swimming pools, tennis courts, bar areas, large living rooms, driving nice cars, all proceeds of the farmworker's sweat and that of the land. Yet they were squatting in some compounds dotted with pole and dagga huts.

Following the takeover of commercial farms, the new beneficiaries adopted very highly developed farms (although, of course, the farm compounds were not as developed). Immediately, they enjoyed unfettered access to social clubs of a very high standard (sports facilities, private bars, gymnasiums, etc.). However, they did not have time to learn that running such infrastructure requires high levels of management skills, money, time and effort, as well as farmer networking to build a community of investors: people willing to part with cash in order to enjoy the benefits. The new beneficiaries simply ran the clubs down. Equally, the ex-farmworkers, by virtue of their class and low income, were excluded from using such facilities before and after *jambanja*.

FDGs with farmworkers (June 2007) showed the nostalgia that ex-farmworkers felt about their former farm 'bosses'. For instance, they pointed out that the farmer used to provide transport for the children to the nearest registered school 10 km away. The 'madam' (wife of the farmer) would run a crèche and a small health facility that workers could access. Social clubs and care for orphans were some of the other cited cases of extra benefits available to farmworkers. Key informant interviews in 2004 revealed a range of social investments by the former farm owners. In some farms, the former owners installed televisions and video recorders in public places, while providing things such as radios to pre-schools. At Mackay[5] Farm, the owners used to invest in social competitions: for instance, house or yard competitions were organised by the 'boss', with prizes being given for the most hygienic house. The winners would be awarded with pots and other items. On a farm called Donitto, the former owner created an old people's home with a dormitory with running water. This significant social infrastructure investment had the cumulative effect of making the farmworkers see life through the lens of the former farm owners.

Changing farm demography and the pressure on social services GoZ has a variety of legislation in place to meet human needs. Access to water, housing, energy, education and health are all regulated by certain statutes that seek to ensure an equitable use of these services. Provision of education, safe drinking water and health are fundamental human rights enshrined in international statutes that GoZ has signed. Experience in the newly resettled areas, however, has demonstrated how it has been difficult to adhere to these statutes. GoZ had neither the money nor the capacity to provide social amenities when the FTLRP started, and, while acknowledging such limitations, it strongly believed that its actions (land takeovers) were necessary. Early in the reforms, the then Minister of Foreign Affairs affirmed that:

> We cannot hide the fact that the Fast Track Programme has room for improvements. For example, the settlers require access roads, water supplies, schools, clinics, dip tanks, draught power, initial seeds and fertilisers, extension services, training and many more which the government is unable to provide at present. If we get some help, some of these facilities can be provided to the settlers.[6]

Farmers settled on the FTFs experienced myriad challenges as they realised how different life really was in the new settlements compared with where they came from. The wider Zimbabwean context over the past ten years has been that a searing economic and political heatwave has led to the suffering of rural people in particular. Those in the newly resettled areas were faced with their own specific problems, due mainly to the inadequacy of basic social services in these areas. The changes in the demographics of the farming communities and the movement of many people into the new resettlement areas led to an increased demand for diverse social services, including health, education, energy and housing, to cater for the increasing population.

The expected mass exodus of ex-farmworkers and the influx of displaced farmworkers into peri-urban settlements such as Harare never materialised. In Mazowe, the research team did not see roadside and river-bank squatter settlements, which means that somehow the ex-farmworkers have integrated with the new communities. Therefore, significant demographic change has occurred, and this has impacted on the social and economic investments expected to service the communities. In Mazowe, on average each of the 6,000 farmer families comprised eight people (including adults and children), which means that in a short space of time 48,000 people moved into the resettlement areas,[7] thus placing pressure on the available physical resources.

The emergence of new resettlement communities was accompanied by the fast track establishment of social services such as health centres and temporary schools. The schools were termed satellite schools because they were linked to the main established centres, but they had inadequate resources (teachers and equipment). The institutions that had previously been provided by large-scale commercial farmers were either no longer available or were unable to cope with the increase in numbers. For instance, before the land reform programme, fewer than 500 farmers with an average of 50 workers each resided in Mazowe District. The infrastructure in these areas was geared to meet the needs of a population of fewer than 24,000 people. After resettlement, there was double this number resident in the commercial farming areas, demanding access to social infrastructure. The numbers included not just the new A1 and A2 farmers, but also their families, farmworkers and service providers such as teachers, nurses and miners. Therefore the existing infrastructure failed to cope with the arrival of huge numbers of people. It must be remembered that forward planning was suspended; the focus was on ensuring that people claimed their land. However, as they moved and settled, the new farmers maintained their original farming homes – if they had such homes – as a risk insurance strategy and to ensure that their children had access to schools.

Conflicts discouraging investment in Fast Track Farms

The FTLRP was a shock to many people, but especially to the financial and services institutions, with their formalised, structured and planned way of operating. Agricultural systems were disrupted as banks shied away from lending to farmers, while service providers and retailers of major agro-capital kept away. Some creditors pushed former landowners for repayment of debts, while some banks went to court to attach equipment to outstanding loans. The case of Barclays of Zimbabwe versus the proprietors of Kondozi Estate in Manicaland was one such example.[8] The *Herald* reported:

> Agricultural machinery and other farm equipment at Kondozi farm was
> yesterday placed under provisional judicial management by the high court.
> This followed an application by Barclays Bank at the high court seeking an
> order compelling ARDA [Agricultural Rural Development Authority] to return
> all the machinery and equipment the bank leased to Mr Edwin Moyo and the
> De Klerk family, the owners of Canvest (Pvt) Ltd which used to run Kondozi.
> Barclays Bank said that it owned the equipment, which Canvest was using on a
> rent-to-buy basis.[9]

In any case, during the early stages of implementation, some white farmers took away with them movable assets such as irrigation equipment, tractors and farm implements. In the course of the fieldwork, the Ruzivo Trust team saw many productive and non-productive assets lying idle and derelict. There were widespread reports of equipment being vandalised, especially during *jambanja*, examples including the pouring of concrete into boreholes at Salaina Farm. At Handa Farm, storage tanks and irrigation pipes lie idle. Attempts at sharing irrigation equipment in particular led to friction and fights among A1 farmers. At Birga Farm, the irrigation equipment available was inadequate due to a lack of pumps, eliciting tussles between the new settlers. At Une and Brent, the farmers managed to find a way of sharing the pipes and ensuring that the irrigation system was functional. In cases where an A2 farmer and A1 farmers were allocated land on the same farm, serious problems of management and ownership of assets arose; this was the case on Chinudu Farm and the ARDA farms. In all cases, the A2 farmers inherited most of the farm assets and refused to share them with the A1 farmers.

In much of the discussion on property loss, the focus has been either on the productive infrastructure or on the social services invested in by the former landowners. Rarely has consideration been given to the asset losses of the poor, particularly the farmworkers. Significant assets were lost during the early years of the FTLRP, as the land occupiers targeted farmworkers as a form of political shock therapy, making the statement clear that they should not support the former landowners. During *jambanja*, farmworkers had to flee their homes, meaning that they often could not take their belongings. At times, as the invasions happened, they had to hide through fear of physical violence. While this was going on, the landowners were not able to protect them as they were also struggling with the land occupiers, who had adopted the twin approach of confronting the owners and isolating them from their farmworkers, so each group was left to literally fight their own battles. In the compounds, some of the farmworkers had their houses demolished and the contents destroyed; pictures appeared on international television networks showing compounds being burnt.

However, in some cases, burning took place as a counterattack against farmworkers who organised themselves to attack resettled farmers, and, in the process, assets were destroyed.[10] Sometimes, the occupiers took food and utensils, and whatever contents they wanted to use while they were on the farms. More generally, as they waited for orderly resettlement, it seems that the settlers began to demand food and transport while they lived on the farms.[11] While in some cases the War Veterans and military discouraged the practice of looting, their numbers were too small for them to properly monitor the civilians (key informant interview, 22 March 2004). As a result, some of the occupiers took some valuable items and destroyed others, with various types of asset falling victim to the raids.

Squabbles among new settlers over inherited assets At the outset, squabbles emerged as land occupiers targeted assets for a variety of reasons. Over time, the land allocation extended to a fight over equipment between the land occupiers and the new owners (those who had been officially allocated the land). Given the importance of such equipment to agricultural production and productivity, both land occupiers and new farmers fought over access to and ownership of equipment. For instance, the settlers at Saratoga Farm on the Shamva road pointed out that some ZANU-PF officials were conniving with senior government officers to deny them farming equipment seized from white former commercial farmers. A row had also erupted among new farmers resettled in Mashonaland East after some farming equipment, which they say was designated for their use, was found hidden on a farm belonging to a top politician. The politician was claimed to have said that 'the equipment was brought to his farm without his knowledge'.[12]

It would appear that the government was relatively unconcerned about the looting. However, it did warn that it was illegal for any farmer to move out or withhold movable assets used for agricultural purposes from acquired farms.[13] This intention was followed by the announcement that the government would compulsorily acquire various idle agricultural equipment and machinery from farms previously occupied by white commercial farmers and was now allocating the equipment to farmers engaged in wheat production. At Saratoga, the equipment identified as idle included 140 tractors, seven combine harvesters, 14 trailers and 3,262 irrigation pipes.[14]

The government decided to put in place a legal instrument in the form of the Acquisition of Farm Equipment and Material Bill, which sought to provide for the acquisition of farm equipment or material not being used for agricultural purposes. According to the Presidential Powers (Temporary Measures) Acquisition of Farm Equipment or Material Regulations 2004, 'no owner or holder of farm equipment or material shall wilfully demolish, damage, alter or impair the farm equipment or material or cause any other person to do this without the permission of the Minister of Lands, Agriculture and Rural Resettlement'.[15]

Several reasons explain why this instrument was enacted. While former landowners saw it as political harassment, the new farmers and bureaucrats in government justified it for the following reasons: a) in the past the government had provided favourable incentives and subsidies for these assets; b) it was alleged that most of the sound agricultural equipment had been smuggled out of the country to neighbouring Mozambique and Zambia by former commercial farmers who migrated following the launch of the FTLRP,[16] and that there was no justification for this, given the subsidies they had received, so there was a need to stop any further movement of equipment out of the country; and c) a lot of equipment that was previously used on the acquired farms was lying idle since most of the resettled farmers could not afford to purchase it owing to prohibitive prices. There was, therefore, a need to ensure that all farm equipment was being used productively, and contributing to economic development, hence the proposal to compulsorily acquire farm equipment at the time of the occupation of the farm.[17] This would also mean that the previous owner would cease all farming activities; the assumption was that at the point of occupation, the previous landowner would be redundant and would not require the equipment anyway, as the land would have been taken away.

New farmers lobbied through political channels for this, yet some politicians were accused of using this legal instrument to loot equipment. Cases of politicians being prosecuted over the alleged illegal takeover of various types of farming equipment continued to be reported up until 2011.

The law referred to earlier had stated that compensation for farm equipment was to be determined within a reasonable time by the evaluating officer assigned by the Acquisition Authority. However, some white farmers were evicted at later stages of the FTLRP implementation and were forced to leave all farming equipment and materials without a valuation being carried out; this was done later and in their absence. This still raises conflicts at the ministerial level today whenever the issue of compensation is raised, as farmers refuse such valuation outcomes.

The government did not have a clear-cut policy on what should happen to immovable assets such as houses, barns and dams. The use and sharing of this property created conflict and tension among the new farmers. Farmhouses were occupied by people who had led the *jambanja*, such as War Veterans, senior army officials and government officials. They were given a caretaking role over all assets on A1 schemes. However, by 2005 the government's stated 'policy on shared infrastructure' reserved homesteads for use by civil servants working on the FTFs. On the A2 schemes, the infrastructure and equipment were taken over by the new farmers, and the government stated that eventually the farmers would pay market values for the properties. It is not clear if this was ever done.

By 2007, conflicts were emerging between some caretakers and the new farmers over the control and use of farm equipment and infrastructure. For example, at Selby Farm the caretaker was accused of removing movable equipment from the farm. Houses were converted for various uses, such as classrooms at Wychwood Farm, a clinic at Davaar Farm and accommodation for civil servants at Hariana.

Investment in agriculture-related assets by new farmers

From an investment and asset-building perspective, the beneficiaries in the A1 scheme in the majority of cases are people who are just about able to meet their basic needs but whose livelihoods are precariously balanced. In other words, these farmers are unlikely to be able to pool resources to invest in public infrastructure and are unable to build or buy complex and expensive assets (combine harvesters), construct farm roads or invest in dams without any form of external support. These farmers are likely to suffer from a lack of access to markets and may not have good crop storage facilities. After a period of time they may be able to improve their housing conditions and afford services (financial, healthcare, etc.) in their vicinity.

Many A1 farmers moved with low-level equipment on to the farms. The new settlers used small types of agricultural equipment (hoes, ploughs, picks, spades, axes, wheelbarrows and ox-drawn cultivators), while a few invested in tractor-mounted discs, trailers, etc. In 2004, the majority of the newly resettled farmers owned small, non-motorised equipment and implements. A few of the newly resettled farmers owned medium to large non-motorised equipment and implements such as cultivators, harrows and scotch carts. An even smaller percentage owned motorised equipment such as water pumps and tractors.

TABLE 6.1 The tractor situation in Mazowe District in 2004

Ownership	Number of tractors
Indigenous	68
Whites	40
Institutions	64
Companies	44
DDF (hired to farmers) (8 working)	15
Resettled farmers (A1 and A2)	123
Total	354

Source: Agritex, 2004.

Most of the new farmers were relying on government sources for tillage units for ploughing and disking. The fleet of tractors and draught animals in the country was not sufficient to till the land of all the needy farmers. The land reform programme stretched tillage resources as more land was cleared to augment existing farming areas. The DDF tillage services could not cope with demand: for example, only about half of the tractors allocated to Mazowe District were in working order during the 2004/05 season (see Table 6.1) and only 26 per cent of the ploughs were working. In the same season, the district had an allocation of only four planters; only one was in working order. As a result, some farmers resorted to practising zero tillage.

The equipment obtained on the farms was used under diverse types of sharing arrangements and on a cost-sharing basis. However, as new farmers continued to invest in their own equipment, a significant number disengaged from sharing, opting for personal ownership of equipment as a basis for eliminating conflicts. Therefore, by 2007, much of the equipment was owned by the new settlers, with fewer incidences of hiring and/or sharing, except in the case of fixed infrastructure. There was an improvement in the type of assets owned by new settlers from 2007 onwards, as the A1 farmers were managing to harvest and market their crops on a commercial and consistent basis. The A2 farmers indicated that when tenure insecurity is resolved, it provides scope for investing resources on their plots.

Some farmers have invested in motorised transport. However, their current income levels do not allow them to purchase good-quality transport that lasts for a long time. Most of the vehicles bought by tobacco farmers in the Mvurwi area of Mazowe tend to be suitable only for urban areas and cannot withstand the rough terrain on the farms. The majority of the second-hand vehicles on the district's roads were cheap Asian imports not suitable for rough, tropical African roads. Before the land reform programme began in 2000, white commercial farmers knew that each season they could purchase new vehicles and high-quality spare parts. This is no longer possible. Interviews with a manager (Harare, March 2007) of a Toyota vehicle retailer showed how the farm vehicle scheme they used to run collapsed after the land reform programme. In the past, each year he would order a certain number of vehicles, and often he could not meet the demand of the farming community. Today, he said, 'You will be lucky to get significant purchases.'

Non-agricultural investments since land reform

Access and investment in education The major finding from the fieldwork in Mazowe and Mangwe is that the children in the newly resettled areas face an uncertain future because of the sorry state of education in the districts. The research revealed a number of outstanding issues, including low enrolment in the newly resettled areas, lack of proper infrastructure for children with special needs, lack of textbooks and teaching materials, poor support from government and councils, and a low rate of fee payment by students. GoZ seemed to have adopted a strategy of resettlement first, services later (GoZ, 2001). Schools in the newly resettled areas were, therefore, set up with only minimum requirements being met, such as sanitation and qualified staff.

There are distinct and important differences between A1 and A2 farmers in terms of accessibility to education. Most A2 farmers are not resident with their families on the farms on a permanent basis, as most retain a home elsewhere. In many cases, distance to social services (schools and hospitals) is not a major hindrance to A2 farmers because they can afford to live off-farm, have transport to get to the nearest service centre, or send their children to boarding schools. These types of farmers have greater social and political connections, and greater skills, education levels and assets, enabling them to pursue economic opportunities, access and benefit from development services, and take positive action to improve their situation (for example, investing in preventative healthcare and educating their children). Children of A1 farmers struggle to access mostly public education facilities. If the distance to the school is great, they opt to leave their children in the communal areas to ensure that they have access to education.

Through an exercise to establish the number of schools in Mazowe District in 2004, it was determined that before 2000 there were 44 schools in the commercial farming area and since the FTLRP some 26 satellite schools had been

Box 6.1 Description of two schools in Mazowe

Hariana school near Mvurwi is situated in the former farm compound. Farm compound houses have been turned into classrooms and offices. The rooms do not have cement floors, so there is a problem of dust and general hygiene. There is an unprotected well less than 200 metres from the school. This was originally dug for the school but is now being used by the whole community, which makes it impossible to maintain the hygiene of the well. The school is using the seven VIP (ventilated improved pit) or Blair toilets that were already part of the farm compound, and they have plans to build their own toilets. Wynchwood in Barwick ICA is located in the former farmhouse, which has several rooms. The school fits into the house because it teaches only four grades (zero to three).

sited and pegged in the new resettlement areas. Children were using farmhouses, sheds and tobacco barns, with some learning under trees. The Prime Minister of Zimbabwe was shocked when he found, in Mazowe Central constituency, that:

> pupils at Maodzwa primary school in Mashonaland Central's Mazowe Central constituency have to endure the smell of raw cow dung as they go about their classes. The conditions at this cattle pen-cum-school are at variance with the top-notch learning institutions attended by children of top government officials … So astonished was Tsvangirai that he could not help but yell at an aide: '*Huya uone zvirimuno*' (come and witness this) as he was negotiating his way round rows of cow dung in what doubled as a classroom …[18]

In general, the schools lack materials such as boards, proper ventilation and stationery. Examples of such schools are given in Box 6.1. In Mazowe there are few secondary schools, while the primary school enrolment is very high. In 2007, there were 28 satellite primary schools[19] in Mazowe compared with eight satellite secondary schools. Due to the serious shortage of teachers, some primary schools have been forced to introduce 'composite' classes. This is when one teacher teaches two grades at the same time, dividing their time between the classes. At Hariana school, the pupils of different grades sat in the same classroom and the teacher took turns to teach them (Box 6.1). There were about 30 to 50 pupils per class with a few textbooks that are given from the 'mother' schools, which are also under severe pressure. In some cases, A1 and A2 farmers tried to provide money for the acquisition of materials. In some of the schools, the only book was the one the teacher used for the instruction of pupils. In grade one, on average 10 to 15 pupils shared one book, while there were no books in grade two in some schools. More worryingly, many of the schools lacked clean water and adequate sanitation, and they did not provide a conducive learning environment.

The Mazowe RDC made rough calculations and found that pupils attending primary school travel on average 2.7 km, while those in secondary school travel 5.9 km. In some cases this led children to drop out, while other children stayed in unsupervised temporary lodgings during the week. The 2004 sample survey (n=539) showed that on average 59 per cent of primary school children were walking less than 1 km to school in the A1 scheme (Table 6.2). In terms of secondary education, the majority of the children walked 2.1 km to 3 km; there was no major difference in distances between the A1 and A2 farms. This reflects the fact that parents risked bringing their children to the resettlement areas in part because the children could then provide labour on the farms. The averages from the sample show that the distance travelled for secondary education was within a reasonable range compared with national averages of more than 6 km. The national results could be attributed to sample coverage: there are some wards without any schools but with significantly high populations.

TABLE 6.2 Distance to primary and secondary schools in resettlement areas in Mazowe

Distance (km)	Primary				Secondary			
	A1		A2		A1		A2	
	No.	%	No.	%	No.	%	No.	%
0–1	24	59	2	10	15	13	14	15
1.1–2	10	24	9	43	37	33	19	21
2.1–3	2	5	3	14	37	33	30	33
3.1–4	0	0	4	19	11	10	11	12
4.1–5	2	5	2	10	5	4	12	13
>5	3	7	1	5	7	6	6	7
Total	41	100	21	100	112	100	92	100

Source: Ruzivo survey, 2004.

In Mangwe, two new schools were established in the new communities. Watershed primary school, for the children of A1 farmers, was developed by surrounding villages that pooled resources and started to build the school from the ground. Each household contributed 300 bricks, and they managed to build two classrooms and a cottage (the teacher's house). Mabhungu school was developed from a farm garage that was renovated and partitioned by A1 farmers to form classrooms. The school was partitioned in 2007 and two classrooms were created for several hundred pupils. However, there was no accommodation for teachers.

In both Mazowe and Mangwe Districts, the schools were built by A1 settlers who pulled their resources together after identifying a real need within their communities. No responsible authority has been defined yet in these cases, i.e. it is not clear whether the schools are government, council, church or privately owned schools. Thus, the two schools in Mangwe were not officially registered by the Ministry of Education because it was said that 'they do not have responsible authorities', an argument that was difficult to interpret. It was also claimed that their sites were not permanent, and that this made it difficult for the Ministry of Education, Sport and Culture to plan and develop these schools. The result was stagnation in the development of the schools.

In Marula Ward in Mangwe there were four primary schools with 528 pupils. As of 2007, there were 23 vacancies for teachers, and the situation showed no prospect of improvement, given that conventional schools (as opposed to satellite schools) were also suffering from a shortage of teachers. It should also be noted that the four villages in this resettlement area were scattered over a large area and it was difficult for children to walk from one village to another to attend school, as the distances involved were very great. The whole area, in which A1, A2 and three-tier (a model resettlement specifically designed for drier areas, where parts of the acquired farms were to be used for cattle grazing) farmers are settled, did not have a secondary school. Farmers were concerned because this negatively affected children through poor socialisation, as children were being sent to live with various relatives in urban centres with variable levels of care and support. Those children who could not be sent to boarding schools ended up getting inadequate schooling, which was reflected in poor school performance and high drop-out levels. This trend is seen particularly where parents decide to migrate to neighbouring countries, leaving their children to be educated in Zimbabwe.

The government has tried to control these schools in a contradictory manner. Although it was not contributing anything to the schools, apart from attempts to provide teachers,[20] the government insisted on maintaining relatively low tuition fees. This means that though education was affordable, it remained inaccessible because of the distances pupils had to walk. In addition, the low fees charged because of government price controls meant that the quality of public education remained very low as schools could not acquire learning materials such as books or chalk.

Access and investment in health infrastructure and services The health system in the newly resettled areas has faced many challenges, especially at a time when the impact of HIV and AIDS was at its peak in the early years of the FTLRP. With surges in the movement of people, the available infrastructure and personnel on the FTFs could not cope with the high demand for health services. However, efforts have been made by government and local authorities to address the challenges. One of the goals of the Ministry of Health and Child Welfare in its 1999–2007 national health strategy was to ensure that at least one health centre is located within 8 km to 10 km of each household. When the FTLRP was implemented, the provision of social amenities such as clinics (GoZ, 2001) appeared to be sidelined. It was only after people had settled that the government began to open clinics within the newly resettled areas using existing structures on the farms such as farmhouses, which were turned into clinics and residences for nurses and their families.

In Mazowe, by 2007 there were 31 health centres in the district; the number had increased by two since the 2004/05 survey. These centres included four hospitals, of which one, Howard, was a mission hospital run by the Salvation Army church, and the other three were owned and run by the government. There were 27 clinics, of which 20 were owned and run by the Mazowe RDC (which also ran one mobile clinic) and the rest were either privately owned or owned by mines or churches. Of these 20 RDC health centres, ten were located in Chiweshe communal lands, another nine were located in the new resettlement farming communities, and one was located in a small town, Glendale.

At the start of the FTLRP, nine sites were approved for the establishment of clinics in the resettlement areas. Of the nine approved clinics, six were functional. Reasons given as to why some clinics were still non-functional about seven years after the resettlement programme included the refusal by some farmers to release farmhouses to be converted into clinics and staff quarters. For instance, at Montgomery a clinic was opened in 2004 and was closed after a week because an A2 farmer refused to release a house that was supposed to be used for the accommodation of health personnel. Five of the six functional clinics are farmhouses that were converted and only one, Holme Eden, was a properly established clinic; this was opened in 1985, well before the FTLRP. No haste was evident in the reinstatement of Holme Eden, in contrast to the health centres established during the FTLRP.

There were other private health facilities offering a regular monthly mobile service in the former commercial farming areas. However, the public health facilities largely depended on public resources, and used farmhouses that were converted into clinics. Many of the buildings did not meet the minimum health standards because the architectural design was meant for residential purposes. For instance, in some of the clinics there were no drug rooms (or refrigerators) and the drugs were shelved in a fitted cabinet. The clinics were underequipped and understaffed. They faced a huge challenge in acquiring drugs, bandages and other necessary items to care for the sick.

In Mangwe, health provision and availability remained a serious problem due to shrinking per capita allocation, high staff attrition and shortages of drugs and equipment due to foreign currency constraints. There was only one clinic (at the Marula Business Centre) that was built before the start of the resettlement programme. Some farmers had to travel more than 50 km to their nearest health centre, while other patients had to visit health centres in Matobo District, as they were nearer than Marula clinic. The mobile clinic offered by the Ministry of Health and Child Welfare and the RDC has been hampered by a lack of funds.

The issue of access to a health facility is related to affordability, which is determined by class and status in Zimbabwe; the differences in access to health services between A1 and A2 farmers is telling. On the other hand, farmworkers and ex-farmworkers had experience of shortages and did not have the same expectations (Amanor-Wilks, 1995; Rutherford, 2001). The A2 farmers in Mazowe are mostly employed, non-resident farmers who have access to urban health centres, specialist doctors, 24-hour ambulance services and pharmacies. Poorer A1 farmers residing in the newly resettled areas in Mangwe and Mazowe do not have access to such services. The survey showed that there are no ambulance services in the newly resettled areas in the two districts, and pharmacies are available only at the business centres. The pharmacies, especially in Mangwe, are also poorly stocked with medication. As shown in Table 6.3, the distance to the nearest health facility decreased between 2004 and 2007. In 2004, 40 per cent of the respondents used to walk 7 km to 10 km, and by 2007 the majority (81 per cent) of respondents in Mazowe walked 1 km to 3 km to the nearest clinic. In Mangwe, there were key challenges with distance, because the area is sparsely populated, which makes it expensive for government and local authorities to establish health facilities. However, while access is very good in terms of distance, the major problem occurs with the quality of healthcare provided by these clinics.

TABLE 6.3 Distance to the nearest clinic in Mazowe

| Distance (km) | 2004 survey (n=251) | | | | 2007 survey (n=539) | | | |
| | A1 | | A2 | | A1 | | A2 | |
	No.	%	No.	%	No.	%	No.	%
< 1	8	10	0	0	5	1	0	0
1–3	11	14	10	20	409	93	26	37
4–6	9	11	14	27	11	3	31	44
7–10	33	41	20	39	10	2	8	11
> 10	20	25	7	14	3	1	6	8
Total	81	100	51	100	438	100	71	100
Not answered	39	32.5	50	49.5	16	3.0	14	2.6

Source: Ruzivo surveys, 2004 and 2007.

In Mangwe there are limited health facilities: for example, in Marula Ward there is one clinic for 1,788 people. There were plans to renovate a farmhouse at Hannyvale into a clinic; however, this was hampered by lack of resources and poor co-ordination. The chief executive officer of Mangwe RDC pointed out that new farmers still owe the RDC huge amounts in rates, which could be channelled into social services provision such as the building and maintenance of clinics. The FTLRP in Mangwe created an emergency health situation in the new resettlement area, yet no agencies – private, public or developmental – have intervened. A key informant interviewee described the health situation as sometimes resembling 'collective punishment of the poor for taking over white farms' (interview, 3 September 2012).

The housing dilemma and efforts at construction With or without the land reform programme, the majority of people have faced a housing dilemma in Zimbabwe. The problem of rural housing necessitated the formation of a ministry specifically to address the housing challenges in 2005. However, the Ministry of National Housing and Social Amenities has been hamstrung by resource challenges, while local authorities have shelved housing construction and are instead selling housing stands for people to develop and construct their own houses. Private developers have also stayed away, because the costs involved are not matched by profits. The FTFs face enormous challenges, as newly resettled people are expected to take responsibility for their own housing needs at a time when housing finance systems are still weak. The movement of people on to the FTFs has created a housing catastrophe that no single farmer is able to shoulder.

The movement of large numbers of people into the newly resettled areas brought with it serious demands on housing and sanitation. Before 2000, one white farmer would have his main farmhouse, cottages, servants' quarters, and farmworkers' compound; together, these could accommodate an average of 60 workers in an area that now accommodates far more people, including A1 farmers, their families and their workers, all of whom require shelter. Due to the adoption of a fast track model, the government openly stated that it would not deliver everything, but instead would provide minimum infrastructure (GoZ, 2001). The government had neither the money nor the time to offer housing to new farmers. The beneficiaries, in turn, were equally unable to plan adequately for their housing needs, since they moved on to the farms very quickly. In the initial stages until around 2003/04, the new farmers merely built temporary shacks, which are now slowly being replaced with permanent structures.

At the inception of the FTLRP, the living quarters in particular houses were occupied by people who spearheaded the *jambanja*; these included ordinary people, War Veterans, senior army officials and government officials. These people were accorded a caretaker role at each farm, with the responsibility for supervising all farm assets, especially on the farms in the A1 schemes. Through the 'policy on shared infrastructure', drafted in late 2005, the government reserved homesteads for use by civil servants. As a result, some of the houses were occupied by government workers and others were turned into schools and clinics. Conflicts over the ownership of the properties were, however, inevitable. Some new farmers took over houses that were being used by farmworkers, while others constructed new houses for themselves. For the A2 farmers, the housing situation did not differ greatly from what had existed before the resettlement, especially where the beneficiary received land that included a farmhouse and a compound.

Before they were officially settled, the land occupiers still had to find shelter in the structures on the farms. This included invading farmhouses and some houses in the compounds that were meant for farmworkers. During this inception phase, the government itself was ambivalent about the whole process of land reform. This was evident when it advised settlers not to build permanent structures on the farms they were occupying; this advice was reported by some interviewees in Mazowe and confirmed by Agritex officers. This policy showed a certain amount of indecisiveness and created ambiguity over the land reform and investment options available to settlers, making it unclear whether they should or should not build temporary or permanent habitation. Most large-scale A2 farmers in Mazowe, however, took over farmhouses, thus facing little challenge in terms of shelter personally, but they did face the challenge of providing housing for their workers, who had to compete with serving and ex-farmworkers in the compounds.

Government policy was such that A1 settlers had to construct houses on stands of 1 acre (0.4047 ha), while A2 farmers could freely choose much larger sites. In Mangwe, those in the three-tier model did not have any problems, since they continued to reside in their communal homes. Civil servants in resettlement areas had their housing requirements given priority, especially on farms with farmhouses. Depending on their needs, settlers who would have occupied farmhouses agreed (willingly or with resentment) to vacate the farmhouses in order to create space for nurses, teachers, police officers, Agritex personnel or natural resources management officials. However, forced movement sometimes met with resistance, and in the process created conflicts between the settlers and government officials in the new resettlement areas.

The external and internal makeup of the farmhouses also determined the nature of occupancy. Civil servants in various ministries were asked to share main farmhouses. The original farmhouses had running internal water and sewage systems, while outside there were manicured lawns and sporting infrastructure (tennis courts, swimming pools, entertainment decks, etc.). One farmhouse with 12 bedrooms was occupied by 12 people and their families, with some of them cooking inside, others keeping goats, and the rubbish left uncollected. The vandalism of houses was phenomenal, and most of the internal and external utilities (taps, electricity points, toilet equipment, etc.) were no longer functioning at the time of the survey. In the compounds, now holding more people than they were designed for, there were shared communal toilets and water facilities; however, maintenance of these communal facilities, especially after the land reform, has deteriorated.

In the 1990s, various writers (Amanor-Wilks, 1995; Rutherford, 2001; Magaramombe, 2003a) complained vehemently about a variety of issues and under-investment in the social welfare of farmworkers. The period since 2000 has not seen any significant investment in the housing and domestic amenities in the compounds, and yet that same infrastructure that scholars complained about more than ten years ago is still being used by the massive numbers of people who moved on to the FTFs. However, due to a lack of institutional support, new settlers who moved into compound houses and a few who have built their own houses have started building their own VIP latrines.

As new people moved on to the FTFs, some farmworkers lost not only their jobs but also their entitlement to housing on the farms and access to basic social services such as health and education. In fact, farmworkers by 2007 were only assured of housing if they worked for the new farmers. In some cases, new farmers took over houses that were being used by farmworkers, while others constructed new houses for themselves. At Hariana Farm, the farm compound was turned into a school, and farmworkers were removed.

Conflicts have arisen over ex-farmworkers' use of the farmhouses inherited by new farmers. First, most farmworkers have retained housing in the compounds and are therefore resident on specific farms. The new farmers on these farms are questioning why a worker who is not willing to work for them should be allowed to continue living in the compound. There were two incidences in 2007 of conditional use of houses in farm compounds: on an A2 farm called Dunberry Park, the farm compound was burned down because the new owner said the ex-farmworkers were refusing to provide their services. On Chigudu Farm, the A2 farmer removed farmworkers from their houses and replaced them with his own workers. In addition, the new settlers allege that farmworkers do not contribute to water bills (or to the repair of boreholes), while they randomly cut firewood, defeating the settlers' efforts to invest in conservation and to halt the wanton destruction of trees.

Such conflicts have led to the forced eviction of a number of farmworkers, who in some cases are replaced by new workers brought in by the farmers. Government policy with regards to farmworkers has not been helpful, as there are no coherent guidelines as to what should happen to farmworkers on acquired farms who continue living in the compounds. This has left farmworkers in a precarious situation where they can be exploited or victimised. Farmworkers may access schools and clinics, but they find it difficult to pay fees. In an interview at Mapere school, the school head indicated that the school has had to allow the children of farmworkers to learn without paying because most are dropping out due to lack of money.

Conclusions

The emerging communities in the former commercial farming areas offer colourful and exciting stories of individual farmers trying to make sense of a harsh and cruel existence. GoZ adopted a 'resettlement first and services later' approach, which meant that, at least for the first occupants, basic amenities such as housing and water were problematic. The initial land occupations had led to widespread vandalism and the theft of property and infrastructure, as War Veterans and like-minded groups took over farms. Life on the frontier on the FTFs has been difficult for most farmers, especially on the A1 schemes. The dream of a better life filled with bumper harvests has not come true for many; they have met with poor service delivery and a daily struggle for inputs and support. Ten years after *jambanja*, most are just existing on the FTFs, but they are optimistic for a better future, one in which they can raise resources to invest in assets. However, for both individuals and families, their survival on the FTFs has been driven by a constant effort to make a better life for themselves. In this struggle, there is a distinct development of classes and power bases forming within the emerging communities, driven by assets acquired through direct and sometimes underhand ways.

The differences between A2 and A1 farmers and farmworkers have crystal-lised into a class divide, with each class facing different life realities and livelihood options. Most A2 farmers are well resourced and remain in cities, where they can access the necessary social services. By contrast, A1 farmers face difficulties in accessing most social services and infrastructures. A major outcome of the FTLRP was that farmworkers' access to resources and services declined. In general, the livelihoods of new farmers in terms of social assets and infrastructures are still underdeveloped years after resettlement. What is intriguing is that the government seemed not to have a plan that clearly outlined how basic services could be provided to improve the lives of new farmers. As the population increased in the former commercial farming areas, there should have been a corresponding increase in the social infrastructure at the very least.

7 | A revolution without change in women's land rights

Introduction

During the last two decades, Zimbabwean women have achieved significant milestones in terms of their rights as a result of greater international efforts to close the gender gap. In response to an increase in international concern, governments have created institutions to specifically deal with gender and women's issues. In Zimbabwe, a Ministry of Women's Affairs, Gender and Community Development has been part of Zimbabwe's cabinet for three decades, since independence in 1980. However, despite these years of investment and greater awareness about women's rights, Zimbabwe's women still face challenges, particularly in relation to property ownership and use and becoming beneficiaries of the land reform programme.

In Africa, it has been observed that women's rights have gained importance in urban spaces because a conglomeration of civil society organisations have largely taken responsibility for addressing the gender gap. Unequal ownership and control of land is a critical factor, which creates and maintains differences between women and men in relation to economic well-being, social status and empowerment. In general, African women produce 60–80 per cent of the continent's food (FAO, undated). At the national level, governments have responded by providing space for both men and women to articulate the rights of women.

Women in rural Africa nonetheless face a myriad of challenges, chief of which is insecurity of livelihoods (Gaidzanwa, 1995; Moyo, 1995b; Goebel, 1998; 1999; Jacobs, 1991), because they still have limited access to land and other productive resources that could improve their welfare. Mutopo (2011) has established that women in Mwenezi District in Masvingo Province, Zimbabwe, use a variety of strategies for accessing and using land. However, Mutopo misunderstands the social differentiation of women as beneficiaries of the Fast Track Land Reform Programme (FTLRP), in that she assumes that the argument in this chapter is that only the powerful women benefited. In fact, the data as presented below show that it was largely 'ordinary' women who benefited. Nevertheless, in Mazowe women were the last beneficiaries, after men were satisfied with their choice of plots. Therefore 'ordinary' women were always at the end of the queue in the allocations and other benefits. Thus, in Zimbabwe, a radical land reform programme did not contribute meaningfully to women's benefit in accessing state land.

This chapter examines some of the dominant tendencies and assumptions of the FTLRP through a 'women's lens'. Broad advocacy statements regarding women's marginalisation need to be anchored by field data that show some of the practices and outcomes. Using evidence from Mazowe District, the chapter examines how women accessed and used the land, as well as the supporting mechanisms for such land utilisation. Issues of land tenure and rights are also examined in terms of how they act as impediments, while the chapter establishes how women tried to circumvent the limitations of the FTLRP in terms of empowerment. The gender approach taken recognised the fact that there is a need to close the gender gap through focusing on women as key actors.

Radical land reform and women's land rights

Land is just one of the assets to be provided through land reform as the foundation for socio-economic equality. In other words, land reform must provide previously disadvantaged groups with new opportunities for employment and to address inequality, resource use inefficiencies and poverty, much of which affects women. Land reform is usually a state-led measure to address specific inequalities and should involve the dismantling of forms of differentiation along lines of class, gender and age in society. Therefore, it fits in with the empowerment discourse. Agarwal (1995) defines empowerment as:

> a process which enhances the ability of disadvantaged ('powerless') individuals or groups to challenge and change (in their favour) existing power relationships that place them in subordinate economic, social and political positions. (In Meinzen-Dick et al., 1997: 1306)

However, in most cases governments do not go all the way in using radical instruments to address specific inequalities that usually relate to gender. Governments become extremely reluctant to address the concerns of women, and usually become defensive, citing culture and custom as forces that they claim should be taken into account in property rights. In practice, Meinzen-Dick et al. (ibid.) noted that lack of access to land mutates into a lack of other productive resources such as water and raw materials. This has a telling effect on women's livelihoods and therefore incomes, which in turn affects their family lifestyles and duties. Land could therefore provide them with a range of opportunities 'at the farm and beyond the farm' if they were to benefit equally from public allocations.

A radical land transfer programme such as the FTLRP could work for women only if there is strong political will to prioritise women in land allocations. This is because, first, the prioritisation of women's access to land through legal backing, which 'radical' governments such as that of Zimbabwe can (and had the opportunity to) push for (Petrie et al., 2003), can provide a firm guarantee that women will benefit from land allocations. And second, radical land reform can help governments redistribute land without fear of a backlash by men who cling to customary systems (mostly derived from land designated as communal lands in Zimbabwe) as a basis for denying women access to land. Since land is acquired for public purposes, it falls outside the jurisdiction of traditional leaders, if the government desires this to be the case.[1]

In Zimbabwe, despite pronouncements against gender discrimination, the constitution permits discrimination against women in land matters (Ncube and Stewart, 1997; Potts, 2000). This is because land matters, including the distribution of land, are deferred to customary law, which dominates in the areas of adoption, marriage, divorce and inheritance. Yet, in the past, gender inequality was used as a justification of the FTLRP, which was based on the premise that men and women would benefit equally. During early years of the FTLRP, government officials would campaign for the reforms on a platform of non-gender discrimination, yet they still promoted such discrimination during the land allocations.

Contradictory radicalism from a gender perspective While the FTLRP qualifies as a political revolution, some (Jacobs, 2000; 2003; Goebel, 2006) hold the view that, from a gender perspective, the programme was not radical enough in terms of empowering women and closing the gender gap.[2] It is a given that the state mobilised its whole machinery (resources, personnel and institutions) to facilitate land transfers and redistribution with a clear political objective of destroying the racial monopoly of land. In order to accomplish this objective, the state put aside formal structures of governance that were seen as a hindrance to land reforms. The land occupations, dominated by men, were backed by the state, and therefore for the first time since independence, the government aligned with the social forces on the ground to push for land takeovers. Through this strategy and tactics, society became highly mobilised and conservative institutions came under attack by forces within and outside government. Human rights and legal structures were put aside and the judiciary was transformed.

ZANU-PF as a political party provided revolutionary leadership to the land reform programme, and in the process maligned, marginalised and captured state bodies so as to rally them behind its objective of taking land for redistribution to the majority. The question is: did women benefit from this revolutionary approach to address the historical challenges hindering access to land? The revolution changed the agriculture-based livelihoods of beneficiaries, including women. Some of the main areas of transformation included gender relations, rural-based life, split households and so on. Yet only a relatively small proportion of women-headed households were resettled under the FTLRP. In 1998, the government had agreed to reserve 20 per cent of land allocated under public resettlement for women (Sithole, 2002). This was promised at a donors' conference in September 1998. Subsequent events proved that the quota of 20 per cent never became a formal policy in the Inception Phase Framework Plan 1999–2000, nor in the land allocations under the FTLRP. Although many organisations, including women's movements, have pointed this out, there has been no defined mechanism to ensure that women are indeed benefiting from the FTLRP.

There have been contradictory statements from politicians about the extent to which women benefit from the Fast Track Farms (FTFs). This is because politicians seek to balance their political interests and say one thing to women's groups – i.e. that they will get access to land – then change their position when they have predominantly male audiences. For instance, President Mugabe announced in October 2000 that female-headed households would receive 20 per cent of redistributed land. Even then it was not clear which categories of women would benefit. However, also in 2000, the late Vice President Msika, from the same political party and in the same government, had this to say about granting women land:

> 'I would have my head cut off if I gave women land ... men would turn against this government,' said Msika. He added that giving wives land or even granting joint titles would 'destroy the family'.[3]

There is an assumption that a household is a single joint unit, people have a common interest, and the head of the household is altruistic. The FTLRP subsumed women's interests under the structure of the unitary household without any reference to women's rights or decisions. The Minister of the then Ministry of Lands, Agriculture and Rural Resettlement, Dr Joseph Made, had this to say:

> Since the family is traditionally made up of two partners, the government cannot say which partner should come forward to apply for land. Such specifics must be left to the families to decide. (Cited by Women and Land Lobby Group, 2001, in Bhatasara, 2001)

Yet President Mugabe, in 2009 and in the light of proposed constitutional reform, strongly supported women's access to land, pointing out:

> our sincere wish that women's food-generating activities can be improved to lead to financial security realised from their sale of their produce. This ... can only occur when and where appropriate policies regarding women's access to land, and the provision of vital farming inputs and credit, are put in place on time. In Zimbabwe, we continue to do our best in prioritising allocation of land and farming inputs to our women and thus empowering them, through our much-maligned land redistribution programme.[4]

Land in Zimbabwe continues to shape socio-economic and political issues relating to the understanding of gender in terms of property rights, against a background of deeply contested cultural constructions of women's position in this regard. In this construction, the land reform policies were paralleled by debates about gender equality in a context in which politicians tried to balance their interests in different constituencies. However, their views were based on a dominant cultural background that subordinates women in terms of owning property. The government has established statutory institutions and laws that can promote gender equality, but they are usually silent when it comes to addressing those inequalities. Women in Zimbabwe still face limited access to land, limited land ownership, insecure land rights and exclusion from the benefits that land provides. This is against the background of a government with strong beliefs in equality, and the FTLRP was supposed to be an example of this.

Land allocation and gender imbalances

In Zimbabwe, there were specific factors that limited women's access to land. The process of land occupations and state expropriation of commercial farming properties created considerable unease in rural areas and fear about loss of property in general. During the early years of the FTLRP, women tended to stay where they were (mostly in communal areas) and had limited participation in processes whose outcomes were, in any case, uncertain in terms of future livelihoods. Other factors that had an impact included the following:

- First, women rarely have a say in the decision-making process in the various land management institutions, dominated by men, where land allocation decisions are made.
- Second, even when provided with land in their own right, they face difficulties in finding key means of production such as finance, labour, inputs and equipment. In resettled areas they compete with men for access to resources and loans. While a few are able to compete, the majority of women are unable to do so.
- Third, women are faced with multiple challenges that make it difficult for them to focus their energies on a single issue. They are farmers, mothers, breadwinners, labourers and entrepreneurs for their families. They try to juggle these roles simultaneously, which makes it difficult for them to compete for space in the resettlement areas.

The transformation of land rights within redistributive reforms has been advanced as a potential means to address pervasive gender inequalities. However, the policy-making process of land redistribution tends to be centred on men, and to clearly import customary attitudes to land reallocation. In fact, although women lack land rights, they are also subject to a range of other insecurities that may be just as important at different times in their lives. The decision about whether to move or not is already a difficult one, but it is compounded by the challenges women face as mothers.

Does land allocation provide a new wave of land concentration in the hands of men? In Zimbabwe, as elsewhere in Africa, the tendency is for women to be treated as part of a male-led household and therefore women are expected to benefit from allocation as proxies; this seemed to be the assumption in the Ministry of Lands and Rural Resettlement (MLRR)/Scientific and Industrial Research and Development Centre (SIRDC) land audit in Zimbabwe in 2006. However, such perceptions of trickle-down advantage might not reflect reality, given the complexities of families and marriage unions, especially in the highly contested FTFs. At the murkier edges of land reform, women tend to be treated as second-class citizens. The redistributed land is first provided to men, and women follow only when men are fully satisfied, having taken, in most cases, the better-quality land (and the infrastructure delivered through the FTLRP). The hierarchy of redistribution mirrors the unequal distribution of all the other resources necessary for farming, and this means that women face a real struggle on the FTFs.

Outcomes of land allocation to women

Women who are involved in farming on the FTFs received land during the farm occupations that began in 2000. Some women participated in the occupations, and then made applications to councillors, land committees, Agritex or chiefs between 2001 and 2003. In Mazowe, in the sample survey in 2004, only 4 per cent (n=251) of the female respondents indicated that they got land through the *jambanja*. There was a view that women were hesitant to join the farm invasions of 2000 due to fears of violence, and that most of them applied after the *jambanja*. Those who had already got plots through the *jambanja* made other women feel that they also had the potential to become plot holders. From the reconstructed Agritex lists of the 4,963 beneficiaries under the A1 model, 13 per cent were women in the wards in Mazowe District. This is equal to the percentage of beneficiaries whose gender was not specified in the list. In the A2 model (n=1,054), 10.9 per cent of beneficiaries were women.[5] This was lower than expected, as it had been anticipated that there would be more women in the A2 commercial model based on statements made by politicians to the effect that women would be prioritised in the allocations. The government policy on land allocation specifically states that farmworkers, women and youths had to be prioritised in the lists of beneficiaries across all the models (GoZ, 2001).

In the A1 model, the sample surveys showed the following patterns: in 2004, 16 per cent (n=121) of the land was allocated to women, and in 2007 it was 18 per cent (n=341). In this model, there was no significant difference over time, unlike in the A2 model (described below). The peri-urban areas had 24 per cent (n=30) women beneficiaries (see Table 7.1). This demonstrates the concerted effort to allocate more land to women in peri-urban areas; urban politicians usually push for such allocations to capture votes, a factor that is particularly pertinent given the dominance of the former opposition party in urban voting constituencies. In fact, women, who usually dominate the low-level informal sector or are unemployed, work many of the plots in peri-urban areas. The women consider these plots as critical for generating supplementary food for their families. Politicians are quite supportive of this kind of land demand, as seen by their desire to allocate such women land and farming inputs.

TABLE 7.1 Land allocated to women in Mazowe, 2004 and 2007 surveys

Sex	Mazowe 2004								Mazowe 2007					
	A1		A2		Peri-urban		Total		A1		A2		Total	
	No.	%	No.	%	No.	%	No.	%	No.	%	No.	%	No.	%
Male	91	84	53	93	19	76	163	86	279	82	167	85	446	83
Female	17	16	4	7	6	24	27	14	62	18	30	15	92	17
Total	108	100	57	100	25	100	190	100	341	100	197	100	538	100
Missing	13	11	43	43	5	17	61	24	0	0	1	1	1	0
Total	121		100		30		251		341		198		539	

Source: Ruzivo surveys, 2004 and 2007.

The Ruzivo sample surveys showed the following patterns in the A2 model: in 2004 some 7 per cent (n=100) women had benefited, yet by 2007 this figure had increased to 15 per cent (n=198). In fact, within a space of three years, the number of women beneficiaries had doubled. The gendered access to land reported in the Ruzivo surveys is very similar to the findings of other studies. In their survey, Moyo et al. (2009) noted that 19 per cent of women acquired land in their own right, with more women getting land under the A2 scheme (15 per cent). In Masvingo District, Scoones et al. (2010) showed that female-headed households constituted 12 per cent of the sample, with 8 per cent of women being A2 beneficiaries compared with 14 per cent in A1 villagised and 13 per cent in A1 self-contained plots. They further noted that while formal legal systems have changed, the de facto situation is that 'traditional' or 'customary' systems, universally overseen by men (as chiefs and headmen), still favour the allocation of land to men (ibid.: 55). As an example, the MLRR/SIRDC 2006 audit of A2 farms noted that in Mazowe, of the total allocations audited (n=868), 86 per cent were held by men and 14 per cent by women. Table 7.2 shows that women in the A2 model were far less numerous than men. The Ruzivo sample survey findings were closer to those of the 2002 Justice for Agriculture (JAG) report, which established that 10 per cent of beneficiaries in the A2 model were women in 2002, while MLRR/SIRDC (2006) indicated that 14 per cent in the A2 model were women.

TABLE 7.2 A2 beneficiaries by gender from Mazowe District

Gender	Ruzivo survey, 2004		Ruzivo survey, 2007		JAG, 2002		MLRR/SIRDC, 2006	
	No.	%	No.	%	No.	%	No.	%
Male	53	93	167	85	43	90	759	86
Female	4	7	30	15	5	10	125	14
Total	57	100	197	100	48	100	884	100
Missing	43	43	1	1	6	11	7	1
Total	100		198		54		891	

Source: Ruzivo survey, 2004; list provided to Parliament of Zimbabwe by an independent MP, Margret Dongo (JAG, 2002); MLRR/SIRDC land audit, 2006.

The data from the MLRR/SIRDC audit made an assumption of broader benefits through marriage, which may imply that there are significant gains by women in any case. The data extracted for Mazowe show that there seems to have been some equity, with 50 per cent of land beneficiaries men and 50 per cent women when marriage is taken into account (Table 7.3). However, the assumption of equity rests on a weak foundation, given that there was a significant difference in the numbers of those benefiting through marriage: 3 per cent were men and 42 per cent women. This meant that men were very unwilling to include their spouses in their allocations, whereas women, even when they sought land on their own, would still include their spouses on the allocation. Of those benefiting in their own right, 48 per cent were men and only 7 per cent were women.

TABLE 7.3 Beneficiaries through marriage in Mazowe District, 2006

Allocations	Category	Number	Percentage
To men	Beneficiaries	748	48
	Beneficiaries through marriage	44	3
	Total	792	50
To women	Beneficiaries	114	7
	Beneficiaries through marriage	667	42
	Total	781	50
	Grand total	1,573	100

Source: MLRR/SIRDC land audit, 2006.

However, to gain a fuller understanding of the differences of benefits between men and women, the MLRR/SIRDC data were further classified into
the different status of the beneficiaries of A2 plots at the time of the survey
(married, widowed, single and divorced) (see Table 7.4). Benefits between men
and women showed even wider differences, with married men comprising 76
per cent of the total number of beneficiaries, compared with just 5 per cent
for married women.

TABLE 7.4 Gender patterns of allocated A2 plots in Mazowe

Allocations	Category	No. of beneficiaries	% by gender	% of total
To males	Single	18	2	2
	Divorced/separated	10	1	1
	Widowed	13	2	2
	Married	673	89	76
	Marital status unspecified	45	6	5
	Total	759	100	86
To females	Single	15	13	2
	Divorced/separated	11	10	1
	Widowed	38	33	4
	Married	44	39	5
	Marital status unspecified	6	5	1
	Total	114	100	13
Allocation to institutions			6	1
Grand total		879		100

Source: MLRR/SIRDC, 2006.

There has to be an explanation for this significant anomaly in the allocation
of A2 plots, but the researchers were unable to discern what this was. The
land committee members were inaccessible for most of the research period.
Therefore, it was not clear whether the allocation criteria specified by government were followed or whether the low proportion of female plot holders
indicated a low proportion of female applicants. Since some of the farms were
occupied by demonstrators who settled wherever they chose, most women
may have shunned activities they considered violent and, as a result, lagged
behind or left it to their spouses to carry out the occupations.

The land allocation criteria for A2 FTFs specifically hindered women's
access to land and failed to address gender equity. Yet, when compared with
the former large-scale commercial farms and previous resettlement, there
was an improvement in women's access. Rugube et al. (2003) had noted that
5 per cent of the approximate 4,500 white large-scale commercial farmers

who owned the land before the FTLRP were women. In the Old Resettlement Areas, the number of women beneficiaries was significantly lower, as usually customary systems were used to allocate land, and therefore mainly male-headed families benefited. The policy of the Government of Zimbabwe (GoZ) stipulated that those who wished to have their applications considered for A2 had to be in a position to mobilise resources such as finance to purchase inputs and machinery. They were also required to have agricultural qualifications and proof of collateral. As a result of these loaded criteria, many women were not able to access land under the A2 model due to lack of resources, capacity and the necessary agricultural qualifications.

Characteristics of women allocated land and the processes they followed The women who benefited fared equally in terms of demographics (age) and social characteristics (education and training) with men. The Ruzivo 2007 survey showed that the majority (91.3 per cent) of female plot holders were within the age range of 15–65 years and the remainder above the age of 65. In terms of educational level, 65.2 per cent of the female plot holders attained secondary education, 2.2 per cent held certificates and another 2.2 per cent also held diplomas. Only one female respondent had a postgraduate degree. This implies that more than half of the women can at least read and write. In terms of agricultural training, female farmers indicated that they underwent master farmer training offered at the farm level, after proving competence in farming based on the extension-cum-training provided through Agritex. At least 7.6 per cent of women held certificates showing that they had completed such training, and 2.2 per cent held certificates awarded by agricultural tertiary colleges.

The origin of the women farmers was critical in terms of how they accessed land and used the land afterwards. Women who were ex-combatants or were civil servants accessed land in both the A1 and A2 schemes. Many of them confirmed that they used their privileged positions to gain access to land, and would not have been successful as ordinary women. Therefore, networking, understanding the processes and having connections were important factors influencing their access to land. In many cases, accessing land meant travelling frequently to Concession, Bindura or Harare to check on the progress of their application. This meant that applicants had to have some financial means as well as time (which they could spend away from their family), which the majority of women did not have. In addition, getting approval from their spouses to apply and travel frequently to the land application offices, which were located in administrative centres such as Concession, was not easy.

However, even though the number of female plot holders is lower than the number of male plot holders, it was noted that the percentage of women who consider farming as a main source of income (86.9 per cent, n=539) is almost equivalent to that of men (87.2 per cent). This implies that, even though there are few female plot holders, women are actively participating in farming and perhaps more would like to farm if land was allocated to them. The majority of women farmers who are involved in full-time farming in the A1 scheme used to be communal farmers or were living in high-density neighbourhoods in urban areas and were not working. The new women farmers employed in the public sector tended to juggle their civil service jobs with farming their plots. Farming had become a way of supplementing their meagre salaries, while others indicated that they were successful in farming to the extent that they saw their formal jobs as being supplementary to their farming businesses.

Men and women in land utilisation Use of land is premised on key factors of production; besides land, these include capital, labour and technology. In the context of the FTLRP, government provided key support for financing, while the new farmers accessed labour from various sources, including the farm-workers who were already resident on the farms. In terms of technology, much of the farming infrastructure was inherited, while the government intervened with schemes such as mechanisation to help the new farmers use the land. In general, there were low expectations that the new farmers, the majority without resources, would invest heavily in these factors of production when they took up their land. This is the background against which these factors of production have to be examined in terms of gender equity.

Studies have established that women landholders may be less likely to be successful farmers, given the discrimination they face in accessing credit and technical assistance. In the A2 allocations, a key consideration was the financial resources an individual had, but this criterion was not strictly adhered to in the land allocation and it has been established that government tended to provide financial support to the new farmers irrespective of their financial status. Relative income (particularly the ability to generate savings) and access to credit, which in turn are conditioned by the income-generating opportunities available to men and women, were crucial aspects in the use of land after the allocations.

Many studies show that plots of land controlled by women have lower yields than those controlled by men, and that these lower yields are usually the result of less labour and fertilisers per acre rather than inefficiency (Commonwealth Secretariat, 1996). Also, a reduction of male labour can lead to a shift in production towards less nutritious crops as well as a decline in yields and output, or an increase in women's reliance on child labour. Women households that are too poor to hire labour resort to this practice and often withdraw their children from school to concentrate on farm work. In most cases, girl children are the main victims, as they become a source of cheap labour.

There are various ways in which women are involved in agriculture on the FTFs. Those who obtained land directly are involved in what can be termed family farming, while those who came in the company of their spouses are also involved in farming activities, mainly as labour. A third of the women involved in farming in both the A1 and A2 models in Mazowe District are plot holders, and the rest are running farming activities on behalf of or together with their spouses. In the 2007 survey (n=539), 35 per cent of the female respondents were fully employed and delegated other people, usually experienced male farmers, to run farming activities on their behalf. The rest were either unemployed or self-employed, especially as full-time farmers. In general, women have to employ people whereas men can use their wives for farm labour while they are absent from the farms, which is most of the time. This represents a continuation of the tendency in rural areas whereby men have sole rights over land and women run farming activities on behalf of spouses employed in urban areas.

Women in Mazowe are a varied group and their experience in terms of agricultural production in the newly resettled areas varies with the political, economic and social power that they wield. There are some women who have connections to political power either directly or indirectly through the patronage of powerful men.

Table 7.5 shows that by 2007 women had considerable experience compared with 2004 when they often had less than five years' experience. However, a lot of capacity development work is still required for women farmers.

TABLE 7.5 Farming experience of women farmers in Mazowe

| Experience (years) | 2004 | | 2007 | |
	Number	Percentage	Number	Percentage
1–5	14	58	13	14
6–10	3	13	28	31
10–15	1	4	12	13
> 15	6	25	37	41
Total	24	100	90	100

Source: Ruzivo surveys, 2004 and 2007.

Newly resettled farmers in Zimbabwe are generally faced with serious challenges in accessing inputs and support services at a time when GoZ has prioritised agriculture in its economic blueprints. In general, there were fewer women beneficiaries in the support programmes, and women on A1 farms complained bitterly about the unclear procedures that were used to choose beneficiaries. The Reserve Bank of Zimbabwe introduced a five-phase Farm Mechanisation Programme, which sought to improve farm technology and was aimed at mechanising both communal and commercial farmers (see Chapter

5). Most women A1 farmers were left out of the programme. Women in focus group discussions (FGDs) in June 2007 claimed that those women who managed to access equipment also had access to the power structures.

The government designed several agricultural support programmes during the FTLRP period. However, there were distributional challenges, exacerbated by corrupt tendencies (FAO, 2006), which resulted in ordinary farmers loathing the government's input support programme. A1 farmers generally had a negative view of the programme, with one commenting that '*tingangoti maguta inzara*' (it is a programme full of hunger). In general, farmers were facing challenges in securing credit, access to inputs, labour shortages and agricultural skills. While men and women shared similar problems in securing farm inputs, women were additionally constrained because they did not have collateral. There were no significant differences between men and women in accessing loans in the A1 model, as they all seemed to face similar challenges. The 2007 Ruzivo survey (n=539) showed that only 3 per cent of female plot holders who obtained assistance got loans from Agribank, compared with 7 per cent of the male plot holders who acquired assistance. At the same time, 37 per cent of the female plot holders and 38 per cent of the male plot holders reported using assets as collateral for loans.

In Mazowe, newly resettled farmers face an acute shortage of labour. For women farmers, even when the farmworkers are available, they face stiff competition from male farmers. In wage negotiations, a key informant at Selby pointed out that there were cases where farmworkers would prefer to work for a male farmer even when they were being offered lower wages compared with what they were offered by female farmers. She attributed this to mindset and attitude, as the farmworkers were schooled in an environment of male white farmers, and this situation is being replicated. Male farmers also had the advantage of offering farm apparel such as protective clothing. In addition, women's low inputs and low outputs mean that labour is often too expensive in relation to their capacity to pay. As a result, most of the female farmers rely on casual and family labour. Female farmers alluded to tense and conflict-ridden relationships with farmworkers, whom they viewed as greedy and lazy. They prefer hiring or bringing their own labour from the communal areas, which is cheaper. Most of these new workers are women – which invites an inquiry into the conditions and nature of their work.

Women farmworkers have taken on the biggest burden of providing farm labour. Landholders (both men and women farmers) preferred women workers whom they regarded as 'soft targets' because they accept what money is offered and work without complaining, unlike male farmworkers. For female farmworkers the land reform has opened up new opportunities for them to improve their earnings. Now they are able to negotiate the price of their labour with the new farmers. Under white farmers, female farmworkers could not work on their own account or get accommodation without being associated with a man. The compound system introduced by white farmers gave a compound house to a family, not to single female workers. To get access to housing on the farms required marriage.

Women's struggles over land rights The government confirmed the allocation of land through the issuing of offer letters. The offer letter to an applicant for land is the interim confirmation of landholding. Every farmer (in both the A1 and A2 model) was supposed to have an offer letter to confirm alloca-tion of land, but not its ownership. The ownership of land was vested in the government, as it explored options of tenure regimes to be given eventually to those allocated land.

It was apparent that the A2 beneficiaries stood a greater chance of obtaining a much more flexible land tenure arrangement, because the criteria favoured those with titled properties elsewhere. The ownership of property was also used in the A2 land applications as a key selection criterion. However, as the interviewed A2 women in Mazowe pointed out, they did not have access to property elsewhere and so this criterion was unfair and discriminated against them. However, in FGDs (Hariana, 16 June 2007, and Selby, 19 June 2007) some married women claimed that they had equal rights and ownership over the land even if the offer letters were in the names of their husbands.

In 2005, the government introduced joint naming on the offer letter, mean-ing that the names of both the husband and the wife appeared on the offer letter. The joint naming on the offer letter applied to both the A1 and A2 farmers. However, it did not apply to applications made before that time, as the government did not retrospectively change previous offer letters, so a large number of women were prejudiced. In any case, the issue of joint naming was not widely publicised (no awareness programmes were carried out by the government). During the FGDs in Mazowe, most women raised the concern that they need their names to appear on the offer letters for them to be guaranteed as co-plot holders (FGDs, June 2007). This issue was being raised on the farms at a time when the policy had already been changed, which means that women continued to be prejudiced despite the pronouncement of this positive policy position by government.

In 2006, the government started issuing 99-year and 25-year leases for the A2 farmers. In the lease documents, married women could have their names registered jointly with the men. However, the offer letters issued until 2006/07 had only the name of the applicant, as joint naming on the offer letter was not allowed. It was not clear whether the leaseholds were being issued based on the name(s) on the offer letter, or whether these could be changed based on new policy allowing joint naming. In Mazowe, officials indicated that for the 54 beneficiaries who had 99-year leases by 2006, those leases were based on the original offer letters. The result was that, despite the progress in policy, women continued to be treated as second class in land ownership.

In any case, joint naming on the offer letter for an A2 leasehold does not guarantee full rights, because the state is the ultimate owner of the land. There is no law to protect the holders of offer letters from eviction by the state. When it was announced as a policy position, joint naming on offer letters was hailed as a progressive move for gender equity, as it established explicitly that FTF rights were vested in both the man and the woman in a couple. The current reality is that, by allowing for joint naming in its policy, there is greater family stability on the FTFs at a time when the most appropriate land tenure system for the FTFs is being explored by government.

If joint naming is adhered to, widely publicised, backed by awareness and mindset change, and is incorporated in future strong land ownership, it can serve to protect women from losing access to what is often the household's most important asset in case of separation or divorce. In either case, joint naming guards against one spouse making decisions with which the other spouse is not in agreement. At present, the offer letter does not allow for sale, rental or mortgage of the farm, because the land remains in the hands of the state. Therefore, the tendency to hail joint naming as positive for women may be premature, until government concedes clearer tenures in which transfers of land by individual plot holders is allowed. In the meantime, joint naming has the potential to increase the bargaining power of women, enhancing their role in household and farm decision-making.

Men's views on women acquiring and owning land In the case of the FTFs, it would seem that men fought to restrict women's sole access to the farms. At several FGDs held in Mazowe in 2004 and 2007, men generally argued that women should not have been prioritised in land allocation. At Mugutu (16 June 2004), they argued that women had to remain behind in the communal or urban areas while the men 'rummaged around' for land under difficult circumstances. According to them, this was enshrined in the culturally defined roles that accord men the role of provider for the household, and it is their responsibility to seek productive resources for the family. In this case, the men argued that the 'homestead belongs to the male head' (*musha ndewababa*), reflecting the dominance of the patriarchal system among the incoming land beneficiaries. At Glengrey (FGD, 27 June 2007), a group composed of both men and women revealed that the nature of the acquisition process naturally discriminated against women because it sometimes involved violence (*jambanja*). Men were therefore at the forefront of land grabbing, and were automatically prioritised for land allocation. Women, who remained in the communal areas to look after the family and home, were largely left out. On the whole, men felt that women had had a fair chance but that some women were afraid of participating in *jambanja.* This was because, according to the men, '*Aidya ndiye anenge aripo*' (one had to be present on the farms when land was being given out to benefit).

Women in resettled areas recognise that men's control over land in both material and symbolic terms is a status issue for them. The manifestation of land control in terms of its administration, management and ownership is a way of maintaining control over women. Men fear that if the idea of women's ownership of land gains momentum, they will lose all authority and control over women. For these reasons, men maintain control and scrutiny over this process within conjugal relations, as well as within patriarchal discourse, in order to restrict women's actions and ownership of land. Thus practices that deny women their land rights are being imported or smuggled in from customary systems at an alarming rate.

Men claim that women are incapable of owning land because of their 'incapacity' as the 'weaker sex', and their 'propensity' to make the 'wrong' decisions in farm management. Within this discourse, men see women as needing to be 'protected' against their 'incapacities' and their 'tendency to roam' with other men in the vicinity (FGDs, March to June 2007). Regarding the question of what happens in the event of divorce, some were of the view that the male plot holder would remain in possession of the land because '*mukadzi agara ndiye anoenda kana vanhu varambana*' (the woman is usually the one who leaves to homestead in most divorce cases anyway). This view was largely supported by male participants. Some women were of the view that the plot should be taken by the wife because women are good caregivers, unlike the men who readily neglect their children when they remarry. Another view expressed was that the plot should be registered in the names of both spouses so that when they divorce they will have to share equally.

Dissolution of marriages and implications on land ownership Women who got land under the FTLRP envisaged FTF areas as commercial land not subject to customary systems. The expectation was that women were to be allocated land in the same way as men on the FTFs, because the customary system that allows land allocation only to men was seen as a communal area construct. In FGDs, both male and female participants agreed that, in the case of divorce, subsequent land ownership depends on the circumstances leading to the divorce. If the divorce were caused by promiscuity on the wife's side (*kubatwa nechikomba*), according to the men the wife should lose everything. However, if divorce occurred because of some other reason, then the properties should be shared equally between the former husband and wife. What was striking about the responses to these questions was that both men and women tended to want to prejudice a female spouse who was promiscuous. In fact, women tended to support men chasing away the spouse. This culturally based view places the majority of women in a lower social group in relation to property rights. In fact, a promiscuous man, divorced by his wife for this reason, is more likely to retain the land, with the injured wife complaining of being thrown off the property. Society generally accepts such prejudice in terms of women's rights.

The land resettlement programme has therefore perpetuated the customary property rights in favour of men. Women can only be equal landowners with their spouses when they are granted leaseholds, rather than title deeds, on which the names of both spouses are indicated as the plot holders. In the 2007 Ruzivo survey (n=539), questions of land tenure security featured prominently, with 45 per cent of female respondents preferring a leasehold type of land ownership and 44 per cent of them indicating that they preferred title deeds. The insignificant difference between those who preferred a leasehold and those who would rather have title deeds suggested that women opted for any type of ownership that gave an advantage in terms of security. The major conclusion drawn by the interviewees and in FGDs was that co-ownership of the plot would work as an incentive to motivate women to participate actively in farming, thus contributing towards agricultural production improvements.

Inheritance, its gender dimension and land rights on the Fast Track Farms The issue of inheritance elicits very emotional responses in patrilineal societies such as those in Zimbabwe. This is more intense in the newly resettled areas, where the state is not sure what form of tenure to provide for the new beneficiaries, given the different customary systems practised by the variety of people who benefited in the allocation of land. A key strength of any tenure system will be its ability to allow beneficiaries to hand over the property to their heirs. This must be clarified in a situation where the state also wants to retain control of the process. While this may appear simple, with property being handed over to family siblings, the actual policy is still to be clearly articulated, especially with respect to the A1 farms.

The fate of a piece of land upon the death of its occupant, divorce or a decision to leave the resettlement area was highly contested in families. When a person was terminally ill, the family usually took over (56.2 per cent) (n=539), and in some cases the wife (32.1 per cent) was given the land (Table 7.6). In some circumstances, the land reverted to the state, with the traditional leader – particularly the chief – exercising the right to reallocate the land.

Women in polygamous unions were of the opinion that, in the case of the plot owner being deceased, the plot should be divided equally among all the wives. However, this decision ignored the fact that the land committee can offer only one letter per plot. Some then suggested that the farm should be given to the first wife, but others argued that there is a strong possibility that the first wife was not involved in the *jambanja* of getting plots but instead

TABLE 7.6 What happens to a piece of land when the plot holder becomes seriously or terminally ill?

| Responses | Type of scheme | | | | Total | |
| | A1 | | A2 | | | |
	No.	%	No.	%	No.	%
Land will be taken by chief	8	2	35	18	43	8
Family will take over	209	61	94	47	303	56
Wife will take over	108	32	65	33	173	32
State will take over	7	2	1	1	8	1
Other	9	3	3	2	12	2
Total	341	100	198	100	539	100

Source: Ruzivo survey, 2007.

remained in the communal lands, only appearing on the land when the situation stabilised. Some participants thought the plot could be handed over to the wife who stood with the husband during the *jambanja*. Male respondents were of the opinion that the A1 plot is not just for the wife/wives but for the whole family, and therefore should be handed over to the first-born son or to any one responsible son who had an interest in farming.

In the interim, the farmers agreed that there is a need for farmers to write a will of inheritance that can be used in the court handling the estate of the deceased so that those left behind will not have problems. If this is not done, then the land should be given to the eldest son. In a polygamous situation, one wife should be chosen to stay, and whatever is harvested should be shared equally among the wives. Table 7.7 explores this further. The spouse normally

TABLE 7.7 What happens to a piece of land if the plot holder dies?

| Responses | Type of scheme | | | | Total | |
| | A1 | | A2 | | | |
	No.	%	No.	%	No.	%
Spouse will continue	130	39	79	40	209	39
Son will take over	73	22	67	34	140	26
Manager will continue	3	1	8	4	11	2
Family will take over	126	38	42	21	168	32
State will take over	1	0.3	1	0.5	2	0.4
Total	333	100	197	100	530	100
Not answered	8	2	1	0.5	9	2
Grand total	341		198		539	

Source: Ruzivo survey, 2007.

assumes the role of the father when he passes away, and this implies taking over the land. However, in some instances, the extended family, which derives most of its welfare from that piece of land, will take it over. Fewer of the respondents indicated that the eldest son would take the land for the family in the event of both parents dying.

In different FGDs, there was a common view that children should take over, and, if they are too young, a guardian can assist them. They argued that if the surviving spouse remarries, the children would not benefit, so it is better to give ownership directly to the children since they are the ones who should be the heirs. Some argued that if the children inherit, they could end up evicting the surviving parent, especially the mother, because control may give them too great a sense of power. It was reiterated that, according to the Shona culture, it is the eldest son who should inherit, and if there are no sons the eldest daughter could take over. Some added that it is even better if the plot is inherited by a female child, because usually the daughters do not neglect their parents. In the case of polygyny, most were of the view that the plot should be registered in the name of the eldest son but the widows should share the land. It is very rare for the state to take over the land, as indicated by the responses from both A1 and A2 schemes. It is for this reason that, in these cases, the state is not the major agency of uncertainty at household level in terms of unfair gender practices.

In the FGDs (15 June 2007, Mooileegte Farm [A2]), men invoked selective aspects of the custom of 'widow inheritance' that focus on inheriting land. This focus ignored other aspects of the custom, which involves 'inheriting' the widow and her children, as these would entail taking on additional financial burdens and obligations. However, in the context of HIV and AIDS, 'widow inheritance' is now largely symbolic, with widows passing on the inheritance to their own elder male children through the symbolic passing of a family knobkerry (*kupa tsvimbo*) to the heir. However, there were cases recorded by the Ministry of Gender in Mazowe where men have 'chased' their deceased brothers' widows with the intention of grabbing the land and other assets left by the deceased. Widows who had not been married long and those who have young children are particularly vulnerable to being 'chased', whereas those with adult sons are in a stronger position to defend their right to the land.

There are cases where the land authorities have had to intervene in inheritance issues. At Three Sisters Farm, a brother responsible for the family of the deceased was failing to look after the family's interests. The District Land Committee (DLC) resolved to transfer the plot into the name of the deceased's child. In the case of Bellavista Farm, where two wives were fighting for the land, the land committee decided to give one of the spouses an A1 plot to end the long-standing dispute. There was a case where a man divorced his wife and married another woman, but he was chased off the land and went to live in the communal area while the wife stayed on the farm.

Radicalism without progress for women in the Fast Track Land Reform Programme

Despite the radicalism of the land transfer programme, the majority of women did not benefit in a country with more women (52 per cent) than men and where most women derive their livelihoods from agriculture (70 per cent). These simple and straightforward demographic facts may make one assume that more women should have benefited in the land allocations. The reality is that largely they did not benefit, despite efforts and gains at regional and international levels in terms of specific protocols setting targets, especially at the Southern African Development Community (SADC) level. The SADC gender protocol provides a number of concrete, time-bound commitments for achieving key strategic objectives. Article 18 relates to agricultural development and food security and states that, by 2015, all member states shall review all policies and laws that determine access to, control of and benefit from productive resources by women in order to end all discrimination, ensure equal access and rights to credit, capital, mortgages, security and training, and ensure that women and men have access to modern, appropriate and affordable technology and support services.

The FTLRP falls short of these policy targets; so to conclude, as Mutopo (2011), Moyo et al. (2009) and Scoones et al. (2010) do, that women benefited to a large extent from the FTLRP fails to address the key challenges that women face in their struggles over access to and control of resources. The facts are straightforward: in Zimbabwe, the largest percentage of users of land are women, and therefore demographically they should be seen to be controlling and using that resource. Yet the control of land by men has been widened not just through access, but also through the importation of customary systems.

There were also pockets of success that should be noted and can be used as a basis for fighting for women's land rights. In Mazowe, male A2 farmers not resident on the land had the farming activities being managed by their wives. For those allocated land, the land reform has brought economic emancipation: for example, one female farmer has risen to become a powerful councillor, whereas before she was an ordinary housewife in town. Men respect her because of her ability to use the land and the farm management capacity she is demonstrating, outcompeting men in the production of tobacco and other crops. She is also sympathetic to the plight of other women, and has been fighting a lone battle in the decision-making forums for women to get better deals in access to land and agricultural support.

In the late 1990s, many organisations, such as the Women and Land Lobby

Group, fought hard for women to be guaranteed land rights in policy as well as in land management institutions. Today, civic organisations such as Women and Land in Zimbabwe are constantly fighting for the rights of women to acquire and benefit from land. However, they have largely remained marginal and have made only a small dent in the land reform programme. In Mazowe, the DLC was dominated by men, although at one stage the district administrator who chairs the committee was a woman. In most cases, the DLC tended to be sympathetic to men: for example, at farm called The Rivers, a plot holder divorced his wife, with whom he had four minor children. Due to the fact that the offer letter was in the name of the wife, the DLC 'felt sorry' for the man and agreed to grant him a plot elsewhere. In most cases, men pushed off the land by their wives when they got divorced tended to get positive redress by the committee; this was not the case for women in similar situations.

At the level of government, there is a real commitment to addressing the gender gap through providing land to more women. Government bases its desire on international and regional precedence, where the uplifting of women in many spheres of society is regarded as a key priority. At the same time, government and local institutions have been forced to reconsider women's access to land because of the civic pressure exercised by women's organisations. However, talk is not often followed up with concrete action to provide women with land. The FTLRP reduced the opportunities for women's empowerment and shrunk the democratic spaces where women could genuinely participate in development processes by denying them rights to land and widening gender inequalities. The proponents and implementers of the FTLRP, in addition to not giving women adequate space on the FTFs, alienated the few women who benefited by denying them access to the resources that would allow them to improve the utilisation of their land. The result is that women farmers are caricatured as incapable, compared with men, of the commercial use of allocated land.

In Mazowe, in all of the FGDs and interviews, no one seemed to know about organisations lobbying for access to land. In the case of Zimbabwe, unfortunately, many of the civic organisations operate at the national (urban) level and do not have organic links to the rural areas, or, more critically, to the FTFs. The result is that women on the FTFs remain unrepresented and have no access to non-governmental organisations (NGOs) that are linked to donors, as these are precluded from doing work on contested FTF land. Yet, in theory, the FTFs provide the greatest scope for the emancipation of women through giving them access to more productive land than the poor soils in the communal areas.

There is a need to identify strategies and tactics that can help women gain access to land, and also to agricultural support from the state and private sector. The mere making of noise, as NGOs do outside the mainstream policy organisation structures, will not address the gender gap in land access. This means there is a need for civil society organisations to adopt a multi-pronged approach, including greater outreach awareness work on the FTFs, so as to engage policy-making institutions and work closely with technical extension and land management agencies to address the gender gap.

Conclusions

In the context of a radical land reform programme, the government of Zimbabwe lost an opportunity to address gender inequities, as this could have been accomplished at the very foundation of the FTLRP rather than later as an add-on. There are three reasons why this happened. First, the fact that the programme was fast tracked made the government compromise on its commitment at international and regional level to address women's concerns and reduce the gender gap through a clear empowerment process by giving them land, and the support necessary for them to thrive in agriculture. Second, it would seem that, although there is an international commitment to address gender issues, the government still has serious work to do in terms of mindset change. This has to start from the level of the state bureaucracy, which failed to push for women and men to benefit equally from the land reform programme, irrespective of the compromise that had been made in 1998 (the promise to reserve 20 per cent of land for women – though this never became a policy or law).

Third, the FTLRP was oblivious to the socio-cultural contexts within which women's access to, ownership of and control of land are mediated, interpreted and negotiated. People were allocated land in a policy vacuum because, aside from one document (GoZ, 2001), the government had no time to develop an elaborate land policy that could have taken women's concerns on board. It was precisely because of this land policy vacuum that men took advantage of land occupations, which had the effect of marginalising women who could not take land by force. Women's lives in marriages and beyond family boundaries needed special consideration in a land reform programme such as the one that Zimbabwe implemented. Yet when it came to actual land allocation, women seemed to become merely spectators of a land and agrarian reform programme that should have addressed their livelihood challenges. Broader issues of social justice, gender equality and democracy must be taken on board if women's rights to land are to be addressed.

The specific trajectory of women's access to land on the FTFs needs to be examined in terms of the three decades of land resettlement. There are clear patterns of continuity in attitudes towards women's access to land. While there are piecemeal policy actions for facilitating women's access to land, customary attitudes among land-allocating authorities hinder moves towards the empowerment of women. Civic society has not focused on gender issues with relation to land struggles and the FTLRP with the same dedication that they have sought gender equity in many other spheres of women's lives. Although there were difficulties for women who sought to engage in the FTLRP, the programme itself was a lost opportunity to articulate women's land rights. In order for women to succeed, there is a need for an ideological and political mobilisation of social forces at all levels of society and for women's land rights to be taken seriously.

8 | Social organisation and reconstruction of communities on Fast Track Farms[1]

Introduction

The Fast Track Land Reform Programme (FTLRP) led to the movement of people from different areas, including urban areas, Old Resettlement Areas (ORAs)[2] and communal areas, across the whole country to the new resettlement areas on land dominated by large-scale commercial farms (LSCFs). People of diverse cultures and backgrounds entered the former LSCFs through different routes and channels (see Chapter 3), and some moved several times before settling on particular farms. For some it started off as *jambanja*, then official allocation, followed by eviction and being allocated other plots at the behest of the state planning processes. The movement of people into new spaces led to new social configurations as they met minority white farmers, corporate farming enterprises and farmworkers with a different culture and systems of farming than those they were familiar with.

While the new settlers had to deal with a maze of government entities that allowed them to enter the Fast Track Farms (FTFs), beyond this first line their most significant encounter was with the white farmers they had to confront, share land with, live with, or see evicted through the FTLRP. However, the land beneficiaries – or settlers, as they are commonly referred to by former farmworkers – have now merged with the commercial farming sector societies populated in the past by the former commercial farmworkers and a few remaining white commercial farmers. The new people, with different backgrounds, culture, values and norms to the pre-FTLRP farmers, have been geographically co-located, while the absolute numbers of people in the former commercial farming areas have increased phenomenally over a short period of time.

This chapter critically analyses the emerging social structure in terms of how the 'new farmer' has forged new social relations on the FTFs, based on the new resettlement areas of Zimbabwe post-2000. Given the complex and multilayered meaning of the FTLRP, land has redefined communities in commercial farming areas. The meeting of 'new' people with 'older' people of different social, cultural and class backgrounds points to the centrality of land being a cause of social production and formation. Social change triggered by the FTLRP is hidden in key assumptions: access to land (size and quality), to the farm resources inherited and/or contested, to markets and networks, all of which contribute to socio-economic development. The second point is that emerging societal relationships are being shaped and reshaped, not by geography but by the behavioural patterns of beneficiaries within the context of new institutional formations and unfamiliar territory.

Influence of the 'socialism' factor in post-independence resettlement

The settlement patterns of Phase I of the Land and Resettlement Programme (1980–97) borrowed significantly from the Ujamaa villagised concept, which in turn had borrowed heavily from the Soviet type of socialism that assumed egalitarian societies and communities.[3] Despite the collapse of the Union of Soviet Socialist Republics (USSR) and the protégés that moved towards capitalism (such as China), Zimbabwe still hangs on to the outdated concepts behind these models, as reflected in the construct of the A1 model. However, a major variation occurred with regards to the FTLRP, which for the first time acknowledged the imperative of developing a pool of black commercial farmers to take over from the former white farmers under the A2 model. Whereas in the first 20 years of independence ZANU-PF, and therefore government, frowned upon the accumulation of wealth; this changed in 2000 as it was accepted that land could be used for black economic empowerment and wealth accumulation.

In the first phase of resettlement up to 1997, the place of origin of the beneficiary was not considered in land allocation. Geza (1986) noted that the independent government had an undeclared policy position regarding beneficiaries of the resettlement programme, which was to view the land schemes as a way of establishing new, cohesive, progressive and dynamic communities out of the many individuals from different parts of the country, all of whom were from the poor sector of the peasantry. The first phase of the resettlement programme had beneficiary selection procedures epitomised by identifying the landless and the rural poor as individuals rather than socially homogeneous groups (e.g. clans, chieftaincies, etc.) as targets for resettlement. In addition, the old resettlement programme (Cusworth and Walker, 1988; Cusworth, 2000; Kinsey, 2004) was implemented in a more orderly manner in terms of technical considerations, unlike the FTLRP, which was initially marred by a level of disorderliness.

Barr et al. (2010: 5) point out that after the Zimbabwean war of independence in 1980, many people displaced by the fighting were resettled in new villages. The resettlement areas were typified by models A, B, C and D, with villages created by government officials selecting households from lists of applicants based on key poverty norms, meaning that there were similarities in terms of wealth status of those selected.[4] A major factor that influenced such a criterion was that government and donors provided equal support from the start to all beneficiaries (inputs, housing, size of land, etc.) as part of a planned resettlement programme.

The new settlements brought together households that were typically unrelated to and unacquainted with each other. They were diverse in terms of wealth (from the rich to the poor) and came from diverse professional backgrounds and livelihoods. These beneficiaries did not command equal support from the time of settlement: each person was responsible for their own resettlement. In order to survive and prosper during the turbulent times of the land reform programme from 2000 to 2005, the new inhabitants in the new villages had to use collective action to solve various problems relating to agriculture and land management, unfavourable access to inputs (seeds, fertilisers, chemicals, technology, etc.) for agricultural production, inadequate access to financial and other services, and the management of risk and uncertainty. On the FTFs, a major principle was to maintain the social and cultural fabric of A1 settlers by, as far as possible, resettling households with common origins in the same village. This was part of the planning process for the creation of villagised settlements.

The need for individualisation by those in the A1 schemes is shown by the wish of most of them to build houses on their plots rather than in designated villages. While, from the point of view of providing efficient services, it would seem rational to put people in villages, the beneficiaries have their own lifestyle preferences that may undermine villagisation. Some A1 farmers who built houses on their plots said they wanted to reduce the time spent moving to and from their fields. They indicated that this would also enable them to protect their crops from both wild animals and thieves. In addition, the settlers' desire for privacy was a factor, as they were not familiar with their neighbours. In many cases, they specifically said they did not want to stay in a compound set-up, which they saw as a foreign construct. They preferred to be scattered over the land, as in the communal areas, where groupings – even when called compounds – are entirely family-based to avoid social friction.

Barr (2001) and Dekker (2004) have argued that in the ORAs in Wedza and Shamva, people tended to have long-lasting relationships based on the need to share farming resources. These relationships were further cemented through marriage as the inhabitants came from different areas and their major goal was farming. This is unlike some areas, particularly in Mazowe, where farmers from Chiweshe strongly felt that they had restitution claims to land and were not happy with newcomers (vauyi).[5] In several focus group discussions (FGDs), sentiments were expressed that if they had any option these people should look for land in their original homes and avoid congesting Mazowe.

The relationships between people in the communal areas of Zimbabwe are founded on historical African values, norms and traditions. The design of the land reform up to 1997 was to allow people/communities to be moved together so as not to break social relationships developed and nurtured for generations. This changed with the FTLRP, as the government sought to resettle people without social consideration. Thus contradictory outcomes emerged, because for some communities the challenges they faced (such as looted farms, hostile ex-farmworkers and lack of government support) provided the impetus for them to co-operate straight away in order to deal with these challenges. On the other hand, in some communities differences and conflicts emerged due to a lack of trust among the beneficiaries (Munyuki-Hungwe, 2011). The evolution of communities on the FTFs was influenced by the multifarious cultural histories of the people benefiting from the allocations, as well as the various ideological forces that intersected with those cultures over time.

The argument then is that community evolution is spatial, temporal and always undergoing hierarchies of change. Based on this view, community evolution was identified as a transitional process, and one that had specific peculiarities in Mazowe District. In addition, the violence and spontaneous redistribution of land by government bureaucrats, traditional chiefs and War Veterans shaped the form of the communities, beyond any cultural basis of the beneficiaries. While the government wanted to see orderly land redistribution taking place (Pazvakavambwa, 2009), the prevailing atmosphere of violence and intimidation meant that any consideration of culture as the 'soft' side of land (Röling, 1997) had to be put aside. In fact, the template of the ORAs was cast aside, and the speed of the FTLRP gave rise to a very different structure on the FTFs, one that will require many years of further study as the process of social fusion evolves.

Forces accounting for the creation of new communities on the Fast Track Farms

The land allocation to new beneficiaries under the FTLRP was the beginning of the merging of incoming and resident people on commercial farms. Many of the communities were created formally, but others were informal. Informal community creation was due to the land occupations, as the occupiers congregated in the compounds that housed the farmworkers, thus creating a community of mostly young and middle-aged men who had led the occupations fused with that of the farmworker families. The formal communities emerged after allocation, when those who benefited joined the compounds, while some of the occupiers moved on or were allocated their pieces of land elsewhere. Thus, this second regime of community creation is what still stands today, where farmworkers and the former white landowner may have given way to the new farmer, but they have also crafted some form of co-existence.

How people came to be on the FTFs has influenced the nature of social relationships in the resettlement areas. In these areas, there are beneficiaries who got land through *jambanja*, and consequently have a different placing in the social hierarchy, which is always in transition. Since 2000, the way people live on the FTFs has been influenced by the behaviour of actors both within and outside them. Some beneficiaries who came after the *jambanja* era experienced a different form of living because social relations had stabilised after the FTFs had been in existence for several years. In general, ordinary people moved on to the FTFs through two streams: A1 and A2. In some cases, the A1 farmers were the first to relocate and establish homes on the FTFs, demonstrating a high ratio of land uptake compared with A2 (Utete, 2003a).

The A2 farmers could afford to commute regularly while they weighed up their options. Therefore, new social formation of a residency type was mostly associated with A1 farmers by virtue of their numbers, the small sizes of their plots, and their limited ability to network because of resource constraints. However, the A2 farmers evaded social and political controls by adopting several strategies: simply being absent physically on the ground; using their workers (and managers) as fronts; appearing only at high-profile meetings; using their cash and donations to speak on their behalf, thereby silencing aggressive opposition; and occasionally playing at philanthropy by allowing their equipment (tractors, vehicles, etc.) to be borrowed for no pay. Thus those with money effectively managed the social networks in the way they wanted.

Nonetheless, the beneficiaries are of different classes and have different connections, which they use to influence not just social life in the newly resettled areas but also specific agrarian relations of production. Some former farmworkers also took advantage of *jambanja* to carve out powerful positions in the areas in which they lived because they could use to their advantage the local knowledge they had built up during their time on the FTFs. Therefore, farmworkers were not the 'lame ducks' they have largely been portrayed as in many studies (Sadomba, 2008; Chambati, 2009; Magaramombe, 2010; Moyo and Yeros, 2007b); they were able to determine the shape and form of the communities. These issues are explored in order to reveal how structure and agency have shaped the nature of the communities emerging on the FTFs in Mazowe.

A new social order as a result of the Fast Track Land Reform Programme

The movement of people due to land reform led to the displacement and replacement of white landowners and some farmworkers. The displacement was also accompanied by insecurity, as previously the white farmers had created a highly secure community, intolerant of theft of any kind (Moyo, 2000b). Farm security had been enhanced through farm radios (Taylor, 2002), investing in private security companies, the erection of electric fencing around properties, and the creation of rapid response teams. The security on commercial farms was complemented by government through the provision of police posts for the Zimbabwe Republic Police, as the government regarded the commercial farms as the engines of the economy. This process led to a sort of physical fortification of the farms. Yet, despite these enormous security resources, the War Veterans and peasants, with all sorts of small arms (machetes, axes, and even just the power of singing and making noise) broke down the barriers.

However, as the new beneficiaries settled on the farms, they became victims of the same insecurity. A key emerging issue in the new resettlement schemes is the problem of security for agricultural infrastructure and property. Given that Mazowe is also a mining area, there are problems between new settlers and gold miners, most of whom are illegal and are protégés of gold buyers with mining claims in the area. There are accusations of thefts from farmers by gold panners and farmworkers who are said to have joined the panning business. In general, beneficiaries complain of wanton destruction of farming equipment, looting of irrigation pipes and conflicts over access to such infrastructure. Access to common or 'free' agricultural infrastructure, especially tobacco-curing barns, is highly contested in farms under the A2 scheme (see Chapter 5). In the A1 resettlement schemes, where only the farmhouses seem to have been retained by the state, there is still competition over irrigation infrastructure and some equipment left by the former landowners. The idea of sharing such infrastructure seems to be unpalatable to the new settlers. Key informant interviews carried out in Mazowe District showed that in most cases the District Land Committee (DLC) had to organise for caretakers to take charge of security on A1 farms during the process of farm demarcation and allocation.

In general, social control seems to have been broken by the *jambanja* approach to everything to do with the FTLRP in the first three years. The wastage in terms of infrastructure was phenomenal. The irrigation systems were idle, either because pumps or pipes had been stolen or damaged, or because the new settlers lacked the necessary skills to run them. Tractors and other farming equipment were appropriated from farms through illegal means, and were literally driven into the ground due to lack of care and maintenance. Some equipment was moved into urban areas and private warehouses by new farmers and former owners who feared insecurity in the farming areas. Ploughs and disc harrows, milking machines, tobacco-curing and tobacco-handling facilities, pumps and generators were largely damaged and some lost through untrained usage or the inability to raise resources to maintain them.

Social forces at work in the construction of social order on the Fast Track Farms

The FTLRP has been seen as an event that was motivated by political power and was driven by what some writers characterise as social movements originating from formalised pressure groups and networks (Murisa, 2007; 2009; Moyo et al., 2008; Moyo and Yeros, 2007b). The networks identified were War Veterans, churches, kinship, political ties, elite networks and professional networks. A variety of social forces influenced the settlement process in the first few years of the FTLRP. On FTFs, political participation became a major determinant in influencing social order. A variety of features come with such participation: independent or compulsory voting; voluntary or involuntary civic participation and involvement; and expected participation in Village Assembly (VA) meetings or Village Development Committees (VIDCOs),[6] scheme management meetings and commodity association meetings. However, participation is also premised on political knowledge, political trust and grassroots political activism.

Notable social processes were influenced by politicisation, which resulted in power struggles, the creation of personality cults based on political connections or liberation war credentials, illegal allocation of land, siphoning of state resources meant for the general public, and intolerance of the government planning authority, especially during farm area demarcations. In other words, there was no natural evolution of social processes, but clearly politically guided social relationships that affected how communities were emerging. The War Veterans, as protégés of the then ruling ZANU-PF party, naturally filled the social space and determined how 'incoming' and 'older residents' lived on the FTFs.

However, class and education were also key in influencing social formation. In terms of educational attainment, those regarded as less educated (some A1 farmers) felt that the most educated undermined them, particularly the elites (most of the A2 farmers), who never really associated with them. Education also emerged as a mechanism that prevented social cohesion, particularly in the case of A1 farmers who felt that they were viewed as backward. The A1 farmers became isolated not only because of the way in which they benefited (through the district administrator at the local level, whereas A2 farmers had been allocated land through the Ministry of Lands at the national level, as discussed in Chapter 3), but also because they were seen as inferior to the A2 farmers (on the basis of resource ownership). The distinction of who allocated land tended to place A1 farmers at the bottom of the social ladder, with the implication that, for any form of support, they came second after the A2s were fully satisfied. However, the A1 farmers' view of marginalisation was also being replicated elsewhere. For instance, the farmers in the communal areas felt that, since the FTLRP, agriculture had become synonymous just with FTFs (FGDs, 27 August 2007).

War Veterans as the organisers of Fast Track Farm communities The War Veterans were prominent as they provided the organising element in the land occupation and subsequently they ran communities following the allocation of land. Chaumba et al. (2003b) and Moyo and Yeros (2005b) argue that the War Veterans helped assert order in a chaotic situation as they used their organising skills learned during the war. The Zimbabwe National Liberation

War Veterans Association is treated as a social movement that has emerged in independent Zimbabwe in order to champion issues of social justice (Moyo and Yeros, 2005a). The War Veterans, though few in number, played a prominent role in organising people, yet at times their mere presence provided confidence (or fear, depending on one's position) to civilians who participated in the *jambanja*. During the land occupations from 2000, the War Veterans organised rural people into constituencies; these were centred around a 'base', a central location where they co-ordinated people and resources for land invasions. This type of structure was developed for co-ordination purposes during the liberation struggle that ended in 1979. Therefore, during the land occupations, people would assemble at central points in different parts of the country before invading farms.

War Veterans were key beneficiaries of the land reform, but were also given further responsibilities to co-ordinate people and communities. During times of elections, they were expected to provide political education. In this context, people on the FTFs, particularly farmworkers, were re-educated about the history of the liberation struggle and why land was a critical resource that had to be a black-owned commodity. At the same time, they also ensured the creation of ordered communities by setting up electable structures that included civilian elements in the communities that were running schemes while waiting for the official allocation of land. In fact, in Mazowe, over time farmworkers gained the confidence of this new social order to the extent of challenging for leadership in some of the new community structures.

Political activists shaping community creation The role of politicians and political parties in shaping the communities on FTFs is known, as shown through their active participation in the processes. In the old resettlement programme that ended in 1997, technical government bureaucrats controlled all aspects. This meant that they influenced social formation by determining who came in and where they settled, as well as the support they got for farming. In the case of the FTFs, the institutional and social formation shifted to ZANU-PF structures. A major objective was to make the land takeover stick through 'political' transformation of the mindset of the civil servant (key informant interview with a War Veteran, 12 May 2004). The new land activists were anti-order, for 'order' meant that the status quo of unequal land ownership would remain (ibid.). Yet the War Veterans also needed civil servants, not just during land takeovers but also afterwards, to help in organising communities so that they could be successful new farmers. A love/hate relationship thus emerged between War Veterans and civil servants.

However, the impact of social organisation and influences on the FTFs began in the places of origin of the beneficiaries. For the A1 farmers, allocation was based on political selection. The screening out of perceived or real opposition party supporters meant that people who were seen as following the ZANU-PF party line were prioritised. In general, as Marongwe (2008) puts it, technical prescriptions that included selecting people with the potential to be good farmers (such as people who had undergone master farmer training) were set aside in favour of political and social criteria in land allocation. For instance, in Mazowe during the initial phases of the land reforms, base commanders who were vicious party supporters or War Veterans would lead the land occupations, mobilising the support of like-minded people. More often than not, these people would become the village chairpersons and start to enact a new form of activism based on managerial control of the schemes, connecting people through patronage networks to gain access to subsidies, and enthusiastically promoting party allegiance through acts of benevolence to the party in the form of donations for party events.

Politics became a strong contributing factor in fostering relationships. In fact, resettled people assumed that everyone belonged to ZANU-PF, and expected everyone to conform to the dictates of the party in many ways. The new resettled farmers expressed allegiance to the then ruling party, ZANU-PF; as one respondent claimed, '*Tiri nhengo dzemusangano nekuti ndiwo wakatipa nyika*' (we are all members of the party as it is the party that gave us land). Being members of one political party united people when it came to national occasions such as Independence Day, Workers' Day, Africa Day and Heroes' Day. The new farmers participated through donating food, money and time to these national celebrations, although, in private, some people complained that they were 'forced' to contribute in cash or in kind. Most of these celebrations were held at business centres, community halls or meeting places (*paruware*). To a great extent, such national events became a marker to establish the support base, with the result that those not seen to be actively participating were viewed as 'sell-outs' (*vatengesi*). In many cases, *vatengesi* faced the threat of eviction, although the participants in the FGDs could not pinpoint specific cases of such politically motivated evictions.

A key role for political activism was to change the mindset of people living on the FTFs. This involved the re-education of farmworkers, in particular on the issues of resource control and empowerment. At the same time, activists wanted to demonstrate to farmworkers that the era of white-dominated farming was over. However, this discourse was aimed not just at farmworkers, but also at new beneficiaries who needed to be schooled on what their access to land meant and what in turn they had to give to their benefactors. Broad support for ZANU-PF was paramount and ended up as a key expectation in the new communities. It was not expected that settlers could challenge 'their land benefactor'. Thus settlers, even those who obtained land through legitimate means, would grumble about the autocratic people taking responsibility for overseeing governance issues in the schemes. A culture of fear (based on political intimidation) became prevalent on the FTFs; this was not conducive to community development, for which trust and tolerance were fundamental.

Re-inventing traditional leadership The government attempted to create order in these new social spaces, at a time when many other issues also had to be addressed. Given the governance problems on the FTFs during the first few years, the government declared that chiefs had no jurisdiction in resettlement areas unless the responsible minister made such a declaration.[6] However, government could not completely ignore traditional leaders. To this end, the traditional leaders in Mazowe become an appendage of the DLC, which was responsible for land allocation and land-related conflict resolution. This provided them with an opportunity to influence land reform and also to shape the emerging communities, based on their presence not only on the committee but also on the farms. They played a significant role in terms of mobilisation, and they also contributed to the minimisation of violence and intimidation (interview with Chief Chiweshe, October 2007).

Yet the traditional leaders were also compromised in various ways, especially when they were given government remuneration, motor vehicles, electrification of their communal area houses, repair of roads to their homesteads, and renovations of their houses through the Ministry of Local Government. This was in addition to the farms they obtained as their second homes on the FTFs (they often received full farms rather than subdivided plots). However, in Mazowe, Chief Chiweshe did not get a farm, while Chief Negomo received a full farm with a farmhouse and was showered with all the farming equipment and inputs he required. The benefits were seen as recompense for their leadership role in the community, but at times the material resources they acquired blurred this role. This remuneration transformed them into semi-politicians, whereas, as traditional leaders, they were supposed to be apolitical. While the then ruling party (ZANU-PF) may not have forced traditional leaders to be political, it was government that incentivised them, and, in turn, traditional leaders may have erroneously felt obliged to serve the political purposes of ZANU-PF. A political activist indicated that, in many cases, the traditional leaders were not compelled to serve the ruling political party, but they did so out of their own volition.

The issue of remuneration and the social role of the traditional leaders has been the subject of widespread concern in Zimbabwe. While there is no problem with remunerating leaders, that remuneration came through a government ministry rather than from independent funding.[8] In other words, the executive then had a free rein in interfering in the affairs of traditional leaders. Of concern, and critical in shaping the emerging social relations in newly resettled areas, is that the Traditional Leadership Act stipulated that traditional leaders should be remunerated for their services. This suggested that they were employees, and therefore they ended up paying allegiance to their government 'employer'.

The manner in which traditional leaders assumed jurisdiction over new re-settlement areas is contested by some land beneficiaries, especially A2 farmers. The A2 farmers indicated that chiefs were supposed to represent and lead A1 farmers, because they lived with them. In fact, the A2 farmers saw themselves as commercial and therefore outside the jurisdiction of traditional leaders. Yet, even on the A1 farms, the effectiveness of chiefs in managing conflicts was already weakened through their incorporation into the DLCs. In many cases, their views, as representatives of the people, were overruled in the commit-tees, thus rendering their social power worthless. Individuals on the FTFs, who were effectively their 'subjects', also contested their power and influence, which made them appear weak.

The village heads were respected on the A1 farms in Mazowe. Many of them were appointees of the chiefs who governed the area, such as Headman Makope, Chief Chiweshe and Chief Negomo. Those A1 areas that chose their own village heads, either someone in a position of political influence or a War Veteran, have found that their village heads are very autocratic and not sensitive to the needs of the people they serve. They are not involved in local traditional ceremonies as they do not have relationships with the ancestors of the land. According to Munyuki-Hungwe (2008), Chief Chiweshe in particular was vocal about the appointment of village heads from outside the Chiweshe communal areas. He argued that the communal areas could not assimilate people from outside unless they learned the values and ways of the local people. He indicated that they required ten to 15 years to become accustomed to the area's traditions and beliefs, before being appointed village heads.

The influence of A2 farmers in the emergence of communities on the Fast Track Farms The A2 model was designed for the elite and the A1 for the masses. A beneficiary's asset base, position in society, wealth and related social level were critical elements in their placing on the social ladder, and therefore their access to land. The composition of this elite class has shaped the characteristics of emerging groups, the relationships within those groups and the relationships that they have with their A1 counterparts, service providers and traditional leadership. The A2 farmers influenced communities in various ways – during *jambanja*, some of them provided resources to land occupiers (Sadomba, 2008). The relationships that emerged at the time of the farm occupations have evolved over the years, and have created specific relationships among A2 farmers, and also between A2 and A1 farmers, that are determined by the spaces in which they live and farm. In fact, common challenges tended to bring the farmers together, as they tried to manoeuvre around the difficulties of new and unfamiliar spaces.

The relationships between A1 and A2 farmers are not always acrimonious. In fact, they are often positive, but only when the *political* circumstances under which they ended up on the FTFs are considered. While resentment of A2 farmers by A1 farmers recurred at different forums, the A1 farmers realised the political weakness of their bargaining power. They became calculating (see Chapter 4) in terms of defending their spaces through passive and active political and social tactics. On the ground, ZANU-PF officials were largely influential in ensuring that members had access to land, and they were seen whenever government organised the provision of 'free' resources (inputs and subsidies) to the FTFs. Sometimes this created fissures, as there was a view among settlers that such resources were biased towards the A2 farmers. However, the fact that in most cases A2 farms existed side by side with A1 farms meant that often the farmers attempted to establish good neighbourly relations. The A2 farmers assisted A1 farmers with farming resources, providing transport and lending tractors and other equipment, depending on what resources they had available.

Relationships between the A2 farmers and farmworkers were also a key issue. The A2 farmers brought in their own workers, which created conflicts with the previous farmworkers in terms of sharing housing, while the ex-farmworkers' rights to housing were weakened due to their resistance to working for the new farmers and paying bills.

Civil servants in charge of creating Fast Track Farm communities A whole range of civil servants in different government departments shaped the FTFs, either through the planning of land settlements or through their presence on the farms. As beneficiaries, they joined the FTF communities and had an impact on those communities from inside, as some sought to effect policy regulations while resident on the farms. In some cases they were thrown off their farms because of their attempts to informally take charge of schemes without having any leadership credentials (key informant interviews, Concession, June 2007).

By joining the scramble for land, many civil servants weakened their technical position in the FTLRP. It is because of this that they faced stiff resistance from the occupiers and those allocated land when they tried to establish their presence on the FTFs by living in the compounds or farmhouses. Many land beneficiaries also claimed that some civil servants lacked professionalism and were attempting to derail the land reform process. The distinction between civil servants and the political party in most cases became blurred. This was because civil servants could be War Veterans, political party leaders or farmers, and they could also play a role in syndicates. The syndicates were a geographically based form of collective organisation for the resource-rich A2 farmers to gain further support from government. They were called 'syndicates' as a deliberate borrowing from corporate language in order to distinguish the social status of their members, some of whom came from the private corporate sector. The prominent syndicates in Mazowe were the Mazowe syndicate and the Nyabira syndicate.

In interviews in Mazowe, the civil servants defended their claim to land and their stay on the FTFs, arguing that: they were Zimbabweans with the same rights as everyone else.

White farmers and co-existence White farmers resident on the commercial farms received and reacted to the shock of the land takeovers in various ways. While some immediately packed and left, others waited to see what would happen. In Mazowe District, intimidation and demonstrations were common, but there was less or even no violence in some areas. The more liberal and less radical white farmers in the Commercial Farmers' Union mooted the idea of co-existence with new landowners. In some areas, farmers negotiated individually and/or collectively; this allowed a few white farmers to remain, and some are still there now. Therefore, in Mazowe in 2004, out of the 459 original white farmers, some 11 remained, but the current figure is not known. At this point in the short history of the FTFs, white farmers are no longer a significant factor in social organisation.

The influence of the white farmers has been severely dented by the FTLRP. The white farmers, and therefore the communities on the LSCFs, were the result of the political construction of colonial Zimbabwe. Many had no homo-geneous roots or a unified history of their own and so they constructed power-ful myths that justified their presence in Rhodes's conquered land. White farmers as settlers created their own exclusive elitist world view, which largely sought to fortify themselves socially against black communities (Taylor, 2002; Selby, 2006). Even after ten years of the FTLRP, they did not attempt to create a new social order in which they would be proactive in aligning themselves with the majority. A few white farmers made limited attempts at providing community assistance (such as donating produce at public events or assisting neighbouring new farmers) but this came too late. Throughout the FTLRP, white farmers saw themselves as rational beings with a better understanding of law and social order than the majority blacks involved in *jambanja*. This fuelled animosity, which Taylor (2002: 7) summed up as follows:

> despite their bid to 'belong' in Zimbabwe, the white farmers also uneasily
> acknowledge their rootlessness and construct themselves as a quasi-Western
> 'other', thus inadvertently collaborating with the state's definition of their alien
> identity.

A somewhat uneasy relationship exists between the beneficiaries and the remaining white farmers. There have been conflicts over continued access to farm housing for farmworkers, and over resources such as land and water.

Thefts, which are said to be rife since resettlement, mean that co-existence comes with its own problems, as the previous security put in place by white farmers no longer exists. Some white farmers ignore minor cases of theft and intrusion and do not report them to the police for fear of instigating hatred and fights with new settlers. However, there are also many instances of peaceful co-existence, with some remaining white commercial farmers participating in local civic issues and providing support to new farmers in the form of training and free access to their infrastructure.

A few black farmers had acquired commercial farms in areas dominated by white farmers; these black farmers were never a significant social force as they tended to keep themselves to themselves in a commercial farming model that had developed a cultural system moulded by white farmers. In many ways, they had remained marginal to the social organisation of white commercial farmers, who had their own clubs, sporting activities, union and commodity associations, all of which shaped their own way of life. The War Veterans sought to take over the social clubs, symbolically striking at the heart of white social organisation and therefore their resistance. Some of the social clubs (in Concession and Glendale) were handed over to the more important A2 farmers or to the council to manage. Such access to and control of social clubs by the A2 elites make their presence on the FTFs highly visible; the majority War Veterans and A1 farmers lack their own spaces based on this form of social organisation.

The paradoxical relationship between ex-farmworkers and new settlers Relationships between former farmworkers and settlers are complex due to a number of factors. Farmworkers remained outside the normal governance structures available to other Zimbabwean communities largely because they were traditionally viewed as 'aliens', even though many of them are Zimbabweans.[9] The FTLRP directly affected their livelihoods in the sense that they lost their main source of employment, while their lives were disrupted, especially in the first years of the programme when the transfer of land was chaotic. In general, ex-farmworkers, of whom about 10 per cent are of foreign descent, were vulnerable due to the arbitrary eviction from their labour-tied accommodation.[10]

In terms of access to land, according to the Government National Land Audit (2006), only 0.03 per cent of ex-farmworkers obtained land. Much of this land was small in size compared with the A1 plots; these 'farmworker plots' were typically less than a hectare and were located on the periphery of the arable land. The farmworkers did not have strong political representation in mainstream national politics, hence there were no national actors to fight for their cause. In Mazowe, most of the former farmworkers have remained on the farms, largely because they did not have anywhere else to go; they chose to work for whoever offered the best rewards for their labour.

Some farmworkers who lost their source of livelihood moved in pursuit of economic opportunities outside farming areas or to other farms where they engage in gold panning, commercial sex work and other income-generating activities. The continued presence of unemployed farmworkers on the farms has been a cause for concern for the authorities and land beneficiaries, and relations between farmworkers and farmers are fraught with tension and conflict. Fast track farmers also hold farmworkers in low social regard: for example, farmers on the Hamilton and Davaar Farms alleged that farmworkers were immoral and promiscuous and changed partners every day. They accused them of being lazy and greedy.

The new landowners accuse ex-farmworkers of theft – both of household goods and farm produce and by overcharging for their labour. On the other hand, the farmworkers accuse the new landowners of not paying them fairly for their labour and of constantly threatening eviction from the housing compounds where they reside. Threats of eviction are rife when the farmworkers choose not to work for the new landowners, opting for *maricho* (casual farm labour) on other farms. This animosity is particularly intense on farms where the farmworkers opted to protect the former white commercial farmer during land occupations instead of being part of the occupations.

The government lacks a clear policy on the fate of former farmworkers. There is an expectation that they should work for the new landowners. The Utete (2003a) report recommended that government urgently address the situation of former farmworkers in the farm compounds. It noted that 'their continued presence on the farms had created numerous problems arising from illegal gold panning, misuse of farm facilities and resources and general criminal activities'. The lack of policy on what happens if a farmworker refuses to work for the new landowners has created mixed fortunes for both the new landowners and the ex-farmworkers. On some A2 farms, former farmworkers refusing to work for new landowners have been forcibly evicted.

Many of the ex-farmworkers have remained on the farms, despite perceptions of insecurity. On some farms, former farmworkers can now negotiate for better wages with an increased number of new landowners, meaning an increased number of potential employers. They also have more freedom of movement than they had under the former commercial farmers. In many cases, they take advantage of the lack of unity among the new farmers on remuneration matters; the previous owners were able to standardise pay. Thus wages and other incentives offered, such as food rations, vary from farmer to farmer, creating room for farmworkers to move rapidly from farm to farm to get the highest remuneration, much to the chagrin of the new farmers. Those new landowners with better resources use this advantage to attract labour at the expense of others. One settler complained that former farmworkers are nurturing mistrust and animosity among settlers because they claim that they are paid a certain fee or wage for a particular task, and in most cases this is not true.

A1 and A2 farmers are failing to share available labour on the farms. The A1 farmers complain about the shortage of labour, mainly because they cannot compete in terms of remuneration and working conditions with surrounding A2 farmers. Most of the former farmworkers are now working for the A2 farmers, who provide them with the protective clothing that the A1 farmers cannot supply. The farmworkers themselves liken their poverty to that of most A1 farmers: one farmworker quipped, '*tosevenzera sei varombo sesu*' (how can we work for poor people like us). Settlers pointed out that labour issues and relations between the settlers should be addressed by the farmers' unions that are now making their presence felt in newly resettled areas.

Skilled farmworkers, such as those who worked as irrigation supervisors, tractor drivers and mechanics in the farm workshops, have benefited from the land reform through access to land but also, more importantly, through being hired by different farms to assist the new farmers. On some FTFs, they are now known as 'consultants', which means that they have moved up a class in the social order of Zimbabwe. In Mazowe District, for example on farms with irrigation infrastructure, the Committees of Seven would in some instances recommend that former farmworkers with relevant specialist skills be allocated land so that the new farmers in the area could benefit from those skills. At the A1 Usk Farm in Mazowe, one such former farmworker heads the irrigation committee. However, this kind of symbiotic relationship between the former farmworkers and the new landowners has not been fully exploited in new resettlement areas.

Fostering new social relationships

The advent of the resettlement programme brought some changes to the nature of family structures. The families in the resettlement areas are more individualised since the communities do not consist of relatives, as is the case in the communal areas. The beneficiaries still maintain their previous homes, creating multiple families, social and economic responsibilities in the process. Initially, most of the plot holders (2007 survey, n=539; 75.13 per cent) indicated that they were no longer farming on the plots they had before resettlement. However, after further probing during FGDs, it was revealed that more than 75 per cent of the farmers are still maintaining their homes of origin due to uncertainty about their permanence in the resettlement areas. At the time of the surveys, the majority of FTLRP beneficiaries were still in transition, having erected only temporary structures on their new lands. Thus, there is still some movement backwards and forwards and interactions with the old communities.

In fact, due to the uncertainty on the FTFs, the nature of families has changed, in that split households have become a significant phenomenon. It was noted that farmers still maintained homes in their places of origin, and usually there are family members maintaining that home. Munyuki-Hungwe (2008) found that the men in the resettled areas left their wives and children when they went in search of new farms. Most have lived as split families since 2000, visiting their families but living as single people. Some have taken in girlfriends or mistresses (who have become known as 'small houses'), a phenomenon that has mushroomed in the new resettlement areas (Munyuki-Hungwe, 2011). Some men have resorted to remitting money and grain to their wives and never visiting their families, as they now have new temporary small houses (i.e. mistresses) in these resettlement areas.

Some of the A1 respondents indicated that, when they become fed up with the pressures of the FTFs, they retreat to the communal areas because they miss their relatives. Others made pragmatic decisions, for example if they had children of school age who had to remain behind so that their education was not disturbed. The non-existence (or inadequacy) in the new areas of social structures such as schools, clinics and community halls justified splitting the families. This usually means that the mother in such families will alternate between the two homes. This is designed to ensure that the children are monitored, while at the same time the mother plays her expected role at the resettlement home. Where this arrangement is not in place, the incidence of extra-marital affairs and divorce can increase, with a resulting destruction of the family structure. Some extra-marital partners become permanent, to the extent that they also get support from the family's income. Traditional leaders noted that this practice is common and a major cause of domestic violence and divorce.

Trust and new social relationships

In Mazowe District, the tendency towards fostering closer relationships was influenced by the origins of the settlers. The class factor was significant in the sense that those from urban areas tended to quickly foster relationships because of common origin: they had the same way of life and the same ways of doing things. Those from the communal areas also used their common background to foster relationships. But, overall, settlers came from different areas, had diverse cultures, norms and values, and different backgrounds, education and other experience, and this created the atmosphere of trust and/ or mistrust between the settlers, between settlers and former farmworkers, and between A1 and A2 farmers. In addition, common participation in *jambanja* fostered close relationships, and this shared history continues to shape such relationships. However, over time the beneficiaries ended up identifying with each other, and so the key issue now is how settlers are responding to a collective opportunity in the form of land as a public good.

Using trust as a key indicator, respondents to a 2007 survey (n=539) were asked if they trusted the other people on the FTFs. At least 60 per cent of the respondents indicated that they do not trust the people around them. When probed further into the reasons why, at least 85 per cent said it was because people steal. Those who had indicated that they did trust other people gave social assistance (29 per cent) as the key reason for this (see Table 8.1). The people on the FTFs did not feel like a community because they originated from different parts of the country. On a comparative basis, the resettled farmers found trust levels higher in their areas of origin, such as the communal areas or urban settlements, than in the resettlement areas. Others trusted only people from their own ethnic grouping or totem.

TABLE 8.1 Issues of trust and mistrust between people on the resettled land

| Why they trust | | | Why they don't trust | | |
Reason	No.	%	Reason	No.	%
Assist each other with social activities	59	29	Some steal	194	82
Assist each other with production	32	15	Some gossip	4	2
Assist each other with marketing	13	6	Some are selfish	5	2
Assist each other with community development issues	13	6	Some former farm workers have dubious characters	34	14
Good social relations	90	43	Total	237	100
Total	207	100			

Source: Ruzivo survey, 2007.

Life on the FTFs has gone through transition, with many getting used to living there. Farmers were asked what they missed most from their places of origin: 63 per cent (n=455) said nothing, while 26 per cent said relatives. This answer partly reflected a defensive posture, given that the respondents feared that they would be labelled 'unpatriotic' and accused of sabotaging the land reform programme if they answered differently. A series of probing questions allowed them to reveal some of their real experiences of living on the farms, both good and bad (see Table 8.2). The new farmers are assisting each other in terms of ploughing and sharing knowledge and transport, especially for transporting produce. Therefore relationships are being fostered based on their shared existence and their desire for successful agricultural production.

It emerged that people in newly resettled areas, especially on A1 farms, had

TABLE 8.2 Contrasting experiences of living on the FTFs in Mazowe

| Benefits of living on the FTFs | | | Social challenges faced since resettlement | | |
Reason	No.	%	Reason	No.	%
Farming	89	17	None	218	53
Easy access to natural resources, e.g. water and firewood	27	5	Theft	71	17
No congestion	67	13	Not having friends	11	3
Improved agricultural production and income	131	25	Limited entertainment	49	12
Better access to inputs	3	1	Long distance to business area (shops, grinding mills)	18	4
Better access to loans	1	0.2	Inadequate accommodation	15	4
Peaceful area	155	30	Poor sanitation	9	2
Other	49	10	Mistrust among farmers	5	1
Total answers	522	100	Building relations with former farmworkers	13	3
			Underdeveloped school infrastructure	2	1
			Total answers	411	100

Source: Ruzivo survey, 2007.

trusting relationships due to having similar totems or by virtue of going to the same church. Yet some farmers in Mazowe felt that strangers had been allowed in their district, which lowered levels of trust. In fact, one beneficiary expressed a common sentiment by declaring that: 'Mazowe belongs to the Zezuru and Korekore' (FGD, June 2007) and one chief passionately argued that *mabvakure* (people from other areas/districts) compromised social relationships. However, Zimbabwean societies develop through natural processes such as marriages between people of different groups and simply from people living in close proximity for a long time.

Thefts and social misdemeanours on the Fast Track Farms

During the first few years of the FTLRP, there were numerous problems of thefts on the FTFs. In fact, thefts were hard to detect, given the mayhem as people took equipment without proper records of handover as the previous owners left the farms. However, most of the blame was placed on ex-farmworkers. In the interviews, respondents pointed out that theft of private and state property was rife. Cases of theft of produce, house breaking and poaching of natural resources were widespread in the new resettlement areas. In the 2007 survey, nearly three-quarters (74 per cent: n=539) of the respondents said that they or their neighbours had had something stolen from them. Of the things stolen, farm produce (43 per cent) and farm equipment (31 per cent) were highest on the list. Other things that were stolen included livestock, food and household goods. In fact, the most common types of theft were thefts of farm equipment (as mentioned above), especially irrigation equipment, fences, gum poles, livestock and crops (in-field and harvested) and breaking into shops and stealing groceries.

While the scheme committee attempted to resolve cases where the perpetrators were known locally, most of the cases were said to involve unknown outsiders, and such cases were referred to the police. The FTF farmers blamed the police for not dealing diligently with reported crimes, including theft. New farmers pointed out that suspected thieves were reportedly released without clear reasons, which upset the victims. In fact, in the FGDs in 2007, many expressed concern that there was a possibility that thieves could have been making deals, given that 'even the police were also suffering from the economic challenges and could do anything to survive'.

At a results feedback workshop at Nzvimbo growth point in June 2005, an officer from the Zimbabwe Republic Police explained the challenges they had in the new resettlement areas, including a lack of resources to carry out patrols and investigations, and the inability to deploy officers throughout the district. In addition, they blamed the lack of a sense of trust among settlers, and low levels of community organisation. This meant that the cost of trying to manage criminal activity was high compared with that in urban areas, and especially when compared with the cost in communal areas, which had relatively fewer police posts. The police envisaged the creation of community policing as complementary to their own work, because at times crime was community specific. By 2006, some FTF communities were offering farmhouses to be used as police posts. This made the police presence more visible on the FTFs and thus reduced crime rates.

Socialisation in the context of a new life on the Fast Track Farms

The former commercial farmers' residency on their farms enabled the establishment of networks and relationships founded on a common cause to make the farms habitable. The former commercial farmers regarded farming as a way of life and a full-time job commitment. The beauty and permanence of their homesteads, as well as other infrastructure investments, epitomised the passion they felt for this lifestyle. To this end, they invested in key social activities, which over time defined a commercial farming culture.

The former farmers established a string of social clubs that helped foster business and pleasure and were platforms for discussing issues of common interest, such as security on the farms, inputs and marketing issues. Extramural activities are, however, affected by lifestyle choices, which in turn are class-based. For example, white farmers used to meet and socialise at farmers' clubs, which provided a bar, various sporting activities and meeting points. They would bring their families, and strong bonds were created among farmers. After the FTLRP, these farmers' clubs continued, albeit with some changes.

There is some difference in the way in which white farmers used these clubs, as important institutions for creating feelings of belonging to a unified class, and the way in which the new farmers use them. The new farmers are now creating artificial differences among those who are supposed to offer a united voice when lobbying for issues that affect agriculture. This has led to the A1 farmers creating and joining various institutions that offer a better sense of belonging, such as religious groups, football clubs, co-operatives, savings clubs and various committees. These institutions have helped with social networking among farmers and have allowed for the emergence of a moral code in the newly resettled areas. While they are important in the lives of new farmers, these institutions nonetheless operate in a fragmented way, without bringing people together as farmers. Therefore, they do not help to create a common 'farmer consciousness'.

However, the new farmers have limited scope for networking, especially as some of them are permanently employed elsewhere. Membership of social clubs on farms has been exclusionary, benefiting mostly A2 farmers rather than A1 farmers. In Mazowe, the Glendale Country Club still operates, with a new membership of A2 farmers who have the money and vehicles to join and attend functions. A1 farmers have limited access to these clubs due to their lack of resources; members are required to pay joining and subscription fees. Even the A2 farmers who are members come only for the bar, as the sporting facilities are now dilapidated. They rarely bring their families, although they do attend some meetings as members.

On many FTFs, social infrastructures that could help in cultivating social capital at a local level are limited. Men have many beer-drinking venues, political party meetings, etc. that they can use as platforms to discuss farming matters. Apart from church, women generally have limited platforms for sharing their experiences. Therefore, associational life in the newly resettled areas is divided along class and gender lines.

The A2 farmers, who have amassed assets from the previous owners, are financially capable of investing their off-farm income to make their farms habitable and are modelling themselves as the new '*varungu*' (new white bosses) to demonstrate their class elevation. The A2 farmers rarely meet and tend to be individualistic and aloof in many ways. In Mazowe, there were atypical cases of A1 farmers sharing a farm with an A2 farmer. Such cases were riddled with conflict between the two classes of farmer, as the A1 farmers complained that the A2 farmers were not bound by the same traditional rules as they were.

Farms can become places for fun and relaxation: some large A2 farms are making use of the therapeutic effects of the countryside and nature by hosting activities such as fishing and partying at weekends. Natural class consciousness has led to A2 farmers investing in their social lives on the farms. This marks the beginning of the building of new communities, different from both those of the past landowners and those of the majority A1 farmers, who are struggling in difficult circumstances.

In Mazowe District, some 76.5 per cent of A1 farmers are full-time farmers and most of them reside on their plots, compared with 26.5 per cent full-time farmers in the A2 model. The implications of this are twofold: on the one hand, it means that a significant number of landowners are not resident on the farms to conduct operations and contribute to community development processes taking place. On the other hand, the landholders could be mobilising resources to support their farming operations from their work incomes and networks away from the FTFs. At a farm in Mazowe, the village head indicated that there are problems with people who are not resident on the farms because they do not attend community meetings that are designed not only to foster better relations among the scheme members but also to help each other in production matters.

Young people found FTFs a social 'pain' (or *marwadzo* in their lexicon) because of the 'social dryness' in areas they describe as 'places without deals' (*hakuna dhiri*). Young people require social engagement, but this is lacking. Some youths found the FTFs to be 'slow and boring' compared with communal areas. They would like to be involved in sports such as football as part of community recreation; sports as entertainment help communities come together when they play and watch games and therefore interact socially, which in turn helps them feel more like a community. The young people would like sport to unify them and would like to play against other farming communities throughout the district. For example, they pointed out that *'tinoda katamba bhora revasikana nevakomana tizive kuti tiri tese'* (we want to play soccer for young men and women so that we can use it to make us feel like a community). The parents of these youths also support sports as they feel that idle young people have tended to get involved in crime, gold panning and alcohol abuse.

Depending on the scheme (A1 or A2), there are certain further differences in how people relate to each other. In the A1 schemes in Mazowe, farmers settled in a villagised model interact on a daily basis. In most cases the relationships in A1 farms arise out of the need for people to unite for a common cause, such as building a clinic, or the sharing of everyday implements. The households on these farms have turned from being strangers to neighbours over the past nine years.

Rebuilding a sense of collective belonging

Farmers in new resettlement areas network through both formal and informal institutions. The 2007 survey showed that 34.8 per cent (n=539) are members of religious groups; this compares with 38 per cent of the farmers being members of agricultural organisations such as agriculture consortiums, farmer irrigation schemes or co-operative projects. Religion is critical in building social capital among newly resettled farmers, and involvement with churches is a sign that new communities are indeed emerging in these areas (Matondi, 2005). The mainstream churches, such as Roman Catholic, Methodist and Anglican, exist alongside numerous apostolic churches (i.e. charismatic, 'born again' or Pentecostal). It seems that the apostolic churches are the most popular in new resettlement areas, especially in the A1 scheme.

It was easier for communities to establish themselves in the A1 schemes because of the higher population numbers. In fact, in the A2 model, farmworkers are the dominant participants, given that the landholders tend to be both physically absent and aloof. Peri-urban areas also have high numbers settlers participating in urban-based church activities. The role of the church can be critical in promoting peace and good relations, which may minimise cases of intolerance and violence. In all parts of the country, various religious denominations are being used as a basis for relationship building between people from diverse backgrounds.

New farmers have taken to organising 'farmer field days' as critical spaces for sharing knowledge and information, showcasing the latest farming technology, comparing farmer production performance trends, rewarding hard-working farmers and encouraging those lagging behind, and sharing advice on issues such as HIV and AIDS. Some respondents (28 per cent; n=475) found field days to be an important source of agricultural information, while some regarded political functions such as national Independence Day (21 per cent) as important platforms for getting political information (Table 8.3). Other important social organisations emerged in the form of burial societies, savings clubs, health committees, school development committees, irrigation committees and churches. These organisations provide the farmers with collective channels to influence policy and to organise their production and the way they live. Networks that are built on trust, such as burial societies and savings clubs, were strong in providing tangible help, which churches were not able to do. The mixed responses to questions about social networking corroborate the high levels of mistrust within newly resettled farming communities that have been observed. Savings clubs and co-operatives are taking time to get established, yet they provide a framework for the mobilisation of financial resources for members of the community.

The presence of farmer organisations and settler participation in those organisations are not well developed on the FTFs. Perhaps this reflects the relative youthfulness of the schemes themselves and the fact that the levels of interpersonal interactions among the settlers might still be very low. Less than 15 per cent of newly resettled farmers in A1 settlements in Mazowe District belong to a farmers' union. Most A1 farmers are not sure whether they belong to the Zimbabwe Farmers Union but use the farming discounts that are offered by the union whenever they are available. Those A1 farmers who participate in collective activities tend to belong to irrigation clubs and commodity associations. This has helped them in pooling resources for fuel, getting inputs from the Grain Marketing Board as a group, and also negotiating for marketing contracts. Some of the A1 farmers have used political platforms to lobby various government parastatals for assistance in agriculture.

On the other hand, the A2 farmers have tended to use their resources and asset base to form 'agricultural consortiums'. Many of these draw potential members based on political affiliation (some of these members are top officials of the former ruling political party) and exclude those who do not belong to their circles. These groupings have a major influence on relationships at the local level, but they are also significant for accessing the necessary government support for farming on the FTFs. In general, the A2 farmers are inclined towards developing as a class based on individualism, while at the same time seeking representation as a group on land tenure security issues, for instance, which may be peripheral to A1 farmers.

TABLE 8.3 Farmers' civic participation in Mazowe District

Community events farmers usually participate in	No.	%	Importance attached to local community events	No.	%
Field days	134	28	Rain making and agricultural information	36	9
Independence Day	101	21	Political information update	70	17
Party meetings (political)	55	12	Social interaction, co-operation and politics	71	17
Funerals	35	7	Getting agricultural information and know-how and grieving together	143	35
Agricultural shows	27	6	Sharing of ideas and information	57	14
Traditional functions	61	13	Upholding culture	31	8
Maintenance of farm infrastructure and equipment	13	3	Physical fitness	1	0.2
Sports	11	2	Total answers	409	100
None	38	8			
Total answers	475	100			

Source: Ruzivo survey, 2007.

Conclusions

The livelihoods of the land beneficiaries have undergone tremendous transformation and new social communities are emerging in resettled areas. It is clear that social reorganisation is taking place, fostered initially by the need for land, but shaped by the realities of new spaces that require co-operation rather than competition. The new social communities that have appeared are alive but not well; they face multiple crises and, without exception, are struggling to meet the demands of the new spaces. The populations in the newly resettled farms in Mazowe came from different geographical backgrounds, reflecting the cultural diversity of the country. The class mix, together with specific differences between A1 and A2 farmers and between serving and ex-farmworkers, has created a social milieu that at times contributes to the failure to establish efficient systems and limits the potential to use available skills optimally.

Social capital emanating from kinship, traditional values, norms and customs faces enormous challenges where people with diverse origins have been forced to co-exist. While past colonial policies of land dispossession involved the separation of the families and relatives of indigenous people, the current land reform programme is creating new communities on the basis of volunteerism in settlement. Yet the same programme has also forcibly uprooted communities of white farmers and farmworkers.

The jury is still out on what type of community is emerging, and how different it will be from both the traditional communities in the communal areas and the old system established by the white farmers and their workers. The new breed of A2 commercial farmers is breaking tradition (Munyuki-Hungwe, 2011) by refusing to be locked into the customary cultural systems that dominate in communal areas. Instead, they are fighting to be left alone in order to concentrate on the business of producing – as did the white farmers. In a way, they are forming a new higher social class.

The FTLRP, due to its magnitude, engendered new perceptions in national governance and population distribution. In Mazowe, communities live as collections of households rather than families, and this is compromising social co-ordination. The result is that there is suspicion, lack of trust and allegations of criminal behaviour, especially against ex-farmworkers. This disdain for ex-farmworkers is shaped by several factors, including the behaviour of some of them during the land occupations (some supported white landowners) and cultural differences. The majority of people on the FTFs are Shona and hold those who adopt 'external' cultural practices in low regard, while ex-farmworkers have cultural connections to Malawi and other countries as a result of labour migration during the colonial period.

The situation today is that there are politically strong institutional structures but socially weak communities, which means less propensity towards collective action that could help agriculture in the medium to long term. Farming in the new resettlement areas has a common purpose and therefore should present an opportunity for networking and co-operation. Improved social capital in the new resettlement areas could have a positive effect on production and therefore on people's development in more general terms.

Conclusion: from a 'crisis' to a 'prosperous' future?

Introduction

In the view of many people in Africa, Zimbabwe has done the 'unthinkable' and its president had the 'guts' to take away land from white commercial farmers. The spectacular takeover of white-owned land has seized the imaginations of ordinary people, the media and intellectuals alike in terms of its significance and the ability of Zimbabwe's agriculture to recover from years of production losses. In 2000, Zimbabwe ditched neo-liberal land reform policies, opting for state-centred compulsory land acquisition and broad land redistribution to the majority. The process has not been neat, as it has been permeated by violence and by the disruption not just of agriculture but of people's lives and livelihoods. At the same time, for the majority this represented a defining moment in their empowerment, even if it were set against the acrimonious circumstances of land occupations and forced land transfers. Violence had the effect of undermining the programme in the eyes of Western countries, still arguing ten years later that they will not assist beneficiaries on 'contested' land, waiting for the issues that emerged from the process to be resolved. Yet, it seems now that there is much more open dialogue about what needs to be done to move agriculture forward; this is demonstrated by the fact that the overhyped land conflicts that were typical of the first five years following the launch of the Fast Track Land Reform Programme (FTLRP) in 2000 have now stopped (both in practice and as reported by the media).

Still, many questions linger: should the land transfers have been carried out differently? Should government have been serious about land reform in the first decade after independence in 1980? Should white landowners have played a bigger and more proactive role in addressing the land inequities through offering land? Should there have been much more serious negotiation prior to the FTLRP? Should the international community have supported the outcomes of the donors' conference in 1998, by committing substantial resources? Or should the landowners have given in during negotiations on the Inception Phase Framework Plan in 1999? While these questions are essentially reactive, looking back at something that has already happened, there is also a series of questions that look forward. These questions are: will the land transfers be sustainable into the future? Are new beneficiaries capable of using the land to its maximum potential? What agrarian model is emerging and is it the

235

best model to meet Zimbabwe's needs? Is government capable of reforming its institutions, moving away from its fast track mode and adopting a more normal system of land administration processes and organisations? Will there be a land policy, and what form will it take? Will land reform be reversed? These questions are not easy to answer, but there is a need for action to resolve the issues relating to land in order to regain prosperity and to improve people's livelihoods.

The questions raised above depend on an accommodation being found in which the land transfers are secure, so that beneficiaries and other farmers can focus on land utilisation. There is no question that the land transfers have provided the majority of people with new opportunities, and also the leverage to enjoy economic freedom over the land, which is an important resource. However, the crisis in Zimbabwe was precipitated by a process of land reform that was supposed to have solved an apolitical and socio-economic malaise caused by an economically divided society. As many have discussed, the history of Zimbabwe since the 1880s perhaps shaped the complexity and mixed results of the massive land transfer programme. The outcomes of that history in 2000 were therefore not surprising, simply because continued inequality together with growing poverty were signs that conflicts were bound to erupt at some stage. Poverty and disgruntlement about its causes and impacts precipitated the land crisis, and, as a result, political actors jumped on to the bandwagon to ensure their own survival. Prior to 2000, this crisis had been predicted in political circles; nevertheless, there was political hesitancy about dealing with it then, and this contributed to the adoption of 'crude' methods for the land transfers when they finally happened. For the government and for the party in power (ZANU-PF), political support had been seriously eroded by years of prevaricating on the land issues, while adoption of neo-liberal economic frameworks had further widened the gap between rich and poor, mainly along racial lines.

Radical land transfers and popular triumph

The FTLRP was associated with radical action and revolutionary language: words and phrases such as 'war for the land' (*hondo yeminda*), 'uprising' (*chimurenga*), *jambanja* (mayhem), and so on. The FTLRP promised to deliver a tangible resource in the form of land, something that resonated with the majority blacks as being the first stage of economic emancipation in a largely agrarian society. Kriger (1992: 237) asks the questions: 'How do revolutionary organisations win popular support, what is the evidence of the popular support, and how satisfactory is it?' Stories on the ground show that the FTLRP gained support from beneficiaries as well as from the local technocrats, most of whom became inextricably linked to the programme; others believed that, from an administrative perspective, the programme's principles were right and any problems could be solved over time. Individual choices had a bearing on how the programme unfolded, but these were made against a background of broad political support obtained, significantly, from ordinary Zimbabweans – it was the ordinary Zimbabweans who largely benefited.

However, important policy signals from government, based on economic support for resettled people through inputs and the mobilisation of machinery, were critical in giving settlers an indication of the value of their stake and its future. The greatest positive signal for beneficiaries was the unwavering support provided by the presidium to the land reform programme in its widest sense. In addition, state control of public media meant that the media consistently 'sold' the programme, to the extent of creating a make-believe world for beneficiaries and a sense of defeat among former landowners. The situation today presents what could be described as a 'done deal' (although behind the scenes government is continuing the process of land takeovers); the Inclusive Government seems to have confirmed the view that the process of land transfers is complete in their power negotiations, as reflected in the Global Political Agreement (GPA) of September 2008.

Gaining access to better quality land was the basis upon which the resettlement process obtained popular support. One generation of the beneficiaries comprised an age group that still has vivid memories of its own dispossession in the 1930s to 1960s to make way for large-scale commercial farms, owned mostly by white farmers in exclusive and highly productive areas. For this group of beneficiaries, the repossession of this land is a triumph and a just process to reverse the injustices of the past. Yet the land issue also resonates with the youth to some extent; many young people have struggled to get jobs in the formal sector and have lived a life of 'doing this or that' (*kukiya kiya*) to make ends meet. The youth are captives of what some would describe as a self-inflicted economic crisis that killed the capacity of the economy to create jobs for them. This was in a context in which agriculture alone could not be the basis for job creation. Therefore, when land emerged as a central issue, young people became involved in various ways: as troopers in land occupations, as black marketeers for government inputs (seeds, fertilisers, fuel, etc.), and as middlemen in the trading of produce. The youth have exploited any opportunity that arose for their economic empowerment, not just the ownership of land.

While challenges have limited the realisation of the full potential of the land taken, the beneficiaries believed that their suffering could be no worse on the land than if they remained on the fringes of an unreformed economic system and infrastructure, where the majority (who, supposedly, had political power) toiled away in declining and overpopulated communal areas. In other words, the promises of the FTLRP reached to the depths of the suffering caused by landlessness, but also drew on the betrayal of war heroes and the virtues they stood for – they had been promised land, but this issue had remained unresolved for 20 years. It was a sore point politically that a large number of mostly white farmers remained on prime land and exhibited an unwillingness to share that land, and in the past the government had seemed to support them in staying there. Thus, when the political fortunes of government shifted to the left and towards the peasants and their supporters, the result was that radical land transfers appeared legitimate in the eyes of the poor.

ZANU-PF as a political party seems to have made it possible for people to settle on the land, and has thus provided a future for ordinary Zimbabweans; however, it has also made it easier for whoever is in power in the future not to deal with the most sensitive parts of the land question, particularly land transfers. This is because the most difficult part of land reform – that of taking over land – has already been achieved politically. Whoever rules Zimbabwe next has been provided with a clean slate as a result of a process that has largely been underpinned by crude methods of land transfer such as violence, forced removals, plunder of state resources, and conflicts over the takeovers and allocations. However, the land reform programme will gain popular legitimacy only when the farmers are producing on the land. At the same time, the international community will need to have sufficient confidence that Zimbabwe is facing up to the challenges of the programme and can therefore regain its place in the global village, not as a pariah nation but as a developing state. There are also other key elements that need to be addressed; for example, land tenure uncertainty and the continuing disputes between the remaining landowners, beneficiaries, farmworkers and others.

Calls for a national land audit to organise the sector relate to the need to resolve the outstanding issues from the land transfers. However, the land audit seems to have been explained in a divisive manner that has implied a reversal of the land reforms: the War Veterans, and others, believe that the audit will result in them being removed from the land. The former ruling party views the call for a land audit as an underhand attempt to torpedo the FTLRP, while the former opposition would like to use the land audit as a way of getting even with the former ruling party (there are allegations that opposition party members did not benefit from the transfers). At the same time, the former opposition view land as an important asset for job creation and food security, and believe that currently it is not contributing fully to these objectives. Caught in between these divisions, the beneficiaries question the dictates of the state and the influence of politicians, especially when land audits are prescribed without any clarity about the fate of the beneficiaries on the farms or any proper explanation of the policies that will be used to assess them. These are issues that can be resolved, given that political players at a central level have opened up a space for dialogue and negotiation, which has stabilised the policy-making environment.

The local drivers spurring success in land takeovers

The question, then, is how did the land revolution gain legitimacy on the ground? There is a view that: 'Revolutionary organisations seek popular support by manipulating peasant grievances' (Kriger, 1992: 238). Balancing this against the FTLRP is not easy, because the peasants *needed* representation for their grievances, which in this case arose from the lack of access to land they viewed as having been appropriated illegally. The War Veterans Association became the vanguard, mostly for reasons to do with unfulfilled promises (better livelihoods, access to land, access to education, health and economic empowerment, etc.) following the liberation struggle; by the second decade after independence, this had become a very real source of discontent. The War Veterans, who had largely given up opportunities (educational and in terms of their normal lives) to go and fight the war, became the main victims of an unreformed economic structure in which lack of access to land was a clear cause of economic problems, stretching back to the time of the Economic Structural Adjustment Programme.

While the land takeovers were a major expression of politics, behind the scenes economics was a key force. Moyo (1999) argued that the major source of formal demands for land were elite black farmers, aspiring black investors and agricultural graduates. This base was broadened during the land occupations; the social action created alliances and made it unfeasible for only those with an agricultural background or those with money to be selected as beneficiaries. The government sought to balance land allocation between those with resources and those without, as reflected in the A1 and A2 models. The result was that a broad social mix of people can be found on the Fast Track Farms (FTFs).

Both classes of land beneficiaries have survived the tribulations of the commercial farms. One could observe a range of behaviours on the part of new farmers in terms of how they took action to 'defend their land rights'; these behaviours showed the extent to which they were prepared to defend what they had received through passive resistance and active political dialogue. Nonetheless, they also benefited from a hesitant but powerful state, creating the basis for ceasefire, dialogue and negotiations. The direct and subtle negotiations between the powerful state and the 'weak' peasants, with the powerful and the War Veterans somewhere between them, reveal the fascinating ways in which the state and the peasants need each other in order to succeed. In a way, the peasants could be said to have triumphed over a powerful state, as they eventually ended up being the key beneficiaries of the land transfers. Yet state officials tried to appropriate the best farms, although they were relatively few in number and obtained a small total land area compared with the ordinary peasants. In fact, peasant demonstrations at district offices had the effect of discouraging some of the excesses of the officials, although at times the officials succeeded by adopting much more cautious methods.

Within the land reform process, there was no coercion but there was persuasion of would-be settlers to move to the FTFs. On the FTFs, the beneficiaries had to conform to a certain way of living, ring-fenced by the interest groups on the ground. Although no one was forced to apply for land, the specific living conditions, together with support to the 'benevolent' groups on the ground, seem to imply that the beneficiaries had no freedom. But for some of the settlers, political and economic freedom come with a price, and many experienced that price not so long ago as veterans of the liberation struggle. Therefore, issues of democracy and rights were inconsequential compared with their need for land. Yet, the poverty and lack of economic opportunities in a society that was becoming increasingly unequal were perhaps reasons enough for the initial land transfers to have obtained broad social support.

Technocracy, the state and elites

The land reform programme had distinctive features that involved potential beneficiaries having to legitimise their access to land through government structures. Given the mayhem that propelled the land reform, one would have expected continued chaos, but that did not occur; the government reasserted control, thereby ensuring that some standards were applied to land acquisition, land allocation and settler emplacement, and offered land through a paper-based system whereby an offer letter demonstrated a basic promise of land to each beneficiary. In addition, there was some support for agricultural production and institutional organisation of settlers at farm level through various committees, as shown through the cases in this book.

Whereas, at the beginning of the reforms, technocrats may have been sidelined from the process of land acquisition, they later regained a foothold, albeit in slightly different ways. They had to contend with extra-legal bodies in the decision-making processes, which meant that at times they lost their influence, but largely they managed to hang on to their roles. For instance, at certain times, some personnel from the Rural District Councils were unable to attend District Land Committees, only being allowed to do so after the intervention of senior politicians. Agritex was reduced to farm planning (and extension) and was completely sidelined from participating in the identification of beneficiaries. War Veterans and senior politicians within the district took over central planning and land allocation.

Technocrats tended to agree to the demands of the extra-legal bodies, simply because these bodies pressured them into delivering the land transfers. In some cases, violence, intimidation and picketing by pressure groups at the offices of district administrators were part of the process of forcing the takeover of land, which was enough for the technocrats to change their attitude towards one that facilitated rather than inhibited. Without celebrating the unfortunate violence or threats, the pressure placed on technical bureaucrats had a domino effect in changing the way they worked in isolated rural environments. They had to make pragmatic decisions for their personal security, and they joined the bandwagon and claimed land for themselves. Nevertheless, land management situations differed from place to place, as some districts, such as Mangwe, sought to adhere to the policy guidelines received from Harare.

In some cases, such as Mazowe District, there was a high level of interest from the elites and the security forces in accessing land, and they were allocated land. This meant that, for the technocrats, the process of land management was subject to pressures from this powerful constituency. Various scholars (Moyo, 2001; Sadomba, 2008; Moyo and Yeros, 2005a; Scoones et al., 2010) have tried to advance the idea that there was negligible violence and also that there was a structure and pattern to the programme. It seems that government had a specific interest in controlling land management so that it would not be completely delegitimised in the eyes of its international friends. It therefore re-engineered its own institutions and incorporated security elements to work with the different interest groups at the district level, precisely to control the chaos. While at the outset there was undeniable violence, over time that violence was curtailed as government put in place various land management institutions, although they largely remained weak, for a variety of reasons.

There has been a misrepresentation of the role of the security forces as beneficiaries in the land reform programme. In fact, as pointed out by the land managers, they competed with everybody else. There was no evidence to show that the members of the security forces bent the rules for self-gain; rather, just like everybody else, they followed the procedures if they wanted to gain access to land. However, they did have the upper hand when it came to accessing state resources such as agricultural inputs under the government subsidies programmes. For instance, they were in charge of distribution, and accusations emerged that they prioritised each other before distributing inputs to civilians (Mutonodzo-Davies, 2010). In general, institutional reforms have had the effect of curtailing such advantages, and the security forces involved in farming are now in the same position as other ordinary farmers, purchasing their farming inputs on the open market. A level playing field seems to have been created, which has had the effect of improving agricultural performance.

Successful farmers on the Fast Track Farms

The FTLRP opened up opportunities for many black Zimbabweans: men, women, youths, elites and the poor. The research sought to establish similarities or discernible patterns characteristic of successful farmers. The aim was to establish why some succeeded and others did not, when probably they had the same opportunities when they settled. For the farmers who have settled successfully, the land has provided hope for them, as their economic circumstances have improved enormously compared with their situation in the communal areas. Even for those from urban areas, who were mostly surviving in the informal sector or in low-paying industrial jobs, the acquisition of land provided them with a new opportunity that led to their abandonment of previous occupations. For those who succeeded, it was because:

- they acquired farmhouses and other infrastructure (or commandeered these for themselves);
- they had agricultural knowledge that they could deploy immediately in farming;
- they had access to personal resources that they invested;
- they got access to government input programmes;
- they employed a farm manager;
- they had better market access than others; or
- they juggled crops and ended up producing products that made better money, such as soya beans, which, unlike maize, were not controlled.

The A2 farmers have had mixed fortunes on the FTFs. There are some farmers who have done very well, judging by the assets they have accumulated over the years. Some farmers have grown their activities to become huge exporters of oranges, while others have established processing plants for milk. There certainly has to be an explanation for why these farmers have succeeded, when the majority of the A2 farmers have been struggling, despite the almost equal opportunities that they enjoyed when they entered the FTFs. First, one needs to understand how they became the new elite farmers. In Mazowe, access to the state was necessary but often not sufficient to establish a successful claim to land. At the height of the land transfers and until 2008, many elite politicians used their access to the state and their knowledge of the land policy to acquire access to farming inputs and land resources. However, clearly some of the new farmer elites must have had open access to workers, to other farmers, to politicians, to bureaucrats and to technical extension workers to make their farming businesses a success. Access to the state broadened their access to the resources of the state, so these farmers were found in the priority lists for everything to do with farming, from tractors and harvesters to inputs and fuel. But it was also essential that the A2 elite farmers redistributed their wealth in order to stay in the political limelight, because success for them depended on their ability to dispense favours and goods, not only at politically expedient moments but all the time.

After years on the FTFs, farmers have invested substantially in buying non-motorised equipment and tools such as hoes, shovels, spades, ox-drawn implements, scotch carts and livestock. However, many farmers have supplemented their farming income with other sources of income, such as remittances from formal work or support from relatives in the diaspora (71 per cent) (Mazowe survey 2007, n=539), which makes it difficult to ascertain whether farming really is the main source of livelihood. Scoones et al. (2010) ranked cropping as the main source of income (70 per cent) but said that it was complemented by various off-farm activities. These activities included formal employment, trading, the sale of firewood, the harvesting of edible mopane worms and basket or pottery making. About 5 per cent of the study sample ranked remittances as the major off-farm activity.

In Mazowe, the successful farmers have an urban background and were formally employed before engaging in farming. Whereas the phenomenon of weekend farming may have been rife, in Mazowe there were some who lived on the farms and were involved in the daily management, because the district is close to Harare and they could commute to their formal jobs. They all have relatively little agricultural experience, unlike the farmers who came from the communal areas. The farmers have varied educational qualifications, with the majority having gone through basic primary education and therefore having a sufficient level of literacy to understand agriculture-related matters, administrative issues relating to land, extension, markets and marketing at a minimum level. In fact, it was not possible to tell whether education made any difference to their performance at the initial stage of settling on the land. What is clear, however, is that the successful farmers had advantages in terms of land resources. Some resourceful A2 farmers resorted to their economic social networks for agricultural support when they realised that agricultural finance was a challenge, as demand outstripped the ability of government to provide these resources.

Struggling beneficiaries on the Fast Track Farms

The defining features of the land reform problems are underperformance and poor production on most of the FTFs. The national figures of production decline (Chapter 5) were an indictment of ongoing production issues, which cannot easily be separated from the FTLRP. There are two major causes for the decline. One is that the FTLRP increased the number of farmers but the government did not pay attention to the capacity of input suppliers to service those farmers. Therefore, more farmers on commercial farmland placed pressure on the few input suppliers at a time when funding from some Western nations dried up. The second cause was that experienced, mostly white, farmers left with their skills, creating an immediate negative impact. Other factors, such as droughts, worsened the crisis and the ability of the country to manage these negative impacts. There was underutilisation of land; one extension officer noted that:

> a farmer with probably 100 hectares of arable land only managed to put 6 hectares under crops. Why would such a person insist on retaining 100 hectares? It boggles the mind. (Personal interview with Agritex official at provincial level, June 2010)

A range of factors account for such land underutilisation, as has been noted elsewhere in this book.

The beneficiaries struggle for a variety of reasons, despite having access to high-quality land. For example, Zikhali (2008) found that there is gender discrimination in access to fertilisers, with male-headed households using more fertilisers than female-headed ones. This means that women struggled on the plots allocated to them because poverty limits their use of fertiliser. In addition, she also established that plot holders with more children used less fertiliser per hectare because they have family commitments that limit their ability to purchase fertiliser.

However, in only one or two cases were interviewed farmers considering quitting resettlement because of the struggles they faced; the majority are hoping for a bright future, in time, given that the land they have is of good quality. Others were already engaged in seeking training, or encouraging their children to train in agriculture-related fields.

The elements required to create a prosperous future for the land transfers

Land acquisition, land allocation and complex compensation issues Land acquisition in Zimbabwe remains inconclusive because of one critical issue relating to the constitutional and legal requirement for compensation for land improvements. In addition, there are still issues to be negotiated politically for compensation for the land itself, despite spirited attempts to put this aside in political terms. In its stated policy, the government agrees to pay compensation for both land and improvements only on land under Bilateral Investment Promotion and Protection Agreements (BIPPAs). However, for the beneficiaries to enjoy total peace of mind on their new land, they need the issue of compensation to be addressed in its totality. The beneficiaries are seeking the strongest form of tenure security, one that affirms their rights in the longer term. Yet, at a time when tenure issues are unresolved, threats are emerging in the form of land audits, re-planning, and eviction of those who are underutilising land. These issues intermix to create uncertainty in complex ways, given that the legal position of the beneficiary remains hazy and weak despite the fact that they have scored 'politically' in having obtained access to land. At this stage, the beneficiaries are waging their own forms of passive resistance, through being reluctant to invest significantly in their plots; this reflects the situation in urban areas, where landowners invest only when they acquire stands with title deeds. Thus, the beneficiaries are making pragmatic decisions that limit their exposure to risk.

Addressing land tenure uncertainties This book demonstrates that the land rights situation in the resettlement areas is very fluid and confusing. There is no particular trajectory to follow and the systems seem to be very unstable; they provide both security and insecurity, depending on the social and political standing of individual settlers. The security of tenure in the current resettlement areas is not comparable with that of the resettlement areas established in the early 1980s; the latter had more security based on the fact that, over time, the state gave up control of the resettlement areas by withdrawing the infamous resettlement officers (Matondi, 2001; Dekker and Kinsey, 2011). The current beneficiaries are continuously juggling land rights, identifying points of state weakness, and sharpening their tools of resistance in case the state decides not to give them their rights. One way in which beneficiaries have dealt with local insecurity is to maintain several homes. When asked why they do this, they claim to have invested a lot of money and therefore cannot just relinquish their communal or urban homes. However, there is also a feeling that settlers are dodging the issue of insecurity of tenure in new resettlement areas. This is because they have noted that the state is uncomfortable about having its land authority questioned by the people who have benefited from its legacy of providing them with land for free.

However, given that there are resource issues to consider in the use of land, it would seem that the overall framework within the new resettlement areas does not provide for security of tenure, especially for the A2 farmers. For A1 farmers there is some level of security based on their numbers. What implications does this have for policy? The problem in Zimbabwe lies in policy neglect and paralysis, because the government intervenes only lightly in the matter of tenure. When it does intervene, it is usually through extra-legal bodies that lack institutional depth and legitimacy, as well as lacking knowledge of local processes. In addition, the government does not hesitate to forcibly remove people (Shivji et al., 1998). On the FTFs, the wealthier and better connected potential A2 farmers have received support from the state to push out weaker A1 farmers, invading and cultivating the plots of the weak A1 beneficiaries. The government argues that it has the leeway to do this because it is 'the government' and the FTFs are still to be completely re-planned, which leaves it with room to revisit land that has been allocated and make any changes that are necessary from a technical perspective.

Land tenure issues are becoming the source of conflict on the FTFs, as farmers employ a variety of tenure bidding strategies. The government tries to settle these with mediation and negotiation, but without much commitment because it views some of the conflicts as too trivial. However, the instigators of such conflicts are now realising that government is too weak to enforce policy or law and they take advantage of this situation. It is an interesting contradiction, that even though government is nominally in control of agricultural land, it is very hesitant to use its power in settling land disputes. In some cases, new farmers have gone on to the land and have asserted their authority and have found ways to co-exist in conflict-ridden situations. Yet, as the state has avoided tackling the core reasons for the conflicts, those reasons are reoccurring due to the unilateral action that beneficiaries take outside societal parameters.

New farmers have had to design their own systems of resistance in order to carve out a niche for themselves in the resettlement areas. Scott (1985) presents a list of what he calls evidence of everyday forms of resistance. This resistance requires little or no co-ordination and, by making use of implicit understandings and informal networks, it typically avoids any form of direct confrontation with authority or the elites. The new settlers confront the state through creating new ways of redefining their rights in spite of central policy designs. However, there are also cases noted in the book where beneficiaries leave resettlement areas at various times because they are suddenly unsure of the extent of their room for manoeuvre or uncertain about the likely reaction of the state, which in the past has used systematic force to remove them from the land. The choice to engage in or disengage from action to protect one's rights is therefore conditioned by the political situation at any point in time. The key challenge today is to determine the extent to which new farmers will have autonomy in the current (and future) dispensation as they settle into the newfound 'glory' of land.

There is a very strong case for the eventual issuing of title deeds, although this elicits robust opposition from advocates against title deeds. The farmers interviewed want title deeds for the properties they are getting, yet armchair critics of title deeds would rather they got leaseholds as a 'halfway house' solution to tenure uncertainty. Most of the debates on freehold title deeds have been monopolised by a few intellectuals and bureaucrats, many of whom preach against freehold title deeds, yet personally prefer such ownership for whatever property they access and own. The issue is not about the rights or wrongs of either title deeds or leaseholds, but the pragmatic reality and demands of beneficiaries on the ground based on their judgement of the FTLRP and the role of the state. This was clearly an emotional issue and they wondered why government could not give them the 'papers' to finalise land takeover. The farmers were also clear about their status in the resettlement areas through distinguishing communal areas (*kumusha*) as places of social living and the new resettlement areas (*kumapurazi*) as places of work and production, which require clear tenure rights.

Farmer advocacy for title deeds emerges from an open economy and a society that believes strongly that ownership comes through 'papers' submitted through some legal process that can then be defended in a court of law. Such a 'paper' can convince the bank manager to release loans, can be used to access inputs from private companies, can convince international investors to partner the farmers, and can be used for personal identity, and so on. It is the flexible use of this 'paper' – a title deed – that provides the potential for stabilising conflicts over land and the pervasive boundary problems. Governments[1] and markets respect this paper very much for the reasons stated above, so why can it not be given to new farmers?

Better land use planning, investments and utilisation The land beneficiaries noted in this book are faced with an uncertain future in the resettled areas. They have had to respond to the rapidly changing situations in their local areas. Some settlers invested in assets (farmhouses, paddocking, farm machinery, etc.) despite the uncertainty. Moyo (2008) has identified a range of investments that the new farmers have made, some of them completely new, on the farms that they were allocated. This is against the conventional wisdom that when farmers are in situations of tenure uncertainty they tend to underinvest or completely stop putting resources into the land. Why do farmers behave in this manner? First, new farmers are in a constant struggle with the state and its agencies and are therefore not passive compliers with policy. They take advantage of the loopholes in blanket policy pronouncements that farmers must be 'weaned off' perpetual state subsidies and go on to invest, knowing full well that they may have no rights on the land they are farming.

Second, the farmers dig into the state subsidies by taking loans from government itself, and then they invest these partly in farming and partly in other things. Government is likely to be sympathetic to these farmers on the basis that, in the last few years, many have taken heavily subsidised government credit and have invested it outside agriculture, so they cannot be thrown off the land when the government has not recovered its money. In any case, during much of the decade of the FTLRP, government was at its weakest and therefore sought beneficiaries who were prepared to put their own resources into agriculture. This has meant that the farmers continue to use the land in the way they wish or even underuse it without any sanctions. Government has tolerated absentee landlords and people who have siphoned off resources targeted for agriculture because it has neither the mechanism nor the capacity to manage activities at the farm level. Third, government was very sympathetic to the beneficiaries because many of them simply did not have the money to invest in capital development; 'illegal' sanctions or restrictive measures were noted to be the key reason for this in the political discourse, as it was claimed that they worsened the position.

Investment in agriculture remains very low, as farmers struggle to get agriculture moving forward without broad support. Commercial land was taken for redistribution to smallholder farmers with a lower level of skills than that of the former owners. Yet, smallholders had proved their success in farming through the smallholder boom of the 1980s (Rukuni et al., 2006). Therefore, the land reform programme provides an important opportunity for the economic development of Zimbabwe, if smallholders receive the correct forms of support within a policy environment that allows them to access inputs, equipment and credit facilities. The reality of the last ten years is that the country has been food insecure, the economy has melted, and agriculture has been at its lowest capacity compared with the situation prior to the reforms. Farmers have shown signs of recovery since 2009, but this comes in the context of an economy that is not operating at its optimum level. The reality is that there is a large amount of idle land, suggesting that there is hardly any farming taking place. In order to address the production challenges, some of the following could contribute to getting agriculture moving:

- There is a need to revisit the models (A1 and A2) and establish their real potential and under what conditions.
- New farmers are perceived as having no capacity to fully utilise the land or to produce diverse crops, including specialised high-value export commodities such as tobacco and horticultural crops. There is a need to audit the skills of the farmers, with a view to establishing how best they can be assisted to develop and broaden those skills.
- The development of learning platforms (education, farming skills, information and training development channels, etc.) for smallholder farmers is key to getting agriculture back on track.
- Farmworkers should not be regarded as saboteurs of the land reform programme and need to be carefully integrated into the new agrarian dispensation. Many of them are Zimbabweans who need to be treated in a fair and just manner.

Institutional reform, stability and growth for effective land management The FTLRP was characterised by top-down and non-participatory policy and planning processes. At the district level, a void in the institutional structures created administrative bottlenecks, which impinged on the basic rights of the beneficiaries. At the farm level, there is a huge institutional void. This is unlike the Old Resettlement Areas of the 1980s that had officers stationed on the farms to co-ordinate activities. In the new resettlement areas there is the Committee of Seven, which a government official referred to as 'the useless group of seven' (key informant interview, June 2007). The official complained that most of the committee members have failed to govern the farms properly because of their selfish personal interests, which they prioritise. They also indicated that the Committee of Seven has become too political. It was suggested that governance of the settlement areas should be the responsibility of apolitical government officials, while the farming unions should be enabled to have a presence on the FTFs.

Yet, at the district level, there is a multiplicity of institutions, some representing the state, some bolstered by state-sanctioned recognition. However, power was fragmented at the local level and was largely used to access state resources that came with the FTLRP. To get access to these resources, the local institutions needed some semblance of institutional order and therefore, at district level, order was created amid what seemed to be chaos. Nonetheless, this orderliness was not aimed at sound or rational planning, but merely served those in control. The relative autonomy provided by central government to the districts was calculated to meet specific government objectives within the land reform programme. When central government saw the autonomy it had given resulting in its own power slipping away, it established 'parallel structures' from national to district level. Many of these parallel structures had no legal standing, but they were well funded with money channelled through the Reserve Bank of Zimbabwe and government itself. This process saw the formation of 'taskforces' or 'specially funded programmes' that competed with or muscled in on local institutions and government itself, which both tended to be underfunded.

However, what seems to be emerging is that tenure uncertainty frequently results not from a lack of institutions, but from the incapacity of beneficiaries to make claims against more powerful actors in the context of struggles over land. For this reason, new and reformed administrative mechanisms that build on Zimbabwe's past successes are required to enhance the capabilities of beneficiaries in protecting and promoting their land rights. These conclusions are made in a context in which institutional arrangements are influenced by the ongoing practices and agency of political social actors. However, the contingent wider ideology of the state and its economic decline make it difficult to predict with certainty whether institutional reform will work or not. Zimbabwe clearly needs a land law to give more rights to beneficiaries. However, law reforms cannot be assumed to have predictable effects on farmers' practices, given the ongoing evolution of other institutions that affect agriculture. Therefore, changes in mindsets and attitudes must accompany key policy shifts.

The need to rebuild the technical and scientific institutions so that they can play a role in resettlement cannot be emphasised enough. These institutions, atrophied by short-term policy choices, need the help of the state to reclaim their space. Agriculture cannot simply be left to extra-legal political bodies in terms of management and decision-making, because the glory of the past (before the FTLRP) will not be achieved in the immediate future. The local authorities have deepened their knowledge of what works in the newly resettled areas, yet they have limited space and scope to influence what happens on the FTFs. Nor can they do much when the decision-making rests with partisan committees bent on protecting and promoting political interests rather than ensuring that agriculture moves forward to feed the nation.

Land administration At the district level, matters of land administration became shambolic, reflecting the state of unpreparedness of local administrators to handle land-related matters. At a certain point, the government introduced the National Land Board for the purposes of assisting in land administration; however, it was never effective. It is therefore necessary to review the current land administration system. The land administration system should provide farmers with reasonable access to legal, judicial, administrative and other institutional entities that deal with land issues. The idea is that both government and land users should have easy access to each other. Access by both to information, data and official transactions is important not only for business but also for enforcing laws and regulations, and for resolving disputes. Ideally, the land administration reviews should yield a policy that effectively addresses historical and potential conflicts, inequities and injustices based on race, social status, gender, political affiliation, and other such differences.

Administrative reforms should aim at improving the capacity of the Ministry of Lands and Rural Resettlement (MLRR) through working on land registration and upgrading cadastral maps so that processes are more cost effective and more decentralised (with links to the deeds registry, surveyor general, etc.). Eventually, this should result in decentralised databases covering all land categories, which will provide leverage for financial services. This information should be shared with the surveyor general to provide cadastral maps in modern systems such as GIS (geographic information system). At the same time, the development of e-government should enable the MLRR to provide services to different stakeholders, while also sharing information with districts such as Mazowe, Mangwe and Shamva in a decentralised fashion. The land information should allow for better agricultural planning, but will require close liaison with the Ministries of Agriculture, Local Government, Economic Planning and Finance.

Land administration should also deal with the issue of multiple farm owners, which the GPA alludes to. However, future multiple ownership cannot be avoided if there are changes in the economic situation, which may necessitate farm consolidation. In the case of a future functioning, productive agriculture system, a limit to single farm ownership could stop the most productive farmers restructuring their land holdings or expanding their farming enterprises. This could particularly affect small-scale emerging commercial farmers, who will need multiple farm ownership in order to compensate for land scarcity in their chosen enterprise. In Mazowe, there were examples where A1 farmers had entered into a range of 'illegal' rental arrangements and had seven or eight plots, because what they were allocated was deemed inadequate. So, in the future, the government will need to discuss policy issues around 'productive' multiple farm ownership arrangements versus politically speculative multiple ownership, and deal with these matters administratively.

In the past, the government has discussed the idea of land taxation, and in fact actually drew up taxation formulae for commercial agriculture (KPMG, 2000). Yet, it has not been able to implement the recommendations because of the politics that surround the issue; there is a fear that taxing mostly poor farmers, who do not necessarily have the capacity to pay, may make government unpopular with farmers. In the past, if land taxation had been introduced it would have limited implementation of the land reform programme, because it works best in private land markets. However, there is a view that land taxation will eliminate land speculators because the tax will mean that beneficiaries will need to use the land in order to pay the tax. However, a strong view exists that central government has an insatiable demand for resources and may take all taxed money from local authorities for the national finances, without ploughing anything back at the local level. In addition, if it is not carefully calculated (and decentralised), taxation may punish cattle ranchers in Mangwe District, for example, who require huge amounts of land to be viable. Zimbabwe is still relying on economies of size, which are the basis upon which yields are being achieved. However, in future land taxation will need to be discussed within the context of a non-land market, given the stalled completion of the process of acquisition of farms by government.

The last point to make is that land administration should be underpinned by a simplified legal framework, efficient administrative processes, modernised technological services, and user-friendly dispute handling arrangements. At the same time, the sharing of information on land matters in an open manner will be key, so that the public at large has access to land information when seeking land rights. The decentralisation to the district level of significant aspects of land administration and the power to discharge related functions will allow authorities in districts such as Mazowe, Mangwe and Shamva to address problems in a timely manner.

Irreversibility of the land reforms

Zimbabwe is in the process of drafting a new constitution, in which land matters will be key. The political parties that formed the Inclusive Government affirmed the irreversibility of the land reforms, which means that actions should be focused on maintaining the gains of the land reform programme. The GPA states that:

Section 5.4: While differing on the methodology of acquisition and redistribution the parties acknowledge that compulsory acquisition and redistribution of land has taken place under a land reform programme undertaken since 2000.

Section 5.5: Accepting the irreversibility of the said land acquisitions and redistribution.

Irreversibility of the land reform programme means that the government has to come up with a way of measuring productivity, and those beneficiaries who do not achieve those measures may lose their land.

However, there is scepticism and fear over land matters born out of the way in which the land was transferred and who has benefited from the land reform. This is one of the outstanding issues facing the Inclusive Government. Any future re-planning of the land sector that may result from the land audit raises the fear of a potential return to the situation before 2000. Now, the agrarian situation demonstrates a balanced racial structure reflecting the demography of the country. On the other hand, investments in agricultural and social infrastructure have been stagnant over the last ten years. Production has also gone down across most agricultural activities. While the racial balance is now acceptable, the situation of agricultural deterioration could reverse the gains of the FTLRP. Land underutilisation could be the basis upon which land is taken away from some individual beneficiaries. However, dealing with these individuals will not constitute a reversal of the land reforms, but rather, provided it is managed with consultations and a clear policy, it will make the reforms permanent in Zimbabwe. Beneficiaries need to be aware of their responsibilities and the acceptable production levels based on the size of plot they now own. There is a need for clear agricultural performance indicators; without these indicators, beneficiaries will continue to view state accusations of land underutilisation as a political ploy to 'get even' with them.

Below, I provide a list of measures that could inform policy to make the land reform irreversible:

- *Using the land optimally:* new farmers should demonstrate their ability to use the land optimally. There should be no room for speculators or farmers who pretend to use the land on commercial agricultural land. In this context, consistent macro-economic policies are key in providing a framework in which agriculture can prosper. A conducive economic environment will provide beneficiaries with the mechanisms to utilise the land productively; this has not been possible during the years of the FTLRP. But such production must be based on national responsibility to produce food for the nation, create employment and mobilise foreign currency through the export of surpluses.
- *Equality in access to land:* for this to be possible, Zimbabwe should uphold the principle of 'one household one farm'. A household is based on an individual over the age of 18 (i.e. the legal age of majority). Land should be guaranteed for all Zimbabweans who deserve it, of all classes, genders and races, as a minimum right.
- *Land ownership:* the transfers have been concluded in principle, but not fully in law, as there are outstanding compensation issues to be resolved.

Land ownership will be premised on resolving the compensation issues; this requires political negotiations among stakeholders in Zimbabwe and should involve the international community.

- *Compensation finalisation:* the GPA has demonstrated that there is a need for a multi-pronged approach to deal with compensation. Certainly, compensation will bring finality to the land contest, but there is no money in government. Therefore, there is a need to negotiate with the landowners while also mobilising broad international financing.

- *Legal and constitutional reforms:* there is a need to establish a supportive legal framework beyond the GPA, including clauses in the laws and constitution that entrench irreversibility. A broad land act based on the constitution should affirm such irreversibility.

- *Future land ownership by foreigners:* there is a view that foreign land ownership in Zimbabwe should be restricted. However, it has been noted that foreigners will be able to acquire land under foreign direct investments, but that they should be subject to a form of tenure that does not allow them uncontrolled expansion; that may lead to the re-concentration of land in the hands of the few, through unregulated land sales by poor and vulnerable groups. Policies on the transfer of land rights, including BIPPAs and the rights of foreigners, must be clear in terms of Zimbabwe's national interest and international relations.

- *Future land reforms:* land reform will be an ongoing process. However, there is a need to halt the FTLRP because its objectives have been achieved. This should give way to 'normal' administrative land transfer that should be handled by the government agency responsible, for example the Ministry of Lands and Rural Resettlement, as well as by the markets, if these are allowed to develop. In future, the right of first refusal in land sales should be reserved for the state. The role of the state is primarily to protect the poor, but also to provide conditions for investment and the development of agriculture for the benefit of the nation, in terms of food security, employment creation and raising foreign currency.

Land tenure policy to consolidate the gains of the land reforms is what the farmers want on the ground. Yet, the government faces a dilemma: on the one hand it wants to release the farmers to produce independently and needs the private sector to come and finance agriculture. On the other hand, the government fears that giving too much freedom to the markets in terms of land ownership will lead to land reform reversal. In the design of a tenure policy, government will have to balance the various interests – the private sector, farmers, women, local authorities and foreign investors, as well as its own political interests. This is no mean task given that Zimbabwe is emerging from a highly contested land reform programme and trust is at its lowest level.

The basis for future optimism

Zimbabweans, through the help of regional partners in the Southern African Development Community, have in the last three years carried out political dialogue and formed an Inclusive Government that, surprisingly, has been able to stabilise the country, making it possible to revisit the land issue. The GPA was the basis for the creation of the current government, which has attempted to address the problems of the FTLRP. However, the land reform programme raises deep sensitivities as part of the political negotiations that saw competing political parties signing the GPA.

The Government of Zimbabwe comprises elements of the former ruling party and former opposition, and may struggle to achieve consensus on issues such as land reform. The political parties exhibit differences in their approaches to land reform, with the former opposition arguing for accountability for what happened during the reform process. One part of government is arguing for support to new farmers, so that they may increase production, and for leaving the land audits to the future; while the other partners see the revisiting of land reform through audits as critical in unlocking donor and foreign investment funding and building confidence, not just in agriculture but also in the economy as a whole. On the other hand, the former ruling party is arguing for consolidation of the reforms and for 'illegal' sanctions to be removed so that financial resources can start flowing on to the FTFs. For example, in Mazowe there were some A2 farmers who were denied access to markets in Europe because they were farming on contested lands.

The political reading of this presents an ideologically divided Inclusive Government. The former opposition is caricatured by the former ruling party as being unduly influenced by external forces. The former ruling party views itself as 'domestic', as illustrated by its political push for indigenisation, which has now spread to most sectors of society. The former opposition party also considers the former ruling party as undemocratic and selfishly using land and other resources to hang on to political power. In my view the ideologies of either state control (ZANU PF preference) or markets with a human face or social democracy (MDC preference) will shape Zimbabwe's future national and local politics and its development as a country. However, there is a basis for optimism due to the fact that an Inclusive Government was formed and has worked, to some extent, over the last three years.

To its credit, the Inclusive Government formulated a series of economic market liberalisation measures including the change from the use of the Zimbabwe dollar to multiple currencies, which seems to have been a policy master stroke that has stabilised the economy and, surprisingly, has also contributed to the recovery of agriculture. Could early market liberalisation and the stopping of cyclical political violence have contributed to consensual land reform and a 'normal' stable country? There are no easy answers, but the political parties have been aware of their responsibility to address the land reform challenges in order to improve agricultural production and economic progress. There are hotly contested issues surrounding the land reform programme, but there is agreement on the following measures:

- conduct a comprehensive, transparent and non-partisan land audit during the tenure of the Seventh Parliament of Zimbabwe, for the purpose of establishing accountability and eliminating multiple farm ownership;
- ensure that all Zimbabweans who are eligible for land and who apply for it shall be considered for allocation of land irrespective of race, gender, religion, ethnicity or political affiliation;
- ensure security of tenure to all landholders;
- call upon the United Kingdom government to accept the primary responsibility to pay compensation to former landowners for land acquired for resettlement;
- work together to secure international support and finance for the land reform programme in terms of compensation for the former landowners and support for new farmers; and
- work together for the restoration of full productivity on all agricultural land (GPA, 2008).

The GPA provides a sound basis for understanding some of the contentious elements of the land reform programme and dovetails with the concerns of farmers with regards to moving the programme forward while ensuring its irreversibility. However, accounts in the press of the tangled negotiations relating to the outstanding issues from the GPA demonstrate that the land question remains unresolved. All the same, the Inclusive Government has been attempting to defuse these problems through linking them to economic recovery as part of the property rights issue.

However, political relations between the parties and the stability of the Zimbabwe political environment will be key to progress (or lack of it) on agricultural recovery. This should be understood against a background in which the land reform beneficiaries have not enjoyed the gains of the land reform programme, although they have received empowerment. The current land administration system is seen as heavily political, and stakeholders have very little information or knowledge about what the Inclusive Government is intending to do from a policy perspective. No one, except those involved in the programme, knows what is going on, making it difficult for broader and more inclusive policy-making. However, there is pressure building from the bottom up, as new farmers want to get on with farming without the hindrances of the past. Thus sugar farmers in the Lowveld of Masvingo, coffee farmers in Manicaland, livestock producers in the Matabeleland and Midlands regions and tobacco 'golden leaf' and cotton producers in Mashonaland are all putting pressure on the government to come up with policy guidelines that help them in their farming enterprises. Bankers and other private players desperately want to invest in agriculture as it starts to regain its global importance, so they too are impatiently waiting for resolution of the land issue. The fact that all these pressures are coming together leads to optimism that policy-makers and bureaucrats in government will address the land question.

Since the FTLRP period, the hype of land transfers has waned, replaced in policy circles by sober reflections on how to move the country forward. In the next 20 to 30 years, agriculture will be important, but it will be linked intrinsically to an urban industrial society, because that is the trajectory that all modern states take in their economic development. Rukuni and Jensen (2003) clearly articulate what needs to be done, noting that Zimbabwe will have to learn from Asian countries whose economies developed speedily because of long-term investments in smallholder agriculture. Modernisation and surplus production allowed greater access to land for the landless backed by massive rural development incentives that resulted in the 'green' revolution and increases in yields and production. Not all Zimbabweans can and should be farmers. Agriculture is currently central to Zimbabwe, but there is a need to reshape the development model centred on agriculture in order to take advantage of Zimbabwe's other natural resources and to instigate a rural industrialisation strategy; this would allow the creation of new economic zones modelled around resources in particular localities.

Conclusions

The FTFs are new places where old institutions and officials have had to change the way they work and relate to farmers. The social and economic barriers existing on the previous, mostly white-owned, large-scale commercial farms have fallen, and the land is now populated by black farmers with different cultural backgrounds and expectations. For the government, there is no doubt that the key objective should be to produce food and other agricultural commodities on the land. Yet the country is emerging from a difficult past. Vijfhuizen (2002: 227) argues that today:

> the most important aim of social actors in everyday rural life in Zimbabwe is to survive, to secure a livelihood and the basics of food, a place to live, money and emotional security and love, for themselves and their families.

The farmers realise that they are sitting on an important national resource, but are manoeuvring to survive on land that is contested nationally and internationally.

For a long time after the new settlement, farmers were subordinated to the state, but there is evidence that, since 2008, the state has literally left them on their own. Since then, notable improvements have been observed at the national level in the production of commodities such as maize, cotton, sugarcane, tobacco, soya beans and sugar beans. Could it then be that settlers should not have received subsidies during the initial period from 2000 to 2008? It would seem that the majority of the farmers in the sample surveys did not access optimal resources from the state, because there was simply not enough for everyone. Elite farmers and non-farmers captured some of the inputs, at a time when government had no consistent or robust institutional capacity to manage subsidies. This means that production outcomes from 2000 to 2008 can largely be attributed to effort and investment on the part of farmers themselves and, in the majority of cases, farmers got access to inputs through informal channels (*kukiya kiya*). In addition, agriculture could not have succeeded in a situation where the private credit markets were not functional, especially as this was coupled with a process of de-industrialisation of input manufacturing companies.

The state-centred land reform programme has given space for markets to operate and for farmers to make independent choices and decisions about what they can do with the land. To judge from the testimony of the farmers, they have not been inhibited by the state; rather, they regard the state as having been the single most important agent in their access to land. Therefore, the struggles they face are not entirely blamed on the state; the farmers see their problems as merely some of the everyday challenges that they face in new and unfamiliar situations. Farmers and the local institutions have created a new environment and way of farming, which is influenced by the alliances that they themselves forge based on the resources at their disposal. However, as they do this, they also learn from historical fragments of experience, extrapolating and inferring what might be relevant to their situations.

The plight of many FTF farmers is tied to the specific history of Zimbabwe that in less than 100 years has seen communities moved in a cyclical fashion of displacement and replacement. The majority of the blacks now on the land have struggled to survive since the country was liberated in 1980, yet they now have productive, large landholdings. However, the beneficiaries have been caricatured, while the reforms and the rationale behind them have been ignored in any discussion of the FTLRP. For the beneficiaries, just as in the historical past, they have no one to whom they can tell their stories of survival, especially on the FTFs. Academia, both in and outside Zimbabwe, has not engaged with the FTF farmers in the manner adopted by Ruzivo Trust through research from 2004 to the present in a few districts such as Mazowe, Shamva and Mangwe. Intellectuals are generally far removed from the FTFs, yet they make strong statements about the farms that sway opinions about what goes on there. In the process, the desk intellectuals, together with partisan and pedestrian news-gathering media, failed adequately to inform the world about the farmers' precarious existence (landlessness, poor soils, overcrowding, water shortages and disease) before the land reform, or about the potential and opportunities provided by the land that they now possess.

As can be seen from the cases quoted in this book, many of the newly resettled farmers are capable of producing crops and feeding themselves and the nation. Yet the food shortages that faced the country were simply blamed on 'incompetent peasants' taking over white farms, rather than on the broader economic context. In some instances, the flight of many Zimbabweans into the diaspora has been squarely blamed on the land reforms, yet there are wider factors beyond farming that conspired to almost destroy the economy. It has become fashionable to present Zimbabwe as a 'bread basket' before the land occupations and a 'basket case' after the occupations and the land transfers. This has helped to support the assumption that, without white farmers, the country could not feed itself. Yet, as can be seen through the current recovery of agriculture, it would seem that the land transfers and FTF communities are sustainable, and there is greater scope perhaps in the next ten years for full production across a range of commodities. Therefore, the stories on the ground show that there is potential for the FTFs to re-create the 'bread basket', if and when all the necessary institutional and structural infrastructure is in place. At present, the infrastructure is strikingly limited, if not absent altogether, but still production is improving.

Therefore, in the case of Zimbabwe, the plurality of sites, rules and modes of governance in the FTLRP period challenged local people's mastery of their livelihoods. It is thus necessary to analyse the simultaneous social processes and power structures in various institutional settings in order to understand the full picture leading up to, during and after the massive land transfers. While this is being done, much work will need to be carried out to change the mindset of people, including intellectuals, who lack sufficient confidence in the beneficiaries allocated land under the FTLRP. At the same time, there is a need to pay serious attention to the ways in which communities construct new lives in a land reform programme that involves massive land transfer in a relatively short period of time and without optimal resources, as was the case in Zimbabwe. However, at the local level, the organisational characteristics of district-based institutions demonstrate how different parts of the same state machinery functioned in markedly different ways to deliver land reform. Therefore, when it comes to redistributive land reform, as in Zimbabwe, the idea of 'state collapse' may not in fact apply, as some state bodies actually grew while innovations emerged during the FTLRP period.

Notes

1 Understanding Fast Track

1 IRIN. 2003. *Zimbabwe: year-ender – chronology of unremitting crisis*. 30 December. www.irinnews.org/printreport.aspx?reportid=47847.

2 *Daily News*. 2012. 'ZANU PF elites in land dog fights.' 26 April.

3 Of course, the reaction of the former owners naturally included taking the government and the new beneficiaries to court; airing complaints in the local and international media; simply resisting vacating the farms; and at times organising reactionary teams to engage in counter-violence (*jambanja*).

4 The term 'new farmer' hides the character and performance of the farmer settled under the FTLRP. The question is: why should they continue to be called 'new' some ten years after the commencement of the reforms? In addition, what would it take for them to be called 'old' or mainstream farmers? In common parlance, 'new' is seen as reflecting solicitations for sympathy in order to get free support, which usually comes via subsidies.

5 Small farms by definition are 'small' within the context of a country, region and society. In the case of Zimbabwe, a farm of less than 6 ha is considered small relative to the average commercial farms that were 2,200 ha before 2000. In the 1980s, the government defined the maximum farm size for model A resettlement as 6 ha (or 12 acres), and this same hectarage has been used for the A1 model for the plots allocated to the beneficiaries.

6 Usually, the A1 farmers reside within the farm compound created by former owners. However, over the years, new areas – some based around a central nucleus and others with a more dispersed

structure – have been established by new farmers, given that the existing compounds could not accommodate all the new farmers on the allocated land.

7 The size of these farms was clarified through Statutory Instrument 288 of 2000 (Cap. 20: 18: Rural Land [Farm Sizes] [Amendment] Regulations, 2000 [No. 1]). In fact, in Zimbabwe, the large-scale commercial farms of an average of 2,200 ha were defined historically based on an income threshold equivalent to income earned by top managers in the industrial sector during the colonial period (1940–50). The land sizes were therefore set to equal income levels and to ensure that white farmers were able to earn an income that was socially acceptable in the context of white settler society. Exceptional cases for large farms were for cattle ranching and wildlife conservancies, which the FTLRP seem also to have maintained but at a reduced size. The FTLRP revised these models by attempting to incorporate notions of viability (combined with land taxation as calculated from the proposals of 1999 by the Ministry of Agriculture) through setting minimum thresholds (KPMG, 2000).

8 Again, the period for the FTLRP remained open, with the dates on which to conclude it constantly changing until the government decided to remain silent on the issue.

9 According to a report by the president of the CFU, Deon Theron, 3 August 2011: 'Records show that the majority of land has been given to senior politicians, senior members of the security forces, judges, so called "War Veterans", civil servants, high-profile clerics and relatives of senior politicians.'

2 Land occupations

1 I have used the term 'squatting' because that was the popular nomenclature of illegal land occupations as defined by the statutes then in use. They were also frowned upon, and did not have popular legitimacy in government or political circles as they were seen to embarrass the leadership.

2 The nomenclature of forceful land occupations called on various lexicons in the language of the political economy of Zimbabwe. Thus there are 'land invasions' (signifying a mass takeover of land), 'squatting' (meaning illegal land occupations based on a legal instrument that prohibits trespassing), 'land mayhem', locally called *jambanja* (meaning demonstration or actual use of violence in the takeover of land), 'land demonstrations' (used by politicians to show that land invasions were a mere demonstration of the need for land by blacks), etc.

3 This is a term used for the farm seizures or forced farm acquisition process where youths and 'cadres' aligned to the ruling party settle themselves on white-owned farms and demand their immediate eviction.

4 The ICAs had varying agricultural systems stemming from variations in soil types and vegetation, which in turn were influenced by the parent materials from which the soils were derived. Thus, both agricultural potential and suitable farming systems were determined on the basis of the ICA.

5 Many white farmers sought refuge in Harare, staying with friends or in their urban houses, and commuted to their farms because of the fear of violence. Some migrated their family while the male members remained as gatekeepers, many without much success.

6 An estimate of 426 farmers largely owning 340,307.42 hectares gives an average of 798.84 hectares per farmer in the most prime lands in Zimbabwe.

7 BBC. 1998. 'World: Africa. Mugabe warns of land reform "anarchy".' 9 September. bbc.co.uk/2/hi/africa/167825.stm.

8 There were, however, no clear-cut operational definitions of how these criteria for compulsory land acquisition were applied by the government-appointed Land Acquisition Committees. Nor was an order of priority established for applying these criteria or for the procedures to be used in identifying farms. In addition to these criteria, various additional explanatory or supportive proposals for the identification of land for acquisition were suggested at various times by government officials.

9 Zimonline quoted a CFU report of 16 February reporting that '16 judges benefit from Mugabe land grab'. www.zimbabwesituation.org/?p=8463.

10 A term generally used in the recording and naming of farms whose deed of grant was divided, with a new deed issued specifying the new farms created.

11 In fact, going by the ward and district boundaries, some suburban areas such as Mount Pleasant Heights are in Mazowe District. Pomona Barracks, parts of Hatcliffe Extension, Wild Geese and the Scientific and Industrial Research and Development Centre (SIRDC) are all in Mazowe.

12 At the time the extent of the swaps for indigenous black commercial farmers could not be established.

13 Jeremy Lovell. 2000. 'Zimbabwean farmers face invasions with stoicism.' AOL: 8 April.

14 *Zimbabwe Independent*. 2007. 'Msika blasts land reform.' 20 July.

3 Interrogating land allocation

1 *Financial Gazette*, 25 June 1998, reported that: 'Unfulfilled promises by Zimbabwe's political leadership are beginning to backfire as some landless peasants forcibly occupy white-owned commercial farms, threatening to plunge the long-delayed resettlement programme into further disarray ... firing the latest salvo on the government's resettlement policy are communal farmers in Nyamandhlovhu in Matabeleland North and those in Svosve in Mashonaland East who have

made clear that they have had enough of empty rhetoric about land redistribution.'

2 *Herald*. 2002. 'Fake offer letters for land surface in Mash West.' 4 December. *The African Aristocrat*. 2011. 'Another white farmer loses farm to ZANU-PF.' 25 May.

3 *Herald*. 2003. 'Resettled farmers stage a demonstration.' 11 February. The article noted that about 112 farmers who were resettled at Mukwene Farm in Goromonzi staged a peaceful demonstration at the DA's office alleging that corrupt officials were privately selling their pieces of land to other people.

4 *Financial Gazette*. 2000. 'Govt official flees as war vets run riot.' 3 August. www.financialgazette.co.zw.

5 This fact was confirmed on 3 July 2011 by Finance Minister Tendai Biti who told the Commonwealth Business Council in London that the land grab was irreversible 'no matter how ugly it was done'.

6 The information management system at the DA's office requires serious investment in the necessary hardware and software for managing the lists of applications for the A1 model. The filing system is archaic, and important information on the applicants is in danger of disappearing from the offices, which makes the job of land administration a mammoth task.

7 The land was allocated to individual beneficiaries. They were plots in the sense that a farm was parcelled to create many plots. These plots act as a reference point for the allocation, and are (new) farms for the new beneficiaries. These terms are used interchangeably in the land reform discourse in Zimbabwe.

8 The response should be viewed with caution because of the threats farmers faced that they should not be 'phone' farmers; the government was threatening farmers with the possibility of a land audit to flush out those under-utilising their farms.

9 The *Standard* newspaper of 10 July 2010 reported the cases that went to court and involved extortion by prominent politicians.

10 *Standard*. 2005. 'Msika blasts invasions while Matonga gets Chegutu farm.' 30 October.

11 *Herald*, 1 August 2003.

12 *Chronicle*, 6 August 2003.

13 *Sunday News*, 7 September 2003.

14 *Daily News*, 17 August 2003.

15 *Sunday Mail*, 24 August 2003.

16 *Herald*, 10 December 2003.

17 *Financial Gazette*, 10 June 2004.

18 *People's Voice*, 18 July 2004.

19 Moyo and Yeros (2007a; 2007b) noted that chiefs were also allocated or gained access to electricity, vehicles and farming inputs as part of their remuneration, which seemed to imply that the government was also trying to buy their support for the agrarian reforms. The contradiction was that the majority of the people under such chiefs did not benefit from the land reform programme.

4 Juggling land ownership rights

1 Ginny Stein. 2010. 'Tobacco adds fuel to Zim's exports.' *Newsday*: 27 December.

2 This is the evidence of permission to occupy land, which resembles land ownership. This letter (which is like gold) is signed by the Minister of Lands for the successful A2 applicant and by the district administrator for the successful A1 applicant.

3 My argument here is not that government must refrain from using land in politics, but rather that agriculture is far more important and needs policies and politics that ensure full use of the land to assure food production. In so many cases where land reform has been carried out, production has been subservient to politics. For this reason, food security, employment, poverty reduction and foreign currency generation – the very objectives of land reform – have rarely been met.

4 A key assumption is that it is the highly productive who may have left the communal area, instead of the land-short or landless. If they continue to maintain split homes, it means that at the family level there is no significant decongestion.

The new settlers will continue to influence land ownership in the communal areas, which inhibits the ability of other family members to benefit from the land.

5 It is in this context that many civil servants, right up to the highest level in government, take leave from their jobs in the summer (November to January) in order to concentrate on their farming.

5 Agricultural production outcomes

1 The research assistance provided by Cuthbert Kambanje is gratefully acknowledged. I also thank Patricia Masanganise, Dr Chrispen Sukume and Professor Carroll Themba Khombe for their initial contributions to the chapter based on their leadership of the research activities in Shamva (2004) and Mangwe (2007).

2 Expected production levels are a proxy measure of the total food requirements of Zimbabwe (2.1 million tonnes of maize per given year). With beef production, for example, the LSCF cattle population dropped from 1.3 million to 0.51 million, a reduction of 61 per cent, while the commercial breeding herd shrunk from 0.72 million to an estimated 0.25 million. Up to 85 per cent of the officially marketed beef and most of the exports have been derived from the LSCFs, hence the current shortage of beef on the domestic market and insufficient export volumes. National milk production in Zimbabwe has experienced a steady decline over the past five years, dropping by 23 per cent from 183 million litres in 1998 to an estimated 140 million litres in 2002. A synoptic overview of dairy producers shows a decline of 44 per cent from 550 commercial farmers in 1990/91 to approximately 310 farmers by 2003.

3 A traditional chief condemned what he described as lazy farmers undermining the land reform programme through their failure to utilise land at a field day in Mazowe (May 2007). He implied that farmers are farming grass, which is a pointless use of the allocated land.

4 The government noted (MLRR, 2009)

some other contributory factors to be inadequate bank loans, poor beneficiary selection, controlled prices, the size and scope of the land reform programme being too large, and the persistent former landowners' legal challenges and the cumbersome legal processes that take a long time to be concluded, which create continued uncertainty.

5 GoZ. 2011. *The 2011 Mid-term Fiscal Policy Review*. www.zimtreasury.org/down loads/Mid-Year-Fiscal-Policy-Review.pdf.

6 Mutenga, T. 2011. 'Land reform erodes property rights: farmers unable to access funding from banks'. *The Financial Gazette*: 15 July.

7 *Zimbabwe Independent*. 2005. 'Army launches Operation Taguta.' 18–24 November.

8 In terms of land allocation, there were 207 beneficiaries for the A1 and 133 for the A2. Mangwe, like the rest of Matebeleland and the Midlands region, has a livestock model resettlement area called a three-tier, which had 437 beneficiaries. Eighteen beneficiaries did not specify their scheme.

9 From the 2008 farming season, tobacco in Mazowe was said to have significantly picked up in terms of production output. This was essentially the result of international prices, with growing demand from the Chinese market. Zimbabwean farmers have responded positively and tobacco has become the key crop of choice for all types of farmer.

10 The findings from Mazowe reflect that the majority of the farmers (75–78 per cent) depended on their own money to finance input acquisition.

11 Figures based on 'Summary of disbursements' at www.rbz.co.zw.

12 In 2010 the Ministry of Agriculture, Mechanisation and Irrigation Development was implementing new cotton legislation which had, however, met with mixed reactions across the cotton farming sector, with contractors seeming to be in support of it and smallholder farmers being against its implementation. The ministry was also in the process of imple-

menting the operation of an agricultural marketing authority, a move that also attracted mixed reactions as to its future role in the partially liberalised market.

13 This was prior to the multicurrency trading regime now being used in Zimbabwe.

6 Access to services

1 I thank Norman Moyo, Gospel Matondi and Memory Mufandaedza who covered aspects relating to assets and investment in farm-productive infrastructure and social services (schools, health facilities, housing and energy) in newly resettled areas from 2007 to 2008.

2 In any case, this is the constitutional responsibility of any government.

3 According to the article 'CFU wants farm compensation plus interest' in *The Zimbabwean*, 25 June 2010: 'Zimbabwe's white commercial farmers last year demanded US $5 billion in immediate compensation from the government before they could vacate their farms' (www.thezimbabwean.co.uk/news/32136/cfu-wants-farm-compensation-plus-interest-.htm).

4 *Daily News*, 8 August 2003. The exchange rate of that year was US$1=Z$750.

5 Some names of farms have been changed.

6 Excerpt from the speech made by Foreign Affairs Minister Mudenge at the dinner held in honour of the former United Nations Development Programme Administrator Mark Malloch Brown, 30 November 2000.

7 These figures would obviously vary because of the split household phenomenon.

8 In 'Battle for control of Kondozi turns ugly' (*Zimbabwe Independent*, 9 January 2004), the newspaper reported that ARDA workers supported by ZANU-PF youths violently clashed with farmworkers at Kondozi Farm. Farm owner Mr Moyo claimed that he did not refuse to be removed from the farm but wanted to make sure that he would leave with all his equipment.

9 *Herald*. 2004. 'Barclays takes ARDA to court over equipment.' 21 May.

10 The *Herald* (15 September 2001) reported that farmworkers at Bita Farm in Hwedza allegedly attacked resettled farmers and ZANU-PF supporters Fanuel Madzvimba and Alexio Nyamadzawo. Both men were assaulted and subsequently killed with axes, steel chains, spears, asterisks, knobkerries and stones. Resettled farmers and War Veteran militants burnt the 60 huts of unnamed farmworkers. The arson attack was in retaliation for the killing of the two resettled farmers by farmworkers.

11 CFU. 2000. 'Farm invasion update.' 5 May. CFU Information Room.

12 *Zimbabwe Independent*. 2004. 'War Veterans squabble over farm equipment.' 2 July.

13 *Sunday Mail*, 21 December 2003.

14 *Herald*, 14 April 2004.

15 *Herald*, 8 June 2004.

16 *New Zimbabwe*. 2009. 'Zimbabwe seizes Zambia-bound farm equipment.' 12 November. www.newzimbabwe.com/pages/farm16.11420.html.

17 *Herald*, 25 May 2004.

18 *Daily News*. 2011. 'PM in shock discovery.' 30 August.

19 Many schools in resettlement areas do not meet the stringent requirements set out in the Education Act, which specifies the number of classroom blocks, teachers' housing, the minimum qualification of teachers, etc. They are therefore linked to a school that *does* meet the criteria.

20 It must be noted that many teachers left the profession or migrated to neighbouring countries during the economic crisis.

7 Women's land rights

1 Before the FTLRP, the traditional leaders had no jurisdiction over large-scale commercial farming areas, and in the Old Resettlements Areas, the Rural District Councils Act 1988 limited their influence. Therefore precedence was set for disallowing customary systems, a situ-

ation that might have worked well in the new fast track areas.

2 The Zimbabwe Minister of Women's Affairs, Gender and Community Development, Olivia Muchena, told a women's conference that the land reform programme had benefited women and that the women's calls for a land audit and redistribution exercise to ensure equity in land ownership were 'driven more by political considerations than a desire to see more women owning land' (*The Zimbabwean*, 18–24 February 2010).

3 Source: http://womennewsnet work.net/2010/08/31/zimbabwewomen farmer-893/.

4 *Chronicle*. 2009. 'Govt to empower women through access to land.' 16 October.

5 The gender of 43 per cent of the people listed for the A2 allocations could not be established.

8 Social organisation

1 I thank Mabel Munyuki-Hungwe for the paper contributed to the Land and Livelihoods Programme, now under the auspices of the Ruzivo Trust. Gospel Matondi also helped in the drafting of the paper, and his contribution is appreciated. Patience Mutopo, together with Gospel, helped in crafting the original chapter.

2 ORAs were schemes implemented by government with the support of donors and Zimbabwean taxpayers as part of a land reform programme that was planned in advance and provided infrastructure and seasonal support to new beneficiaries. This became known as the Phase I of the Land and Resettlement Programme (1980–97). Market-led approaches (willing seller and willing buyer) were used for the acquisition of land from mostly large-scale white farmers for redistribution to blacks, the majority of whom were poor or landless and had come back from the war as refugees.

3 This was a Tanzanian experiment of reorganising traditional villages through moving people into settlements, on the assumptions that peasants where the same and therefore needed to live and work together.

4 This work is based on the data on resettlement, land and livelihoods developed by Bill Kinsey of the Ruzivo Trust since 1982. This is the most comprehensive longitudinal data set that has been developed in Africa. Recent field visits were concluded in June 2010 by Dekker and Kinsey.

5 This refers to farmers who are not originally from the surrounding communal areas of Mazowe such as Chiweshe. The original settlers from Mazowe feel that their space is being encroached upon.

6 Note that a VIDCO is a smaller committee of the VA. In the VA all village members over 18 years of age are expected to attend meetings.

7 The Traditional Leadership Act (Chapter 29: 17) and the Rural District Councils Act (Chapter 29: 13) define what resettlement areas are and their administration.

8 A good example will be the Judiciary Services Commission, which has its own independent budget. In this case, public funds are allocated to the commission and are independent from government.

9 They are born in Zimbabwe but some to parents from Malawi, Mozambique and Zambia.

10 In other words, accommodation is guaranteed only if they work for the beneficiary.

Conclusion

1 Although the Government of Zimbabwe has taken over land by force, accessing title deeds from former landowners has been a problem. This makes it difficult to conclude the land reform as the government wants to follow legal precedents of getting the title deeds and finalising cases in a legal sense.

References

Agarwal, B. 1995. 'Women's legal rights in agricultural land in India.' *Economic and Political Weekly*, March.

Alexander, J. 2003. 'Squatters, veterans and the state in Zimbabwe.' In A. Hammer, B. Raftopoulos and S. Jensen (eds). *Zimbabwe's unfinished business: rethinking land, state and nation in the context of crisis*. Harare, Zimbabwe: Weaver Press.

Alexander, J. 2006. *'The unsettled land': state-making and the politics of land in Zimbabwe 1893–2003*. Harare, Zimbabwe, Oxford, UK, and Athens, USA: Weaver Press, James Currey, and Ohio University Press.

Alexander, J. 2007. 'The histography of land in Zimbabwe: strengths, silences and questions.' *Safundi* 8(2): 183–98.

Alexander, J. and J. McGregor. 2001. 'Elections, land and the politics of opposition in Matebeleland.' *Journal of Agrarian Change* 1(4): 510–33.

Alexander, J. and J. McGregor. 2005. 'Hunger, violence and the moral economy of war in Zimbabwe.' In V. Broch-Due (ed.). *Violence and belonging: the quest for identity in post-colonial Africa*. London, UK: Routledge.

Amanor-Wilks, D. 1995. *In search of hope for Zimbabwe's farm workers*. Harare, Zimbabwe: Dateline Southern Africa and Panos Institute.

Amanor-Wilks, D. 2009. 'Land, labour and gendered livelihoods in a "peasant" and a "settler" economy.' *Feminist Africa* 12: 31–50.

Barr, A. 2001. *Trust and expected trustworthiness in rural Zimbabwe: an experimental investigation*. WPS/2001.12. Oxford, UK: Centre for the Study of African Economies, University of Oxford. www.csae.ox.ac.uk/working papers/pdfs/2001-12text.pdf.

Barr, A., M. Dekker and M. Fafchamps. 2010. *The formation of community-based organisations in sub-Saharan Africa: an analysis of quasi experiment*. Working Paper 90/2010. Leiden, Netherlands: African Studies Centre.

Bartle, P. 2007. *What is a community? A sociological perspective*. Consulted at http://cec.vcn.bc.ca/cmp/whatcom.htm.

Berry, S. 1993. *No condition is permanent: the social dynamics of agrarian change in sub-Saharan Africa*. Madison, USA: University of Wisconsin Press.

Bhatasara, S. 2001. 'Women, land and poverty in Zimbabwe: deconstructing the impacts of the Fast Track Land Reform Programme.' *Journal of Sustainable Development in Africa* 13(1): 316–30.

Bolding, A. 2004. *In hot water: a study on sociotechnical intervention models and practices of water use in smallholder agriculture, Nyanyadzi Catchment, Zimbabwe*. Amsterdam, Netherlands: Wageningen University.

Bruce, J. W. 1993. 'Do indigenous tenure systems constrain agricultural development?' In T. J. Basset and D. E. Crummey (eds). *Land in African agrarian systems*. Madison, USA: University of Wisconsin Press.

Bruce, J. W. and S. E. Mighot-Adholla (eds). 1994. *Searching for land tenure security in Africa*. Dubuque, USA: Kendall Hunt.

Bryceson, D. F. 1999. *Sub-Saharan Africa betwixt and between: rural livelihood practices and policies*. Working Paper No. 43. Leiden, Netherlands: De-Agrarianisation and Rural Employment Network, Afrika Studiecentrum.

Bryceson, D. F. 2000. 'Rural Africa at the crossroads: livelihood practices and policies.' *ODI Natural Resources Perspectives* 52 (April).

Buka, F. 2002. *A preliminary audit report of land reform programme*. Buka Report. Harare, Zimbabwe: Government Printer.

Centre on Housing Rights and Evictions. 2004. *Bringing equality home: Promoting and protecting the inheritance rights of women*. Geneva, Switzerland: COHRE. www.wri.org/property-rights-africa/wriTest_Ghana/lessons/lesson3/documents/Promoting_and_Protecting_the_Inheritance_Rights_of_Women.pdf.

CFU (Commercial Farmers' Union). 1991. *Proposals for land reform*. Harare, Zimbabwe: CFU.

Chambati, W. 2009. *Agrarian labour question in the new resettlement areas in Zimbabwe*. Harare, Zimbabwe: African Institute for Agrarian Studies.

Chambati, W. and G. Magaramombe. 2008. 'An abandoned question: farm workers.' In S. Moyo, K. Helliker and T. Murisa (eds). *Contested terrain: land reform and civil society in contemporary Zimbabwe*. Pietermaritzburg, South Africa: S&S Publishers.

Chaumba, J., I. Scoones and W. Wolmer. 2003a. 'New politics, new livelihoods: agrarian change in Zimbabwe.' *Review of African Political Economy* 98: 585–608.

Chaumba, J., I. Scoones and W. Wolmer. 2003b. *From jambanja to planning: the reassertion of technocracy in land reform in southeastern Zimbabwe*. Research Paper 2. Brighton, UK: Sustainable Livelihoods in Southern Africa Programme, Institute of Development Studies. www.ids.ac.uk.

Chavunduka, C. and D. W. Bromley. 2010. 'Beyond the crisis in Zimbabwe: sorting out the land question.' *Development Southern Africa* 27(3): 363–79.

Cheater, A. P. 1984. *Idioms of accumulation: rural development and class formation*. Gweru, Zimbabwe: Mambo Press.

Cheater, A. P. 1990. 'The ideology of communal land tenure: mythogenesis enacted.' *Africa* 60(2): 188–206.

Chimakure, C. 2010. 'Candid comment: Audit won't reverse land reform.' *Zimbabwe Independent*: 7 January.

www.theindependent.co.zw/comment/2010/01/07/audit-wont-reverse-land-reform/.

Chingarande, S. 2008. 'Gender and the struggle for land equity.' In S. Moyo, K. Helliker and T. Murisa (eds). *Contested terrain: land reform and civil society in contemporary Zimbabwe*. Pietermaritzburg, South Africa: S&S Publishers. pp. 275–304.

Chitiyo, K. T. 2000. 'Land violence and compensation: reconceptualising Zimbabwe's land and war veterans debate.' *Track Two* 9(1): 1–27.

Chiweshe, M. K. and P. B. Matondi. 2008. *Education and skills development in the newly resettled areas in Mazowe District, Zimbabwe*. Mimeo. Harare, Zimbabwe: Ruzivo Trust.

Cliffe, L., J. Alexander, B. Cousins and R. Gaidzanwa. 2011. 'An overview of Fast Track Land Reform in Zimbabwe: editorial introduction.' *Journal of Peasant Studies* 38(5): 907–38.

Commonwealth Secretariat. 1996. *Women and natural resources management: the overview of a pan-Commonwealth training module*. London, UK: Commonwealth Secretariat.

Cusworth, J. 2000. 'A review of the UK ODA evaluation of the land resettlement programme in 1988 and the land appraisal mission of 1996.' In T. A. S. Bowyer-Bower and C. Stoneman (eds). *Land reform in Zimbabwe: constraints and prospects*. Aldershot, UK: Ashgate.

Cusworth, J. and J. Walker. 1988. *Land resettlement in Zimbabwe: a preliminary evaluation*. Evaluation Report No. EV 434. London, UK: Overseas Development Administration.

Daloz, J.-P. 2003. '"Big men" in Sub-Saharan Africa: how elites accumulate positions and resources.' *Comparative Sociology* 2(1): 271–85.

Dekker, M. 2004. 'Sustainability and resourcefulness: support networks during periods of stress.' *World Development Journal* 32(10): 1735–51.

Dekker, M. and B. Kinsey. 2011. 'Contextualizing Zimbabwe's land reform:

long-term observations from the first generation.' *Journal of Peasant Studies* 38(5): 995–1019.

Derman, B. 2006. *After Zimbabwe's Fast Track Land Reform: preliminary observations on the near future of Zimbabwe's efforts to resist globalization.* Montpellier, France: Colloque international 'Les frontières de la question foncière/ At the frontier of land issues'.

Derman, B. and A. Hellum. 2007. 'Livelihood rights perspective on water reform: reflections on rural Zimbabwe.' *Land Use Policy* 24(4): 664–73.

FAO (Food and Agriculture Organization of the United Nations). 2006. Fertilizer use by crop in Zimbabwe. Food and Agriculture Organization of the United Nations. Land and Plant Nutrition Management Service Land and Water Development Division. Rome.

FAO (Food and Agriculture Organization of the United Nations). Undated. *Gender-sensitive indicators for natural resources management.* Rome, Italy: FAO.

FAO (Food and Agriculture Organization of the United Nations). Undated. 'Women and sustainable food security.' Prepared by the Women in Development Service (SDWW), FAO Women and Population Division. www.fao.org/ sd/fsdirect/fbdirect/FSP001.htm.

FAO/WFP (Food and Agriculture Organization of the United Nations/World Food Programme). 2009. *Crop and food security assessment mission to Zimbabwe.* FAO Global Information and Early Warning System on Food and Agriculture: Special Report: World Food Programme. Rome, Italy: FAO.

FAO/WFP (Food and Agriculture Organization of the United Nations/World Food Programme). 2010. *Crop and food security assessment mission to Zimbabwe.* FAO Global Information and Early Warning System on Food and Agriculture: Special Report: World Food Programme. Rome, Italy: FAO.

FES (Friedrich-Ebert-Stiftung). 2004. *The 'Look East Policy' of Zimbabwe now focuses on China.* Policy briefing paper Harare, Zimbabwe: FES.

Fontein, J. 2009. 'We want to belong to our roots and we want to be modern people: new farmers, old claims around Lake Mutirikwi, southern Zimbabwe.' *African Studies Quarterly* 10(4). www.africa.ufl.edu/asq/v10/v10i4a1.htm#_edn1.

Fortmann, L. 1995. 'Talking claims: discursive strategies in contesting property.' *World Development* 23(6): 1053–63.

Gaidzanwa, R. B. 1994. 'Women's land rights in Zimbabwe.' *A Journal of Opinion* 22(2): 12–16.

Gaidzanwa, R. B. 1995. 'Land and the economic empowerment of women: a gendered analysis.' *Southern African Feminist Review* 1(1): 1–12.

Gelfand, M. 1973. *The genuine Shona: survival values of African culture.* Gweru, Zimbabwe: Mambo Press.

Geza, S. 1986. 'The role of resettlement in social development in Zimbabwe.' *Journal of Social Development in Africa* 1: 35–42.

Goebel, A. 1998. 'Process, perception and power: notes from "participatory" research in a Zimbabwean resettlement area.' *Development and Change* 29(2): 277–306.

Goebel, A. 1999. '"Here it is our land, the two of us": women, men and land in a Zimbabwean resettlement area.' *Journal of Contemporary African Studies* 17(1): 75–96.

Goebel, A. 2006. *Gender and land reform: the Zimbabwe experience.* Montreal, Canada: McGill-Queen's University Press.

Gono, G. 2005. *Monetary policy statement for fourth quarter 2004 and roadmap for 2005.* Harare, Zimbabwe: Reserve Bank of Zimbabwe.

GoZ (Government of Zimbabwe). 1982. *Transitional national development plan. Vol. 1.* Harare, Zimbabwe: Government Printer.

GoZ (Government of Zimbabwe). 1986. *The first five-year development plan, 1986–1990.* Harare, Zimbabwe: Government Printer.

GoZ (Government of Zimbabwe). 1991. *Second five-year national development plan.* Harare, Zimbabwe: Government Printer.

GoZ (Government of Zimbabwe). 1998. *Land Reform and Resettlement Programme Phase II. A policy framework.* Harare, Zimbabwe: Government Printer.

GoZ (Government of Zimbabwe). 1999. *Statutory Instrument 419 of 1999; Rural Land (Farm Sizes) Regulations.* Harare, Zimbabwe: Government Printer.

GoZ (Government of Zimbabwe). 2001. *Land Reform and Resettlement, Revised Phase II.* Harare, Zimbabwe: Ministry of Lands, Agriculture and Rural Resettlement.

GPA (Global Political Agreement). 2008. Agreement between the Zimbabwe African National Union-Patriotic Front (ZANU-PF) and the two Movement for Democratic Change (MDC) formations, on resolving the challenges facing Zimbabwe. 15 September.

Greif, A. 2006. 'Chapter 1: Introduction.' In A. Greif. *Institutions and the path to the modern economy: lessons from medieval trade.* Cambridge, UK: Cambridge University Press.

Hagedorn, K. 2003. *Integrating and segregating institutions. A concept for understanding institutions of sustainability.* Paper presented at the Workshop in Political Theory and Policy Analysis. Bloomington, USA: Indiana University.

Hammar, A. 2007. *The day of burning: land, authority and belonging in Zimbabwe's agrarian margins in the 1990s.* PhD dissertation. Roskilde, Denmark: Department of International Development Studies, Roskilde University.

Hammar, A. 2008. 'In the name of sovereignty: displacement and state making in post-independence Zimbabwe.' *Journal of Contemporary African Studies* 26(4): 417–34.

Hammar, A. 2010. 'Ambivalent mobilities: Zimbabwean commercial farmers in Mozambique.' *Journal of Southern African Studies* 36(2): 395–416.

Hammar, A., J. McGregor and L. Landau. 2010. 'Introduction. Displacing Zimbabwe: crisis and construction in southern Africa.' *Journal of Southern African Studies* 36(2): 263–83.

Hammar, A., B. Raftopoulos and J. Stigen (eds). 2003. *Zimbabwe's unfinished business: rethinking land, state, and nation in the context of crisis.* Harare, Zimbabwe: Weaver Press.

Hardin, G. 1968. 'The tragedy of the commons.' *Science* 162: 1243–8.

Hellum, A. and B. Derman. 2004. 'Land reform and human rights in contemporary Zimbabwe: balancing individual and social justice through an integrated human rights framework.' *World Development* 32(10): 1785–805.

Herbst, J. 1989. 'How the weak succeed: tactics, political goods and institutions in the struggle over land in Zimbabwe.' In F. Colburn (ed.). *Everyday forms of peasant resistance.* London, UK: M. E. Sharpe.

Herbst, J. 1990. *State politics in Zimbabwe.* Harare, Zimbabwe: University of Zimbabwe Publications.

Hooghe, L. and G. Marks. 2003. 'Unravelling the central state, but how? Types of multilevel governance.' *American Political Science Review* 97(2): 233–43.

Human Rights Watch. 2004. *The politics of food assistance in Zimbabwe.* Briefing paper. New York, USA: Human Rights Watch.

Jacobs, S. 1991. 'Changing gender relations in Zimbabwe: the case of individual family resettlement areas.' In D. Elson (ed.). *Male bias in the development process.* Manchester, UK: Manchester University Press.

Jacobs, S. 2000. 'The effects of land reform on gender relations in Zimbabwe.' In A. T. S. Bowyer-Bower and C. Stoneman (eds). *Land reform in Zimbabwe: constraints and prospects.* Aldershot, UK: Ashgate.

Jacobs, S. 2003. 'Democracy, class and gender in land reform: a Zimbabwean example.' *Research in Rural Sociology and Development* 9: 203–28.

Jones, L., P. Koegel and K. Wells. 2008. 'Bringing experimental design to community-participatory research.' pp. 67–84. In M. Minkler and N. Wallerstein (eds). *Community-based participatory research for health.* New York, USA: Jossey-Bass/John Wiley & Sons.

Justice for Agriculture (JAG). 2002. *Confirmed VIPs' allocations – the landless poor?* Harare, Zimbabwe: JAG.

Kinsey, B. H. 1983. 'Emerging policy issues in Zimbabwe's land resettlement programs.' *Development Policy Review* 1(2): 163–96.

Kinsey, B. H. 1998. *Determinants of rural household incomes and their impact on poverty and food security in Zimbabwe.* Resource paper for a discussion on Rural Household Dynamics. Bronte Hotel, Harare, Zimbabwe, 15–16 June.

Kinsey, B. H. 1999. 'Land reform, growth and equity: emerging evidence from Zimbabwe's resettlement programme.' *Journal of Southern African Studies* 25(2): 173–96.

Kinsey, B. H. 2004. 'Zimbabwe's land reform program: underinvestment in post-conflict transformation.' *World Development* 32(10): 1669–96.

Kinsey, B. H. 2010. 'Who went where ... and why: patterns and consequences of displacement in rural Zimbabwe after February 2000.' *Journal of Southern African Studies* 36(2): 339.

KPMG. 2000. *Draft report on land tax study. Volume 1.* Ministry of Lands and Agriculture, Department of Land and Technical Services. Funded by Danida.

Kriger, N. M. 1992. *Zimbabwe's guerrilla war: peasant voices.* Cambridge, UK, and Harare, Zimbabwe: Cambridge University Press and Baobab Books.

Langa, V. 2010. 'Police warn panners.' *The News Day*: 3 August. p. 2.

Leftwich, A. 2008. *Developmental states, effective states and poverty reduction: the primacy of politics.* Project on Poverty Reduction and Policy Regimes. Geneva, Switzerland: United Nations Research Institute for Social Develop-ment (UNRISD). www.unrisd.org/unrisd/website/projects.nsf.

Lloyd, P. C. 1966. *The new elites of tropical Africa.* Oxford, UK: Oxford University Press.

Lockwood, M. and J. Davidson. 2010. 'Environmental governance and the hybrid regime of Australian natural resource management.' *Geoforum* 41(3): 388–98.

LTC (Land Tenure Commission). 1994. *Report of the commission of inquiry into appropriate land tenure systems.* Harare, Zimbabwe: Government Printer.

Madhuku, L. 2004. 'Law, politics and the land reform process in Zimbabwe.' In M. Masiiwa (ed.). *Post-independence land reform in Zimbabwe: controversies and impact on the economy.* Harare, Zimbabwe: Friedrich-Ebert-Stiftung and University of Zimbabwe Institute of Development Studies.

Magaramombe, G. 2003a. *Resource base and farm production: farm labour relations, use and needs.* Discussion series paper. Harare, Zimbabwe: African Institute for Agrarian Studies.

Magaramombe, G. 2003b. 'Farm workers: the missing class in Zimbabwe fast track resettlement.' pp. 277–82. In F. Gonese and M. Roth (eds). *Delivering land and securing rural livelihoods: post-independence land resettlement in Zimbabwe.* Harare, Zimbabwe, and Madison, USA: Centre for Applied Social Sciences (CASS), University of Zimbabwe, and Land Tenure Center, University of Wisconsin.

Magaramombe, G. 2010. 'Agrarian displacements, replacements and resettlement: "displaced in place" farm workers in Mazowe District.' *Journal of Southern African Studies* 36(2): 361–75.

Magaramombe, G. and M. Chiweshe. 2008. *HIV and AIDS issues in the newly resettled areas in Mazowe District, Zimbabwe.* Mimeo. Harare, Zimbabwe: Ruzivo Trust.

Makombe, L. 2010. 'Poor resource usage: a potential cause of conflict.' *Zimbabwe*

Independent: 20–26 August. Harare, Zimbabwe.

Manzungu, E. 2004. 'Environmental impacts of the Fast-Track Land Reform Programme: a livelihoods perspective.' In D. Harrold-Barry (ed.). *Zimbabwe: the past is the future. Rethinking land, state and nation in the context of crisis.* Harare, Zimbabwe: Weaver Press.

Marongwe, N. 2002. *Conflicts over land and other natural resources in Zimbabwe.* Harare, Zimbabwe: ZERO Regional Environment Organisation.

Marongwe, N. 2003. 'Farm occupations and occupiers in the new politics of land in Zimbabwe.' In A. Hammer, B. Raftopoulos and S. Jensen (eds). *Zimbabwe's unfinished business: rethinking land, state and nation in the context of crisis.* Harare, Zimbabwe: Weaver Press.

Marongwe, N. 2008. *Beneficiary selection in the Fast Track Land Reform Programme in Goromonzi District, Zimbabwe.* DPhil thesis. Cape Town, South Africa: Institute of Poverty and Agrarian Studies, University of Western Cape.

Marongwe. N. 2011. 'Who was allocated fast track land, and what did they do with it? Selection of A2 farmers in Goromonzi District, Zimbabwe and its impacts on agricultural production.' *Journal of Peasant Studies* 38(5): 1069–92.

Masanganise, P. and C. Kambanje. 2008. *Agricultural production and land reform in Zimbabwe: a case of Mazowe District.* Mimeo. Harare, Zimbabwe: Ruzivo Trust.

Masiiwa, M. (ed.). 2004. *Post-independence land reform in Zimbabwe: controversies and impact on the economy.* Harare, Zimbabwe: Friedrich-Ebert-Stiftung and University of Zimbabwe Institute of Development Studies.

Masuko, L. 2004. *The role of the state in land reform: the case of land reform in Zimbabwe, 1998–2002.* Dakar, Senegal: CODESRIA.

Matondi, G. H. M. and P. B. Matondi. 2008. *The energy question and agriculture in new resettlement areas of Mazowe District, Zimbabwe.* Mimeo. Harare, Zimbabwe: Ruzivo Trust.

Matondi, P. B. 2001. *The struggle for access to land and water resources in Shamva District, Zimbabwe.* Unpublished PhD thesis. Uppsala, Sweden: Swedish University of Agricultural Sciences, Department of Rural Development Studies.

Matondi, P. B. 2005. *Agriculture and rural development transformation: findings from Mazowe District.* Mimeo. Harare, Zimbabwe: Ruzivo Trust.

Matondi, P. B. 2008a. *The question of tenure and land rights in the resettled areas in Mazowe district in Zimbabwe.* Mimeo. Harare, Zimbabwe: Ruzivo Trust.

Matondi, P. B. 2008b. 'Institutional and policy issues in the context of the land reform and resettlement programme in Zimbabwe.' In C. T. Khombe and L. R. Ndlovu (eds). *The livestock sector after the Fast Track Land Reforms in Zimbabwe.* Bulawayo, Zimbabwe: Institute of Rural Technologies.

Matondi, P. B. 2011a. 'Land, agriculture and rural development.' In G. Kanyenze, T. Kondo, P. Chitambara and J. Martens. *Beyond the enclave: towards a pro-poor and inclusive development strategy for Zimbabwe.* Harare, Zimbabwe: ANSA, Labour and Economic Development Research Institute of Zimbabwe, Zimbabwe Congress of Trade Unions and Weaver Press.

Matondi, P. B. 2011b. *Livelihoods diversity in Zimbabwe.* Paper commissioned by Oxfam Canada. Harare, Zimbabwe: Ruzivo Trust.

Matondi, P. B. and S. Moyo. 2002. 'Experiences with market based land reforms in Zimbabwe.' In F. Barros, S. Sauer and S. Schwartzman (eds). *The negative impacts of World Bank market-based land reform.* Washington, USA: Environmental Defense.

Matondi, P. B., K. Havenvik and A. Beyene. 2011. *Biofuels, land grabbing and food security in Africa*, London, UK: Zed Books and Nordic Africa Institute.

Matondi, P. B. and T. Khombe with

G. H. M. Matondi, N. R. Moyo and M. Chiweshe. 2008. *The land reform and resettlement programme in Mangwe District, Matebeleland South.* Lands and Livelihoods Research Programme: Mangwe District report. Harare, Zimbabwe: Ruzivo Trust.

Matondi, P. B., G. H. M. Matondi and M. K. Chiweshe. 2008. *Housing in new resettlement areas of Mazowe District, Zimbabwe.* Mimeo. Harare, Zimbabwe: Ruzivo Trust.

Matondi, P. B., M. Mufandzedza and N. Chiweshe. 2008. *Voices from the field: reflection on the land resettlement programme in Mazowe District, Zimbabwe.* Mimeo. Harare, Zimbabwe: Ruzivo Trust.

Meinzen-Dick, R. S., L. Brown, H. Feldstein and A. Quisumbing. 1997. 'Gender, property rights, and natural resources.' *World Development* 25(8): 1303–15.

Mgugu, A. 2008. *Women's land and economic rights in Zimbabwe: gender audit report.* Harare, Zimbabwe: Women's Land and Water Rights in Southern Africa.

Migot-Adholla, E. and J. W. Bruce. 1994. 'Introduction: Are indigenous African tenure systems insecure.' In J. W. Bruce and S. E. Migot-Adholla (eds). *Searching for land tenure security in Africa.* Dubuque, USA: Kendall Hunt.

MLRR (Ministry of Lands and Rural Resettlement). 2009. *Some of the major themes proposed for the retreat.* MLRR Planning Retreat. Caribbea Bay Hotel, Kariba, Zimbabwe, 11–13 June.

MLRR/SIRDC (Ministry of Land and Rural Resettlement/Scientific Industrial Research and Development Centre). 2006. *A2 land audit report.* Harare, Zimbabwe: Government of Zimbabwe.

MLRR/SIRDC (Ministry of Land and Rural Resettlement/Scientific Industrial Research and Development Centre). 2007. *Mashonaland Central Province: A2 land audit report.* Harare, Zimbabwe: Government of Zimbabwe.

MLRR/SIRDC (Ministry of Land and Rural Resettlement/Scientific Industrial Research and Development Centre). 2008. *Consolidated: national A2 land audit report.* Harare, Zimbabwe: Government of Zimbabwe.

Moyo, S. 1995a. *The land question in Zimbabwe.* Harare, Zimbabwe: SAPES Books.

Moyo, S. 1995b. 'A gendered perspective of the land question.' *Southern African Feminist Review (SAFERE)* 1(1): 13–31.

Moyo, S. 1998. *The land acquisition process in Zimbabwe 1997/8.* Harare, Zimbabwe: UNDP Resource Centre.

Moyo, S. 1999. *Land and democracy in Zimbabwe.* Southern Africa Political Economy Series. Harare, Zimbabwe: SAPES Books.

Moyo, S. 2000a. *The interaction of market and compulsory land acquisition processes with social action in Zimbabwe's land reform.* Paper presented at the Southern African Regional Institute for Policy Studies (SARIPS) of the SAPES Trust annual colloquium on 'Regional integration: past, present and future'. Harare, Zimbabwe: Sheraton Hotel and Towers, 24–27 September.

Moyo, S. 2000b. *Land reform under structural adjustment in Zimbabwe.* Uppsala, Sweden: Nordic Africa Institute.

Moyo, S. 2001. 'The land occupations movement and democratisation: the contradictions of the neoliberal agenda in Zimbabwe.' *Millennium* 30(2): 311–30.

Moyo, S. 2006. *Land redistribution and public action in Zimbabwe.* Montpellier, France: Colloque international 'Les frontières de la question foncière/At the frontier of land issues'.

Moyo, N. 2008. *Investing and rebuilding assets in times of uncertainty in newly resettled areas: case of Mazowe District.* Mimeo. Harare, Zimbabwe: Ruzivo Trust.

Moyo, S. 2011a. 'Land concentration and accumulation after redistributive reform in post-settler Zimbabwe.' *Review of African Political Economy* 38(128): 257–76.

Moyo, S. 2011b. 'Changing agrarian relations after redistributive land reform in Zimbabwe.' *Journal of Peasant Studies* 38(5): 939–66.

Moyo, S. and P. B. Matondi, 2003. 'The politics of land reform in Zimbabwe.' In M. Baregu and C. Landsburg. *From Cape to Congo: International Peace Academy*. New York, USA: International Peace Academy.

Moyo, S. and T. Murisa. 2008. 'Civil society: public action towards a transformative agenda.' In S. Moyo, K. Helliker and T. Murisa (eds). *Contested terrain: land reform and civil society in contemporary Zimbabwe*. Pietermaritzburg, South Africa: S&S Publishers.

Moyo, S. and P. Yeros. 2005a. *Reclaiming the land: the resurgence of rural movements in Africa, Asia and Latin America*. New York, USA: Zed Books.

Moyo, S. and P. Yeros. 2005b. 'Land occupations and land reform in Zimbabwe: towards the National Democratic Revolution.' In S. Moyo and P. Yeros (eds). *Reclaiming the land: the resurgence of rural movements in Africa, Asia and Latin America*. New York, USA: Zed Books.

Moyo, S. and P. Yeros. 2007a. 'The radicalised state: Zimbabwe's interrupted revolution.' *Review of African Political Economy* 34(111): 103–21.

Moyo, S. and P. Yeros. 2007b. 'The Zimbabwe question and the two lefts.' *Historical Materialism* 15(3): 171–204.

Moyo, S., W. Chambati, T. Murisa, D. Siziba, C. Dangwa, K. Mujeyi and N. Nyoni. 2009. *Fast Track Land Reform baseline survey in Zimbabwe: trends and tendencies, 2005/6*. Harare, Zimbabwe: African Institute for Agrarian Studies.

Moyo, S., K. Helliker and T. Murisa. 2008. *Contested terrain: land reform and civil society in contemporary Zimbabwe*. Pietermaritzburg, South Africa: S&S Publishers.

Moyo, N., G. Matondi, C. Kambanje and P. B. Matondi. 2009. *Mazowe District farmer feedback and policy dialogue outcomes*. Unpublished. Harare, Zimbabwe: Ruzivo Trust.

Mufandaedza, M. and P. B. Matondi. 2008. *Health delivery services in the context of land resettlement in Mazowe District*. Mimeo. Harare, Zimbabwe: Ruzivo Trust.

Munyuki-Hungwe, M. N. 2008. *Challenges in constructing social space in newly resettled areas: empirical evidence from Mazowe District*. Mimeo. Harare, Zimbabwe: Ruzivo Trust.

Munyuki-Hungwe, M. N. 2011. *In search of 'community' in Zimbabwe's Fast Track resettlement area of Mazowe District*. Unpublished PhD thesis Sweden, Lund: Lund University.

Murisa, T. 2007. *Social organisation and agency in the newly resettled areas of Zimbabwe: the case of Zvimba District*. Harare, Zimbabwe: African Institute for Agrarian Studies.

Murisa, T. 2009. *An analysis of emerging forms of social organisation and agency in the aftermath of 'fast track' land reform in Zimbabwe*. Unpublished PhD thesis. Grahamstown, South Africa: Rhodes University, Faculty of Humanities.

Murombedzi, J. C. 1994. *The dynamics of conflict in environmental management policy in the context of CAMPFIRE*. Unpublished PhD thesis. Harare, Zimbabwe: University of Zimbabwe.

Mutangadura, G. 1997. *Meeting development objectives with agricultural research: priority setting in Zimbabwe*. DPhil dissertation. Blacksburg, USA: Virginia Polytechnic Institute and State University.

Mutonodzo-Davies, C. 2010. *The political economy of cereal seed systems in Zimbabwe: rebuilding the seed system in a post-crisis economy*. Working Paper 15. Brighton, UK: Future Agricultures.

Mutopo, P. 2011. 'Women's struggles to access and control land and livelihoods after fast track land reform in Mwenezi District, Zimbabwe.' *Journal of Peasant Studies* 38(5): 1021–46.

Ncube, W. and J. Stewart. 1997. *Paradigms of exclusion: women's access to resources in Zimbabwe*. Harare, Zimbabwe: Women and Law in Southern Africa Research Trust.

Ndlovu-Gatsheni, S. 2009. 'Mapping cultural and colonial encounters: 1880s–1930s.' In B. Raftopoulos and A. Mlambo (eds). *Becoming Zimbabwe: a history from the pre-colonial period to 2008*. Harare, Zimbabwe: Weaver Press.

Nemarundwe, N. 2003. *Negotiating resource access. Institutional arrangements for woodlands and water use in Southern Zimbabwe*. DPhil thesis. Uppsala, Sweden: Swedish University of Agricultural Sciences.

North, D. 1990. *Institutions, institutional change and economic performance*. Cambridge, UK: Cambridge University Press.

Nyambara, P. S. 2001. 'Immigrants, "traditional" leaders and the Rhodesian state: the power of "communal" land tenure and the politics of land acquisition in Gokwe, Zimbabwe, 1963–1979.' *Journal of Southern African Studies* 27(4): 771–91.

ODA (Overseas Development Administration). 1988. *Land resettlement in Zimbabwe: a preliminary evaluation*. London, UK: ODA.

ODA (Overseas Development Administration). 1996. *Report of ODA land appraisal mission to Zimbabwe, 23 September to 4 October. British Development Division in Central Africa*. London, UK: ODA.

Okoth-Ogendo, H. W. O. 2000. 'Legislative approaches to customary tenure and tenure reform in East Africa.' In C. Toulmin and J. Quan (eds). *Evolving land rights, policy and tenure in Africa*. London, UK: International Institute for Environment and Development.

Okoth-Ogendo, H. W. O. 2007. *The last colonial question: an essay in the pathology of land administration systems in Africa*. Keynote presentation at a workshop on Norwegian land tools relevant to Africa. Oslo, Norway: 3–4 May. www.statkart.no/filestore/Eiendomsdivisjonen/PropertyCentre/Pdf/HWOOkoth-Ogendo_THELASTCOLONIALQUESTION.pdf.

Ostrom, E. 1990. *Governing the commons: the evolution of institutions for collective action*. Cambridge, UK: Cambridge University Press.

Ostrom, E. 1992. *Crafting institutions for self-governing irrigation systems*. San Francisco, USA: ICS Press.

Pazvakavambwa, S. 2009. *The food security and land debate in Zimbabwe*. Paper presented at a regional seminar on food security at the Multi-Donor Trust Fund seminar organised by the World Bank office in Harare, Zimbabwe.

Pazvakavambwa, S. and H. Hakutangwi. 2006. 'Agricultural extension.' In M. Rukuni, P. Tawonezvi, K. Eicher, M. N. Munyuki-Hungwe and P. B. Matondi (eds). *Zimbabwe's agricultural revolution revisited*. Harare, Zimbabwe: University of Zimbabwe Publications.

Petrie, R., M. Roth and K. Mazvimavi. 2003. 'Seeking women land owners and ownership in Zimbabwe: case studies of women's access to land and land use.' In F. Gonese and M. Roth (eds). *Delivering land and securing rural livelihoods: post-independence land resettlement in Zimbabwe*. Harare, Zimbabwe, and Madison, USA: Centre for Applied Social Sciences (CASS), University of Zimbabwe, and Land Tenure Center, University of Wisconsin.

Pilossof, R. 2012. *The unbearable whiteness of being: farmers' voices from Zimbabwe*. Cape Town, South Africa: University of Cape Town Press.

Platteau, J.-P. 1996. 'The evolutionary theory of land rights as applied to sub-Saharan Africa: a critical assessment.' *Development and Change* 27(1): 29–86.

Potts, D. 2000. 'Worker-peasants and farmer-housewives in Africa: the debate about "committed" farmers, access to land and agricultural production.' *Journal of Southern African Studies* 26(4): 807–32.

PoZ (Parliament of Zimbabwe). 2003. *Second report of the portfolio committee on lands, agriculture, water development, rural resources and resettlement. Third session – fifth parliament. Presented to parliament on Wednesday 11 June 2003*. S.C. 11, 2003. Harare, Zimbabwe: PoZ.

PoZ (Parliament of Zimbabwe). 2006. *Fourth report of the portfolio committee on lands, land reform, agriculture, resettlement and water development on the viability of the sugar indus*try. *First session – sixth parliament. Presented to parliament on 6 June.* Harare, Zimbabwe: PoZ.

Prosterman, R. and J. Riedinger. 1987. *Land reform and democratic development.* Baltimore, USA: Johns Hopkins University Press.

Putnam, R. 2000. *Bowling alone: the collapse and revival of American community.* New York, USA: Free Press.

Raftopoulos, B. 2003. 'The state in crisis: authoritarian nationalism, selective citizenship and distortions of democracy in Zimbabwe.' In A. Hammar, B. Raftopoulos and J. Stigen (eds). *Zimbabwe's unfinished business: rethinking land, state and nation in the context of crisis.* Harare, Zimbabwe: Weaver Press.

Raftopoulos, B. and A. Mlambo. 2009. *Becoming Zimbabwe: a history from the pre-colonial period to 2008.* Harare, Zimbabwe: Weaver Press.

RBZ (Reserve Bank of Zimbabwe). 2005. *Monetary policy statement for fourth quarter 2004 and roadmap for 2005.* Harare, Zimbabwe: RBZ.

RBZ (Reserve Bank of Zimbabwe). 2009. 'The role of property rights in investment.' Supplement No. 2 of the January 2009 monetary policy statement. Harare, Zimbabwe: RBZ.

Richardson, C. 2004. *The collapse of Zimbabwe in the wake of the 2000–2003 land reforms.* Lewiston, USA: Edwin Mellen Press.

Richardson, C. 2005. 'The loss of property rights and the collapse of Zimbabwe.' *CATO Journal* 25: fall. www.cato.org/pubs/journal/cj25n3/cj25n3-12.pdf.

Röling, N. 1997. 'The soft side of land.' *ITC Journal* 3 & 4 (special congress issue): 248–62.

Roth, M. 1990. *Analysis of agrarian structure and land use patterns in Zimbabwe.* Background paper prepared for the World Bank Agricultural Sector Memorandum. Washington, USA: World Bank.

Roth, M. and J. Bruce. 1994. *Land tenure, agrarian structure and comparative land use efficiency in Zimbabwe: options for land tenure reform and land redistribution.* Land Tenure Center Research Paper 117. Madison, USA: Land Tenure Center, University of Wisconsin.

Rugube, L. and W. Chambati. 2001. *Land redistribution in Zimbabwe: five census surveys of farmland transaction, 1996–2000.* Madison, USA: BASIS CRSP Management Entity, Land Tenure Center, University of Wisconsin.

Rugube, L., S. Zhou, M. Roth and W. Chambati. 2003. *Land transactions monitoring and evaluation of public and private land markets in redistributing land in Zimbabwe.* Harare, Zimbabwe, and Madison, USA: Centre for Applied Social Sciences (CASS), University of Zimbabwe, and Land Tenure Center, University of Wisconsin.

Rukuni, M. 1994a. 'The evolution of agricultural policy: 1890–1990.' In M. Rukuni and C. Eicher (eds). *Zimbabwe's agricultural revolution.* Harare, Zimbabwe: University of Zimbabwe Publications.

Rukuni, M. 1994b. *Report of the commission of inquiry into appropriate agricultural land tenure systems.* Harare, Zimbabwe: Government Printer.

Rukuni, M. and C. Eicher (eds). 1994. *Zimbabwe's agriculture revolution.* Harare, Zimbabwe: University of Zimbabwe Publications.

Rukuni, M. and S. Jensen. 2003. 'Land, growth and governance: tenure reform and visions of progress in Zimbabwe.' In A. Hammar, B. Raftopoulos and J. Stigen (eds). *Zimbabwe's unfinished business: rethinking land, state, and nation in the context of crisis.* Harare, Zimbabwe: Weaver Press.

Rukuni, M., J. M. Nyoni and E. Sithole with P. B. Matondi and M. Mutema. 2009. *Policy options for optimisation of the use of land for agricultural productivity and production in Zimbabwe.*

Submitted to the Agrarian Sector Technical Review Group (ASTRG). Harare, Zimbabwe: World Bank.

Rukuni, M., P. Tawonezvi and C. Eicher with M. Munyuki-Hungwe and P. B. Matondi (eds). 2006. *Zimbabwe's agricultural revolution*. Second edition. Harare, Zimbabwe: University of Zimbabwe Publications.

Rutherford, B. 2001. *Working on the margins: black workers, white farmers in postcolonial Zimbabwe*. London, UK, and Harare, Zimbabwe: Zed Books and Weaver Press.

Sachikonye, L. M. 2003. *The situation of commercial farm workers after land reform in Zimbabwe*. Report prepared for the Farm Community Trust of Zimbabwe (FCTZ). Harare, Zimbabwe: FCTZ.

Sachikonye, L. M. 2004. 'The promised land: from expropriation to reconciliation and jambanja.' In B. Raftopoulos and T. Savage (eds). *Zimbabwe: injustice and political reconciliation*. Cape Town, South Africa: Institute for Justice and Reconciliation.

Sadomba, W. Z. 2008. *War veterans in Zimbabwe's land occupations: complexities of a liberation movement in an African postcolonial settler society*. Unpublished PhD thesis. Wageningen, Netherlands: Wageningen University.

Sadomba, W. Z. and N. Andrew. 2006. *Challenging the limits of the state's market-based land resettlement programme in Zimbabwe: the War Veterans as catalyst of the land movement*. Paper for presentation to the workshop on 'Market-oriented changes in land policies in developing and transition countries: understanding the varied views and reactions "from below".' Part of the International Conference on Land, Poverty, Social Justice and Development, 9–14 January.

Sanyanga, R. 2008. *Water issues in the context of land resettlement: the case of Mazowe District*. Harare, Zimbabwe: Ruzivo Trust.

Scoones, I. 2008. *Lands and livelihoods programme*. Cape Town, South Africa:

University of the Western Cape and Institute of Development Studies, University of Essex.

Scoones, I., N. Marongwe, B. Mavedzenge, F. Murimbarimba, J. Mahenehene and C. Sukume. 2010. *Zimbabwe's land reform: myths and realities*. London, UK: James Currey.

Scoones, I., N. Marongwe, B. Mavedzenge, F. Murimbarimba, J. Mahenehene and C. Sukume. 2011. 'Zimbabwe's land reform: challenging the myths.' *Journal of Peasant Studies* 38(5): 967–93.

Scott, J. C. 1985. *Weapons of the weak: everyday forms of peasant resistance*. New Haven, USA, and London, UK: Yale University Press.

Selby, A. 2006. *Commercial farmers and the state: interest group politics and land reform in Zimbabwe*. DPhil thesis. Oxford, UK: Oxford University Press.

Shivji, I., S. Moyo, W. Ncube and D. Gunby. 1998. *Draft national land policy for the Government of Zimbabwe, Ministry of Land and Agriculture and Food and Agriculture Organisation (FAO)*. Unpublished draft discussion paper. Harare, Zimbabwe.

Sithole, E. 2002. *Gender analysis of agrarian laws in Zimbabwe: a report*. Harare, Zimbabwe: Women and Land in Zimbabwe (WLZ). www.kubatana. net/docs/women/wlz_gen_analysis_agrilaws_zim_0207.pdf.

Sukume, C. 2005. *Agrarian transformation and emerging constraints: a case study of Shamva District*. Collaborative project of the Shamva Rural District Council. Harare, Zimbabwe: Ruzivo Trust and Department of Agricultural Economics and Extension, University of Zimbabwe.

Sukume, C., S. Moyo and P. B. Matondi. 2004. *Farm sizes, land use and viability considerations: Utete presidential land review committee*. Working Paper. Harare, Zimbabwe: African Institute for Agrarian Studies.

Taylor, J. J. 2002. *The politics of uncertainty in a white Zimbabwean farming community. Part IIB. Dissertation: Social*

Anthropology. Presented by Jesus College, University of Cambridge, Cambridge, UK.

Tiffen, M. 1996. 'Land and capital: blind spots in the study of the "resource-poor" farmer.' In M. Leach and R. Mearns (eds) *The lie of the land: challenging received wisdom on the African environment*. Woodbridge, UK: James Currey and International African Institute.

Tshuma, L. 1997. *A matter of (in)justice: law, state and the agrarian question in Zimbabwe*. Harare, Zimbabwe: SAPES Books.

Utete, C. M. B. 2003a. *Report of the Presidential Land Review Committee on the implementation of the fast-track land reform programme 2000–2002*. Harare, Zimbabwe: Presidential Land Review Committee.

Utete, C. M. B. 2003b. *Report of the Presidential Land Review Committee. Volumes I and II: main report to his Excellency the President of the Republic of Zimbabwe, August*. Harare, Zimbabwe: Presidential Land Review Committee.

Van Zyl, J., J. Kirsten and H. P. Binswanger (eds). 1996. *Agricultural land reform in South Africa*. Cape Town, South Africa: Oxford University Press.

Vijfhuizen, C. 2002. *The people you live with: gender identities and social practices, beliefs and power in the livelihoods of Ndau women and men in a village with an irrigation scheme in Zimbabwe*. Harare, Zimbabwe: Weaver Press.

Weiner, D., S. Moyo, B. Munslow and P. O'Keefe. 1986. 'Land use and agricultural productivity in Zimbabwe.' *Journal of Modern African Studies* 23(2): 251–85.

World Bank. 1991. *Zimbabwe: agriculture sector memorandum: vol. I and vol. II, no. 9429 – Zimbabwe*. Washington, USA: World Bank.

World Bank. 1995. *Zimbabwe achieving shared growth: country economic memorandum: vol. 2*. Washington, USA: World Bank.

Yeros, P. 2003. *The political economy of civilisation: peasant-workers in Zimbabwe and the neo-colonial world*. PhD thesis. London, UK: London School of Economics, University of London.

Zamchiya, P. 2011. 'A synopsis of land and agrarian change in Chipinge District, Zimbabwe.' *Journal of Peasant Studies* 38(5): 1093–122.

ZCBC (Zimbabwe Catholic Bishops Conference). 2008. *The effects of party-state on democracy and human rights: the case of in Zimbabwe. A report on the harmonised elections in Zimbabwe*. Conference held on 29 March 2008, Harare, Zimbabwe.

ZEC (Zimbabwe Electoral Commission). 2005. 'Results for parliamentary elections, March 31.' Published in *Sunday Mail*, April 3.

ZESN (Zimbabwe Elections Support Network). 2005. *March 2005 parliamentary elections: preliminary report*. Harare, Zimbabwe: ZESN.

ZESN (Zimbabwe Elections Support Network). 2008. *Report on the Zimbabwe 29 March harmonised election and 27 June 2008 presidential run-off*. Harare, Zimbabwe: ZESN.

Zikhali, P. 2008. 'Fast Track Land Reform and agricultural productivity in Zimbabwe.' In P. Zikhali. *Land reform, trust and natural resources management in Africa*. Economic Studies 170. Gothenburg, Sweden: University of Gothenburg.

Index

A1 farm classification, x, 8–10, 41, 44, 52, 54, 55, 58, 60, 64, 84, 101, 110, 111, 112, 115, 116, 117, 125, 133, 135, 141, 144, 151, 153, 154, 156, 161, 171, 173, 174, 175, 182, 209, 227; class divide with A2 farmers, 184; community-building in, 230; conceptualisation of, 98; eviction of farmers, 108; farmers' access to education, 177; farmers' access to healthcare, 180; farmers' relations with chiefs, 218–19; land allocation, in Mazowe, 64–9; model of, 212 (need to revisit, 248); social and cultural fabric of, 210; social institutions in, 228; socialisation of farmers in, 229, 231; women as beneficiaries in, 190–4, 196

A2 farm classification, x, 8–10, 12, 41, 52, 54, 55, 58, 59, 60, 63, 64, 84, 85, 86, 89, 90, 98, 100, 110, 111, 117, 126, 135, 143, 144, 146, 150, 152, 153, 156, 157, 161, 171, 173, 174, 182, 209, 212, 242; abandonment of, 112; applications for plots, 62; beneficiaries in Mazowe District, 70; class divide with A1 farmers, 184; community-building in, 230; distribution of farm sizes, 72; eligibility criteria for, 69; elites, 221; farmers reject customary cultural systems, 233; farmers' access to education, 175; farmers' access to healthcare, 180; farmers' formation of agricultural consortiums, 231; farmers' movement to A1 farms, 113; farmers' redistribution of wealth, 242; farmers' relations with chiefs, 218–19; farmers' relations with farmworkers, 219; increasing numbers of, 127; influence of farmers on community emergence, 218; land allocation in, 68 (in Mazowe District, 69–73); model of, need to revisit, 248; socialisation of farmers in, 229; women as beneficiaries in, 190–4, 195, 196

abandonment of land, 111–14
absentee farmers, 230, 247
academics, lack of interest in agrarian reform, 257–8
Acquisition of Farm Equipment (or) Material Act (2004), 162, 172
administrative mechanisms for land acquisition, 38–40
Affirmative Action Group, 15
agrarian base, changed and expanded, 8–12
agrarian model, emergence of, 235
agrarian reform: complexity of, 236; future shape of, 253
agrarian relations, new, 11–12
agrarian transformation, definition and character of, 130–4
Agribank, 148, 150; loans to women farmers, 197
agricultural extension, 12
agricultural graduates, selection of, 10
Agricultural Land Settlement Act (2000), x
agricultural production, shift in, 10–11
Agricultural Rural Development Authority (ARDA), 29, 170, 171
Agricultural Sector Productivity Enhancement Facility (ASPEF), 149–50
agricultural shows, revival of, 159
Agricultural, Technical and Extension Services (Agritex), 41, 48, 49, 57, 68, 69, 83, 89, 90, 98, 108, 151, 152, 182, 190; data on beneficiaries, 70; field days, 110; gathering of data, 66–7; role of, 60; sidelining of, 240
agro-ecological regions, x
all-night vigils, as part of land occupations, 24
assets: asset stripping by former owners, 162; for cropping, 163; for livestock, 163–4; inherited, conflicts over, 171–3

Ballineety scheme, 57
bankability of land, 97, 128

banks: unwillingness to lend, 96, 146, 170, 246; wish to invest in agriculture, 256

Barclays of Zimbabwe, 170

basket making, 243

Bayle Farm, occupation of, 47

beer drinking, provision of spaces for, 167

beneficiaries, 13, 23, 51, 63, 102, 109, 153, 208, 223–4, 238; 'big guys', 24; caricatured, 257; classes of, 63–4; cronyism among, 74–81; debate about, 5; distribution of, 56; in Mazowe, 70; listing of, 87; managers as, 77; numbers of, 9, 55; passive resistance of, 244; public announcement of, 65, 68; raffle for, 60; reconstruction of allocation lists, 66; responsibilities of, 252; security forces as, 241; under A2 scheme, 12

Berea Farm, 120

Bilateral Investment Promotion and Protection Agreements (BIPPAs), 18, 43, 50, 244, 253

biofuels, promotion of, 6

black farmers, 133, 209, 221; characterisation of, 7–8; elite, 239

black market, in agricultural inputs, 123, 147, 237

Blackfordby Institute, 164

books, lacking in schools, 176

building: of health facilities, lacking health standards, 179; of housing, 120; permanent structures eschewed, 106

Buka land audit, 13, 86

burial of dead, 116

burial societies, 231

cadastral maps, updating of, 250

Canvest (Pvt) Ltd, 170

capacity-building, 12, 13

captivity of farmworkers, 167

cash preference of farmers, 158

Cattle Levy Act (1931), 34

cereal production, 136–8

Certificate of No Present Interest (CONPI), 31

Champion Farmer Programme (CFP), 149

chaos, in land allocation, 13–14, 40, 49, 88, 93; control of, 21, 58–61, 241

chiefs, as policy elite, 89–90

child labour, used by women farmers, 195

children, inheritance by, 203

Chiweshe, 61, 65–6, 210; decongestion in, 117

Chiweshe, Chief, 89, 217, 218

churches, 230; apostolic, 230; as social venue for women, 229

citrus production, 44–5, 48, 136, 161

civil servants, 215; approaches to land allocation, 67, 82 (self-interest in, 64, 123); as beneficiaries of land allocation, 92, 219; housing requirements of, 182; in creation of Fast Track Farm communities, 219–20; self-claiming of land, 241

co-existence between farmers, 25, 27

co-operatives, 231

coffee, 255

collateral, need for, 96, 106, 150

collective belonging, rebuilding of sense of, 230, 230

collective organisation of settlers, 125

command agriculture, use of term, 135

Commercial Bank of Zimbabwe, 106

Commercial Farm Settlement Scheme (CFSS), 99

Commercial Farmers' Union (CFU), 7, 25, 48, 165, 220

Committees of Seven, x, 38, 40, 223, 248

communal areas, xi, 61, 218, 246; A1 farmers' movement to, 113; agrarian structures in, 118; maintaining links with, 116, 224; maintaining homes in, 115

communities, evolution of, on Fast Track Farms, 211–12

community share schemes, 15

compensation, 9, 21, 30, 35, 97, 124, 165–7, 244; for farm equipment, 173; need for finalisation of, 253; settlement of, 255

compounds, 211; burning of, 171; seen as foreign construct, 210; system of, 197–8

compulsory acquisition: farms spared from, 44–5; in Mazowe District, 40–6; of agricultural equipment, 172; politics of, 32–4; reaction of white farmers to, 46; resistance to, 31; state-centred, 235

computerisation of data, 87

Constitutional Amendment No. 11 (1990), 31

Constitutional Amendment No. 17 (2005), 49, 94

continuous grazing, 144

184; abandonment of, 111–14; access to services on, 161–84; agrarian patterns of, 16; as sites of struggle, 94; housing catastrophe in, 181; labour issues in, 153–7; living experiences in, 226; mix of peoples represented in, 239; political participation in, 214; seen as boring by young people, 230; social organisation in, 208–34; socialisation in, 228–30; struggling beneficiaries in, 243–4; successful beneficiaries in, 241–3; thefts and social misdemeanours in, 227–8; transition of life processes in, 225; women benefit from, 188; women unrepresented in, 205

Fast Track Land Reform Programme (FTLRP), x, xi, xv–xvi, 35–8, 94, 101, 157, 158, 159, 161, 169, 179, 208, 210–11, 220; affects livelihoods of ex-farmworkers, 221; as top-down policy, 248; as viewed in international discourse, 7–8; associated with radical action, 236; background to, 1–17; benefits of, 90–1; characterised as chaotic, 13–14; continuity of state policy in, 99; criticism of, 54, 69, 75; declining access to services as result of, 184; disinvestment as a result of, 162; driven by social movements, 213–14; engenders new notions of governance, 233; extends state land ownership, 95; founding document of, 11; gender inequity of, 206; lack of guidelines for, 129; lack of progress for women, 204–6; loss of housing infrastructures in, 127; need to halt, 253; oblivious of socio-cultural contexts, 206; origins of, 18; overlooks need for inputs capacity, 243; politics of, 77, 78; price controls introduced, 147; provision of housing during, 181; reduces empowerment of women, 205; shift in agricultural production under, 10–11; allocation of land under, 51–93; transforms state-society relations, 15

female-headed households, 244

fertiliser, 101, 138, 148, 169; black market in, 147, 237; gender inequity in access to, 244; wrongly applied, 155

financing of agriculture, contradictions of, 148

focus group discussions (FGD), 105, 111, 115, 122, 154, 168, 197, 199, 203, 210, 227

food shortages, 248, 258

foot and mouth disease, 145

Forrester Estate (Mazowe District), 43–4

freedom farming, use of term, 23

freehold title, 94, 95, 96, 97, 99, 108, 128, 246–7

Galloway Farm, 57

gazetting of farms, 18, 34, 39, 42, 50

gender equity issues, 12, 115; as justification of FTLRP, 187, 189; in land rights, 185–207

Glendale Country Club, 229

Global Political Agreement (2008), 124, 135, 165, 237, 250, 251, 253, 254

gold mining, illegal, 103

gold panning, 155, 156, 213, 222

Gono, Gideon, 149

Good Husbandry Act (1944), 34

government: assertion of control by, 240; controls commercial agricultural lands, 95; negotiation with, 122–3; weakness of, 245, 247, 249

Government Input Scheme, 149

Government National Land Audit, 221

government-to-government agreements, 39

Grain Marketing Board (GMB), 98, 119, 146, 148, 157, 158, 231

grazing land, access to, 20

greenhouses, investment in, 74

groundnuts, production of, 139

Gubbay, Anthony, 35

Harare, 107, 143; proximity of farmland to, 41, 61; residential development in, 73–4; urbanites seek land, 29

healthcare, 175; affordability of, 180; clinics, 167; investment in infrastructures, 178–81

Henderson Research Institute, 44, 164

HIV/AIDS, 115, 203; advice about, 231; disrupts labour market, 156; during period of FTLRP, 178; problems for farmworkers, 155

horticulture, 11, 48, 136, 248

housing: building of, 20, 146; disaster area in Fast Track Farms, 181–3; for female farmworkers, 198; shortages of, 20; vandalism of, 182

land grabbing, use of term, xi, 22
Land Identification Committees, 38–9
Land Information Management System, 50
land invasions, use of terms, xi, 22
land law, need for, 249
land market, segregated, 30
land occupations, xi, 16, 19, 182, 187, 215; by proxy, 24; control of, 51; driving factors of, 239–40; Mugabe's support for, 21; peasant and elite approaches to, 23–6; reaction of white farmers to, 46–9; resistance to, 28
land ownership rights, uncertainties of, 94–129
land pirating, 83, 91
land reform: as theatre of contestation, 3; first phase of programme, 53–6; radicalism in, 4–5
land registration, 250
land sales by the poor, 96
land speculators, elimination of, 251
land squatting, 19–21; use of term, xi, 22; violence against squatters, 33
land tenure see tenure of land
land use, planing of, 247–8
land utilisation see utilisation of land
landlessness, 54, 237, 256, 258; pressure of, 61
large-scale commercial farms (LSCF), xi, 95, 97, 130, 154, 208, 220
large-scale land ownership, breaking of, 135
laws regarding land issues, 6
learning platforms, need to develop, 248
leasehold land, 95
leasehold tenure, 10, 95, 128, 246; 25-year, 198; 99-year, 95–6, 108, 126–7, 198; power of state in, 96
legal and constitutional reforms, need for, 251, 253
liberalisation, economic, 254–5
lineage, development of, 116
literacy, 243
litigation, 59, 94, 97, 109, 131; by elites, 82; hindrance to growth of assets, 166
livestock, 141, 161, 255; beef cattle, 164; cattle ranching in Mangwe District, 251; in Shamva District, 142; loss of cattle to disease, 145; production of, 143–6

local politics of land issues, 3
'Look East' policy, 107
looting, 171, 172, 211
Lowdale Farm, 85

Mackay Farm, 168
Made, Joseph, 188
maize, 11, 131, 136–7, 141, 146, 157, 161, 164; difficulties of production of, 146–7; hybrid, marketing of, 164
Maize Control Act (1931), 34
Makope, Headman, 218
malnutrition, 133
managers of farms: as beneficiaries, 77; caretaker managers, 166; employment of, 153, 242; wives as, 204
Mangwe District, 3, 6, 10, 11, 80–1, 126, 157; cereal production in, 136–8; education in, 175, 177–8; election results in, 81; healthcare provision in, 179–80, 180–1; production of livestock in, 143–4
maps, drawing of, 30
market structures, ambiguity of, 157–8
marriage: between different groups, 227; dissolution of, 200–1 see also divorce
Maryvale association, 27
Mashonaland Central Province, land allocations in, 41
Masvingo, land occupations in, 21
maximum farm sizes, 44, 85
Mazowe Citrus Estates, 42–3, 45
Mazowe District, 3, 6, 10, 11, 19, 27, 31, 40, 146, 154, 158, 159, 165, 210–11; A1 land allocation in, 64–9; as bread basket of Zimbabwe, 59; attraction for land applicants, 61–74; cereal production in, 136–8; changing demographics of, 169; class mix in, 233; compulsory land acquisition in, 40–6; education in, 175, 176–8; election results in, 79; elite interest in securing land in, 241; extension services in, 151–2; farmers' social participation in, 232; gold panning in, 213; healthcare provision in, 179; insecurity of tenure in, 106–11; irrigation committees in, 223; labour supply in, 156; land acquisition in, 34; land conflicts in, 108–9; lease preferences in, 126; lobbying for land access in, 205; new social relationships in, 224; oil crop production in, 138–40;

poverty, 20, 33, 236, 240; of women, 244; reduction of, 15
presidential inputs programme, 150
Presidential Land Review Committee, 40
Presidential Powers (Temporary Measures) (Amendment of Electoral Act) Regulations (2008), 35, 172
press-ups, as part of land occupations, 24
prices: control of, 147; determined by government, 157; of agricultural commodities, 148
private property, seen as sacrosanct, 20
private sector, 253; in agricultural investment, 164–5; restricted space for, 159
production, agricultural, 136–43; complexity of outcomes, 130–60; complexity of factors, 146–58; decline of, 17, 161, 243, 248, 252; lack of predictability in, 128; recovery of, 258; trends in, 132
Productive Sector Facility (PSF), 149–50
productivity, agricultural, 160; restoration of, 255
property rights, 20, 35
protective clothing, 197, 223
Provincial Land Committees (PLCs), 38
proxy occupations of land, 24
Public Services Commission, 92

racial mapping of culture of production, 8
racialism, 30, 49, 52
raffle for land allocation, 60
registration systems, 86
religious groups, 228; membership of, 230–1
remittances, 224, 242
renting of cattle, during land audits, 119
re-planning of farms, 84, 85, 124, 127, 244, 245, 252
Reserve Bank of Zimbabwe, 91, 149, 249; Farm Mechanisation Programme, 77, 196
resettlement, 20, 30, 45, 54, 209–11; abandonment of, 114; of ex-farmworkers, 67–8; stability of, 129
resistance, everyday forms of, 246
restitution, 57, 61, 210; use of term, 20
Rio Tinto Agricultural College, 164
roads: lands adjacent to, avoided, 83, 113; maintenance of, 164; paved, 29; poor networks of, 103; provision of, 61

Robertson, John, 134
Rockland Farm, 88
roving occupying leaders, 23
Rural District Councils, xi, 164, 240
Rural Land Occupiers (Prevention from Eviction) Act (2001), 33
rural rich, as beneficiaries, 64
Ruzivo Trust, xiv; surveys (2004–2009), 3, 18, 42, 53, 68, 73, 103, 141, 156, 191, 194, 197

sabotage, by white farmers, 131
Salvation Army, 179
sanctions, 100, 247, 254
Saratoga Farm, 171–2
savings clubs, 231
scaling, politics of, 15
scheme, use of term, xii
Scientific and Industrial Research and Development Centre (SIRDC), 13, 57–8
security forces: as beneficiaries of land allocation, 241; presence of, 61
seed, farming of, 48
self-allocation of land, 13, 51, 65; by civil servants, 77
services: minimum, provision of, 136; on Fast Track Farms, access to, 161–84
sex work, commercial, 222
Shamva District, 3, 6, 10, 11; cereal production in, 136–8; election results in, 80; extension services in, 152; fertiliser financing in, 150; labour hiring in, 153–4; lease preferences in, 126; livestock production in, 142; oil crop production in, 138–9; production of livestock in, 143–4; usage of permanent labour in, 156
Shona people, 233
shrines, importance of, 58
simulation of land usage, 118–19, 143, 146
singing, as part of land occupations, 24, 25
size of farms, 46
skills: audit required, 248; development of, 12; lack of, 134, 143, 151, 154, 213, 243; of farmworkers, 223; of managers, lack of, 153; skills gap, 131
smallholder agriculture, xii, 46, 100; contribution to economy, 134; success of, 247–8
social clubs, 221; of former farmers, 228–9

Veterinary Services Department, 145
village, as governance unit, xii
Village Development Committees, 214
villagisation, 209, 210
violence associated with land occupations, 13, 22–3, 24, 28, 33, 47–8, 94, 190, 131, 199, 235, 238, 240; reduction of, 217; stopping of, 241, 254
VIP latrines, 183
voting patterns, on Fast Track Farms, 78–81

War Veterans, x, 5, 15, 19, 20–3, 23–4, 40, 51, 64, 65, 69, 71, 75, 89, 96, 98, 125, 167, 168, 171, 173, 181, 184, 213, 216, 221, 238, 239, 240; allocation of land to, 72, 215; as organisers of Fast Track Farms communities, 214–15; in land occupations, 26–7; relations with civil servants, 215
War Veterans Association, 239
ward, subdivision of district, xii
water, access to, 168–70, 186, 258
weapons of the weak, 122
weekend farming, 119–20
wheat, 11, 136, 146, 157, 161
white farmers, 7–8, 25, 30, 45, 99–100, 164, 208, 216, 235, 238, 258; and co-existence, 220–1; challenges faced by, 147; classified as indigenous, 45; compound system under, 197–8; dispossession of, 1, 8; elitist world view of, 220; exodus of, 243; expropriate original landowners, 237; harassment of, 82; reaction to land occupations, 46–9; remove assets, 170; security systems of, 212, 221; social activities of, 228
widow inheritance, 203
wildlife protection, 118
wildlife sanctuaries for tourism, 74
wills of inheritance, writing of, 202
women: allocation of land to, 200; as

beneficiaries of FTLRP, 185; as farmers, training of, 194; as percentage of white farmers, 193; avoid violent situations, 193; challenges faced by, xvi; church as social venue for, 229; exclusion of, 199–200; expectations of access to land, 17; in context of customary law, 187; in land allocation, characteristics of, 194–5; land allocation to (outcomes of, 190–204; men's views on, 199–200); land rights of, 185–207; named on offer documents, 198; poverty of, 244; prioritisation of, 186; role as mothers, 224; struggles over land rights, 198–9
Women and Land Lobby Group, 204–5
women-headed households, 187
World Bank, Learning and Innovation Fund, 32

young people: allocation of land to, 67; involvement in land occupations, 237; role in land occupations, 67; subject to economic crisis, 237
young women, alienated from Fast Track Farms, 230

Zimbabwe African National Union – Patriotic Front (ZANU-PF), 2, 19, 20–1, 26, 33, 78–80, 82, 86, 87, 91–2, 122, 125, 159, 171, 187, 209, 214, 215, 216, 217, 219, 236, 238; allegiances to, 216; Land Allocation Joint Committee, 60; supporters of, as beneficiaries, 74–8
Zimbabwe Farmers Union, 231
Zimbabwe Investment Centre, 31
Zimbabwe Joint Resettlement Initiative, 32
Zimbabwe National Army, allocation of land to, 70, 85
Zimbabwe National Liberation War Veterans Association (ZNLWA), 26
Zimbabwe Republic Police, 24, 212
Zumba people, 29